THE CRITICAL READING INVENTORY

Assessing Students' Reading and Thinking

SECOND EDITION

Mary DeKonty Applegate
St. Joseph's University

Kathleen Benson Quinn
Holy Family University

Anthony J. Applegate
Holy Family University

PEARSON
Merrill
Prentice Hall

Upper Saddle River, New Jersey
Columbus, Ohio

Library of Congress Cataloging in Publication Data

Applegate, Mary DeKonty.
   The critical reading inventory: assessing students' reading and thinking / Mary DeKonty
Applegate, Kathleen Benson Quinn, Anthony J. Applegate.
        p. cm.
Includes bibliographical references.
   ISBN-13: 978-0-13-158925-4
   ISBN-10:   0-13-158925-3
1. Reading—Ability testing.   2. Critical thinking.   3. Reading comprehension.   I. Quinn,
Kathleen Benson. II. Applegate, Anthony J. III. Title.
   LB1050.46.A64 2008
   372.48—dc21   2007015955

Vice President and Executive Publisher: Jeffery W. Johnston
Senior Editor: Linda Ashe Bishop
Senior Production Editor: Mary M. Irvin
Senior Editorial Assistant: Laura Weaver
Design Coordinator: Diane C. Lorenzo
Project Coordination: Carlisle Publishing Services
Cover Designer: Jeff Vanik
Cover Image: SuperStock
Production Manager: Pamela D. Bennett
Director of Marketing: David Gesell
Marketing Manager: Darcy Betts Prybella
Marketing Coordinator: Brian Mounts

This book was set in Galliard by Carlisle Publishing Services. It was printed and bound by
Courier/Kendallville, Inc. The cover was printed by Phoenix Color Corp.

Pearson Education Ltd.
Pearson Education Singapore Pte. Ltd.
Pearson Education Canada, Ltd.
Pearson Education—Japan

Pearson Education Australia Pty. Limited
Pearson Education North Asia Ltd.
Pearson Educación de Mexico, S.A. de C.V.
Pearson Education Malaysia Pte. Ltd.

10 9 8 7 6 5 4 3 2 1
ISBN 13: 978-0-13-158925-4
ISBN 10:   0-13-158925-3

To Tony, who in love wrote this with me to help me heal.
To my Mom, Dad, sisters, and brothers who love and believe in me.

— *Mary DeKonty Applegate*

To my Mom and Dad, for teaching me to read and so much more.
To my children, for teaching me the meaning of life.
To my husband for teaching me to love.
To my teachers, students, and colleagues, for teaching me that
I have so much to learn every day.

— *Kathy Quinn*

To Mary: my colleague, my inspiration, my best friend, and my love.
In loving memory of my parents, Edmund and Anne,
who never failed to encourage me to love learning.

— *Tony Applegate*

Introduction

The Critical Reading Inventory is, above all, an invitation to educators to delve deeply into the thinking skills of their students and help them to grow in their ability to respond to text. Our aim in constructing the CRI has been to enable teachers and reading specialists to identify with confidence those children who do not think about what they read. Armed with that understanding, teachers will be able to model solid thinking for their students and challenge them, through their own questioning, to understand text at new and deeper levels. It is our hope that more and more teachers will experience the thrill of hearing first graders discuss the mistakes that characters in their books have made or middle school students discussing the links between their reading and current events. Most of all, we hope that more teachers will experience the pure joy of seeing children learning to think about text and overcoming the sometimes stubborn belief that it is beyond their capability.

Ultimately, we must acknowledge the skill and insight of the educators who use the CRI. No reading inventory can ever be better than the people who use it, and the CRI is no exception.

So many people have helped with this project along the way and deserve special thanks. Marjorie Seddon Johnson and Roy Kress, our major professors at Temple University, literally "wrote the book" on informal reading inventories. All three of us had the good fortune to be counted among their students. Eleanor Ladd Kress modeled instructional practices rooted solidly in diagnostic information. Elizabeth Davis taught us the principles of conscientious research. They were our mentors, our friends, and our inspirations; in short, everything that one can hope for in professors. Throughout the development of the CRI, we reread their words and reflected on their guidance. It is important to us that they know how much they empowered us.

Our editor, Linda Bishop, has been a godsend to us, providing guidance and encouragement at every step, even to the point of dreaming up the title for our text. Linda's assistant, Laura Weaver, has always been a model of helpful and pleasant professionalism. We owe special thanks to Mary Tindle of Carlisle Publishing Services for her infinite patience and conscientious preparation of the text.

The following professional reviewers provided much-appreciated encouragement and praise along with invaluable insights and many valuable suggestions: Bonnie Armbruster, University of Illinois at Urbana-Champaign; Mary Ann Dzama, George Mason University; Laveria Hutchison, University of Houston; Michael W. Kibby, University at Buffalo; Margot Kinberg, National University; Timothy Rasinski, Kent State University; Barbara V. Senesac, Central Michigan University; and Timothy Shanahan, University of Illinois at Chicago. We know from experience that doing book reviews can be a time-consuming and difficult task. Please accept our deepest thanks for your time and efforts on our behalf.

We are deeply indebted to many colleagues who contributed in very significant ways to the evolution of CRI 2. Mike Alft lent his programming genius to the Automated Scoring and Interpretation Interview. He literally adopted the project as his own and put untold hours into refining, expanding, and polishing the program and providing us with new ideas about how to use it. We could never begin to repay him for his help. And at every step along the way, Mike was assisted by his wife Mary Teresa, a former student in whom we take much pride and a highly accomplished teacher and reading specialist. Mary Teresa also provided us with exceptionally insightful critiques of the CRI as a whole.

Kyle Warren was a model of meticulous professional skills in the preparation of the DVD that accompanies the CRI. His patience and expertise were absolutely essential in the preparation of a valuable professional tool for educators. Kyle's students and staff at ChARTer Tech High School also assisted him in the editing and special effects for the DVD. Our expert scorers, particularly Pat Erickson, Cathy Pinto, and Sue Stackhouse, gave up many hours of their time to provide us with invaluable feedback and insights. Pat and Sue even served as our model test administrators on the DVD and volunteered their sons, Scott and Brendan, as models for the same DVD.

No reading inventory can progress very far without the help of colleagues and students. We are much indebted to Conne Broderick, Harriet Goldberg, Helen Hoffner, Eileen Baker, and Roger Gee and their graduate students for the feedback and suggestions they so generously provided. To our professional colleagues who shared so many insights with us: Virginia Modla, Cathy McGeehan, Kelly Doyle, Lisa Freeman, Janine Sack, Noreen Farkas, and the reading specialists from Upper Merion School District. To our own long-suffering graduate and undergraduate students we owe much: your conscientious work and willingness to share ideas and critiques are much appreciated. And seldom is a project of this magnitude completed without the work of a graduate assistant. Lauren Rogan served this role with an exceptional level of conscientiousness and skill.

In addition, we have had much valuable technical assistance from Michelle Perkins, Gary Coleman and Jason Mills of Holy Family University as well as Dan Parker and Susan Watkins from Prentice-Hall. We were also the benefactors of the photography of Pat Getty and Thomas Jenkins, Jr., and original art work created by Walter Benson and Rob Ferguson. We are most grateful for all of the many special talents that have been contributed to this text by so many special people.

Preface

Since the 2004 publication of the first edition of *The Critical Reading Inventory (CRI 1)*, we have been overwhelmed and gratified by the sheer intensity of interest among practicing as well as prospective teachers in the ability of their students to think about what they read. It is impossible to discern whether the interest of teachers has been sparked by the emphasis on higher-order thinking in standardized accountability assessments, or whether those measures are simply responding to the demands of educators for assessment of thoughtful literacy. In any case, it seems that an emphasis on thoughtful responses to literature and informational text is here to stay, and that assessments of those responses have the potential to promote fundamental changes in the shape of the literacy classroom.

We would like to think that the CRI has made a significant contribution to the reshaping of classroom instruction and assessment in the United States. We undertook from the very beginning to develop an assessment instrument that refused to label items that called for mere translation and a simple recall of ideas as higher order thinking. Instead we attempted to assess whether readers could achieve the often delicate balance between the use of textual information and the use of their own background experiences and concepts. We were not satisfied with the assessment of recall; we aimed for a more accurate and complete picture of comprehension, an assessment of the reader's ability to critically respond to text. The feedback we have received from users and reviewers on the value of assessing thoughtful literacy has been overwhelmingly positive and immensely valuable to us in our undertaking of a major revision of the CRI. Outlined below are the features users will find in our second edition, CRI 2.

- **Expanded Number of Passages** Reviewers and users alike called on us to expand the number of passages available so that they could use the CRI for gathering pretest and posttest assessment information. Consequently, we added a third passage to each level of narrative and informational text carefully crafted to parallel the other two passages in both conceptual and linguistic complexity. The increased use of informal assessments of reading and literacy at the junior and senior high school levels also led to a call for expanded grade levels that was too insistent to ignore. As a result, CRI 2 includes, instead of only generic passages at "junior high school" and "senior high school" levels, passages at grade levels 7 through 12. Thus CRI 1 has seen its 40 passages more than doubled to 86 passages in CRI 2.
- **Revised Word Lists** With the addition of passages at the 7th through 12th grade levels came the need for word lists to assess sight vocabulary at those same levels. With the inclusion of two forms of word lists, users can gather pretest and posttest data. In addition, the word lists at every level are divided into graded words that appear in context in the narrative passages and graded words that appear without context. Users can compare the reader's performance in both types of word recognition.

- **Revised Items and Analyses of Student Responses** We used the results of an analysis of literally thousands of readers' responses to the passages included in CRI 1 to strengthen the overall effectiveness of measurement in CRI 2. We identified comprehension items that did not produce results that were congruent with other items and either revised or replaced them. Items that seemed to cause confusion among readers or that encouraged readers to respond based solely on their own experience without reference to the text suffered a similar fate. As a consequence we have been able to tighten the scope of assessment of the instrument and produce results that are more conceptually congruent.

  The analysis of reader response also led to the discovery of a set of patterns of thinking that readers consistently evidenced in response to higher order questions. These *Profiles in Comprehension* (Applegate, Quinn, & Applegate, 2006) can serve as a framework for the analysis of a student's thinking, allow users to identify patterns of weakness, and encourage them to address that weakness through a well-developed program of instruction.

- **Retelling Rubrics Revised** The CRI 1 introduced retelling rubrics that allowed users to assign a numerical value to a retelling based on text structure. Retellings of narrative passages were scored based on a structure that approximated a story grammar and included only key information related to story structure. Retellings of informational passages were organized around a macro-concept and micro-concept structure that encouraged the reader to be selective in recalling what was central to the spirit and content of the text.

  To ensure that any revisions to CRI 1 would make the scoring of retellings more reliable, we conducted an exhaustive analysis of student retellings and derived a set of guidelines that could be used to calculate a numerical value for a retelling. To simplify the assessment and further increase the reliability of the scoring of retellings, we developed an automated scoring system that calls for the user merely to identify and click on the story elements that were present in a student's retelling. The program will automatically calculate the numerical value of the retelling based on the detailed rubric included in the CRI 2 text.

- **Automated Scoring and Interpretation Interview (ASII)** Mindful of the demands on time that informal assessment can make of teaching professionals, we set out to simplify the process. Our aim was to remove much of the time-consuming drudgery associated with scoring, calculating, and reporting the results of an informal reading inventory. Our solution is the Automated Scoring and Interpretation Interview (ASII). Windows users who have completed the assessment and scoring of the CRI can access the ASII and click on appropriate boxes to input the number of word list miscues, the oral reading miscues, and the comprehension items for which the reader has received full or partial credit. The ASII will automatically calculate the percentage scores for the word lists, the Reading Accuracy Index (RAI), and Meaning Maintenance Index (MMI) for each passage read aloud, and the oral, silent and/or average comprehension item scores at each level. The tool will further break down comprehension performance to indicate Text-Based, Inferential, and Critical Response scores. Users of the ASII can also easily access the Automated Retelling Scoring tool from within the program.

  At the conclusion of the interview, the ASII will respond with a completed and professionally formatted Recapitulation Record that can be printed and used as part of each student's academic records. The Recapitulation Record is a visual tabular summary of a child's reading performance suitable for use in the child's formal academic records. The ASII will also calculate and print a Level One Analysis Worksheet that juxtaposes key information from the Recapitulation Record and facilitates the interpretation of a child's reading performance. The ASII is easily accessible for PC users only at www.prenhall.com/readinginventory/scoringassistant.

- **Tutorials for the Scoring of Miscues, Retellings, and Comprehension Items** Professors who teach the use of an informal reading inventory as a diagnostic assessment are not immune to their own kind of drudgery. Valuable class time can often be consumed by the task of teaching users how to score student responses reliably and consistently. We would certainly never argue that this kind of instruction is unimportant, but it can expend a significant amount of class time that could be used for more crucial issues such as interpretation of results and instructional planning based on those results. We have attempted to address this problem by developing detailed tutorials that provide users with extensive practice in the scoring of miscues, retellings, and comprehension items.

The Miscue Tutorials present users with a record of a child's oral reading with miscues noted using the system as explained and illustrated in the CRI 2 text. The user must interpret the miscue as either maintaining or violating the meaning and syntax of language. Answers will be submitted in a multiple-choice format and the program will respond with the correct response and explanatory feedback after each answer.

The Retelling Tutorials present users with a student retelling and ask them to judge whether each of the text elements included in the Retelling Rubric is present, partially present, or absent in the student's retelling. It will then ask the user to calculate the retelling score or submit the results to the Automated Retelling Scoring tool. The program will respond with the correct answer and instructive feedback after each user response.

The Comprehension Item Scoring Tutorials present users with actual student responses to CRI 2 items and ask them to score the responses as meriting Full, Partial, or No Credit. The tutorial includes a sample of responses to Text-Based, Inferentials, and Critical Response items at three different grade levels, representative of the range of levels that can be tested on the CRI 2. Once again, the program will respond with the correct answer and a detailed explanation of the scoring of each item included in the tutorial.

- **Expanded Technical Data for the CRI 2** The opportunity to collect more than two hundred test protocols administered by trained educational professionals under well-controlled conditions has enabled us to develop a set of data that support the reliability and validity of the CRI 2. Among the analyses we have conducted are:
  1. A comparison of user scoring of test items and retellings to those of expert scorers with extensive training in the use of the CRI 2.
  2. Correlation of retelling and comprehension scores on the CRI 2.
  3. A study of the overall reliability of the scoring of retellings.
  4. A study of the effectiveness of the word lists as an estimate of a staring point in reading.
  5. A study of the construct validity of the Meaning Maintenance Index (MMI)—comparison of reader retelling and comprehension scores of readers low in MMI to readers high in MMI.
  6. A comparison of reader scores on narrative versus informational passages.
  7. An analysis of scores to determine the extent to which grade-level passages are increasingly challenging to readers.
- **Inclusion of DVD** Users of the CRI 2 can access an authentic video demonstration of the administration of the instrument to children at two different grade levels. The DVD illustrates the administration of interviews, word lists, oral reading, retelling, and comprehension items.

Contents

Part I

Section 1 **Introduction to The Critical Reading Inventory**   **1**

What Is Critical Reading?   **1**

Why Assess Critical Reading?   **2**

Why a Critical Reading Inventory?   **3**

Who Will Use the CRI?   **4**
   Preservice Teachers   **4**
   In-Service Teachers   **5**
   Reading Specialists and Graduate Students   **5**
   Researchers   **5**

Special Features of the CRI   **5**
   Three Measures of Comprehension   **5**
   Complete and Extended Text   **6**
   Automated Scoring and Interpretation Interview (ASII)   **6**
   Scoring Tutorials   **7**
   Retelling Rubrics   **7**
   Levels of Interpretation   **7**
   Interviews   **8**
   Reading Accuracy Index (RAI) and Meaning
   Maintenance Index (MMI)   **8**
   Scoring Aids   **8**
   Case Studies   **8**
   DVD Demonstration of Administration Procedures   **8**

Potential Impact of the CRI   **8**

Conclusions   **9**

Section 2 **Description of The Critical Reading Inventory**   **11**

Word Lists   **11**
   Flash   **11**
   Untimed   **11**

What Word Lists Cannot Do   **12**

Form A: Narrative Passages   **12**

Form B: Informational Passages   12

Oral Reading and Miscue Analysis   13

The Nature of Miscues   13

Comprehension Check   15

    Three Dimensions of Comprehension   16

      Text-Based Items   16

      Inference Items   16

      Critical Response Items   17

    Profiles in Comprehension   17

      1. Literalists   18

      2. Fuzzy Thinkers   18

      3. Left Fielders   18

      4. Quiz Contestants   18

      5. Politicians   18

      6. Dodgers   19

      7. Authors   19

      8. Minimalists   19

Conclusions   19

Section 3   **Administration and Scoring of The Critical Reading Inventory**   **21**

Interviews   21

    Student Interview   21

    Parent/Guardian Interview   21

    Teacher Interview   22

Word Lists: Flash and Untimed   22

Oral Reading   23

Scoreable Miscues   24

Nonscoreable Miscues   24

Miscue Analysis: Calculating and Interpreting the RAI and MMI   25

    Miscue Analysis Worksheet   27

    Examining Miscues: Using the Miscue Analysis Worksheet   28

Fluency   29

Silent Reading   29

Comprehension Assessment: Retellings   30

    Scoring Retellings   30

    The Nature of Retellings   31

Practical Guidelines for Scoring Narrative Retellings in the CRI   32

    Key Characters and Setting   32

    Character's Problem or Goal   32

    Problem-Solving or Goal-Meeting Process   32

    Personal Responses   33

Practical Guidelines for Scoring Informational Retellings in the CRI   34

    Macro-Concepts   34

    Micro-Concepts   34

    Personal Responses   34

Comprehension Questions   35

    Scoring Comprehension Questions   36

Practical Guidelines for Scoring Comprehension Questions in the CRI   37

    Text-Based Questions   37

Inference Questions 37
Critical Response Questions 37
Administering the Listening Comprehension Test 38
Lookbacks 38
Using the Recapitulation Record 39
Word Lists 40
Comprehending and Responding to Text: Oral and
Silent Reading 40
Oral Reading 40
Estimating Reading Levels 41
Recording Scores in the Analysis Table 41
Word Lists and Miscue Analysis 41
Recording Comprehension Scores and Retellings 41
Oral Comprehension and the MMI 43
Question Type 43

Section 4   Interpretation of Test Results   45

Levels of Analysis on The Critical Reading Inventory 45
Level One: Numerical Interpretation 45
Level Two: Analytical Interpretation 46
Level Three: Comprehensive Interpretation 46
The Analysis of Reading Performance: What a Good Reader Does 47
Reading Levels in The Critical Reading Inventory 49
Independent Level 49
Instructional Level 49
Frustration Level 50
Listening Comprehension Level 50
Setting Reading Levels with the CRI 51

Section 5   Technical Features of The Critical Reading Inventory: Development and Validation   53

Construction of the Components of the CRI 53
Word Lists 53
Interviews 54
Graded Passages 54
Passage Readability 54
Assessment of Comprehension 55
Retelling Rubrics 55
Postreading Questions 56
Estimating Reading Levels 56
Reliability and Validity of the CRI 2: Standardization Study 57
Word Lists 58
Scoring of Miscues 59
Reliability 59
Validity 59
Scoring of Comprehension Items 61
Reliability 61
Validity: The Existence of Different Item Types 61
Scoring of Retellings 62
Reliability 62

Retelling Rubrics 62
   Reliability 62
   Validity 63
Fluency Rubric 63
   Reliability 63
   Validity 64

References   **65**

Part II

Test Materials   **69**

Summary of Administration Procedures for The Critical Reading Inventory 70

Student Interview, Grades K–4 72

Student Interview, Grades 5–12 73

Parent/Guardian Interview 74

Teacher Interview 75

Oral Reading Fluency Rubric 76

Critical Reading Inventory—Recapitulation Record—Narrative Passages 77

Critical Reading Inventory—Recapitulation Record—Informational Passages 78

Critical Reading Inventory—Completed Sample Recapitulation Record—Narrative Passages 79

Narrative Retelling Scoring Guide 80

Informational Retelling Scoring Guide 81

Word Lists Set A 82

Word List Set B 89

Narrative Passages Examiner's Copy   **97**

Informational Passages Examiner's Copy   **247**

Section 1

Introduction to The Critical Reading Inventory

What Is Critical Reading?

If we examine the historical roots of reading instruction in the United States, we will find a long tradition of assessing the reading comprehension of children on the basis of how much of their reading they could recall and recite (Allington, 2001). Few reading experts would argue that a clear recollection of the points that an author makes is not important. But fewer still would argue that recall of information is sufficient to define a good and effective reader. Instead of a rather simple and passive gathering of information, reading is now viewed as "an active process that requires an intentional and thoughtful interaction between the reader and the text" (Report of the National Reading Panel, 2000, pp. 4–5). In addition to the text, the raw material that we use in that interaction is the collection of our past experiences and concepts, rooted in our culture and language (Anderson, Osborn, & Tierney, 1984; Pearson, 1992).

But as complex as this interaction of reading systems may be, it is still only the beginning of our job as readers. After we construct a plausible explanation of the text, we must react and respond to what we have read, and this reaction and response is the heart of what we describe as critical reading. C. S. Lewis described the literary experience in this way: "In reading great literature I become a thousand men and yet remain myself . . . I see with a myriad eyes, but it is still I who see" (Lewis, 1961, p. 141). Critical reading of literature involves the exploration and analysis of characters, their histories, their motivations, their values, and their actions. Critical readers react dynamically to characters, loving some and despising others, forgiving some and condemning others. In short, critical reading expands our knowledge of ourselves as it develops our understanding of others, enabling us to live vicariously through the lives of others (Rosenblatt, 1983). But we also assess the craft of the writer, analyzing techniques that the writer uses to elicit our responses and frequently judging the validity or quality of the writer's reasoning on the basis of that analysis.

And critical reading is not restricted to literature. When we react and respond to informational text, our aim is to incorporate new information into our existing frameworks of understanding. In many ways this task is more challenging than it is when we are reading narrative text. Informational text often presents ideas so new that we must create new schemata in order to actively process the ideas (Bransford, 1984). We have all had the experience of effectively memorizing information and passing tests, only to find that the information is gone from our memories a few days later. But critical readers look for links between new ideas and their own experiences and may even make judgments or propose alternatives in response to informational text. When they do this, they arrive at a level of ownership that essentially ensures that the information they have studied will be more easily accessible to them (Allington & Johnston, 2000).

In short, critical reading as we are defining it for The Critical Reading Inventory (CRI) involves at its root a personal response to text that takes the reader far beyond mere memory for facts. We are intentionally avoiding the traditional definition of critical reading as an analysis of the logical support provided by writers to shore up their theses. We simply find that definition too narrow. For us, critical reading is thoughtful literacy, a dynamic process of thinking about what we read and how it fits in with our own ideas and values, the ideas of others, ideas we have encountered in the past, and ideas that we accept or reject. And critical reading for our purposes is also related to *engaged reading,* in that we must not ignore the simultaneous functioning of motivation, concepts, and social interaction during reading (Alvermann & Guthrie, 1993). The level of engagement in reading is predictive of the amount of reading that children do, and children who are engaged and read more are likely to continue to do so (Wigfield & Guthrie, 1997). Not surprisingly, research has suggested that engagement in reading is predictive of achievement (Anderson, Wilson, & Fielding, 1988; Cipielewski & Stanovich, 1992; Cunningham & Stanovich, 1997). At the core of critical reading is an interest and curiosity that leads readers to go beyond the surface of the text and to try to understand its meaning, its significance, and its relevance to their own lives (Schiefele, 1991).

It is not difficult to envision a reciprocal relationship between thoughtful, critical response to text and motivation to read. The more you are inclined to think about reading, the more you are likely to find it rewarding. The more you find it rewarding, the more you are likely to engage in it. The more you engage in it, the better you are likely to become at it, which in turn enhances the level of thinking you bring to reading. At the center of this complex string of relationships is your view of reading that must include at its very core thinking about and responding to what you are reading. Consequently, reading teachers and reading experts alike have called on assessment professionals to expand their tools to include an assessment of the extent to which readers think about, not simply recall, what they have read. The response to this call has been broad and extensive.

Why Assess Critical Reading?

In response to reading research and theory, critical reading and thoughtful literacy are being more and more widely assessed on national, international, and state levels. At the international level, for example, the National Assessment of Educational Progress (NAEP) Reading Framework assesses four different stances or ways of responding to text: (a) forming an initial understanding; (b) developing an interpretation; (c) generating personal reflection and response; and (d) taking the critical stance. The framework's target distribution of items for the fourth-grade 2000 NAEP Reading Test was 33% critical stance, 33% personal reflection, and 33% combined initial understanding and interpretation (National Center for Education Statistics, 2002).

At the national level, the Stanford Achievement Test–9 (SAT–9), a widely used nationally normed achievement test, includes open-ended items as well as more traditional multiple-choice measures. Each open-ended item on the SAT–9 measures one of three reading processes: initial understanding, interpretation, or critical analysis (Harcourt, 2002). The Terranova Performance Assessments in Communication Arts assess the ability to establish understanding, explore meaning, extend meaning, and examine strategies, and to evaluate critically (CTB McGraw-Hill, 2002). A random sampling of 20% of the frameworks that guide the construction of state tests reveals that 90% of the statewide measures include open-ended or reader response items.

This increased emphasis on the ability to think about and respond to text represents a challenge for future success in reading instruction in the United States. For although the assessments are increasingly emphasizing critical thinking, classroom instruction does not seem to be responding. Allington (2001) reported that in study after study of the nature of classroom tasks, the overwhelming emphasis has been on "copying, remembering and reciting with few tasks that engage students in thinking about what they have read" (p. 94). And whereas the NAEP performance of American students has risen to historically high levels of achievement with regard to literal comprehension, "only a few students can demonstrate even minimal proficiency with higher-order literacy strategies" (p. 8). It stands to reason that students who are asked more often to explain or discuss ideas from their reading are more likely than their counterparts to demonstrate proficiency in higher-order tests (Donahue, Voelkl, Campbell, & Mazzeo, 1999). It appears that the challenge to develop thoughtful literacy is landing squarely in the schools.

But with the NAEP, national and state tests acting as summative assessments, it appears that little is being done in the way of formative assessment, assessment that can redirect the teaching curriculum as it is being delivered. In fact, Black and Wiliam (1998) found that classroom assessment tends to be characterized by measures of rote and superficial learning. Questions that teachers use tend to be noncritical, focusing instead on the narrow learning that teachers believe will ensure short-term success on high-stakes tests (Black, 2000). If Black and his associates are correct, not only is there a gap between what is being assessed and what teachers are teaching, but there is also a fundamental misunderstanding on the part of many teachers about the kinds of learning that are now being assessed on national and state tests.

It is precisely this gap in formative assessment that The Critical Reading Inventory has been designed to fill. There appears to be widespread agreement among experts that reading involves a thoughtful response to and interaction with text (Flippo, 2001) and because of this agreement, the assessment of thoughtful response had been included in national and state assessments. But if there is indeed a mismatch between assessments that emphasize critical response and classrooms that do not address it, we must find a means for teachers and administrators to identify and approach the issue.

Why a Critical Reading Inventory?

The decision to add yet another reading inventory to a field where more than a dozen well-known and widely used inventories already exist was a difficult one. We had used several different informal reading inventories (IRIs) in our advanced diagnosis courses, courses that in our programs led to study in instructional strategies and techniques. Our orientation toward critical thinking and thoughtful literacy shaped our study of instructional strategies, but we perceived a heavy weighting toward literal comprehension in inventories that we had used. We even modified one such inventory, adding items that called for higher-level thinking and thoughtful responses. But such modifications eliminated the benefits of the validity or reliability data that had been gathered on the original instrument. And so the mismatch between our concern for critical reading and our use of instruments that did not seem to measure it effectively led us to a more formal investigation of the problem (Applegate, Quinn, & Applegate, 2002).

We identified eight of the most widely used and cited IRIs and developed detailed descriptions of items that were text-based and items that were response-based. Text-based items called for readers to recall information verbatim from the text or to make simple and rather obvious low-level inferences. Response-based items required the reader to draw logical conclusions based on a combination of information from the text and ideas from their experience; or they called for readers to express and defend their reactions to the underlying significance of the key ideas in the text. From a sample of nearly 900 open-ended questions taken from the eight IRIs in the study, we found an overwhelming emphasis on text-based thinking (see Table 1–1). More than 91% of the items required only literal recall of information or low-level inferences. Items that required readers to draw a logical conclusion or to discuss the significance of a story occurred at a rate of less than 9%.

Needless to say, we found the results of our study disconcerting. We saw the use of open-ended questions to assess literal recall as a missed opportunity to make maximum use of the diagnostic potential of such items. Even aside from the fact that literal recall can be measured more easily and more reliably by objective test items, we concluded that the IRIs we studied were unable to distinguish between readers who could *remember* what they read and those who could *think about it*.

But even more crucial is the missed opportunity to use assessment data as a spur to instructional reform. If we cannot demonstrate that many children are unable to think about and respond to text, we will have no compelling reason to convince teachers that they need to adjust their instruction to address such needs. And because research suggests that classroom questioning is largely literal (Allington, 2001; Brown, 1991; Elmore, Peterson,

Table 1–1 Percentage of Item Types Found in Informal Reading Inventories

Informal Reading Inventories	Total Text-Based	Total Response-Based
Bader (1998)	92.5%	7.5%
	($N = 136$)	($N = 11$)
Burns & Roc (1993)	88.1%	11.9%
	($N = 111$)	($N = 15$)
Flynt & Cooter (2001)	89.6%	10.4%
	($N = 86$)	($N = 10$)
Johns (1994)	91.8%	8.2%
	($N = 123$)	($N = 11$)
Leslie & Caldwell (2001)	81.6%	18.4%
	($N = 93$)	($N = 21$)
Shanker & Ekwall (2000)	99.2%	0.8%
	($N = 121$)	($N = 1$)
Silvaroli & Wheelock (2001)	98.5%	1.5%
	($N = 66$)	($N = 1$)
Woods & Moe (1999)	90.1%	9.9%
	($N = 73$)	($N = 8$)
TOTAL	**91.2%**	**8.8%**
	($N = 809$)	($N = 78$)

& McCarthey, 1996; Knapp, 1995; Tharp & Gallimore, 1989), the cycle of poor performance on assessments that call for thoughtful responses is likely to remain unbroken. Fortunately, the research into exemplary literacy classrooms suggests that teachers who engage children in reading, problem solving, and linking ideas across texts routinely obtain superior performance on standardized achievement tests (Gottfried, 1990; Pressley et al., 2001; Ruddell, Draheim, & Barnes, 1990; Taylor, Pearson, Clark, & Walpole, 2000). But we still must be able to provide a reason for teachers to learn to use effective literacy strategies in their classrooms.

The American Educational Research Association (AERA) has advised that "tests should be aligned with the curriculum as sct forth in standards documents representing intended goals of instruction" (2000, p. 3). We noted that the experts agree, the developers of curriculum standards agree, and the writers of national and state tests agree that thoughtful response is a central part of the act of reading. We did not find an equal emphasis on critical response in the inventories we studied. We concluded that the challenge for reading specialists and experts is clear: We can lead the way toward fundamental changes in our approach to the assessment of thoughtful literacy, or we can wait until external assessments force us to follow.

Who Will Use the CRI?

We envision the CRI as useful to four distinct groups: preservice teachers; in-service teachers; reading specialists and graduate students; and researchers.

Preservice Teachers

The CRI can be useful in helping prospective teachers develop the skills of diagnostic teaching rooted in the ability to identify student strengths and weaknesses. More specifically, we envision the CRI as a structured way to introduce students to the role of informal assessment as a guide to instruction. The diagnostic data they gather can be used as the basis for the development of instructional plans and programs. An important offshoot of the use of the CRI is the development of greater sensitivity to the notion of reading as thinking and the types of questions that distinguish literal and critical readers. It is our hope that the study and use of these kinds of questions will promote the ability of preservice teachers to develop thought-provoking questions for use in their own classrooms.

In-Service Teachers

The variety of uses to which in-service teachers may put the CRI calls attention to the flexibility of the instrument itself. Classroom teachers are frequently asked by their schools or districts to gather assessment data on their children. They may find it useful to use only a numerical or abbreviated version of the CRI, testing children, for example, only at their grade level, only on oral or silent reading, or to contrast performance on narrative and informational text. In other circumstances they may wish to assess critical thinking in response to silent reading for students at those grade levels selected for state or local assessments. But teachers may also need to confirm or estimate reading levels for students with specific needs (e.g., new students). This task calls for a much different alignment of CRI features. It would be unusual for teachers to be asked to do a comprehensive diagnostic analysis on each of their students, but they may need to complete such analyses on some of their students.

As a consequence, the CRI should be seen as a tool to be tailored to meet a wide variety of demands and not as a rigidly formulated instrument. For example, if CRI results are being used as evidence of student growth, then steps should be taken to ensure that the test is administered and scored as consistently as possible. If the CRI is being used to gather general diagnostic insights to inform a teacher about her program of instruction for a given child, then the teacher could exercise a good measure of latitude in selecting and administering those elements of the test that best meet her needs. Further discussion of the various uses of the CRI is included in Section 4.

Reading Specialists and Graduate Students

Reading specialists and specialist candidates are or will be in the position of providing full-scale diagnostic analyses or estimating reading levels for students whom they assess. They may be called upon to provide instructional direction to classroom teachers or to instructional support groups. They may help school or district personnel make decisions about instructional materials, programs, or strategies. Finally, they may also engage in research at a variety of levels and their need for reliable and valid assessment data may be met by the CRI. Reading specialists and graduate students or even those seeking master teacher status would normally use the CRI in its most comprehensive form and it is to these individuals that the full-scale directions for test administration are generally directed. However, the flexibility of the CRI allows for decision making to be guided by the needs of the user and the demands of the situation (Bean et al., 2002; Bean, Swan, & Knaub, 2003).

Researchers

Researcher and school administrators who wish to gather pretest and posttest data to assess the progress of readers will be able to do so through the use of additional passages at all levels of the CRI. Electronic tutorials have been demonstrated to enhance the reliability of the scoring of comprehension items, retellings, and miscues. Automated calculation of retelling and fluency scores can minimize errors, further enhancing the reliability of the scoring of the CRI.

Special Features of the CRI

Three Measures of Comprehension

The most salient feature of the CRI is its use of three distinct item types in the assessment of reading comprehension. *Text-based items* require the reader to recall information from the text or to make fairly obvious connections between and among the ideas in the text. Factual information and readers' concepts comprise the building blocks upon which critical thinking is based. Thus, text-based items are also included in the CRI for the purpose of contributing to differentiated diagnosis. Users of the CRI will discover, as we have, many students who can recall text and answer text-based items but who cannot think about the text in any other way.

The CRI measures higher-level thinking in two different ways: *Inference items* require readers to draw conclusions by relating the information in the text to what they already know by, for example, predicting events, explaining ideas, or devising alternative solutions to problems. *Critical response items* require readers to address the "big picture" and arrive at statements of the broader significance of the text. They then must defend their ideas, based on information in the text that is linked with their background experiences. A common critical response item will, for example, require readers to make a judgment about a character or a character's actions and to defend that judgment. Thus the CRI can effectively measure a child's ability to recall the text, but at least 40% of the items assessing comprehension of a selection will require inferences and at least 20% of the items will require critical responses.

Complete and Extended Text

The CRI includes, as most inventories do, selections that can be used for oral as well as silent reading, and passages that are narrative as well as informational in nature (Johnson, Kress, & Pikulski, 1987). In the CRI we have developed original passages centered on topics chosen for their potential appeal to readers, but also that were not overly familiar. We were mindful of the criticisms leveled at the short and sometimes choppy passages that are used in reading assessment measures (Goodman & Goodman, 1994; Klesius & Homan, 1985). We were also aware that research had found that the nature of children's miscues changed as they began to develop a sense of the context of the text that they were reading (Goodman, 1970; Goodman & Burke, 1972). Because many informal reading inventories include passages that tend to be short or even incomplete in terms of story elements, children who read them do not always have an opportunity to develop a solid sense of the semantic and syntactic elements in the text. These observations create something of a dilemma for the constructors of IRIs because they must balance the demands for complete text with the demands of time spent in the diagnosis of reading difficulties. In the CRI, we opted for longer, more fully developed text, mindful of the need to match our assessment with the text that characterizes most instructional materials, as well as national and state standardized assessments in reading. Longer stories enable us to assess the reader's ability to construct meaning and develop a greater sense of story, content, and context. Because the longer and more fully developed text resembles actual reading tasks, we feel that they provide a higher level of usefulness in the assessment of comprehension.

Automated Scoring and Interpretation Interview (ASII)

As former reading specialists and teachers, we were very much aware of the demands upon time that informal assessment can make on professionals. In order to make up for the extra time that testing with somewhat extended text would take, we developed a procedure to streamline the calculations and recording that the use of an inventory would normally involve. The Automated Scoring and Interpretation Interview (ASII) gives the CRI user the opportunity to input information about the child's performance in a modified interview format. The ASII then calculates and displays for the user a completed Recapitulation Record, a visual summary of a child's reading performance suitable for use in the child's academic records. The Recapitulation Record includes the child's chronological age, the total comprehension scores for oral and silent reading, the average comprehension scores for each level, the number of each item type that the child has answered correctly at each level, and two types of miscue analysis data.

The ASII includes an option for automated calculation of retelling and fluency scores. The ASII will display the results of its calculations in tabular form to facilitate further analysis of data. Of course, the ASII cannot replace the professional judgment of the examiner in assessing the correctness of the child's responses or the value assigned to a retelling, but it can save considerable time with the mechanical and mathematical tasks associated with informal reading assessment. The ASII is readily available for download by CRI Windows users. Simply log on to *www.prenhall.com/readinginventory/scoringassistant* and follow the instructions for loading the program into your computer. The ASII program includes a detailed user's manual, and a variety of help functions to provide users with extra instruction in scoring and interpreting reader responses.

Access the Automated Scoring and Interpretation Interview at www.prenhall.com/readinginventory/scoringassistant *for scoring help, tutorials, and case studies (ASII is accessible to Windows users only).*

Scoring Tutorials

The CRI web site as well as the DVD that accompanies the CRI include 44 separate tutorials that can give users extensive practice in scoring miscues, comprehension item responses, and retellings. Twenty-four tutorials provide practice on narrative text and eighteen use informational text. Each tutorial requires the user to assign a score to authentic reader responses and includes the opportunity to compare the user's scoring to that of expert users of the CRI. After each response, the tutorial provides the expert scoring and a detailed explanation of the rationale for that scoring. Hypertext features allow the user instant access to the story text at any time as well as access to scoring principles and guidelines.

Professors who teach courses in which the CRI is used can assign tutorials to their students to give them practice in scoring student responses. In their present form, the tutorials include a mechanism for professors to track the progress of their students and to maintain a record of which tutorials the students have completed.

Retelling Rubrics

For each narrative and informational passage, the CRI includes a rubric to guide the user in assigning a more consistent numerical value to retellings. The rubrics are built around the central story elements of the narrative passages and the key factual data included in informational passages. The rubrics are thus designed to move users away from a reliance on verbatim recall as a measure of the worth of a retelling; the rubrics assign greater weight to the most significant ideas in the text. Included in the rubric is the element of student response to the text which is factored into the final scoring. The use of the rubric to assign a numerical value to a retelling in no way replaces the careful analysis that can provide qualitative insights into a child's thinking, but it can lessen the wide range of values that might be assigned to retellings in the absence of any guidance. It also provides another source of comparative data that may be useful, given the different purposes for which the CRI can be used. To calculate a numerical value for a retelling, use the extensive Narrative or Informational Scoring Guides in the Test Materials section of the text. Each Scoring Guide also includes a description of the meaning of the numerical values.

For users who may wish to avoid the calculations associated with assigning a numerical value to a retelling, the *retelling help* feature of the ASII provides an alternative. Simply locate on the ASII the title of the passage that you are working with and click on the retelling help button. A window will open which allows you to identify those elements of the text that are present in the retelling and the program will automatically calculate the retelling score.

Levels of Interpretation

The CRI includes case studies on the DVD-ROM and the CRI web site that illustrate the three distinct levels of interpretation that are designed to serve the different needs and purposes of CRI users. For situations where assessment data are the primary objective of testing, examiners may choose to carry out a Level One numerical interpretation of the test data. This allows the examiner to compare a child's reading performance on several distinct dimensions of reading (e.g., performance on different item types, oral vs. silent, narrative vs. informational, unprobed comprehension vs. probed comprehension). Level One is far from superficial but it can save a great deal of time for users who must administer numerous assessments, particularly when it is used in conjunction with the ASII. A Level Two analytical interpretation is called for when the user needs detailed information about a child's reading performance. Level Two calls for users to expend the time to examine the child's responses in detail and draw conclusions about the nature of the child's thinking on the basis of those responses. A Level Three comprehensive interpretation is more detailed still, representing an attempt to piece together all available information that may be contributing to a child's reading performance, including personal view of and attitude toward reading, parental involvement, and classroom instruction. Levels of interpretation are simply another means of maximizing the flexibility of the CRI to meet the needs of a wide range of professionals involved in the reading assessment of children.

Interviews

Included as part of the CRI are interview forms that may be used for children (both older and younger), parents/guardians, and teachers. If the purpose of the CRI administration is to obtain a comprehensive picture of the child's entire reading situation, the interviews can provide some valuable insights. Under optimum conditions, the interviews are designed to support and supplement the CRI user's inquiry into the child's overall reading milieu, but they can also be used in their present form as stand-alone instruments. Ultimately, the interviews can, at the very least, give the CRI user information about children's view of and attitude toward reading, the level of parental support for and awareness of any reading problems, and the type of instruction that the children receive on a daily basis.

Reading Accuracy Index (RAI) and Meaning Maintenance Index (MMI)

The CRI includes a percentage that reflects the sheer accuracy of a child's reading, the extent to which the reading is free from miscues. This we have termed the Reading Accuracy Index (RAI). But we have also acknowledged the research that suggests that not all miscues are created equal (Goodman & Burke, 1972). That is, less serious miscues, although they may deviate from the text, still represent a successful attempt on the part of the reader to make the reading meaningful. For other miscues, however, the need to preserve meaning breaks down and these miscues may violate the sense and syntax of the text. A significant number of this type of miscue may indicate a distorted view of the nature of reading itself. To differentiate between the two types of miscues, we have included a percentage of the reader's attempts to maintain meaning during reading, called the Meaning Maintenance Index (MMI). The MMI provides at a glance an indicator of the extent to which the reader views reading as an active process of constructing meaning in response to text.

Scoring Aids

For those who opt not to use the ASII, the CRI examiner's materials include charts to facilitate the calculation of comprehension scores as well as the calculation of the RAI and MMI. Once the examiner has tallied the reader's responses, it is a simple matter to locate the appropriate percentages on the charts that accompany every passage.

Case Studies

Two complete sample case studies which represent detailed analyses of CRI data are available to users of the CRI web site at *www.prenhall.com/readinginventory/scoringassistant* as well as on the DVD that accompanies the CRI.

DVD Demonstration of Administration Procedures

The DVD that accompanies the CRI includes two authentic demonstrations of the administration of the CRI, ranging from interviews and word lists to oral reading and retellings. Users who wish to become familiar with assessment techniques or professors who are preparing students to administer the CRI will find the DVD demonstrations most helpful.

Potential Impact of the CRI

It is our hope that the publication and use of the CRI will help educators focus on the wisdom and efficacy of assessing and teaching the ability to think critically about one's reading. If it is true that we are tending toward the assessment of traits that we are not effectively teaching (Allington, 2001), then accurate assessment is one of our most effective means of establishing the facts and stressing the need for change. Thus we envision the CRI as a potential change agent in that it can provide evidence that thoughtful analysis of and response to reading is not part of the view of reading held by a significant number of children. Without such data, it will be difficult to ask teachers to reassess the notion that literal recall is the central issue in reading assessment.

We acknowledge that teachers widely recognize the importance of critical reading and our hope is that the use of the CRI will add to that level of recognition. But if professional preparation programs have overemphasized a linear conceptualization of reading, that framework may hinder some teachers from addressing thoughtful literacy. That is, some theorists and researchers believe that the process of reading involves a kind of taxonomy. Within the confines of that taxonomy, children must master all the details of the text and acquire a baseline skill level before they can do any thinking about the text. Under these circumstances, many children may not progress to the point where they are required to engage in critical thought.

It appears that these concerns have invaded the realm of teacher preparation itself. In a study of nearly 400 sophomores who had declared elementary education as their major, researchers investigated reading habits and attitudes (Applegate & Applegate, 2004). The findings suggested that more than half of the would-be teachers who participated in the study could be euphemistically labeled as "lukewarm" readers. The authors concluded that many prospective teachers are being placed in situations where they are called upon to promote an enthusiasm for reading that they do not have themselves. It is our hope that the CRI will serve as an effective model for teachers of the kinds of questions that engage and challenge students and serve as an incentive for some teachers to examine their own view of reading.

We also hope to spark debate about the link between thinking about one's reading and one's ability to find rewards in reading itself. We believe that the CRI can ultimately help teachers distinguish between readers who can read and those who are likely to do so. Specifically, if children see reading as little more than storing and retrieving the details of text, they will have a very limited incentive to engage in the activity (Schraw & Bruning, 1999; Wigfield & Guthrie, 1997). Fortunately, a child's view of reading can be changed in response to effective instruction, but it must be identified first.

Ironically, the very tendency to read may well be at the heart of performance on reading tests. For example, research comparing the amount of reading that children do with their performance on achievement tests (Anderson et al., 1988) revealed that the amount of time a child spends reading is related to the child's reading level in 5th grade and overall growth in reading proficiency from the 2nd to the 5th grade. And although correlational studies do not establish causal links, few experts will minimize the logical link between motivation to read and growth in reading (Guthrie, Wigfield, Metsala, & Cox, 1999; Meece, Blumenfeld, & Hoyle, 1988).

Conclusions

We believe that the CRI can be an effective measure of a child's ability to think about text at a variety of levels, an ability that is measured widely in summative but much less so in formative assessments. And because it is formative assessments that are designed to have a more direct impact upon classroom practice, it is at this level that we believe the CRI can make its greatest contribution. If the CRI can provide evidence that significant numbers of children are not thinking about what they read, then teachers will have the opportunity to develop both the tools and the incentive they need to effectively address the problem in their classrooms. Conversely, and even more important, the CRI may help demonstrate to teachers that many of their children (about whom they may have presumed otherwise) can effectively think about what they read. Once teachers recognize this potential on the part of their students, they may become more comfortable incorporating thoughtful literacy instruction on a regular basis in their classrooms.

Section 2

Description of The Critical Reading Inventory

Word Lists

The CRI begins with an assessment of the child's word recognition level in isolation from text. A graded list of words is presented to the readers in 1-second flash and untimed formats and their performance determines the starting point of the actual reading assessment. There are two word list forms at each grade level from Pre-Primer through Grade 12 to allow for pre- and posttest assessment. Each of the graded word lists contains 10 words from the narrative passages at corresponding grade levels of the CRI. Thus, users have the opportunity to contrast a student's ability to read words in isolation to the ability to read them within the context of a passage. Words used in the reading passages are designated with an asterisk in the Examiner's Copy of the word lists.

Flash

The Flash administration of the graded words lists is designed to provide a relatively quick and easy estimate of the level of the child's sight vocabulary. Sight vocabulary is defined as the fund of words that the child can recognize immediately, without the need for any word analysis skills. To administer the Flash segment of the test, you provide the child with a 1-second exposure to each word in a list of 20 words per grade level. The words have been chosen because of the frequency with which they appear in actual grade-level materials typically used in classroom instruction (see the discussion in Section 5). Because the word lists take very little time and are easy to administer and score, we also use the results to obtain an estimate of the level at which we should begin the reading of graded passages.

This estimate is based on an assumption that works most of the time: If children can identify all of the words in a specific grade level given just flash exposure, the chances are good that they will be able to read materials written at that grade level with very little difficulty. Of course, there are always exceptions to that rule, but because you want the reading segment of the CRI to be administered with maximum efficiency, a fairly good estimate of the appropriate starting point will be well worth your while as you will see in greater detail when we discuss the process of estimating reading levels.

Untimed

If children do not immediately recognize a word (or do not respond after about 5 seconds), give them an opportunity to use their fund of word analysis skills to identify the word. This is the Untimed segment of the Word List test. Note that you are not assessing reading; there is no real text involved and thus no context. When you give children unlimited time (in reality 10 to 15 seconds) to decode a word, they can do one of two things: They can use either word analysis skills (breaking a word into component parts—prefixes, affixes, root words, etc.) or phonics skills (linking the correct sounds and syllables to the combination of letters). Obviously, there can be no syntactic (grammatical) or semantic (meaningful) clues involved if there is no real text.

Use the DVD that accompanies this text for guidance on how to use *The Critical Reading Inventory*.

Nonetheless, giving the Untimed word list can give you some additional information about the level of the child's decoding skills, how that child approaches decoding, how flexible the child is in trying different pronunciations or techniques, and even how effectively that child handles frustration. You can observe whether children try everything in their repertoire or whether they simply glance at a word, look up at you, and tell you they don't know what it is (and presumably will not know at any time in the near future). You can observe how the child deals with success as well as a lack of success. For all of these reasons, despite the limitations discussed below, you will want to administer a list of graded, isolated words. A video demonstration of the administration of the word lists is available on the DVD that accompanies the CRI.

What Word Lists Cannot Do

We need to discuss what Word Lists cannot do. Word Lists cannot be used as the basis for the analysis of a child's pattern of errors in word recognition. We cannot develop a thorough program of word recognition instruction based on the Word Lists for one simple reason: The word lists are not actual reading. There is no coherent meaning in a list of words. Nor is there a grammatical structure in a word list; a reader cannot use context clues in word lists because the context does not exist. Frankly, based on the Word Lists alone, you will have no idea whether a child really knows what a word means. And until you observe children actually reading text, you will have no idea of the skills and strategies they use in the act of reading. All you are measuring at this point is whether the child can pronounce the word correctly. Needless to say, this is not the foundation upon which you want to build an instructional program. You use the Word Lists because they can give useful information about the starting point of The Critical Reading Inventory. But you cannot draw conclusions about a child's specific word recognition ability based solely on the recitation of a list of words.

Form A: Narrative Passages

Form A of the CRI includes three Narrative Passages for each grade level, beginning with Pre-Primer and ending with Grade 12. Narrative Passages are designed to include the major story elements associated with a relatively simple story grammar. These include characters who experience a problem of some type, take action to solve that problem, and meet with varying levels of success in their progression toward a resolution. This action also occurs within a time frame and at a given place, either of which may influence actions or outcomes in the story. The story grammar structure enables the examiner to note which of the elements of a story are central and which are less so. Consequently, you will want to assess the effectiveness of a retelling by determining to what extent the child recalled or reacted to the central story elements. The scoring rubric for retellings that accompanies each passage is built upon these central story elements. In addition, we recommend that the first of the passages at each grade level be administered as oral reading and the second as silent reading. Although we acknowledge the contributions of miscue analysis research and the role of oral reading in that research (Goodman, 1970; Goodman & Burke, 1972), we also endorse Allington's (2001) observations about the authenticity of silent reading. Administering in both oral and silent format will offer you the opportunity to contrast the child's performance in two very different reading modes.

Form B: Informational Passages

Form B of the CRI includes three Informational Passages for each of the grade levels. These passages are designed to convey information to the reader, preferably information that is rather unusual so as to minimize the effects of prior knowledge insofar as that is possible. Informational Passages tend to be more complex in structure than Narrative Passages because they can be organized around one structure or a combination of structures, including comparison, contrast, cause-effect, examples, or enumeration. Thus children's recall of and ability to react to informational text often depend upon the skills they demonstrate in organizing the information around a logical structure. This alone makes the evaluation of retellings of informational text both more challenging and a very rich source of diagnostic information about any given child's reading.

Oral Reading and Miscue Analysis

It is at this point that you are ready to make some judgments about the child's word recognition ability since there is a meaningful context and a somewhat authentic task involved. Now you can obtain some insight into how a child handles unknown words and uses (or fails to use) the meaningful context of a passage. We can, of course, make no claims that having a child read aloud in front of an adult who is furiously noting any deviation the child makes from the printed text is a very authentic reading situation. But it is the best you can do under the circumstances to gather some insights into the child's overall approach to word recognition. And it is the overall perspective on reading and word recognition that matters at this point, not the specific skills that the child appears to have deficiencies in.

It may be helpful to think that at least part of your work as test administrator will be to identify the child's place along a continuum of proficiency in word recognition during oral reading. At one end of the scale are those children who read with fluency, accuracy, good pacing, and expression and who use their ear for the grammar and meaning of the language to monitor their reading and ensure that it "sounds right." These are the children who will immediately self-correct most miscues that violate the context of the passage, whether semantic (meaningful) or syntactic (grammatical). Consequently, they will earn consistently high marks when you assess their word recognition in the context of oral reading. Keep in mind that these high marks are no guarantee that these children have processed or critically reacted to what they have read. Rather, you will need to determine that later in the test.

Naturally, there are those children who stand at the opposite end of the word recognition spectrum. These children seem to see the task of oral reading as a one-word-at-a-time pronunciation task with little or no attention paid to the meaning or flow of the language. The oral reading of these children tends to sound as if they are reading a list of disconnected words with almost no intonation or inflection. The miscues that these children make are much more likely not to make sense in the context of their reading. These children may even create pseudo-words for the sake of attaching sounds to letters, particularly if their instructional program includes the use of nonwords. Their self-correction and consequent monitoring for the sense of what they read may be virtually nonexistent. Reading for these children appears to be word-by-word decoding and little more.

Of course, as you have probably suspected all along, there are innumerable gradations along the continuum of word recognition we have begun to define. But a key insight that you can hope to gain by engaging in *miscue analysis* of oral reading is that of the child's view of reading. This is where self-corrections come into play. Self-corrections occur when children notice that what they have read aloud violates either the sense of the language (semantics) or the grammar of the language (syntax). That is, children who self-correct are indicating that they expect what they read to make sense and to fit in with the grammar of the language and that, when it does not, they know that they must do something to correct the situation. This is a healthy perspective on reading. For this reason, every self-correction is important: It may indicate an emerging view of reading as a process of making meaning.

The Nature of Miscues

Aside from an overall assessment of a child's perspective on word recognition, you can also gain some insight into the child's view of the nature of reading by analyzing the miscues that have occurred (Goodman & Burke, 1972). Not all miscues are identical in terms of their importance or their interpretation. When you look at the overall pattern of a child's miscues (a miscue is defined as any deviation from the printed text), you will find some that change the meaning intended by the author of the text but still fit in grammatically and make logical sense. For example, the text reads: *The boat was floating near the dock* and Reader A reads: *The boot was floating near the dock*. The reader has clearly altered the intended meaning but has substituted a noun (*boot*) for a noun (*boat*) and thus has created a sentence that keeps the grammar of the language intact. The reader has also created a sentence that makes some logical sense because it is entirely possible that a boot could be floating in the water near a dock. When we discuss the scoring of miscues in Section 3, we make the point that this type of miscue, even though it deviates from the actual text, can be classified as acceptable on the basis of both syntax and semantics. It can be viewed as the reader's attempt to make sense of the text. If a pattern of this type of miscue is evident, it suggests that the reader is developing some sensitivity to the structure of the language and expects what he or she has read to make sense. A pattern of these miscues does suggest that the reader is struggling to use words that fit logically or grammatically, and is demonstrating some elements of a view of reading as meaning making. In any case, you can observe whether the reader's confusion is cleared up by the context clues provided in the remaining text. If the story goes on to say that three boys jumped into the boat and the reader continues to read "boot," then you have a different type of problem.

Reader B, on the other hand, may demonstrate a consistent pattern of miscues that violate both grammar and logic. For example, the text reads: *The man rode the horse into town* and the child reads: *The man robe his horse into town*. In this case, the reader has substituted a noun (*robe*) for a verb (*rode*) and created a sentence that is not grammatically correct and makes no sense. Such a miscue fails to maintain meaning and suggests that the reader is not attempting to make sense of the text. Readers who make significant numbers of such miscues and who do not self-correct are suggesting that they view reading as a simple decoding task wherein once the words have been pronounced, the task is over. The difference between Reader A and Reader B discussed earlier is significant. Children who demonstrate either of these patterns of miscues will require instructional programs that are very different from one another if you are to help them become better readers.

Of course, there are numerous variations in the nature of miscues. Our first concern at this point is to gather diagnostic information centering on whether children, in spite of the number and nature of their miscues, still attempt to make sense of what they read. Once we have answered that question, it will be worth our while to seek out patterns in the reader's approach to unknown words. In this case, the Miscue Analysis Worksheet (discussed in detail in Section 3) will be helpful in that it provides a visual display of all of the miscues that the reader has made. It is then easier for us to identify when children use sounding out, for example, as their prime strategy in decoding words. Other children may take care to substitute syntactically appropriate words or word forms. Others may take care to consistently attempt to identify word parts or break unknown words into syllables. When these strategies are used with some degree of consistency, it allows us to identify the reader's overall approach to the identification of unknown words and shed some light on the child's instructional needs.

Readers will frequently use context clues and self-correct at reading levels that they find rather easy or only mildly challenging. However, when the reading becomes challenging they frequently focus more closely on graphophonemic cues and are much more likely to violate sense and language in their miscues. This is not a particularly unusual or alarming pattern.

In order to facilitate the analysis of miscues, we ask CRI users to calculate two different indices. The first is the Reading Accuracy Index (RAI). This is simply the percentage of the words in the passage that the child has read with complete faithfulness to the text. It is calculated by subtracting the number of scoreable miscues from the number of words in the passage, dividing by the number of words in the passage, then rounding off to the nearest whole number (see sample in Figure 2–1). The second index is the Meaning Maintenance Index (MMI). This is calculated by subtracting the number of scoreable miscues that violate the sense or grammar of the text from the total number of words, dividing by the total number of words, and then rounding off to the nearest whole number. Both of these indices will be discussed in greater depth in Section 3.

Figure 2–1

Sample Calculations
of the RAI and MMI

Second Grade II. "The Roller Coaster Ride" is 244 words in length.
If Student A makes 13 scoreable miscues, the RAI is calculated in this way:

RAI

244 words − 13 scoreable miscues = 231 words read accurately
231 words ÷ 244 total words = 94.67%
= **95% is Student A's RAI for this passage**
(rounded off to the nearest whole number)

MMI

If 7 of those 13 scoreable errors alter the grammar or meaning of the language, the MMI is calculated in the following way:

244 words − 7 meaning-violating errors = 237 words read in a manner that
preserves meaning
237 words ÷ 244 total words = 97.13%
= **97% is Student A's MMI for this**
passage
(rounded off to the nearest whole
number)

Note: To simplify the calculations, we have included a miscue calculator box with every selection in the CRI. Simply find the number of scoreable miscues first, then the number of or meaning-violating miscues in that box and you will find the corresponding percentage for the RAI and the MMI, respectively. The ASII performs this calculation automatically.

Comprehension Check

We have included a statement in the Examiner's Copy of the CRI passages to introduce each assessment. In it we say, for example, prior to oral or silent reading of a passage: *"Would you read this passage about _____ (to yourself/out loud). When you are finished, I'll take away the passage. Then I'll ask you to tell me about what you read and what you think of it. After that, I'll ask you some questions about the passage."* Once the reader has completed the reading, you remove the Reader's Copy of the story and begin the assessment of comprehension.

See ASII

Access the Automated Scoring and Interpretation Interview at www.prenhall.com/readinginventory/scoringassistant *for scoring help, tutorials, and case studies (ASII is accessible to Windows users only).*

There are several objectives for your use of the introductory statement. The most important of these is to give your readers a clear idea of what will be expected of them. Specifically, they will need to prepare to give a retelling and be ready to answer questions without the benefit of the passage in front of them. The objective in asking for the retelling is to try to determine which elements of the text that the reader felt were important enough to recall. You do not ask the child, for example, to "tell me everything you remember" about the story. You do not want to encourage the child to try to remember everything; at least some of the passage contains relatively incidental information or details. Instead, you want to see what children decide to emphasize in their interaction with the text. If the retelling lacks logical structure or emphasizes elements that are not central to the essence of the text (see examples of retellings and scoring rubrics in the Retelling Scoring Tutorials), then you have diagnostic information that can be valuable in framing a course of instruction.

For each of the selections in the CRI, we have provided a scoring rubric. In it you will find the elements of the text that are central to the intended message of the author. Instructions for translating the retelling into a numerical value are included in the Retelling Scoring Guides in the Test Materials section of this text, or you may wish to use the Automated Scoring and Interpretation Interview (ASII) available online to CRI users. We have found that most children will anticipate that you are asking for a verbatim recall of the details of the text. For this reason, you extend an invitation ("Tell me about what you just read and what you thought about it.") for the student to respond to the text. If the child does not provide a personal reaction in the initial retelling, you repeat that invitation and specifically ask the child what he or she thought of the story or text. Any hint of reaction to or interpretation of the message of the text is a welcome sign of a child's development of a healthy view of reading. Even a laugh or grimace or any expression of like or dislike for the text can be viewed as a most encouraging personal response. But in order to receive credit for a personal response in the retelling scoring, readers must be able to support their responses. Simply stating an opinion without an accompanying justification does not meet the criteria for a personal response.

After the unaided retelling of the selection, begin the open-ended questions that comprise the comprehension check of the CRI. As discussed earlier, we believe that remembering the details of what one has read is not a complete measure of one's understanding. Instead, comprehension involves the ability to remember what one reads, to think about it, and to respond to it. For these purposes, you will utilize three different types of items in your comprehension check.

Three Dimensions of Comprehension

Text-Based Items. As their name suggests, these items call for the children to recall information that they have read in the passage. In the CRI we have limited text-based items to include only information that is important in light of the central story elements or the key factual information related to the passage. Text-based items call for information that is stated either verbatim in the passage or so nearly verbatim that the item would require little more than translation of the text into different words. In asking text-based items, you are attempting to find out if children can, without benefit of the passage in front of them, remember specific elements of what the author said. Text-based items assess memory for information, not the ability to use that information or even think about it. For example, in the narrative titled "The Race," the main character brags whenever he wins a race and he always wins. Consequently none of the other characters want to race against him. An example of a text-based item would be "Why didn't any of the other characters want to race against him?" Because the relationship between winning and bragging is stated explicitly in the text, an acceptable answer would be that the character bragged about his speed.

You ask text-based questions because these items measure part of the reading comprehension process. Many children, however, have come to believe that memory of the facts is the essence of reading. Children with this view of reading are likely to perform much better in the text-based comprehension arena than they are at levels that require thought and analysis.

Specifically, text-based items are those that
- require the reader to recall explicitly stated information from the text.
- involve the recognition of information in different words from those used in the original text. Such items require of the reader only a translation of the printed text.
- require the reader to identify relationships that exist between ideas in the text. Such items as these are not completely verbatim. For example, the text reads: *I was late for the meeting. My car wouldn't start.* A question such as "Why was the character in the story late for the meeting?" would not be strictly verbatim only because the writer has not made the relationship explicit by using a grammatical marker (e.g., *because*). This is not to say that the skill of making such connections is unimportant. Classification of such an item as text-based merely reflects the fact that the writer assumes that at a given grade level, the reader can and will make the connection (Applegate et al., 2002).

Inference Items. Inference items require children to draw logical conclusions about elements of the passage they have read. These items frequently demand that children draw upon experiences that they have, but the link between experience and text is more logical than interpretive. Consequently, the inference items most often have a clearly identified link between experience and text. For example, in the narrative "The Race" already cited, the main character is finally beaten by a female cat who smiles when the main character challenges her to a race. An example of an inference item would be: "Do you think this is the first time this character has ever raced against anyone? Why or why not?" One can infer that the smile signifies a certain level of confidence that could be based on a record of prior successes. An inference item requires a response that is not stated verbatim in the text and which requires the child to do more than merely paraphrase the text. Children must link experience with the text to draw a logical conclusion about what they have read.

Inferences are those items that require the reader to

- devise an alternative solution to a specific problem described in the text.
- describe a plausible motivation that explains a character's actions.
- provide a plausible explanation for a situation, problem, or action.
- predict a past or future action based on characteristics or qualities developed in the text.
- describe a character or action based on the events in a story.
- identify relationships between or among pieces of information in the text. (Applegate et al., 2002)

Critical Response Items. Critical response items require children to analyze, react, and respond to elements of the text based on their experiences and values. Because responses to these items can be based on the link between text and the child's unique experiences, critical response items do not generally lend themselves to single correct answers. What makes answers to critical response items correct is the children's ability to justify their responses by providing a clear and coherent rationale (which still includes elements from the text) for their thinking. For example, in "The Race" the main character loses several rematches before he walks away angry. The cat who beat him is disappointed because she had hoped he would become her friend. An example of a critical response item would be: "If another new family moved into the jungle, do you think Spencer would ask them to race or not? Explain." Both affirmative and negative responses could be justified, based on the character's actions and statements. Critical response items invite discussion about characters, situations, or ideas. But the reader must select information relevant to the question and ignore information that may be important in the story but not germane to the issue addressed in the question. If children can state opinions but are unable to discuss or support them, then their response is considered inadequate.

We regard critical response items as requiring the reader to

- describe the lesson(s) a character may have learned from experience.
- judge the efficacy of the actions or decisions of a character and defend the judgment.
- devise and defend alternative solutions to a complex problem described in a story.
- respond positively or negatively to a character based on a logical assessment of the actions or traits of that character
- use information in a passage in support of a judgment about the efficacy of an action or a solution to a problem (Applegate et al., 2002).

The use of three types of items in the CRI will enable you to seek patterns of responses that give evidence of strengths and weaknesses. Many children, for example, will be able to answer only text-based items. Other children, particularly verbally proficient children, will respond effectively to text-based and critical response items, largely because they can link experiences to text and justify their thinking naturally. If that is all they can do, however, they will experience difficulty with inference items that require them to draw logical conclusions and that frequently require multiple text connections. Other children will recall and draw logical conclusions but may not have the slightest idea that they are supposed to think about and discuss ideas that are implied in the text. Thus the pattern of a child's comprehension response will often enable you to develop a plan of instruction that is specifically geared to their needs.

Profiles in Comprehension

In the course of their assessment, teachers can often identify obstacles to clearer and more sophisticated thinking, and ultimately adjust their instruction to meet the needs of their students. For example, in the course of our preparation of this edition of the CRI, we conducted an extensive study of the responses of more than 400 students to CRI comprehension items (Applegate et al., 2006). From this analysis there emerged eight distinct profiles of thinking that we believe represent pitfalls that readers can encounter on their way to thoughtful literacy.

1. Literalists. The Literalist is characterized by the fundamental belief that all answers to all types of questions will ultimately be found in the text. Literalists often express the belief that their thoughts and reactions to text are of little consequence and that their primary objective as readers is to commit the details of a story to memory. They often find it very difficult to distinguish between questions that require them to think and those that require them to find information. Before responding to a question they will engage in a systematic search of their memories or of the text in an attempt to locate answers. Literalists will frequently refer to "what the story said" in their responses or explanations. They often respond to thought-provoking questions with statements such as "I don't remember that part" or "It didn't say anything about that," occasionally with indignation that they had been asked a question that could not be answered on the basis of pure recall.

A final point about Literalists is in order. Accomplished Literalists are often viewed by teachers as exemplary readers because they recall all or most of what they have read. Equally often these same teachers are stunned by the poor performance of Literalists on accountability measures of reading comprehension that focus less and less on literal reading at higher grade levels.

2. Fuzzy Thinkers. Fuzzy Thinkers are characterized by vague and imprecise concepts that are often expressed in vague and imprecise language. Fuzzy Thinkers will nearly always respond to any type of question they are asked, but the thinking behind their responses will be elusive and ambiguous. If they are asked questions that follow up on their initial responses, they are often unable to explain what they meant, probably because they never had a clear idea of the significance of their original answer. Frequent use of trite descriptors such as *happy, sad, nice, mean, good,* and so on is often a red flag indicating the presence of a Fuzzy Thinker.

3. Left Fielders. Left Fielders are so named because their unpredictable responses seem to come from the deepest recesses of that part of the baseball playing field. Their responses frequently have nothing whatever to do with the text and may even seem incoherent or illogical. Left Fielders often deliver these responses with remarkable confidence and assurance. They may even elaborate upon them when asked to do so, but their elaborations will often be equally incoherent. Left Fielders seem to believe that any answer will serve in response to any question. They differ from those readers who make a personal, idiosyncratic link with the text that others cannot easily understand. These readers can explain their thinking; Left Fielders have a great deal of difficulty doing so.

4. Quiz Contestants. Quiz Contestants respond to questions about text by searching their memory banks for any explanation that will serve as a plausible response, whether it is alluded to in the text or not. Thus Quiz Contestants most certainly use their background experiences, but they do so without consideration of the text they have read. Quiz Contestants are related to Left Fielders in their disconnection from the text, but Quiz Contestants differ significantly in that they feel compelled to provide a logical response to a question. In that sense their view of reading is more accurate than that of the Left Fielder because they are monitoring their responses to ensure that they are logical. The problem is that they believe that their task is to provide a plausible answer to a question without using the details included in the text. An intriguing observation we made of Quiz Contestants is that they are frequent underachievers in state and national accountability assessments. It seems that Quiz Contestants are susceptible to a form of distractor that is common in standardized multiple-choice tests: answers that sound logical but have little or nothing to do with the text. Helping children identify such distractors can be beneficial as long as you encourage them to apply the skill in more authentic reading.

5. Politicians. These readers weigh the question and then do their best to tell you what it is that they believe you want to hear. Politicians often quote or devise slogans or platitudes that sound meaningful and weighty, but which have rather vague connections to the themes of the text they have read. It sometimes seems that the objective of Politicians is to convince you that they can think profoundly on issues related to the text, but when you ask them to explain what they mean, they are often unable to do so with clarity.

6. Dodgers. Dodgers are those readers who focus on the comprehension question itself. If it is not to their liking, they change the question into one that they feel is more suitable and then respond to the new question. Dodgers are often very voluble in their responses, and their sheer verbiage can sometimes overcome teachers and distract them from the fact that the Dodger has not actually answered the question at hand. Dodgers can be creative in their efforts to avoid questions that they cannot answer. One ploy that they commonly use is to paraphrase the question and try to pass it off as a valid answer.

Less sophisticated Dodgers may miss the point of the question because they have misunderstood or misinterpreted it in the first place. Others may have little or no realization of the role of the question in setting up the parameters of the reader's thinking.

7. Authors. Authors are those readers who add details, characters, and even entirely new story lines to the text that they have read. Authors may create entirely new stories, some of which have a markedly tenuous link to the text they have read. When they are questioned, they frequently show remarkable consistency by using their idiosyncratic text as the basis for their responses. Authors sometimes seem to be embarrassed by the fact that they have not comprehended what they have read, and they attempt to compensate by elaborating on the few details that they do recall.

8. Minimalists. Minimalists, on the other hand, are characterized by simple and unelaborated responses to even the most complex and thought-provoking of questions. Minimalists are maddeningly reluctant to elucidate their responses or explain their thinking. When they are asked to do so by teachers, they frequently respond with "I don't know" or "That's all I can think of." The difficulty with Minimalists (and the source of much teacher frustration) is that some elements of their responses may be correct. The problem is that they leave it to the questioners to create the logical links between their thoughts. Consequently Minimalists are difficult to instruct because they give teachers so little to work with in terms of diagnostic information. They are further complicated by the fact that they may be of two distinct types.

Type A Minimalists refuse to elaborate because they have little or no confidence in their language skills. Teachers can find Type A Minimalists particularly frustrating because they often feel that these children are capable of much more effective thinking. Indeed, Minimalists differ from Fuzzy Thinkers in that they may show tantalizing glimpses of their ability to think clearly and articulate their thinking effectively. But their unwillingness to elucidate their responses is rooted in the fear that they will "say the wrong things" or "say the things wrong."

Type B Minimalists have a profound fear of being wrong. They have somehow internalized the notion that reading, and indeed all of education, is about "getting it right" and getting it right the first time. Type B Minimalists often show physical signs of frustration such as fidgeting or frequent requests for breaks when they are faced with questions about what they have read. They will be particularly uncomfortable or frustrated if they believe that their responses are wrong (Applegate et al., 2006).

Conclusions

If anything at all is evident from our analysis of student responses, it is the power of the higher-level question as a tool for identifying habits of reading and thinking that merit your attention as a teacher. If you can remove some of the obstacles to thoughtful literacy that students experience, you will be able to offer them more opportunities for engaged reading. Thoughtful reactions to text are more than simply mechanisms to sort out good readers from poor readers. There are many instructional tools in a teacher's professional arsenal to teach virtually all students to respond thoughtfully to what they read. Well-timed and well-executed lessons from teaching professionals who are themselves thoughtful readers is often all it takes to begin the process of altering the fundamental view of reading that children hold (Applegate et al., 2006).

Section 3

Administration and Scoring of The Critical Reading Inventory

Interviews

Student Interview

In the Student Interviews we distinguish between younger (kindergarten–4th-grade levels) and older children (5th grade–12th grade), but the overall intent is identical. The interview offers you an opportunity to develop a rapport with the child whom you are about to test. That rapport often spells the difference between a thoroughly enjoyable intellectual inter-action with a child or one that is terse or unpleasant. In the course of the interview, you want to encourage the child to relax and to develop a sense of trust in you. For that reason, the interview should be conducted as an informal conversation rather than an interrogation. But at the same time, the questions that you ask are not frivolous and the information that you obtain may be significant when it comes time for you to piece together an educational profile of the child. Not surprisingly, the most significant items for you are often those that ask the child about reading, reading habits, and views of reading. The fact that you also in-terview parents and teachers gives you an opportunity to compare the children's responses to those of the adults who observe them on a regular basis.

You should record the child's responses to each interview question verbatim in the space provided on the interview form. You may also want to note any other interesting dimensions of the child's behavior in the margins of the form, such as the ease with which rapport was established, the level of confidence with which the child responded, or any signs of anxiety demonstrated by the child.

Parent/Guardian Interview

One objective of the Parent/Guardian Interview is to provide a counterpoint to the child's interview responses. But more important is your attempt to gain some insight into the level of parent awareness of, interest in, and support for the child's efforts in read-ing. The interview offers opportunities for the parent to react to the type of instruction and support the child is receiving at school as well as to demonstrate a level of awareness of any difficulties the child is experiencing in reading. The parent's responses should provide some idea of the extent of support that the child is receiving at home as well as some insight into the view of reading held by the parents. All of this information can be-come part of your overall picture of the child in a comprehensive diagnosis of reading performance.

Once again, the interview should be conducted insofar as possible as an informal conversation between a parent and a professional who is very much interested in helping that child achieve higher levels of reading competence. Keep in mind that the interview questions are guidelines, and need not be followed slavishly. If conversations with par-ents or teachers are providing the information you need, you should feel free to abandon the interview format. The Parent/Guardian Interview would, of course, be most helpful if it were conducted face-to-face, but you may often find yourself in situations where telephone interviews are the only viable option. Parent responses should be recorded in as much detail as is feasible on the interview form. Any observations about the parent's behavior, such as confidence level, willingness to elaborate, awareness of the child's school performance, and so on can be noted in the margins as well. Again, we emphasize that the interview is not designed as a lockstep procedure. Any follow-up questions that can help clarify responses will enhance the level of information you obtain from interviews. It is also worthwhile at this point to note that you need to avoid being judgmental about what you discover through the interviews. The more objective you remain in your analysis, the more value it will be likely to have for you and for the individuals whom you assess.

Teacher Interview

The Teacher Interview brings the third highly significant player in the child's reading journey into focus. You are most interested in gaining some insight into the teacher's view of reading, the instructional approaches regularly used in the classroom, and the match between that instruction and the child's needs. Ask the teacher to briefly assess the child's ability, attitude, interests, needs, and behavior in the classroom and how these relate to reading. Also ask the teacher to describe the instructional emphases that characterize her classroom, particularly with respect to the assessment of the children's reading comprehension. Your objective is to ascertain the level of the match between the child's needs as you determine them and the instruction that the child is receiving on a daily basis.

The Teacher Interview may need to be conducted via telephone, but personal interviews are always preferable. The interview is best conducted as a conversation between two professionals who have a mutual interest in the academic growth and achievement of a child. Responses should be recorded verbatim on the interview form, as with all interviews, along with any anecdotal observations that you may note in the course of your conversation.

Word Lists: Flash and Untimed

The technique for administering the Word Lists segment of the CRI is fairly straightforward. You will need the Reader's Copy of the word lists to show to the student and the Examiner's Copy of the word lists to record the student's responses. Seated across from or beside the child (experiment here to decide which position is best for you), use a pair of 3 × 5 cards to expose each word for a 1-second period. We have found over the years that the easiest way to expose the words effectively is to drag the bottom card down the page far enough to expose the first word and then, after a silent count of "one thousand one," to drag the top card down to cover the word. Be sure to cover the word after 1 second; a common error in the administration of this test is the tendency to leave the cards open for longer than 1 second. When that happens consistently, you are no longer gaining an estimate of sight vocabulary, the fund of words that the child instantly recognizes. For a video demonstration of the administration of the word lists, see the DVD-ROM that accompanies the CRI.

Use the DVD that accompanies this text for guidance on how to use *The Critical Reading Inventory.*

For younger elementary school children, begin the word list assessment at the pre-primer level or, for upper-level elementary children, 2 or 3 years below their current grade level. It is good to begin the test at a level at which most children can achieve success so you will be able to observe them in a more relaxed situation. Of course, if your reader is a junior or senior high school student, beginning at the pre-primer level is not appropriate. If you have reason to believe that your reader is likely to be insulted by a list of very easy words, you will need to make the adjustment and choose a starting point that will, when possible, ensure some level of success. There is, of course, always the possibility that some children will struggle even at the most elementary of levels.

In the interest of time efficiency, it is best to administer the word lists in this way:

1. Begin the Flash test at the point where you have reason to believe that the child will be successful but not insulted (usually 2 to 3 years below the child's grade level). It is always possible, of course, that the child is a nonreader and must begin at the lowest possible level.
2. Continue Flash exposure of words until the child makes a miscue. (Do not bother at this point to record each correct response on the Examiner's Copy of the list.) Remember that if the child self-corrects in response to the Flash exposure of a word, score the response as correct.
3. At the point of the miscue, open the cards that cover the missed word and say, "Let's take another look at that one."
4. While the child is trying to decode the word, record phonetically in the space next to that word in the "Flash" column what the child said in response to the Flash exposure.
5. Record the child's response after the Untimed exposure in the space next to that word in the "Untimed" column.
6. Discontinue the test once the child scores 70% or lower on the Flash portion of the lists.

Once you have selected a starting point, you are ready to begin the test administration. In the interest of conserving time, it is not necessary to pause after each correct response to record a (+) on the Examiner's Copy of the Word Lists. Instead, record only what the child says that is incorrect; you can always fill in the plus signs later when you score the responses after the entire test has been completed. Some children may become overly concerned that you seem to be recording only when they respond incorrectly. If you see that this is happening, you may wish to place a mark on the line for every one of the child's responses.

During the test administration, if the child gives a response that is different from the word on the list, use the space provided next to that word in the "Flash" column to record what the child said. A phonetic spelling of the miscue will allow you or anyone reviewing your test materials to reproduce the child's performance later when you are analyzing test results. Any response that deviates from what is printed on the list and which is not attributable to variations in pronunciation or dialect is scored as a miscue. If the child responds with "I don't know," then record the letters *DK* for "don't know" in the space provided; if the child does not respond at all, record the letters *NR* for "no response."

Scoring of the word lists means simply calculating a percentage of words on the list that were identified correctly. Because every list has 20 words, the Flash score for a child who identifies 17 of the words in a list would be 85% for that particular level. If the child correctly identifies two additional words in the Untimed segment of the test, simply add those two to the 17 correctly identified words in the Flash portion. Thus the child's score would then be 95% for Untimed for that level.

Oral Reading

Begin the oral reading segment of the CRI at the highest level where the child received a score of 100% on the Flash segment of the word lists. Again, your objective is to arrive at your best estimate of a level that is unlikely to present great challenges because of oral reading and word recognition. Unlike the word lists, the reading segments at each level of the CRI take a good deal of time to administer and if you can acquire even a decent guess at an appropriate starting point, you may save yourself and your readers considerable time and effort. Once you have identified the appropriate level for your starting point, locate the Reader's Copy of the story, present it to the child, and read aloud the introductory statement that accompanies each passage. Note that you are telling the child the topic of the passage but you are not engaging the child's background knowledge relative to the passage or attempting to help the child set a purpose for reading. At this point, you are in diagnostic mode and not in teaching mode and it is of great interest to you to observe for what purpose, if any, the child may read without any prompting. Furthermore, testing in this manner

Use the DVD that accompanies this text for guidance on how to use *The Critical Reading Inventory*.

may predict how children will perform on formal, standardized accountability measures where no activation of prior knowledge occurs.

It is a good idea to use a tape recorder to give yourself a second chance in case you should miss some elements of the reading. Even very experienced test users can find themselves hard pressed to keep up with a rapid reader who makes a significant number of miscues. In any case, it takes considerable practice to master any notation system, but the effort will be worth it in terms of time saved and diagnostic information gathered. For a video demonstration of oral reading assessment, see the DVD that accompanies the CRI.

Scoreable Miscues

With the Examiner's Copy of the story in front of you, listen carefully to the child's oral reading and note any miscues the child makes in the space provided. Because you are likely to be sharing some of your results with professors, teachers, colleagues and/or fellow students, it is important to learn a common set of notations for different types of miscues. Then, anyone looking at your Examiner's Copy will be able to reproduce the child's responses.

With this in mind, during the test administration, you need to identify the miscue types used in the CRI for your miscue analysis. A miscue, once again, is defined as any deviation from the printed test, no matter how major or how minor. You will interpret the proportion of major and minor errors later when you score the measures. Miscues may be classified and noted as follows:

> *Substitutions* The most common type of miscue, a substitution, occurs when a child reads a word that is different from the word in the text. To note a substitution, simply draw a line through the word that was read incorrectly and write the substitution in the space directly above the word. Once again phonetic spellings may be necessary for those occasionally creative substitutions that are not part of our language. *Reversals* are considered a variation on substitutions.

> *Omissions* These occur when the child skips one or more words that are in the text. To note an omission, put an *X* through the word or words that have been skipped.

> *Insertions* These occur when the child includes in the oral reading a word or words that are not part of the text. Note insertions by writing the added words in the appropriate space in the passage and use an editor's carat (^) to mark the place of insertion.

> *Teacher-Provided* Readers who cannot identify words will sometimes wait for help from the examiner. If a child cannot identify a word within a reasonable time span (usually about 5 seconds or so), simply give the word to the child. Then record the event by circling the word that you have provided and writing the letters *TP*. We have found that circling teacher-provided words gives the examiner a useful visual cue to the presence of significant numbers of this particular miscue.

> *Special Cases* Occasionally a child will make *the same error on the same word* time after time throughout the passage. Although you record every instance, you score only the first miscue. So if a child reads *weather* for the word *water* and does so consistently for a total of four times throughout the passage, score it as only a single miscue. If a child *skips an entire line,* score it as only a single miscue although it is, of course, a very serious one.

Nonscoreable Miscues

Several other types of miscues should be noted during the oral reading but not scored. The most important is the *self-correction*. Self-corrections occur when readers notice that what they have said does not make sense or does not fit in with the grammar of the language. As we suggested earlier, self-corrections are indicators that the children are engaging in self-monitoring and that they may be developing or have developed a view of reading as something that must make sense. Consistent self-correction is an indicator that children, even if

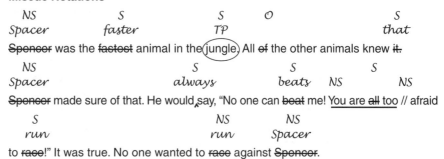

Figure 3–1

Sample Miscue
Notations

The child reads:

Spacer was the faster animal in the . . . [waits for examiner to help] . . . jungle. All the other animals knew that. Spacer made sure of that. He would always say, "No one can beats me. You are too [long pause] You are too afraid to run!" It was true. No one wanted to run against Spacer.

Miscue Notations

they are a bit sloppy in their oral reading, at least have a solid view of the act of reading as something that is supposed to convey meaning. In that respect, even a single self-correction is significant and must be noted. Because of the speed of the oral reading test and the need to keep up the pace in noting miscues, you will almost certainly have begun to note the miscue that the child eventually corrects. In the case of a self-correction, mark it with a check mark or *SC* to indicate that the child has made the correction. Once again, self-corrections are not scored as miscues.

As noted in the discussion of the word lists, you should not score as miscues *variations in pronunciation or dialect* or miscues children make on *proper names*. When readers *ignore punctuation marks* and read through the end of a sentence, for example, without any change in pace or inflection, note it by circling the skipped punctuation mark. Do not, however, score it as a miscue. By the same token, you may note in the margins of the Examiner's Copy certain characteristics of the child's oral reading, such as word-by-word reading where the children read as if they are pronouncing a list of words, or finger-pointing during reading, or pacing that is very fast or very slow. These notations will prove useful if you are using the Oral Reading Fluency Rubric to assess the reader's fluency (see our later discussion of fluency), but again these are not scoreable miscues. Children will frequently *repeat what they have read* as they try to process information; these can be noted by underlining each part of the text that is repeated, but they are not considered scoreable miscues. Hesitations or inappropriate pauses in reading can be noted with a slash mark at the point of the hesitation as a mark of the overall fluency of the oral reading. Figure 3–1 shows a sample of miscue notations with additional marks for scoreable miscues (*S*) and nonscoreable miscues (*NS*). For a thorough preparation and instruction in the scoring of miscues, Windows users should see the self-paced Miscue Scoring Tutorial available on the Prentice-Hall website.

Use the DVD that accompanies this text for guidance on how to use *The Critical Reading Inventory*.

Miscue Analysis: Calculating and Interpreting the RAI and MMI

Scoring for the miscue analysis involves making a decision about the nature of each of the scoreable miscues the reader has made. For a brief review of scoreable and nonscoreable miscues, see Figure 3–2.

First you must determine whether each scoreable miscue represents an attempt on the part of the child to maintain the meaningful sense or the grammatical integrity of the sentence. These types of miscues are more positive and less serious than the miscues that occur

Figure 3–2

Summary of Miscue
Scoring Conventions

Scoreable Miscues		Nonscoreable Miscues	
Substitutions/Reversals	Self-corrections	Repetition of words
Omissions	Repeated miscues	Ignored punctuation
Insertions	Proper nouns	Finger-pointing
Teacher-provided	Dialect differences	Subvocalization

when the reader has lost all sense of meaning and language. We recommend that you mark all of these meaning-maintaining miscues with a plus sign (+) in the margin of the line where they occur. Those more serious miscues that fail to maintain sense or linguistic integrity in the passage should be marked with a zero (0) in the margin of the line where they occur.

To perform your calculations and to arrive at a numerical expression of the child's oral reading, simply count the number of miscues (both pluses and zeros). Subtract this number from the number of words in the passage to arrive at the number of words that the child has correctly identified in the context of the reading. Then divide the remainder by the total number of words in the passage, round it off to the nearest whole number, and the result is the Reading Accuracy Index (RAI) percentage for that grade level. It is even easier to refer to the miscue chart that accompanies each passage. Simply find the number of scoreable miscues on the chart; the accompanying percentage will be the RAI.

Then count the number of miscues that violated the meaning of the language (only those that are marked with zeros) and subtract that number from the number of words in the passage. Then divide the remainder by the total number of words in the passage and round off the result to the nearest whole number. This will be the percentage for the Meaning Maintenance Index (MMI) for that grade level. Once again, to simplify the calculation of both the RAI and the MMI, we have included a miscue chart for each reading passage in Form A and Form B. To use the chart, simply look up the total number of miscues (both pluses and zeros) to find the RAI percentage and look up the number of meaning-violating miscues (only those marked with zeros) to find the MMI. Then note the corresponding percentages on your recording form.

Note that the RAI and the MMI are simply screening devices that allow you to identify at a glance any potentially serious problems. They are not designed to replace the more detailed analysis that may be called for if a problem arises. The RAI itself is a fairly simple measure of the faithfulness of a child's oral reading with respect to the text. The RAI makes no attempt to distinguish between incidental miscues that do not change the meaning of the text and those that are more serious. That task is left to the MMI.

For example, a child who makes 10 scoreable miscues in a 200-word passage would have an RAI of 95% (200 words − 10 miscues = 190; 190/200 = 95% total words). If each of those miscues turned out to be fairly minor variations from the text, and each one indicated an effort to maintain both the sense and the syntax of the language, you would have no miscues that distorted meaning. Thus your MMI would be 100%. If, however, 6 of those 10 miscues altered the meaning of the text, you would have an MMI of 97% (200 words – 6 meaning-violating miscues = 194; 194/200 = 97% total words). Both the RAI and MMI can be calculated automatically by the ASII program that accompanies the CRI.

As the test progresses, pay attention to the reader's word recognition and comprehension levels in order to guide your decisions about whether to continue to test. In the interest of the most efficient use of testing time, you will not have the opportunity to calculate actual scores while the reader waits for the testing to resume. Comprehensive calculations will have to wait until you have completed the testing and you have the opportunity to score all responses and even to listen to tape recordings as needed. But as a rule of thumb, when readers begin to struggle seriously with word recognition and when they begin to comprehend only half of what they read, it is probably time to either end the testing or switch to Listening Comprehension (which is discussed later in this section).

Miscue Analysis Worksheet

The Miscue Analysis Worksheet (MAW) is an optional form that may be used to visually represent patterns in the child's word recognition strategies. It can also indicate at a glance whether there are significant changes in these strategies as the reading material becomes more challenging. Some users of the CRI may find it most useful to facilitate the analysis of miscues by summarizing them on the worksheet.

In order to use the MAW effectively, you must have estimated tentative reading levels for the highest Independent, highest Instructional, and Frustration levels. To facilitate the analysis of miscues, as well as to prepare for the use of the worksheet, we suggest that you use the margins on the Examiner's Copy of the selections to tabulate all miscues.

As a quick review, you should complete the following steps:

1. When you come to a scoreable miscue, determine the extent to which it reflected an attempt on the part of the child to make sense of the text.
2. If the miscue was an attempt to make the reading meaningful, place a plus sign (+) in the margin of the appropriate line in the Examiner's Copy.
3. If the miscue violates the meaning or sense of language, place a zero (0) in the margin of the appropriate line in the Examiner's Copy.

When you complete this process, you will be able to easily tally the scoreable miscues and meaning-violating miscues. Locate those numbers in the Miscue Chart and determine the student's RAI and MMI. In the example shown in Figure 3–3, the first scoreable miscue was a substitution of *faster* for *fastest*. Because the substitution maintained meaning, you would record a plus sign. Keep in mind that teacher-provided miscues reflect no attempt on the part of the reader to use context or make meaning, so they cannot be evaluated from a meaning-making perspective. A teacher-provided miscue is always marked with zero. However, all other miscues must be analyzed to determine if they do reflect attempts to use the context. You then *total all miscues marked with zeros* and locate the number of miscues and the accompanying percentage figure in the Miscue Chart on the Examiner's Copy of the texts. This percentage represents the MMI.

The child reads:

Spacer was the faster animal in the . . . [waits for examiner to help] . . . jungle. All the other animals knew that. Spacer made sure of that. He would always say, "No one can beats me. You are too (long pause) You are too afraid to run!" It was true. No one wanted to run against Spacer.

Miscue Notations	Type		Explanation
			Spacer/Spencer is non-scoreable—proper noun
Spacer *faster* TP	+	S	faster/fastest
~~Spencer~~ was the ~~fastest~~ animal in the (jungle.)	0	TP	jungle
that Spacer			
All ~~of~~ the other animals knew ~~it.~~ ~~Spencer~~ made sure	+	O	of
		S	that/it
always *beats*			
of that. He would ˰say, "No one can ~~beat~~ me! <u>You are</u>	+	I	always
	+	S	beats/beat
run			
~~all~~ too // afraid to ~~race~~!" It was true. No one wanted to	+	O	all
	+	S	run/race
run *Spacer*			
~~race~~ against ~~Spencer.~~			repeated substitution—non-scoreable

Figure 3–3

Sample Miscue Analysis

Examining Miscues: Using the Miscue Analysis Worksheet

After you have administered the entire test and you have completed the initial calculations of the RAI and MMI, you are ready to perform an even more careful analysis of the miscues that the child has made. The first thing you do is record the miscues that the reader has made at his or her highest Independent, highest Instructional, and Frustration levels in the first two columns of the Miscue Analysis Worksheet (see sample in Figure 3–4). Be sure to record only scoreable miscues in these columns. For those miscues marked with a plus sign to indicate that they are meaning maintaining, place a plus sign in column 3 under *MM*. For those miscues marked with a zero to indicate that they violate meaning, place a zero in column 4 under *MV*. Remember that teacher-provided words are always regarded as meaning violating. If any of these meaning-violating miscues are nonwords, place a zero next to that word in column 5 under *Non*.

At this point you have a complete visual display of the reader's miscues and the nature of many of those miscues. It is now a fairly straightforward process to examine those miscues and determine if the reader is using a particular pattern of strategies in the decoding of unknown words. You will want to determine if the reader is (a) overusing phonological clues in decoding, (b) attending to syntactic relationships by substituting nouns for nouns, etc. or (c) utilizing word analysis strategies by attempting to break down words into their smallest component parts. For instance, the example MAW in Figure 3–4 shows that the reader experiences few difficulties at his Independent Level but uses nonwords frequently when he

---

Miscue Analysis Worksheet

Student ___John___ Grade ___5th___ Age ___10.8___

Highest Independent Level __2nd__   Highest Instructional Level __N/A__   Frustration Level __3rd__

Miscue	Text	MM	MV	Non	Miscue	Text	MM	MV	Non	Miscue	Text	MM	MV	Non
again	against	+	—	—						hears	heard	+	—	—
I am	I'm	+	—	—						vis—iting	visiting	—	0	0
and	but	+	—	—						ez-citied	excited	—	0	0
growled	groaned	+	—	—						a	his	+	—	—
										ru-sha	rush	—	0	0
										ju-lupt	gulped	—	0	0
										touring	turning	—	0	—
										po-sto-les	postholes	—	0	0
										tru-dy-ing	trudging	—	0	0
										her	to	+	—	—
										early	eager	+	—	—
										too	so	+	—	—
										rep-lied	replied	—	0	0

RAI ____   MMI ____   RAI ____   MMI ____   RAI ____   MMI ____

RAI: Count the number of scoreable miscues from column 1 and use the Miscue Chart for that passage to obtain the RAI.

MMI: Count the number of meaning-violating miscues and use the Miscue Chart for that passage to obtain the MMI.

Non: The number of meaning-violating miscues that were nonwords.

MM: Miscue that represents an attempt to maintain the sense of the text.

MV: Miscue that violated the sense of the text.

Figure 3–4

Miscue Analysis Worksheet

attempts to read at his frustration level. Some CRI users may be able to obtain the same information by analyzing the miscues as they are noted on the Examiner's Copy. But the MAW can be particularly useful for teaching miscue analysis techniques or for simply providing an overview of the bigger picture of an important dimension of the child's reading.

Fluency

Allington (1983) has identified reading fluency as an important factor for reading comprehension. In his view, a child's fluency and automaticity of word identification contributes to comprehension by freeing up mental resources that would otherwise be occupied with word identification. Once these resources are available, readers can then utilize them to concentrate on comprehension and thoughtful response. Fluency is composed of rate, accuracy, and expression and has been cited as an important goal for reading instruction (Allington, 1983, 2001; Rasinski, 1989).

Teachers using the CRI can easily evaluate fluency in a qualitative manner by taking anecdotal notes during the student's oral reading. Particular attention should be paid to the reader's expression, phrasing, and attention to punctuation during oral reading. CRI users can also time oral reading and compare a reader's rate to well-established average reading rate tables (Harris & Sipay, 1990, p. 634). Qualitative analysis and measurement of reading rate can contribute, along with the RAI and MMI, to a thorough assessment of a reader's fluency.

For users who prefer a more structured approach to the assessment of fluency, the CRI includes an Oral Reading Fluency Rubric designed to help users assign a numerical value to a reader's fluency. That same value can be calculated automatically as part of the Automated Scoring and Interpretation Interview (ASII). Oral reading fluency should be assessed at the reader's Instructional Level, the level that challenges but does not overwhelm the reader. It is difficult to see how the assessment of fluency in response to very easy reading or very difficult reading is likely to add a great deal to the overall assessment of any reader.

But most important, fluency should never be discussed in isolation from comprehension. Although fluent readers often comprehend materials effectively, that is not always the case. Nor is it true that children who are "dysfluent" are necessarily weak in comprehension. Word recognition and comprehension function in a complex interaction that can vary widely among readers. It is tempting to conclude that teachers must teach all readers fluency before they can "free up the resources" to truly comprehend, but such a conclusion would be a profound oversimplification. The interaction between fluency and comprehension is so complex that teachers must avoid conceptualizations that are simple and linear. It is equally tempting to conclude that poor readers need more intensive drill in sound, letter, and word instruction. Research has suggested that good readers are more likely to be given instruction that focuses on meaning (Alpert, 1974; Gambrell, Wilson, & Gantt, 1981) and to have their teachers emphasize the need for oral reading to make sense and sound right (Allington, 1983). In short, fluency assessed apart from comprehension and language is likely to be of little value in contributing to the picture of any reader's functioning.

Silent Reading

Asking children to read passages silently offers them the chance to focus more of their attention on comprehension because they are relieved of the need to demonstrate their ability to pronounce aloud the words in the text. It also offers users of the CRI the chance to observe whether readers can take advantage of the situation and focus more effectively on comprehension. Silent reading forces readers to read without the help that can be obtained through teacher-provided words; it is not unusual for children with severe word recognition problems to demonstrate an inability to deal with text silently. Subvocalization during silent reading is common in such circumstances. But above all, silent reading offers the CRI user the opportunity to observe children reading alone, to note their habits and idiosyncrasies, and to compare their comprehension performance after oral reading and silent reading.

Comprehension Assessment: Retellings

After you have read the introductory statement and the children complete either the oral or silent reading, say "Tell me about what you just read and what you thought about it" and record their retellings verbatim. Note that we specifically ask the child to respond to the text, express an interest in it, or react to the content. We are simply issuing an invitation to do so. It is of vital interest to you to determine if the children see reading as a task that requires them to use their background knowledge and thinking skills. Children who view reading as a passive activity will almost never accept the invitation to comment about "what they thought" of the passage or its content. If they do not, repeat the invitation after the initial retelling as noted on the Examiner's Copy of the test.

We advise you to have a tape recorder available for this part of the test as children who speak very quickly or give a lengthy retelling can severely challenge your hand and wrist strength as you try to write down everything. The purpose of the retelling is to ascertain, without the benefit of the jog in memory that accompanies the asking of open-ended questions, what the child has determined is important enough to remember and how it is organized. When you score the test, you will analyze the retellings both qualitatively and quantitatively as another window into the thinking of the child during and after reading. As an aid to analysis of the retellings, use the unique rubric provided for each story in the Examiner's Copy and look for signs of how the child perceived the structure of the text, the level of importance of the ideas included in it, and any personal response to the text the child may have expressed. You will often gain a great deal of insight into the organizational processes used by the child in your analysis of the child's retelling.

Access the Automated Scoring and Interpretation Interview at www.prenhall.com/ readinginventory/ scoringassistant *for scoring help, tutorials, and case studies (ASII is accessible to Windows users only).*

Use the DVD that accompanies this text for guidance on how to use *The Critical Reading Inventory.*

Scoring Retellings

Score the retelling by using the scoring guides for either narrative or informational passages on pages 80 and 81 in the Test Materials section. In the interest of more efficient use of the examiner's time and more reliable numerical calculation of scores, we have included an Automated Scoring Program as part of the ASII. Users simply indicate on the rubric the presence or absence (or partial presence) of text elements for each passage retold. The program returns the calculated numerical score for the retelling.

As an aid to mastering the technique of scoring retellings, we have included self-paced Retelling Scoring Tutorials on the CRI website. The tutorials provide numerous opportunities to score actual children's retellings and provides instructional feedback on your scoring as well. Retellings are demonstrated on the DVD that accompanies the CRI.

Use the story structure (narrative) or the macro-concept/micro-concept structure (informational) rubric to calculate the student's retelling score in Figure 3–5, based on the scoring guide. We suggest that you mark a "+1" next to each text element listed in the rubric that you judge as having been addressed in the retelling. If the category is partially covered, you may find it necessary to award partial credit by marking $\frac{1}{2}$ next to the appropriate text element. If the category is omitted entirely, place a "0" next to the appropriate text element.

Description of the significance of numerical retelling scores are included in the Scoring Guides found in the Test Materials section of the text. For more examples of retellings and application of scoring critetia, CRI users can consult the Retelling Scoring Tutorials.

The Nature of Retellings

The optimum retelling, that done by our hypothetical ideal reader, includes all of the important elements in the text and also includes a well-supported personal response to the text. This is a rather tall order for most children in that surprisingly few children respond spontaneously to what they read. Most children who are familiar with the concept of an un-aided retelling will strive to faithfully reproduce the information that they have read. They will often do so without commenting on whether they enjoyed reading it or not, whether it matched their belief system, or whether they found it in any way interesting. For this

Sample Narrative Retelling Rubric

Child's Retelling:

"Spencer brags to the other animals about how fast he is and tries to get them to race so he can brag more. Then a new family moves in and he asks them to race and Annie races him and wins. All the animals were happy 'cause they thought he would stop bragging but Spencer was mad and he went away. He came back the next day and bragged about how high he could jump and all the animals rolled their eyes and groaned." *Examiner*: "Tell me what you thought about the passage." *Child*: "It was about a cat who bragged a lot."

Scoring and Discussion

This is a very good retelling that includes the key characters, the character's goal, and 4½ steps in the Problem-Solving Process. The reader fails to note Annie's disappointment in Spencer's reaction. This results in the partial credit score for step 4 in the Problem-Solving Process. The other piece that is missing is the personal response; in its place the reader simply relates a very brief summation of the story.

Score: 2.5

Retelling Rubric

Story Structure:

According to the Scoring Guide, the Starting Score (SS) for this retelling is 2.0. Because the reader has included 4½ steps in the Problem-Solving Process, we add .5 to the SS to make it 2.5. Without the additional credit of a Personal Response, however, the final score is 2.5.

1. **Key Characters and Setting:** Spencer, other animals, and Annie who moved into jungle. +1
2. **Character's Problem or Goal:** Spencer wants to be able to brag about his abilities. +1
3. **Problem-Solving or Goal-Meeting Process:**
   - Spencer brags and gets others to race with him so that he can brag more. +1
   - Annie moves in and Spencer races with her. +1
   - Spencer loses the race. +1
   - Spencer walks away angrily and Annie is sad because she had wanted a friend. +1
   - Spencer returns the next day and brags about jumping. +1/2
4. **Personal Response:** Any well-supported positive or negative response to the characters or events in the story or to the story as a whole. no

Figure 3–5

Sample Retelling Scoring Rubric

reason, you will often find it necessary to remind readers that you would like to hear their personal response.

Although you will use the Retelling Rubric box that accompanies each passage as the first step in assigning a numerical score to each retelling, it is important to emphasize that the retelling is only one piece of information that you can use in the analysis of a child's reading performance. Seldom is the retelling sufficient in itself as a diagnostic tool, although it can offer you glimpses of the child's thinking processes that can be gained in no other way. Retellings are often insufficient in themselves because of extraneous variables that may affect a child's performance on any retelling. For example, the child's confidence and willingness to elaborate on responses may be affected by the rapport developed with the examiner. If a child is characterized by a fear of making incorrect responses, you may obtain nothing more than minimal retellings from that child. Children with little confidence in their ability to verbalize or explain their answers may score poorly on retellings. Children who are simply unaccustomed to doing a retelling and more comfortable with the memory jog that comprehension questions provide may do poorly as well. In any of these cases, it is not necessarily the child's reading ability that is affecting the retellings. For this reason alone it is important that you verify, insofar as possible, any observations you make in one area of the test with performance in all other related areas. For examples of comprehensive analyses of CRI results, read the case studies available on the CRI web site.

Practical Guidelines for Scoring Narrative Retellings in the CRI

Key Characters and Setting

The primary objective of this assessment is to determine if the reader has been able to fit into the retelling the major characters in the story and the general time and place where the story has occurred. There are several issues to be taken into consideration in the scoring.

1. Readers need not recall the name of a character so long as their description makes it clear that they have acknowledged that character. For example, after having read *The Race*, one child talked about "the cat who was really fast and always bragging." She could not remember that the cat's name was Spencer, but her description of the character is unmistakable.
2. The omission of one or even two key characters often results in the awarding of partial credit. For example, in the story entitled *The Vacation*, there are four key characters: Juan, Maria, Mr. Ruiz, and Mrs. Ruiz. The omission of any one of these characters would result in a half-credit score.
3. The setting of a story is a part of the core of the story grammar. We need, however, to be sensitive to the fact that many readers imply rather than directly state the elements of the setting. For example, in the story entitled *The Little Fish*, the characters are swimming in the ocean. The reader need not specifically mention the ocean in the retelling but may imply the fact by describing the home of the fish and talking of other fish swimming nearby. In such cases the setting is implied and we can exercise considerable flexibility in our interpretation of the identification of the setting.

Character's Problem or Goal

1. The problem that characters try to resolve and/or the goals that they try to achieve are central elements of any narrative retelling and they are essential to the idea of the story grammar.
2. The most common error in identifying the problem or goal is the incomplete response. Many goals are complex and require more than one proposition in the sample statement in the scoring rubric. For example in *The Race*, Spencer's goal is not only to be the fastest animal but to be able to brag about it. The omission of either element results in a half-credit score.

Problem-Solving or Goal-Meeting Process

1. This is one of the most straightforward steps in scoring narrative retellings in the CRI. The user must simply determine whether the step in the process is clearly stated or implied in the reader's retelling.
2. The most common error in scoring steps in the Problem-Solving Process is awarding full credit when only half of the step is stated or implied in the retelling. For example, in the story entitled *The Roller Coaster Ride*, one step in the Problem-Solving Process reads as follows. "Jessie becomes frightened and she promises she will never ride again." A retelling that includes only that Jessie became frightened qualifies for a score of half credit.

Personal Responses

A Personal Response to a story is defined as a well-supported positive or negative reaction to the characters or events in a story or to the story as a whole. For the most part, the difficulty in scoring the Personal Response hinges on the issue of how well-supported the reader's ideas are. A positive or negative opinion is always easy to come by, but solid support for that opinion is often a different story. A solid Personal Response should make use of elements from the story and draw conclusions that are not stated directly in the story itself. The following guidelines and examples should help you in distinguishing between a scoreable and a nonscoreable Personal Response.

1. Any unsupported statement of opinion about the story is not scored as a Personal Response. The reader who says, "I liked that story. It was funny." or "That was a stupid story" has not provided support for the stated opinion.

2. A statement drawn from pure experience without reference to other story elements is not scored as a Personal Response. Responses such as "I like this story because I like baseball" or "I went on vacation to Florida once" have not provided any solid link to what went on in the story.

3. A response that links to or identifies with a character or event in a story is scored as a Personal Response. One reader responded to *The Race* by stating, "I like to race like Spencer did but I don't think people should brag like he does." This is a solid response.

4. A generalization or a moral that can be drawn from the story is scored as a good Personal Response. If a reader responds to *Getting What You Want* by stating, "You should be careful what you wish for," he has clearly grasped the essence of the story.

5. Literary criticism with no support is not considered a Personal Response. Readers who say such things as "I don't like stories with a twist like that" or "It was a good short story but not suspenseful" should not be awarded credit.

6. Responses that restate facts from the story are not credited as Personal Responses. One reader, after reading *Getting What You Want*, stated, "I liked how she entered the contest and the prize was to marry the emperor's only daughter." This reader has done little more than express an opinion and try to support it with information lifted almost directly from the text.

7. A scoreable Personal Response need not be a profound analysis of the underlying significance of a story. All we are looking for is a tendency to think about the story beyond the level of mere recall of details. Of course, we will still assess the depth of a reader's thinking under any circumstances. After reading *The Championship Game*, one reader observed, "I don't really know what lesson she could have learned." This response simply demonstrates the reader's willingness to think about the unstated lessons that the experiences in the story might have taught. That type of thinking is what we hope to see in the Personal Response.

8. We must be on our guard against responses that sound profound but have little support or substance behind them. One young philosopher, in response to *The Championship Game*, stated, "It is something like what I do in my life. I have a lot of championship games." Without a follow-up question to elicit some further explanation of the reader's thinking, it is impossible to award credit for this response.

9. Solid text-to-text connections are scored as successful Personal Responses. But the reader must be able to explain how the connection came about. It is not enough for the reader to say, "This story reminded me of *Snow White*" without explaining how the story did so.

Practical Guidelines for Scoring Informational Retellings in the CRI

Macro-Concepts

1. Readers are often more challenged by informational retellings than by narratives, simply because they are more familiar with the stable story structure than with

the variety of expository structures they are likely to encounter. Consequently they are under greater pressure to organize independently the ideas they read about in informational text.

2. Macro-concepts are the central ideas around which the content of a passage is built. Since they do not serve the same function as details, they do not have to be recalled verbatim. We can exercise a good deal more judgment and give greater leeway in our interpretation of a reader's retelling when we are dealing with Macro-concepts.

3. A frequent error in retellings of Macro-concepts is the omission of the logical connectors that link Macro-concepts together and form the ideational fabric of the passage.

4. Examiners must be on their guard since informational text is more likely to elicit pure background knowledge from readers than is narrative text. That is, when readers are under stress to recall information, they find it easy to digress, particularly if they have a well-developed background related to the topic in the passage.

Micro-Concepts

1. Micro-concepts are, by definition, factual statements that support or elucidate the Macro-concepts that form the conceptual framework of the passage. As such, we need to be a bit more stringent in our interpretation of retellings to insure that the factual underpinnings of key ideas are present.

2. Do not be reluctant to ask follow-up questions. Readers tend to view Informational retellings as a recall of the central topics of a passage. As such, they frequently recall a good deal more than the initial retelling reveals. Remember that an informal reading inventory is a maximum performance test. We want to see what children are capable of and we need not be overly concerned about the "fairness" of test procedures because our purpose is seldom to compare one child to another.

3. The assessment of Micro-concepts often provides us with the opportunity to observe the organizational skills of the reader. Look for retellings that are scattered or disjointed as a sign of potential problems with informational text.

4. The retelling of Micro-concepts presents a temptation to substitute background knowledge for the information included in the text. Examiners must be on their guard.

Personal Responses

A Personal Response to a passage is defined as a well-supported positive or negative reaction to the ideas or details in the passage or to the passage as a whole. For the most part, the difficulty in scoring the Personal Response hinges on the issue of how well-supported the reader's ideas are. A positive or negative opinion is always easy to come by but solid support for that opinion is often a different story. A solid Personal Response should make use of elements from the text and draw conclusions that are not stated directly in the passage itself. The following guidelines and examples should help you in distinguishing between a scoreable and a nonscoreable Personal Response.

1. Any unsupported statement of opinion about the passage is not scored as a Personal Response. The reader who says, "I liked that passage. I don't know anything about that" or "That was boring" has not provided support for the stated opinion.

2. A statement drawn from pure experience without reference to other passage elements is not scored as a Personal Response. Responses such as "I like this one because I like bears" or "I saw a Beluga whale once" have not provided any solid link to what went on in the passage.

3. A response that links to or identifies with ideas or details in a passage is scored as a Personal Response. One reader responded to *The Immigrants* by stating,

"My grandfather was an immigrant and he was mistreated just like the people in the passage." This is a solid response.

4. A generalization or a moral that can be drawn from the story is scored as a good Personal Response. If a reader responds to *Child Slaves* by stating, "Laws should protect people who can't fight for themselves," she has clearly grasped the essence of the story.

5. Literary criticism with no support is not considered a Personal Response. Readers who say such things as "I don't like to read about ants" or "It was good but it didn't have enough information in it" should not be awarded credit.

6. Responses that restate facts from the story are not credited as Personal Responses.

7. A scoreable Personal Response need not be a profound analysis of the underlying significance of a passage. All we are looking for is a tendency to think about the text beyond the level of mere recall of details. Of course, we will still assess the depth of a reader's thinking under any circumstances.

8. We must be on our guard against responses that sound profound but have little support or real meaning behind them. Without a follow-up question that might elicit some further explanation of the reader's thinking, it is impossible to award credit for this kind of response.

9. Solid text-to-text connections are scored as successful Personal Responses.

Comprehension Questions

You then ask the comprehension questions that accompany each passage in the order in which they occur. For each question, record the child's response verbatim in the space provided on the Examiner's Copy. This is another instance of furious writing on your part, but it is well worth it in the long run. We have found that at this point a tape recorder provides an excellent and necessary backup. It is an impossible task to try to rely on your memory when it comes time to analyze the child's performance on the CRI. You can take one short-cut, however: If the child's response is the same as the suggested sample response that accompanies each item, simply underline that part of the suggested answer that the child used. This is likely to save you at least some writing, particularly for the literal items for which there is usually only one correct response.

See ASII

Access the Automated Scoring and Interpretation Interview at www.prenhall.com/ readinginventory/ scoringassistant *for scoring help, tutorials, and case studies (ASII is accessible to Windows users only).*

Another major difference between the CRI and most standardized tests is the extensive use of open-ended questions. Open-ended questions are really an attempt to open a window to the child's thinking processes. In the course of responding to open-ended questions, however, children may be vague, evasive, fuzzy in their thinking, or simply lacking in confidence in their ability to express themselves verbally. In these cases the examiner is encouraged to ask follow-up questions to try to elicit more information or more clarity from the children. When you do ask a follow-up question, you should note the question by a circled question mark when you are recording the child's responses. Then record the child's response to the follow-up immediately after the question mark. Because the CRI is an assessment that attempts to measure the maximum performance of the reader, give the child credit for any correct answers given in response to a follow-up (see Figure 3–6).

A need for many follow-up questions may be evidence of imprecise thought or expression that may be addressed in your instructional plan for that child. In order to know when it is appropriate to ask for more information, it is essential that the examiner be familiar with the CRI selections and the range of acceptable answers for the comprehension questions. For this reason, you are likely to become a more effective diagnostician the more you administer the CRI. If you are a beginner with the CRI, time allotted for reading and studying selections, questions, and sample responses will be time well spent. The more familiar you are with the test materials, the more efficient and effective your testing will be. And because your time with any given child may be limited, you will need to be aware of testing techniques that make the best use of that time. An examination of the follow-up questions noted in the case studies will also be helpful to you in identifying appropriate times to ask follow-up questions.

Figure 3–6

Sample Follow-Up
Questions on the CRI

Example 1

In the second-grade story titled "The Race," the child is asked "What did the animals do when Annie won the race?" She responds, "They were happy." The examiner notes that the child is correct based on the information in the story but that she has not really addressed the text-based question about what the animals *do*. The examiner follows up with a question: "Good, but can you tell me what the animals did that let you know they were happy?" When the child responds "They cheered her," the examiner records the response as correct.

Example 2

In the same story, the child is asked, "Do you think this was the first time Annie had ever raced against anyone?" She responds, "No, because she knew she would win." This response hints that it was confidence behind Annie's smiling acceptance of the challenge to race, but the link is not clear. Thus the examiner follows up with the question: "But why would Annie think she would win?" When the child responds with "She had probably raced other people before and so she knew she was fast," the logical link is complete.

In a typical administration of the CRI, once you have completed the comprehension check for an oral reading selection for a particular grade level, you progress immediately to a silent reading selection at that same grade level. Once again, you *use the printed introductory statement to introduce the reading* and then you observe while the child reads silently. At this time you may jot down any behaviors that are worthy of note, such as subvocalization, finger-pointing at words and lines, unusually fast or slow pace of reading, and so forth.

The comprehension check after silent reading is identical to that following oral reading. That is, you ask the child for a retelling and then follow with the open-ended comprehension questions. A sample administration of the CRI is included on the DVD that accompanies the test manual.

Scoring Comprehension Questions

Use the DVD that accompanies this text for guidance on how to use *The Critical Reading Inventory*.

Scoring comprehension questions can range from being very simple to being very complex, depending on the nature of the reader's responses. Most scoring of text-based items is quite straightforward; either the child remembers the details or does not. One notable exception occurs when readers interpret a text-based question as calling for an inference or critical response. A follow-up question redirecting the reader to "what the *passage* said" is usually very effective in eliciting an appropriate response. But inference and critical response items can often be quite another matter. Even in those inference items that have a single correct response, the range of creative ways in which the children can express their ideas can often present a challenge to scorers.

For this reason, we include sample correct responses in the Examiner's Copy for each item in the CRI, but we encourage you not to follow them slavishly. They are by no means the only answers that can be correct. Often you will find yourself considering a logical interpretation of both the question and the response. This individual variation in scoring is the most often cited weakness of any informal reading inventory, but it is also its most valuable strength. You simply need to keep in mind that the ultimate objective for CRI users is to gather diagnostic information that will make your instructional program more effective in the long run.

Scoring critical response questions can be even more challenging than scoring literal and inferential ones. A good answer to a critical response item is one that provides solid and logical support for one's ideas. It is not sufficient to answer a critical response item by stating an opinion; in the CRI, opinions are of no consequence unless readers can back them up with reasons. It is up to you to make judgments about the extent to which readers have supported their responses. The completion of the self-paced Comprehension Item Scoring Tutorials (Available on the CRI web site as well as on the DVD-ROM that accompanies the CRI) will go a long way toward developing your skill and confidence in scoring comprehension responses.

As we have noted, you may at any time choose to ask children follow-up questions in search of more complete or precise responses. Readers are not penalized when they arrive at a correct response as a result of a follow-up. We are interested more in gaining insights into how the child is thinking than in the "fairness" of the scoring. You are also free to assign partial credit to any of the child's responses. It is often possible for the examiner to recognize in retrospect that a child's response may be logical but also incomplete.

Scoring involves once again the calculation of a simple percentage. For both oral and silent reading, simply add the number of correct responses (or partially correct responses) and divide by the number of comprehension questions used at that grade level. To arrive at the average comprehension for a grade level, add the oral and silent percentages, divide by two, and round off to the nearest whole number. For your convenience we have included percentage boxes to facilitate your calculations. You will, of course, wish to differentiate between the child's text-based and higher-level responses, but you can also use the Automated Scoring and Interpretation Interview (ASII) included at the web site that accompanies this text.

See ASII

Access the Automated Scoring and Interpretation Interview at www.prenhall.com/ readinginventory/ scoringassistant *for scoring help, tutorials, and case studies (ASII is accessible to Windows users only).*

Practical Guidelines for Scoring Comprehension Questions in the CRI

Text-Based Questions

The essence of the Text-based question is that it calls for the reader to recall information stated or obviously implied in the text.

1. Occasionally, a reader will respond to a text-based item as if it were calling for an inference. In this case, a simple reminder that the question is looking for "what the story said" is enough to re-direct the reader.
2. Responses to text-based items that include both accurate and inaccurate information are generally scored as $\frac{1}{2}$ credit responses.
3. The sample responses provided in the CRI Manual are only examples and the examiner need not insist on verbatim replication of those responses. Any adequate paraphrases are sufficient for our purposes.

Inference Questions

The effective response to an Inference question involves two elements: it must draw upon information included or implied in the story and it must draw a logical conclusion based on that information. If the reader draw a logical conclusion based solely upon experience, it does not meet the criteria for a scoreable response.

1. Answers drawn from pure experience are described as Quiz Contestant responses in Profiles in Comprehension. It is entirely possible to arrive at answers that are logically plausible but not even suggested in the story. These kinds of responses are never credited as valid inferences.
2. Logical inferences that include both correct information and inaccuracies are generally scored as $\frac{1}{2}$ credit.
3. Difficult inference questions sometimes tempt readers to rephrase the question into a statement and attempt to pass it off as a response. Examiners must be on their guard.
4. Vague, fuzzy, or unclear responses beg for a follow-up question to allow the reader to clarify the thinking that went into the responses. In the absence of the reader's ability to explain the response, it is scored as no credit.

Critical Response Questions

The Critical Response item forces the reader to take a stand and state an opinion. Of course, the opinion is not nearly as valuable as the support that the reader uses to shore up the response.

1. The reader must draw a logical conclusion that is valid and draws support from the story. When asked if Jill (from *The Championship Game*) had a chance of becoming a professional player, one reader responded in the negative "because Jill is not nice to her team." Being nice to your team has no real connection to one's performance as a player.
2. Struggling readers who are skilled at masking their difficulties sometimes alter the thrust of the question and reply at some length to the new question. Examiners must be on their guard.
3. Vague support for opinions does not qualify for credit.
4. Readers who are unfamiliar with Critical Response questions are sometimes tempted to use platitudes as support for their responses. When asked if he thought Mr. Singer (from *The Player*) should let his young son make his own decisions, one reader answered, "Yes, because you can do whatever you want to if you try hard." This response simply does not support the opinion.

Administering the Listening Comprehension Test

You should administer the Listening Comprehension assessment of the CRI to those children whose Instructional Level is lower than their current grade-level placement. In such cases, administer the Listening Comprehension test by selecting a passage at the grade level where the child is currently placed. Your purpose is to assess whether children are able to comprehend adequately in their current classroom and thus if they are benefiting from oral instruction in the classroom. It is also advisable to use the Listening Comprehension for children whose word recognition problems appear to be overwhelming their ability to comprehend text.

We have found that the easiest way to phase into the Listening Comprehension test is to simply say to the child, "Because you have read to me it is only fair that I should read to you for a change. When I'm finished, I'll ask you to tell me about what you've heard and I'll ask you questions, just as I did when you read." Then you proceed to read one passage per grade level, followed by a retelling and the comprehension questions.

Lookbacks

It is clear that the practice of taking the text from students and then asking them to retell and to respond to questions about what they have just read taxes the memory. It is equally clear that as diagnosticians, teachers want to know how and where readers have allocated their memory resources in response to text. But it is also enlightening to assess the extent to which readers are able to function when the sheer memory task is relieved and they are allowed to look back at the text they have just read. In other words, you want to see if their test performance has been largely due to difficulties with memory or difficulties with comprehension.

And so users of the CRI may wish to expand their assessment to include *lookbacks*. You simply return the text to students after they have responded to all comprehension questions related to the passage. Because a student who has responded correctly to all questions has already demonstrated a solid level of comprehension, you would normally use lookbacks only when a reader has experienced some difficulty with several of the comprehension items. Lookbacks are likely to be particularly helpful in assessing the comprehension of students who tend to respond frequently with "I don't know" or "I don't remember." To utilize lookbacks, simply return the passage to the reader and say, "Let's see if looking back at the passage can help you with some of these questions." Then repeat those questions with which the reader experienced initial confusion. Any additional responses the student makes can be noted on the Examiner's Copy. A simple slash and a notation of *L* will make it easy for you to distinguish between unaided responses and responses that followed lookbacks (see Figure 3–7).

Your objective in utilizing the lookback convention is, of course, to add to your overall diagnostic profile of the reader. During lookbacks, you want to see if the reader is able to use the text in a meaningful way. Some readers will, for example, quickly and easily locate information relevant to the comprehension item, particularly if the item is text-based. Others will struggle and may even read the entire passage in search of helpful information. Some readers will demonstrate clearly during lookbacks that they believed their initial

Figure 3–7

Sample Notations
After Lookback

> **Comprehension Questions**
> 1. Why was everyone in the family excited about the vacation in Florida? Text-Based: It was their first family vacation; first trip to Florida.
> *I don't really remember.*
> *L // It was their first trip to Florida.*
>
> Located information quickly and efficiently.

response to be more than sufficient to answer the question. Still others will read in an attempt to locate answers directly in the text, even when the item calls for them to draw conclusions or respond to ideas in the text. All of these types of behaviors, of course, add valuable information to your overall diagnostic profile of any reader.

It goes without saying that rereading the entire passage in search of answers to questions is a poor strategy and you would normally stop using lookbacks with students who consistently reread passages. You would gain little or no further information about these readers as a consequence of lookbacks.

Comprehension after lookbacks can be considered a more authentic type of assessment as it replicates more closely the kind of reading that a student will normally engage in. But you must realize that lookbacks will provide some readers with clues that their responses are wrong or incomplete. For readers with a great deal of confidence, or readers who project a high level of confidence, the realization that all is not well may be disconcerting. In these cases you would generally stop using lookbacks as well.

Whereas lookbacks may give information that will help in the process of estimating a student's reading level, scores after lookbacks should not be used as the basis for these estimates. The authenticity of such reading is not in question, but the data are simply not available that relate comprehension after lookbacks to actual classroom performance in reading. Nor are traditional criteria for estimating reading levels based on comprehension after lookbacks.

Lookbacks are particularly valuable in the assessment of students who overrely on memory in their attempts to comprehend text. Retellings that include scattered details, significant gaps, or clear attempts at verbatim recall of the text are telltale signs of such readers. If their inferential and critical response comprehension improves significantly after lookbacks, then you can include in their instructional program tools to help them use their memory more effectively. These might include story grammars, graphic organizers, sketch to stretch, the use of sticky notes to encourage self-questioning, or even more extensive prereading activities during instruction. Readers who do well in text-based comprehension but who do not improve in response-based comprehension after lookbacks will require a different approach. They are likely to benefit from prereading that builds on an examination of their own experiences as these relate to the text and their own ideas related to the underlying significance of the text. Such an approach is designed to lead readers to a full-scale reexamination of their view of reading itself.

Using the Recapitulation Record

See ASII

Access the Automated Scoring and Interpretation Interview at www.prenhall.com/ readinginventory/ scoringassistant *for scoring help, tutorials, and case studies (ASII is accessible to Windows users only).*

The Recapitulation Record simply provides a summary of the child's overall performance on the CRI and facilitates some relevant analyses of those scores as well. The Recapitulation Record, as the name suggests, provides a recap of the child's performance that is useful for what we will discuss in Section 4 as numerical interpretation. An examination of the Recapitulation Record can provide you with an overview of any child's performance, but it should actually be used in conjunction with a careful analysis of the child's comprehension responses. The more sources of information you bring to bear on the case, the more effective your proposed program of instruction is likely to be. And, as you will see, there is far more information available in the CRI beyond the numbers alone that can give you valuable insights into any child's strengths and weaknesses in reading. After you have graded and calculated all scores for the CRI, you are ready to begin to fill out the Recapitulation Record. If you prefer, you can access the Automated Scoring and Interpretation Interview (ASII) that accompanies the CRI. The ASII will perform many of the calculations involved in filling out the Recapitulation Record and will allow you to print a clean and professional-looking copy suitable for student records.

Word Lists

If you fill out the Recapitulation Record manually, simply transcribe the flash and untimed percentages you have calculated and place them in the appropriate boxes under the heading "Word Lists" as illustrated in Sample Box 1.

Comprehending and Responding to Text: Oral and Silent Reading

Oral Reading. After you have analyzed the miscues the child made during oral reading, you can calculate an RAI and MMI score for each level the child has completed. Place these numbers in the appropriate columns on the Recapitulation Record (see Sample Box 1).

Sample Box 1 From Recapitulation Record

Level	Flash	Untimed	RAI	MMI
Pre-Primer	100	100	99	100
Primer	90	95	98	99

After you have graded the oral comprehension questions, calculate the overall oral reading comprehension percentage score and put it in the first column as illustrated in Sample Box 2. Then move to the retelling. Place the score you have assigned in the column titled "Retelling Score." Then fill in the number of questions that were correctly answered in each of the three question types.

Sample Box 2 From Recapitulation Record

Oral Comp. %	Retelling Score	Oral Text-Based	Oral Inference	Oral Critical Response
90	2.5	4/4	3/3	2/3
70	1.5	4/4	1/3	2/3

When you have completed the oral comprehension, simply move on to the silent passage and follow the same procedures (see Sample Box 3). Then calculate the average percentage value of the oral and silent comprehension and put it in the appropriate column. Repeat the process for all additional passages, oral and silent. Finally, identify the grade level used for listening comprehension (if administered), and fill in the comprehension percentage and number of items in each category for that level.

Sample Box 3 From Recapitulation Record

Silent Comp. %	Retelling Score	Silent Text-Based	Silent Inference	Silent Critical Response	Average Oral and Silent	Listening Comp. %
80	2.5	4/4	2/3	2/3	85	—
75	2.0	3/4	2/3	2.5/3	70	—

Estimating Reading Levels

After the completion of the recapitulation table, use the recorded data to identify tentative reading levels (see Section 4 for a complete discussion of level setting). We suggest that you use the Betts criteria shown here as the basis for these levels.

Betts Criteria for Estimating Reading Levels		
Level	Average of Oral and Silent Comprehension	Reading Accuracy Index (RAI)
Independent	90%	99%
Instructional	75%	95%
Frustration	50%	90%
Listening comprehension	N/A	75%

Recording Scores in the Analysis Table

Once you have estimated reading levels, you are ready now to transcribe the scores from the Examiner's Copy of the CRI to the Level One Numerical Interpretation tables on the second page of the Recapitulation Record (see Figure 3–8). At this level you will be looking primarily at the story told by the numbers you have gathered and not necessarily at the reasons why the reader obtained these scores. That will occur in the Level Two interpretation. The Level One table is structured to promote a systematic look at the data and to raise some important questions about contrasts in reading performance.

Word Lists and Miscue Analysis

After you have estimated the child's reading levels, transcribe these levels in columns 2, 3, and 4 for the highest Independent, highest Instructional, and the Frustration levels, respectively. Begin with scores from the highest Independent Level and transcribe the Flash, the Untimed, RAI, and MMI for that level from the main body of the Recapitulation Record. Then retrieve the number of self-corrections and the number of nonwords from the record of miscues in the Examiner's Copy for that level. The same data will be included on the Miscue Analysis Worksheet if you used that instrument. Repeat this process for the highest Instructional and Frustration levels.

When this part of the table is complete you will see at a glance the contrast between the child's performance with words in isolation and words that the child has encountered in the context of actual reading. This part of the table will also facilitate the contrast between attempts to make meaning and failure to do so, with particular attention to the use of nonwords. These contrasts are designed to provide insight into the child's view of reading.

Recording Comprehension Scores and Retellings

For this part of the analysis, transcribe the oral and silent comprehension percentage score for the Independent Level and average the two. Then take the oral and silent retelling scores for the same level and average the two. Repeat this process for the Instructional and Frustration levels.

The key contrast that this part of the table is designed to highlight is the difference that might exist between the child's unaided recall of the text (the retelling average) and the structured assessment provided by specific comprehension questions. You can also compare at a glance the differences that might exist between the child's oral and silent reading comprehension. This contrast is becoming increasingly important as national, state, and local measures rely more and more on silent reading as their means of assessment. Any significant changes that occur in the child's pattern of comprehension between Independent and Instructional or even Frustration levels can be invaluable in setting up an effective program of instruction for the child.

Level One Numerical Interpretation

Level	Highest Independent Level	Highest Instructional Level	Frustration Level
Word List and Miscue Analysis	Flash ___ MMI ___ Untimed SC ___ Comp. % RAI ___ Nonwords ___	Flash ___ MMI ___ Untimed SC ___ Comp. % RAI ___ Nonwords ___	Flash ___ MMI ___ Untimed SC ___ Comp. % RAI ___ Nonwords ___
Comprehension and Retelling Scores	Comp. % ___ Retelling ___ Oral: ___ Silent: ___ Average: ___	Comp. % ___ Retelling ___ Oral: ___ Silent: ___ Average: ___	Comp. % ___ Retelling ___ Oral: ___ Silent: ___ Average: ___
Oral Comprehension, Fluency, and MMI	Oral comp. % ___ MMI ___	Oral comp. % ___ MMI ___ Fluency ___	Oral comp. % ___ MMI ___
Question Type	Oral ___ Silent ___ Text-Based: ___ ___ Inference: ___ ___ Critical: ___ ___	Oral ___ Silent ___ Text-Based: ___ ___ Inference: ___ ___ Critical: ___ ___	Oral ___ Silent ___ Text-Based: ___ ___ Inference: ___ ___ Critical: ___ ___

Figure 3–8

A Method for Systematically Examining and Comparing Numerical Data from the CRI

Oral Comprehension and the MMI

Transcribe the oral comprehension score and the MMI from the body of the Recapitulation Record for the highest Independent level, the highest Instructional level, and the highest Frustration level.

This segment of the table facilitates the observation of any discrepancy that might exist between overall comprehension following oral reading and attempts at meaning making on the part of the reader. For example, a child who directs most of her energy toward accuracy and fluency and fails to comprehend effectively may be signaling the teacher about a view of reading that does not include thinking about or responding to text. Although the MMI and oral comprehension are usually quite similar at the Independent Level, discrepancies at the Instructional and/or Frustration levels are typically a clear signal for instructional intervention.

Question Type

See ASII

Access the Automated Scoring and Interpretation Interview at www.prenhall.com/ readinginventory/ scoringassistant *for scoring help, tutorials, and case studies (ASII is accessible to Windows users only).*

Transcribe the fractions from the body of the Recapitulation Record for the three different question types for the oral and the silent reading at the Independent, Instructional, and Frustration levels.

This segment of the table is designed to provide at a glance the extent to which comprehension is balanced across the ability to recall, the ability to infer, and the ability to respond. Once again, it is important to look for discrepancies that might exist across different reading levels.

The analysis table on the second page of the Recapitulation Record is the basis for what we will define in Section 4 as the Level One or Numerical Interpretation of CRI data. Although the numbers are largely redundant with respect to the body of the Recapitulation Record, their juxtaposition allows us to isolate issues that will be of the greatest interest during Level One interpretation. In any case, examiners who use the ASII will find the analysis table completed automatically for them.

Section 4

Interpretation of Test Results

Levels of Analysis on The Critical Reading Inventory

Teachers and reading specialists will use the CRI for a variety of different purposes and so the type of interpretation they use will vary as well. If, for example, you use the CRI to investigate the reading needs of children with whom you will be working on a daily basis, you may not need a thorough and detailed analysis of results. You can presume that your daily teaching and observation of the children will provide you with ongoing insights into their needs. If, on the other hand, you are administering the CRI at the request of a teacher who needs comprehensive and structured input as to strengths, weaknesses, and optimum instructional strategies, your analysis will need to be thorough and detailed. The chances are good that you will not encounter those children in an instructional setting on a regular basis, so the more insights you can share with the teacher, the more helpful you are likely to be.

Because of your different needs for depth and detail of analysis, we have designated three different levels of interpretation of the CRI. These levels, although distinct, are by no means mutually exclusive. They are simply an attempt to address specific purposes.

Level One: Numerical Interpretation

The first level of analysis we have identified is *Numerical Interpretation*. Numerical Interpretation is, in some respects, a concession to the fact that a rather artificial assessment constrained by time and circumstances can never replace the insights you can gain by means of daily interaction with children. But some schools and districts use informal reading inventories to gather assessment data on the reading performance of their children. If the CRI is used for this purpose, it can provide a broader cross section of a child's comprehension performance than can most inventories. It can do this because of the distinction among question types and the Retelling Rubric that is included with each passage. Numerical Interpretation will include comparisons of a child's performance on several different dimensions of the CRI, such as performance on different comprehension item types, on oral versus silent reading, on reading in relation to grade level, on retellings, and so on.

It is important to note that Numerical Interpretation is by no means superficial, but that it seldom stands completely alone. Any insights you gain from a comparison of numbers should be verified on the basis of your observations of the child's actual performance. But numerical analysis can save a great deal of time and enable less experienced professionals to use the CRI effectively, while still providing a solid level of diagnostic information. Users may wish to employ the Automated Scoring and Interpretation Interview (ASII) feature of the CRI in cases where numerical analysis is called for.

Level Two: Analytical Interpretation

In cases where teachers or reading specialists will require a higher level of insight into a child's strengths and weaknesses (a situation that is nearly universal), we recommend the *Analytical interpretation* of CRI results. The analytical interpretation goes beyond numbers to an examination of children's actual responses and their significance as evidence of processing skills, thinking strategies, or reading habits. For example, you will frequently find children who are capable of answering virtually any text-based items but who experience difficulty with inference or critical response items. The fact that there is a significant numerical difference in their performance on these items is important to note. But if you want to delve deeper into the nature of their difficulty, you must examine their responses to the questions that they could not answer. Many children, for instance, will regularly respond to difficult items with "I don't know." (Possible translation: "I have no idea how to approach this item or how I would even arrive at an answer.") Others may reply with "It didn't say in the passage." (Translation: "I expect every question to have a clear and direct answer and I expect to find it stated in the text.") Still others will respond with marvelously detailed and creative answers that have absolutely no connection to what they have just read. (Translation: "I have no idea that I must use information from the text to support my thinking.") Clearly there are different problems implicit in the patterns of responses elicited from these three types of children.

An Analytical Interpretation of CRI results will note signs of frustration or annoyance on the part of readers. It will attempt to describe the strategies that a child uses in response to unknown words, ranging from the lack of strategy indicated by frequent teacher-provided words, to an overemphasis on graphic cues from text, to the detriment of context clues. Whereas Level One interpretation can tell you, for example, that the child is making numerous meaning-violating miscues, including nonwords, Level Two interpretation can give you insight into the source of those problem areas. You can find out if the child is overemphasizing syllabication rules in his creation of nonwords. Or you might observe insensitivity to the syntax of the language that is reflected in the child's oral reading performance. Analytical Interpretations also require you to examine retellings in detail, looking for signs of strategies such as attempts to memorize every detail as if they were equal, inclusion of extraneous details, or the inability to logically link ideas presented in text. It will include observations such as very fast oral or silent reading, a reluctance to elaborate on responses, a lack of enthusiasm or inflection in reading, or even the lack of an emotional response to text.

Analytical Interpretation of all these factors, and many more, will play a part in the detailed analysis of any child's responses. Coupled with creative insight and a firm grasp of the nature of reading, Analytical Interpretation will enable teachers and specialists to draw a much clearer picture of any child's needs. It will, of course, also enable them to justify and explain more effectively the differences in the programs of instruction most likely to address those different needs.

Level Three: Comprehensive Interpretation

 *See ASII*

Access the Automated Scoring and Interpretation Interview at www.prenhall.com/ readinginventory/ scoringassistant for scoring help, tutorials, and case studies (ASII is accessible to Windows users only).

Finally, there is a third level of analysis that we have termed *Comprehensive Interpretation.* Comprehensive analysis goes one step beyond the qualitative assessment of children's responses to include the multiple sources of data that are available as a consequence of the time spent administering the CRI. For example, the children who consistently respond to inferential and critical response items with "I don't know" may be telling you that they have no idea how to respond. But your examination of their retellings during your Level Two analytical interpretation may indicate that they do not have a strategy for recalling or responding to text in an organized way. Your observation of these children during the CRI administration may lead you to conclude that they are reluctant to attempt anything associated with a risk of failure. Interviews with teachers, parents, or the children themselves may provide evidence of a regular avoidance of reading. Performance on district and state assessments of reading may provide further insights into the nature of the child's view of reading. In other words, comprehensive analysis is, as its name suggests, an exhaustive examination of all relevant factors that may be contributing to a child's performance on the CRI. More specifically, it is an attempt to piece together any and all facets of a child's performance to arrive at an educational profile that underlies that child's performance as a reader. Comprehensive Interpretation is the most challenging and in many respects the most rewarding use of the CRI. And needless to say, the greater your depth of understanding of the nature of reading and the factors that influence it, the more valuable your analysis is likely to be. Examples of all three levels of CRI interpretation (numerical, analytic, and comprehensive) can be found in our discussion of case studies available on the CRI website.

The Analysis of Reading Performance: What a Good Reader Does

Any analysis of a child's reading performance on the CRI must begin with an examination of the fundamental elements of good reading. At the same time, you need to be aware of the ways that these traits are evidenced throughout the administration of the CRI. We will first identify those traits of the good reader that we regard as axiomatic and then identify elements of CRI performance that may act as "red flags" relative to each trait.

1. *Good readers achieve a balance among text-based, inference, and critical response items in their comprehension of text.*

High achievement in text-based reading to the exclusion of inference and critical evaluation often indicates a reader whose view of reading is rooted in remembering factual information (Durkin, 1978–1979; Guthrie, 2001; Singer & Donlan, 1982). Inference items require the reader to draw logical conclusions based on both text and experience. Success in this arena is often associated with precision in concepts. Critical response items require that the reader express a point of view and defend it logically, using both experience and information from the text.

Warning signs:
- Consistent and large differences between scores in text-based, inference, and critical response items (for example, text-based scores that are consistently 20 or more percentage points higher than inference or critical response scores)
- Inability or unwillingness to elaborate on or explain responses to higher-level items
- Annoyance or frustration in response to items that have no clear answer stated in the text
- Retellings that may be characterized by attention to less significant details or that may reflect attempts to memorize the passage
- Reports from parents and/or teachers that proficient literal readers are viewed as "good readers"

2. *The good reader demonstrates solid comprehension in both oral and silent reading relative to his or her grade level.*

A consistent pattern of higher performance after oral reading may indicate that children are overly dependent on listening skills (Armbruster & Wilkinson, 1991; Lynch, 1988; Miller & Smith, 1990; Stauffer, 1969). This pattern is more likely to occur among younger children, particularly those with limited experience with silent reading. A pattern of higher performance after silent reading is more common among older children (Allington, 2001). Weak silent reading may suggest that the reader lacks strategies to approach word recognition and comprehension independently.

Warning signs:
- Consistent and large differences between average oral versus average silent reading comprehension scores (for example, average oral comprehension scores that are consistently 20 or more percentage points higher than silent comprehension scores)
- Very fast or unrealistically fast silent reading
- Consistently high MMI coupled with low comprehension after oral reading
- Frequent teacher-provided miscues during oral reading
- Expressions of annoyance or frustration at the need for silent reading

3. *The good reader responds or reacts to the ideas included in text.*

Other than the acquisition of knowledge, there is little purpose or joy in reading if one does not think about text, evaluate its messages, compare its ideas to one's own, or respond to it, whether positively or negatively (Anderson, Wilkinson, & Mason, 1991; Cross & Paris, 1988; Hansen, 1981; Morrow, Tracey, Woo, & Pressley, 1999; Stauffer, 1969). Such thoughtful response to text lies at the heart of active thinking and construction of meaning.

Warning signs:

- Admission of a dislike for reading in the course of the interview
- Inability or reluctance to elaborate on or explain responses
- Frequent questions about when the testing will be over, sometimes even at the start of the testing
- Negative response to the testing situation
- Report from parent or teacher that the child is uninterested in reading

4. *The good reader detects the logical structure inherent in text and uses it as an aid to the organization and retrieval of ideas.*

Sensitivity to the ways that the writer has linked ideas together can go a long way toward promoting a reader's ability to process and retrieve those ideas (Beck & McKeown, 1991; Carnine & Kindler, 1985; Kame'enui, Carnine, & Freschi, 1982). Passive reading or attempts to memorize ideas in text are far less effective because the ideas are not linked to existing schemata in the reader's mind.

Warning signs:

- Frequent responses of "I don't know" to higher-level questions
- No demonstration of Personal Response to text
- Obvious demonstrations of frustration or anxiety as reading materials become more challenging
- Low retelling scores and higher comprehension scores on same passage (child may use questions themselves as an aid to memory rather than the organization of ideas)
- Recall of extraneous details in retellings or attempts to memorize passage
- Omission of major story elements or central factual information
- Little or no evidence of logical links between ideas in retellings

5. *The good reader uses a range of strategies for recognizing unknown words and frequently self-corrects miscues that alter the sense or grammar of the text.*

Monitoring for comprehension is a hallmark of good reading and when a reader does this type of monitoring, miscues that make no sense are immediately detected and corrected (Adams, 1990; Allington, 1983, 2001; Biemuller, 1994; Clay, 1979; Eldredge, Quinn, & Butterfield, 1990; Foorman, Nory, Francis, & Liberman, 1991; Goodman & Burke, 1972; Gray & Moody, 2000; Stahl, Duffy-Hester, & Stahl, 1998). By the same token, miscues that do not fit the grammatical structure of text simply do not "sound right" and will be corrected.

Warning signs:

- Lack of inflection in reading or word-by-word reading
- Overemphasis on graphic cues in word recognition
- Infrequent correction of even serious miscues
- Frequent teacher-provided miscues during oral reading, particularly at more challenging reading levels
- Identification by parents and/or teachers as a struggling reader (may even be labeled as "learning disabled")
- History of avoiding reading

6. *The good reader has developed an extensive sight vocabulary relative to his or her grade level.*

Sight vocabulary tends to grow as a consequence of solid attention skills and frequent reading. Much of a child's sight vocabulary is learned incidentally as a consequence of that reading. The broader the sight vocabulary, the easier and more fluent one's reading tends to be and the more likely one is to engage in the activity (Adams, 1990; Allington, 1983, 2001; Betts, 1954; Morrow et al., 1999). Thus the level of a child's sight vocabulary tends to be a classic case of the rich getting richer (Stanovich, 1986).

Warning signs:

- Flash percentage at child's current grade level lower than 70%
- Word recognition does not improve significantly when reading in the context of the actual selection (Flash consistently higher than MMI)

- No demonstration of a systematic or consistent strategy for recognizing unknown words
- Infrequent or sporadic independent reading on the part of the child
- Low self-concept related to school

7. *The good reader enjoys reading and engages in it regularly for a wide variety of purposes.*

The ultimate goal of reading instruction is to help children arrive at the conclusion that reading is a rewarding and enjoyable activity (Allington, 2001; Baker & Wigfield, 1999; Gray & Moody, 2000; Guthrie, 2001; Wigfield & Guthrie, 1997). In order to arrive at this belief, children must experience the joys and rewards of seeing their own lives mirrored in those of characters about whom they read. They must be drawn in (Langer, 1996) to the transaction that will demand of them a full participation in the world of ideas that reading represents.

Warning signs:
- Failure to elaborate on or explain responses to test questions
- Lack of ease or comfort in the testing situation
- Tendency toward low sight vocabulary relative to grade level
- Expression of a dislike for reading in the interview
- Avoidance of reading in classroom and home settings

You can use these seven characteristics of the good reader as a starting point in the analysis of reading performance.

Reading Levels in The Critical Reading Inventory

As we mentioned earlier, setting reading levels with the CRI (as with any IRI) requires thoughtful attention to a fairly wide range of factors. Not only do you have to consider the children's reading performance on the CRI itself, but at the very least you must also take into consideration the type of instruction and the teacher expectations that the children encounter on a daily basis. It goes without saying that any diagnostic information you gather about the child's reading and thinking, no matter what level of interpretation you use, will matter little if the child is expected only to recall details of the text in the classroom. If you do not have all the necessary information related to the instructional milieu, level setting can be tricky. Still, you must recognize that level setting is one of the most common uses of informal reading inventories, particularly because standardized test performance is unlikely to provide you with a great deal of help in determining the reading level at which you should instruct a child.

Independent Level

Informal reading inventories are generally used to distinguish among three different reading levels (Johnson et al., 1987). The first is the *Independent Level,* where children can identify the vast majority of the words they encounter without difficulty, can develop a sense of the semantic and syntactic content of the text, can grasp the meaning intended by the author, and can think about and respond to what they have read. And they can do all of this without the help of either a teacher or a parent. The Independent Level is, of course, the level where homework should be assigned as well as where children should be doing a great deal (but by no means all) of their leisure reading. It is important for you to observe, when possible, your readers on the CRI reading at their Independent Level, most particularly to see if the strategies they are using when the material is fairly easy for them differ from the strategies they use when the material is more challenging.

Instructional Level

The second reading level that you want to estimate through the use of the CRI is the *Instructional Level.* This is the level where you can achieve the optimal match between the child's needs and the instruction that you provide in response to those needs. The Instructional Level is very much akin to Vygotsky's oft-cited Zone of Proximal Development (Vygotsky, 1978) in that the instruction that you provide matches the child's needs so well that you help the child achieve a slightly higher level of competence in reading. Of course, your first requisite is a firm grasp of your students' needs, and those needs are best demonstrated when they are reading material that challenges and stretches their reading competence beyond their comfort level. In other words, children experience Piagetian disequilibrium (Piaget, 1973) in the instructional setting; otherwise, they have no reason to accommodate and change their way of doing things. A savvy observer who is in the presence of children reading at their Instructional Level will soon be able to spot shortcomings, confusions, strategic gaps, or distortions that are preventing children from progressing to the next stage in reading achievement. Of course, this type of diagnostic insight can be gained only when children are reading at their Instructional Level in the presence of a skilled teacher of reading. Consequently, instructional-level reading is most often meant for instructional situations, situations where skilled professionals can guide children and help meet their needs.

Frustration Level

The third level that you want to identify through the CRI is the *Frustration Level*. Children reach their frustration level when the reading material, whether by virtue of difficulty in word recognition or comprehension, becomes too difficult for them to handle and too complex for them to even benefit from instruction. There are simply too many things going wrong at the frustration level for teachers to address at one time. In the course of the administration of the CRI, you will ask children to read materials at their Frustration Level. You do this simply for the sake of the insights that you may gain when you observe how (or if) the children adjust to frustration in reading. For example, some children may revert to less sophisticated views of reading and attempt to use only graphophonemic clues when they encounter unknown words. Others increase their use of nonwords, simply attaching sounds to collections of letters with no attention to syntactic or semantic fit. Still others revert to attempts to memorize instead of think about what they have read. Others may shut down completely and give up any attempt to read what they perceive as materials that are beyond their scope. In any and all cases, you can gain some insights into their view of reading, their motivation to succeed, and the strategies that they fall back on when the going gets tough. It is our hope that the short-term discomfort of reading at one's Frustration Level will yield enough diagnostic information to make it worthwhile.

Use the DVD that accompanies this text for guidance on how to use *The Critical Reading Inventory*.

Keep in mind that your ultimate goal is to help every child read those very materials with a high level of success as soon as possible. The diagnostic information you gain may help bring about this ultimate success. It also never hurts to tell the children whom you test that no one expects them to succeed at every level, that you know they are reading at very high levels, and that mistakes are okay. You should even feel free to tell them that the authors who created this test insist that you make them read such difficult materials. Anything you can do to reassure the children may eventually pay off in solid diagnostic insights. For a video demonstration of the administration of the CRI, refer to the DVD that accompanies the CRI.

Listening Comprehension Level

The fourth reading level that we can use in certain circumstances is the *Listening Comprehension Level*. You estimate the Listening Comprehension Level by reading the passages aloud to the children and then measuring their comprehension just as you would if the children themselves had read the text. You will undoubtedly encounter children whose word recognition skills are so seriously problematic that they become insurmountable obstacles to comprehension. In such cases, it is beneficial to know what kinds of materials or conceptual levels the children could handle if they were relieved of the burden of sheer word recognition. When you observe that children are struggling mightily with word recognition and you suspect that they can comprehend at a much higher level if the materials are read to them, it is time to try to estimate the Listening Comprehension Level. It is also valuable to use listening comprehension assessments at the reader's current grade level, if that level has not been tested as part of the typical CRI administration.

Setting Reading Levels with the CRI

The traditional approach to level setting utilizes a combination of (a) the overall percentage of successful word recognition during oral reading, or the Reading Accuracy Index (RAI); and (b) the percentage of accurate responses to comprehension questions averaged across oral and silent reading at any given grade level (Betts, 1954). Thus, the numbers associated with different reading levels look like this:

Level	Reading Accuracy	Average Comprehension
Independent	99%	90%
Instructional	95%	75%
Frustration	90%	50%
Listening Comprehension	N/A	75%

Even given the frequently stubborn refusal of numbers to fit neatly into the patterns just described, it is often a fairly straightforward process to estimate a child's reading levels using a combination of these two data sources. But you must also consider the nature of the reader's word recognition problems. Even though reading experts long suspected that not all miscues were equal in importance (Johnson, et al., 1987), that realization did not have widespread impact until the work of Goodman and Burke (1972) on miscue analysis became widely disseminated. Now the equation becomes a bit more complicated: One reader with 95% accuracy in oral reading at a given grade level may have made no serious miscues, whereas another reader with an identical score may have made many. In spite of the identical numbers, the problems experienced by each reader are very different and so, of course, are the instructional strategies that you would use to address them.

Therefore, in the CRI we ask you to consider not only the pure percentage of words that a child reads correctly (RAI), but also the percentage of words the child reads that preserve the sense of the text (MMI). Significant discrepancies between these two numbers, accompanied by problems with comprehension, may signal a failure to monitor for meaning that could severely hinder a child's growth in reading. Under these circumstances, the word recognition problems are often more severe and will affect the judgment you make about a child's ability to handle materials at any given reading level.

For example, the RAI for a child who reads a 200-word passage and who makes 12 scoreable miscues would be 94%. The RAI is calculated by subtracting the number of scoreable miscues from the number of words in the passage and then dividing by the number of words in the passage (200 − 12 = 188; 188/200 = 94%). Then you calculate the MMI by first examining each of the miscues and determining whether the miscue preserved the sense and grammar of the language. In this case, the child exhibited the tendency to look at the first part of any difficult word and simply guess at the rest. He frequently used nonwords in these cases and 8 of the 12 miscues noted were serious; that is, they distorted the meaning of the text. Therefore the MMI for this child would be 96% because the MMI is calculated by subtracting the number of meaning-altering miscues from the number of words in the passage and then dividing by the number of words in the passage (200 − 8 = 192; 192/200 = 96%).

An MMI score of 96% coupled with reading comprehension problems is a red flag. It suggests that readers are not actively monitoring the reading to ensure that what they read makes sense. Note that the MMI in this child's case is actually higher than the RAI. This will happen frequently. The RAI is based on the sum of the meaning-maintaining and meaning-violating miscues; the MMI is based on only meaning-violating miscues. Thus the MMI can never be lower than the RAI. But you should be less concerned with the absolute value of the MMI and more concerned with the fact that it represents a departure from the quintessential purpose of reading: making meaning. It is a teacher's hope that every miscue a child makes is relatively minor and does not affect the overall sense of the text. In such cases, the child scores 100% on the MMI every time. If the child does not score 100% then you would do well to examine the nature of the miscues that took place during the oral reading and to contrast the MMI with overall comprehension scores as well as performance on different comprehension item types.

Another consideration in level setting is that the CRI attempts to identify not only the absolute comprehension of passages but also three different types of thinking called for by comprehension questions: text-based, inferential, and critical response. It is fairly common for children to demonstrate solid proficiency in text-based comprehension but serious difficulties with inferential and critical response comprehension. On a typical reading inventory, such children might be expected to perform quite well (Applegate et al., 2002). If these same children are taught in a classroom where the primary emphasis is on the recall of the details of text, they would be likely to perform equally well. However, their inability to think about or respond to text would be a significant disadvantage on the CRI (not to mention in their growth as readers and in their performance on state and national reading tests) and would clearly lower their overall reading level identified by any user of the CRI.

Thus users of the CRI would be well advised to think of diagnosis and level setting as an interaction between the child's instructional situation and the child's test performance. For example, many children are instructed in classrooms where teachers expect them to critically respond to ideas in text, discuss those ideas, and defend their interpretations. For these children, the CRI would be an effective diagnostic instrument that could predict their performance. If, however, a child is instructed in a classroom where text-based reading assessment is the norm, then that child's level may be underestimated by the CRI. Because research suggests that a significant amount of the nation's classroom reading instruction is characterized by text-based assessment (Brown, 1991; Allington, 2001), this is an issue that should be considered during the estimation of estimating reading levels.

It is our hope that users of the CRI become change agents who can effectively address the preponderance of literal thinking in the reading classroom. It is becoming increasingly important for teachers to foster a greater balance between thoughtful responses to text and memory for text details, particularly in light of the increased emphasis on the former that is beginning to emerge in state and national assessments of reading.

Section 5

Technical Features of The Critical Reading Inventory: Development and Validation

Construction of the Components of the CRI

The primary purpose of the CRI is to assist teachers and reading specialists in their assessment of children's reading ability, strengths, needs, and interests. To determine the extent to which this purpose is met, we conducted extensive field testing of the original test materials, including word lists; interviews for children, parents/guardians, and teachers; narrative and informational text selections; three types of comprehension questions; retelling rubrics and a fluency rubric.

Test materials were evaluated by 20 practicing reading specialists, who averaged 15 years of experience and who administered informal reading inventories an average of 100 times per year. All had at least one master's degree and two were enrolled in doctoral programs. All were certified reading specialists, with 14 also certified in elementary education, 6 in secondary education, 4 in special education, 2 in early childhood education, and 7 seeking educational leadership certification. Their teaching assignments included urban, suburban, and rural districts ranging in grade level from Kindergarten to Grade 12, ranging in family income from low to high, and including several schools with diverse populations.

In addition to this wide-ranging professional evaluation, the authors engaged in an extensive analysis of student responses to comprehension questions and retellings. Our objective was twofold: (1) to identify items and passage segments that were not effective in discriminating between accomplished and struggling readers, and (2) to identify patterns of thinking that could guide users in the instruction of all readers (Applegate et al., 2006).

As a consequence of the input from the initial field testing and the analysis of responses, we made numerous changes in passage wording, readjusted several reading levels, increased the clarity of directions for administration and scoring, and revised numerous comprehension items for both narrative and informational assessment.

Word Lists

The Word Lists in the CRI 2 were designed to allow users to gain insights into two dimensions of a reader's context-free word recognition ability. The first 10 words in each graded word list were selected at random from high-frequency word lists such as Fry's Instant Words, the Dolch word lists (Dolch, 1948), Frances and Kucera's word lists (1982), and the core reading vocabulary lists compiled by Taylor et al. (1989). The final 10 words in each list were drawn from the graded narrative passages. This format is designed to allow users to compare the reader's word recognition in isolation to word recognition within the context of reading. We used only narrative passages as sources for these words in order to avoid very specific content-related vocabulary that may underestimate the starting grade level for reading. Words that appear in the passages are marked with an asterisk in the Examiner's Copy of the Word Lists.

CRI 2 includes two sets of word lists, Form A and Form B, that allow users to administer the word lists in pretest and posttest format.

Interviews

We created the Student Interview questions as a means of gathering (1) background information on the child, (2) information about the child's view of reading, and (3) information about the child's interests and attitudes. Our intent was to add a more balanced and affective dimension to the analysis of the data collected. To enable users to obtain multiple perspectives rather than just a self-report, we included both a Parent/Guardian and a Teacher Interview form. The Teacher Interview is designed to uncover the teacher's perception of the child's ability and classroom performance, a description of the classroom reading program, and an indication of the teacher's theoretical orientation to reading instruction. Parent/Guardian information includes the parent or guardian's perception of the child's reading and classroom performance, the level of parental involvement, and literacy/school activities in the home. These sources contribute to a triangulation of key information to lend to the CRI 2's credibility and practical value in diagnosis. Examples of typical responses to interviews are included in the case studies on the DVD that accompanies the CRI.

Graded Passages

All graded passages were written by the authors based on more than 20 years of observational notes in classrooms and clinics for Grades K–12 and over 30 years of professional experience in classrooms per author, including supervision of reading practicum experiences at their respective institutions. These observations included notes regarding curriculum, materials, topics, themes, and children's interests and developmental responses toward the curriculum and activities, in addition to personal experience. Key ideas for the content of the passages were brainstormed among the authors; then each author wrote several passages on agreed-upon themes or content for a particular age or grade level. We then met, shared, and revised the passages collaboratively. Three narrative and three informational passages were written for each level, Pre-Primer through Grade 12. At the lower levels, Pre-Primer through Grade 1, we made an effort to include repetitive text and structural elements that would be appropriate for the emergent reader (Fountas & Pinnell, 1996). Throughout the CRI 2, but particularly at the higher level of the informational passages, we attempted to include high-interest but less familiar topics in order to avoid potential reader overexposure to topics, a difficulty we had noted in other recently published IRIs.

Passage Readability

We initially evaluated passage readability using multiple formulas included in the MicroLight software for readability, but we found many inconsistencies across formulas. We decided to use the Flesch-Kincaid Formula found on Microsoft Word software (1997). The formula itself is similar in formulation to the Fry Readability Scale and the SMOG Readability Formula (*http://www.med.utah.edu/pated/authors/readability/html*). This choice allows the CRI users easy access for checking the readability of materials they wish to use with their students. It is important to note that the 1997 software package was used to determine CRI passage readability. Subsequent versions of the Flesch-Kincaid Formula on later editions of Microsoft Word tend to significantly overestimate readability. Exact information regarding readability and passage length is provided on the introductory page of the Examiner's Copy of both the narrative and informational passages. Passages were written in an attempt to maintain a .2 or less difference between the readability estimates at each level and to ensure that there would be equal intervals in readability between levels (Gerke, 1980; Klesius & Homan, 1985).

In addition to readability considerations, we used content, appeal, interest, background knowledge, text structure, overall length, and print format/layout in determining appropriateness for each passage at each grade level. It is well established that sentence length, word frequency, and number of syllables and words per sentence are not the only factors that should be considered in evaluating the difficulty of text (Jitendra et al., 2001; Johnston, 1997; Kinder, Bursuck, & Epstein, 1992; Lynch, 1988).

Illustrations were included at the Pre-Primer through Grade 1 levels for several selections of narrative passages, and photographs were included for some passages at the same levels and beyond for the informational passages. Thus, the examiner can compare a child's performance with and without picture clues at each of these three levels. The pictures and photographs were specifically created to support the text in a meaningful way.

For the narrative passages, we used a variety of genre types, including familiar childhood experiences as well as folk tales and fablelike stories. All passages were created by the authors in order to eliminate the concern for past exposure to stories by our intended audience. Passages were written with an eye toward gender fairness and ethnic diversity. The informational texts include original social science and science content as well as biography. All informational selections were thoroughly researched for accuracy of the facts presented.

During field testing, we also assessed children's interests, background knowledge, and performance on the materials as a means of determining level appropriateness. As we discussed earlier, several passages were modified for ease or difficulty.

Selection length was also an issue that we discussed and examined. Based on previous recommendations (Jitendra et al., 2001; Johnson et al., 1987; Jongsma & Jongsma, 1981; Klesius & Homan, 1985), it is important to have adequate length (more than 125 words) at each level except for Pre-Primer so that there will be substantive content to serve as the basis for comprehension assessment. In addition, passage length is important in that the majority of materials that children will be expected to read in their classrooms (from mid-first grade on) will have well over 100 words. State and national assessments also tend to include longer passages. Research has suggested that shorter IRI selections tend to overestimate children's reading ability for regular classroom materials and show inaccurate miscue patterns (Bowden, cited in Klesius & Homan, 1985). Jitendra et al. also found that most recent basal series have selections that are well over 100 words in length and most content text chapters also fit this pattern. Because the intention of IRIs is to estimate placement into curriculum materials, suitable length was an important factor in the development of the CRI.

Assessment of Comprehension

Because comprehension is the most important aspect of reading that is being evaluated, we developed two tools to assess comprehension: retelling rubrics and postreading questions. An Oral Reading Fluency Rubric is included to accompany assessment of the reader's comprehension.

Retelling Rubrics

Rubrics for the scoring of retellings are included for each passage in the CRI. In the case of narrative selections, the elements assessed in the retelling are based on essential story grammar components (i.e., characters, character goals or problems, and the key steps characters take toward the solution of the problem or the attainment of the goal). The final component of the retelling rubric is the presence or absence of a well-supported personal response to the text.

Rubrics for informational passages draw a distinction between Macro-concepts and Micro-concepts. Macro-concepts are defined as superordinate ideas that are central to the information presented in the text and which are supported, illustrated, or further explained by additional information in the text. The supporting details are defined as Micro-concepts, not because they are unimportant but because they act as support for the more general and inclusive Macro-concepts.

In the case of either narrative or informational text, test users will consult the retelling rubric that accompanies each passage. Users must note the presence or absence of each of the text elements listed in the rubric, and then consult the Retelling Scoring Guides in the Test Materials section of the CRI Manual. These guides provide detailed instructions for assigning a numerical score to a retelling. Users also have the option of downloading the Automated Scoring and Interpretation Interview (ASII) from the Prentice Hall website listed in the manual. The ASII automatically calculates retelling scores.

The formulas included in the guides were developed as a part of the authors' analysis of student responses to retellings and comprehension items. Our objective was to create a reliable and valid numerical representation of a retelling score that could inform users at a glance of a reader's proficiency in unaided recall of text. We will discuss the results of our tryout of the scoring guides in our subsequent discussion of the standardization study of the CRI.

Because reader response to text is central to our definition of critical reading, we have included an invitation to readers to discuss their personal response to the text. Assessment of the personal response is included in the rubric used for scoring retellings. During field testing of the CRI, this component was identified by participants as a positive feature that provided reliable information about a reader's view of and attitude toward reading.

Postreading Questions

After examining several current IRIs and analyzing their methods of comprehension assessment, we determined there was a need for a more structured assessment of higher-order thinking in the form of inferential and critical response items (Applegate et al., 2002; Manzo, Manzo, & McKenna, 1995; Nessel, 1987). We then applied the questioning criteria we had developed (see Figure 5–1), along with the recommendations from Klesius and Homan (1985), to create Text-Based, Inference, and Critical Response questions for each passage. All questions are labeled as to type and possible correct responses, many of which were actually given by children during the field testing. These are included in the Examiner's Copy of the CRI.

For levels Pre-Primer through Grade 1, there are 8 questions for each passage at each level and for each type of text. For Grades 2 through 12, there are 10 questions for each passage at each level for each type of text. For narrative passages, when there are 8 questions, there are 3 Text-Based, 3 Inference, and 2 Critical Response items; when there are 10 questions, there are 4 Text-Based, 3 Inference, and 3 Critical Response items. For informational text, when there are 8 questions, there are 3 Text-Based, 3 Inference, and 2 Critical Response items; when there are 10 questions, there are 4 Text-Based, 4 Inference, and 2 Critical Response items. There are more Critical Response items for narrative text at the upper levels because there is more opportunity for this type of thinking in response to this type of text (Rosenblatt, 1983). No direct assessment of vocabulary was done because these types of questions are often dependent on a child's background knowledge and language ability (Duffelmeyer, Robinson, & Squier, 1989).

Virtually all questions require that the child actually read the passage and use information from it in order to avoid one of the pitfalls of many IRIs regarding passage dependency (Klesius & Homan, 1985). No questions rely totally on a child's past experience or background knowledge, although we know that some children will and should make use of their experiences in order to help them comprehend and respond to the passages. Passage dependency of questions was also evaluated by asking 16 children and 6 adults the comprehension questions without affording them the opportunity to read the passages. More than 90% of the questions could not be answered. Questions from the informational passages at the lower levels (Pre-Primer through Grade 2) were more readily answered correctly without reading the passages; however, this was done more frequently by older children and adults who for the most part would not be evaluated by those passages.

We also noted that lookbacks could be utilized as an additional dimension of the assessment of reading comprehension. Lookbacks can be most useful with students who have recurring difficulty with literal recall and who frequently respond with "I don't know" or "I don't remember." Lookbacks enable the user to assess whether the reader is experiencing difficulty with remembering or with comprehending the text. It also enables you to assess the reader's ability to quickly locate information relevant to questions that he or she had been unable to answer (Alvermann, 1988; Bossert & Schwantes, 1995–1996; Swanson & De La Paz, 1998).

Estimating Reading Levels

We have chosen to use the Betts criteria for estimating reading levels, even though there are studies that have both supported (Bader & Wiesendanger, 1989; Johns, 1991; McKenna, 1983) and critically examined them (Johns & Magliari, 1989; Lowell, 1969; Pikulski, 1990). Because they

Text-Based Question Types (TB):

1. **Literal Items:** Answers to these items are stated explicitly (verbatim) in the text. They simply require that the readers recall what they have read.

2. **Low-Level Inference Items:** The answers to low-level inferences are not stated verbatim in the text but may be so close to literal as to be very obvious. All inference items require that readers draw a conclusion on the basis of the text and use their background experiences to some extent as well. However, low-level inferences require very little in the way of drawing conclusions. We classified as low-level inferences, for example, items that

   - involve the recognition of information in different words from those used in the original text. Such items require of the reader only a translation of the printed text.
   - require the reader to identify relationships that exist between ideas in the text. Such items as these are not literal only because the writer has not made the relationship explicit by using a grammatical marker (e.g., *because*). This is not to say that the skill of making such connections is unimportant. Classification of an item as low-level merely reflects that the writer assumes that at a given grade level, the reader can and will make the connection.
   - deal with details largely irrelevant to the central message of the text.
   - require that the reader draw solely on background knowledge or to speculate about the actions of character without the benefit of information in the text that may transform speculation into a logical prediction.

Inference Question Types (I):

3. **High-Level Inference Items:** These items call for the reader to link experience with the text and to draw a logical conclusion. Answers to these items require significantly more complex thinking than low-level inferences. Examples include those items that require the reader to

   - devise an alternative solution to a specific problem described in the text.
   - describe a plausible motivation that explains a character's actions.
   - provide a plausible explanation for a situation, problem, or action.
   - predict a past or future action based on characteristics or qualities developed in the text.
   - describe a character or action based on the events in a story.

Critical Response Question Types (CR):

4. **Response Items:** These items call for a reader to express and defend an idea related to the actions of characters or the outcome of events. Response items differ from high-level inference items in that they are usually directed toward broader ideas or underlying themes that relate to the significance of the passage. Although high-level inference items are directed toward a specific element or problem in the passage, response items require a reader to discuss and react to the underlying meaning of the passage as a whole. Examples include items that ask the reader to:

   - describe the lesson(s) a character may have learned from experience.
   - judge the efficacy of the actions or decisions of a character and defend the judgment.
   - devise and defend alternative solutions to a complex problem described in a story.
   - respond positively or negatively to a character based on a logical assessment of the actions or traits of that character.

Figure 5–1

Criteria for Determining Question Types

are the most frequently used criteria, we believe that they are useful for comparative purposes. In addition, many of the other criteria that have been tried are very close to Betts's original criteria. We wish to emphasize that, in any case, these criteria are only guidelines for estimating levels. Many other factors enter into such estimates, including qualitative information, knowledge about the student's actual performance in the classroom, and observations about reading strategy use and behavior (Goodman, 1997; Harris & Lalik, 1987).

Reliability and Validity of the CRI 2: Standardization Study

We assessed several dimensions of the reliability and validity of the CRI 2 by conducting a broad standardization study that involved the administration of the CRI to 215 students ranging from Grade 1 through Grade 12. The following analyses were carried out on 1,255 passages administered to this standardization sample. The sample for this study included a nearly equal proportion of males and females, representing a wide range of ethnic groups, most of whom attend public schools in the tristate area including Pennsylvania, New Jersey, and Delaware. The sample included just over one quarter of its students who had been identified by teachers

Table 5–1 Demographic Characteristics of Standardization Sample (*N* = 215)

Gender	Male	Female			
	N = 105	*N* = 110			
Ethnicity	Caucasian	Black	Hispanic	Asian	Other
	N = 150	*N* = 38	*N* = 15	*N* = 6	*N* = 6
School	Public	Private	Parochial		
	N = 156	*N* = 21	*N* = 38		
Reading level	High	Average	Low	N/A	
	N = 56	*N* = 68	*N* = 89	*N* = 2	
Grade level	1 to 3	4 to 8	9 to 12		
	N = 93	*N* = 95	*N* = 27		

or parents as high-achieving readers. The remaining three quarters of the sample fell into the average and low-achieving groups, those most likely to be assessed by an informal reading inventory. Thirty of the 215 students in the sample were eligible for special education services, whereas 5 were enrolled in programs for the gifted. For 14 of the students in the sample, English was not their native language. Demographic data for the sample are included in Table 5–1.

All tests were administered by graduate students who had been trained in the use of the CRI through demonstrations of test administration similar to those found on the DVD that accompanies the main text. In addition, all students had completed several tutorials for scoring miscues, retellings, and comprehension items, tutorials that are included on the same DVD.

Interrater reliability for scoring the CRI was assessed by comparing the scoring of miscues, retellings, and comprehension items of the test administrators to those of six trained and experienced experts in the administration and scoring of the CRI. Three of the expert scorers were practicing reading specialists; three were former reading specialists. All expert scorers worked independently. The aim of the comparative scoring study was to establish the extent to which users of the CRI can, with a few hours of instruction and practice, administer the instrument correctly and score the results with consistency.

Word Lists

Whereas the ability to administer and score the Word Lists segment of the CRI 2 is a straightforward matter, there still remains the issue of whether the lists achieve what they are designed to do. We focused on two specific issues in our validity study of the lists. First of all, users need assurance that the lists become progressively more difficult as the grade levels increase. Second, because we use the lists specifically to determine a starting point for the reading portion of the CRI, we needed to determine if they can act as accurate indicators of that starting point.

To address the first question, whether the lists become increasingly difficult, we considered presenting data drawn from the graded word lists that we used as sources to demonstrate increasing difficulty of the words on our lists. However, the standardization study data provide more accurate and direct evidence of the issue. We reasoned that if the word lists are progressively more difficult, that fact would be reflected in the scores that students achieved during the flash and untimed presentation of the lists. Specifically, we assumed that the progressive difficulty of the word lists would be demonstrated if children who read consecutive graded word lists would achieve progressively lower scores as the grade level increased.

We examined the Flash and Untimed Word List scores of all subjects and compared the scores of lists administered at consecutive grade levels. We then simply tallied the number of times that a score on a higher grade level was matched or exceeded by the score at the lower grade level. For example, if a reader was given a third-grade word list followed by a fourth-grade list, we would not expect the fourth-grade score to exceed the score on the third-grade list that was designed to be easier.

An analysis of the data from the standardization study yielded a total of 864 paired comparisons. In 804 cases, or 93.1% of the total observations, the score from the higher-grade-level list did not exceed the score from the lower-level list. We concluded from this analysis we could have a high level of confidence in the progressive difficulty of the CRI Word Lists.

What remained to be demonstrated was the usefulness of the lists in identifying a starting point for the onset of the CRI oral reading and reading comprehension measures. We advise CRI users to begin the reading test at the highest level where the reader achieves a perfect score of 100% during the flash presentation of the words. Our reasoning is that if readers can flawlessly identify a list of words drawn from instructional materials at a given grade level, the chances are good that they will be able to read those materials with a high degree of competence. Of course, as any teacher knows, flawless word recognition does not guarantee flawless comprehension. However, the investment of time involved in testing a child's reading and comprehension makes any good estimate of a starting point worthwhile.

We examined the standardization study data and found that 200 subjects had achieved a perfect score on the flash presentation of the word lists. When we assessed their reading performance at that beginning level, we found that 84.5% of the students were reading at their Instructional or Independent Level. Thus we concluded that the use of the Word Lists as an estimate of a beginning level for the CRI, although by no means perfect, was both valuable and valid.

Scoring of Miscues

Reliability

A total of 604 of the passages administered to the standardization sample were administered as oral reading. The examiners were instructed to use a tape recorder to capture the oral reading of the children and to note any deviation from the text on the Examiner's Copy of the passage in question. The examiners were then instructed to distinguish between miscues that maintained meaning in the context of the passage (to be marked with a plus sign) and miscues that violated meaning (to be marked with a zero). The job of the expert scorer was to determine if he or she agreed with the judgment of the graduate students who administered the tests and scored the miscues.

A total of 3,827 miscues were noted in the oral reading of the subjects and the expert scorers agreed on the assessment of the examiners 3,624 times for a total interrater reliability percentage of 94.7. This very high level of reliability can be explained in part by the nature of the task. We did not ask graduate students to identify the source of miscues or to analyze miscues at any deeper level other than to judge whether they maintained or violated meaning. In the CRI we interpret the tendency of readers to violate meaning in their oral reading as indicative of a potential loss of comprehension. Because the percentage of meaning-maintaining miscues is the primary component of the Meaning Maintenance Index (MMI), these results suggest that teachers can, without inordinate amounts of instruction, identify meaning-violating and meaning-maintaining miscues with a high degree of reliability.

Validity

The Reading Accuracy Index (RAI) is equivalent to a form of reading assessment that has long been associated with the use of informal reading inventories to estimate a child's reading grade level (Betts, 1954; Johnson et al., 1987). The RAI is a simple baseline measure of the percentage of words read aloud that accurately replicate the text. The MMI, on the other hand, allows the examiner to distinguish between types of miscues and to assess the percentage of words read aloud that represent an attempt on the part of the reader to maintain the sense of the language. Thus, the MMI would seem on the surface to be a more useful tool in level setting because a high MMI suggests a reader who views the task of reading as one of constructing a meaningful message in response to text.

The problem with using the MMI for level setting is that there are virtually no data to support its use or even to validate its worth as an educational construct. We designed the data analysis that follows as an attempt to establish the MMI as a worthwhile estimate of a reader's view of reading as a meaningful activity. We reasoned that if two readers made equal numbers of miscues, but Reader A's miscues preserved the syntax and sense of language whereas Reader B's frequently violated them, then there would be some measurable difference in the overall comprehension of these two readers. Otherwise, there would seem to be little value in distinguishing between the RAI and MMI.

We reviewed the CRI protocols that had been administered by our graduate reading specialist candidates for the past 2 years. The sample tested represented an exceptionally wide range of students and an equally wide range of socioeconomic and achievement levels in reading and language arts. Our students selected subjects from among their own students, the children of friends and family, and students in schools in which they happened to be working.

We posited the following distinction between levels of achievement in the RAI and MMI: If a pair of readers read the same passage and achieved the same RAI level, it would mean that they had made nearly the same number of miscues. If, however, one reader's MMI score was at least two percentage points lower than the other's, it would mean that the miscues made by the latter reader included a significant number of violations of sense. For example, if a pair of readers read a passage that was 300 words in length, and achieved an RAI score of 97, that would mean that each of them had made 9 miscues. If the first reader scored an MMI of 100, it would mean that virtually none of his miscues violated sense. If the second reader scored an MMI of 98, it would mean that 6 of her miscues represented a distortion of semantics or syntax. We reasoned that such a number of meaningful distortions would be likely to affect the reader's comprehension of the text.

We asked a graduate assistant to review the records of the administration of the CRI to more than 400 students, ranging from Grade 1 through Grade 12. We asked her to seek out matched pairs of students who had read the same passage aloud, had the same RAI score, but had an MMI score that differed by no fewer than two percentage points. We did not reveal to her the reason for her search or the details of the analysis that we had planned. Thus it was not likely that she intuited the purpose of the search or could use that intuition to screen the comprehension scores of potential candidates for the study.

The screening yielded 32 matched pairs of readers, with the grade level of the oral passages they read ranging from Pre-Primer to Grade 6. The retellings and responses to comprehension questions were graded by two expert scorers working independently. The level of interrater agreement was 96% for the comprehension items and 95% for the retellings with all differences resolved by discussion.

The results of the analysis were unequivocal. For the high MMI group, 28 of the 32 readers scored higher in their overall percentage of comprehension items scored correctly, with an average difference in scores of 28.94%. The results of comparative analyses are presented in Table 5–2. A one-way Analysis of Variance (ANOVA) suggested that differences between groups were highly significant ($F = 61.21$, $p < .0001$). We must note that a comparison of comprehension scores based on only 8 to 10 comprehension items and a single retelling is not an optimum situation. However, the powerful and consistent results seemed to us to minimize this disadvantage. This dramatic difference in comprehension scores seems to confirm what many reading professionals may view as the obvious: Readers who view reading as a meaning-making process are likely to be more successful at comprehending materials than readers who do not demonstrate that view in their processing of text.

A comparison of the retelling scores of both groups yields equally compelling, if not equally dramatic evidence. For the high MMI group, 26 of the 32 readers scored higher in their retelling scores with an average difference in scores of more than 1.20 points on a scale of 4.00. A one-way ANOVA suggested that differences between groups were highly significant ($F = 52.30$, $p < .0001$).

Table 5–2 Comparison of Reading Comprehension and Retelling Scores for High MMI and Low MMI Readers

Mean Score: Comprehension

High MMI ($N = 32$)	Low MMI ($N = 32$)	Difference	F-Ratio	Significance
77.5%	48.6%	28.7%	61.21	<.0001

Mean Score: Retelling

High MMI ($N = 32$)	Low MMI ($N = 32$)	Difference	F-Ratio	Significance
2.02	.81	1.21	52.30	<.0001

In retrospect, we were not surprised by the results of our analysis. It stands to reason that text comprehension is clearly related to the extent to which a reader views reading as requiring comprehension. The high MMI readers avoided the types of miscues that violated sense precisely because they were monitoring their reading to ensure that it made sense. These preliminary results provide some encouraging evidence for the overall worth of the construct of the MMI, and suggest that further research may be warranted into its value as a factor in the estimation of reading levels.

Scoring of Comprehension Items

Reliability

A major issue in the standardization study of the CRI 2 was the extent to which expert scorers would agree with the examiner scoring of comprehension item responses. This is an issue that cuts to the heart of the CRI as a useful assessment tool because the proportion of higher-order items in the CRI significantly exceeds that of other informal reading inventories (Applegate et al., 2002). By definition, text-based items and low-level inferences have a clearly stated or obviously implied answer, but inference and critical response items in the CRI lend themselves to far more creative and challenging responses, and often allow for multiple correct and partially correct responses. The ability of examiners with a reasonable level of professional preparation to score these items with reliability can go a long way toward determining the value and usability of the instrument as a whole.

Examiners were prepared to score comprehension items largely via the completion of 12 tutorials very similar to those included on the DVD that accompanies the CRI. Examiners were instructed to score each response as meriting full credit, partial credit (1/2), or no credit. Expert scorers then independently assessed each response and determined whether they fully agreed, partially agreed, or completely disagreed with the scoring of the examiners. The inter-rater reliability was calculated as a percentage of agreement between expert and novice users.

The six expert scorers assessed a total of 11,905 responses and agreed on the scoring of 11,328 for a total percentage of agreement of 95.2. When results were divided between narrative and informational passages, the total percentages of agreement were 94.8 for narrative passages and 96.1 for informational passages. These are exceptionally high levels of agreement and suggest that the CRI can be used with confidence by professionals who have a modest but reasonable level of preparation in the interpretation and scoring of item responses. These data also suggest that the tutorials that accompany the CRI are useful tools in preparing professionals for the reliable scoring of comprehension items.

Validity: The Existence of Different Item Types

Davis (1968), in his landmark attempt to isolate distinct factors in the assessment of reading comprehension, discussed at some length the nature of reading as a unitary process. Specifically, he suggested that further attempts to empirically validate different types of comprehension items may be an exercise in futility for several reasons. First of all, there is powerful evidence that reading develops as a unitary skill, with the vast majority of children learning to read in an integrated fashion, combining skill development in word recognition with the development of a full range of comprehension skills. More specifically, it seems that most children will seamlessly transition from an oral language system that is pragmatic and meaning-centered to a written language system that requires the same levels and types of thoughtful response.

If Davis is correct, then the attempt to isolate different types of thinking skills and empirically validate their existence in a broad sample of the population is indeed doomed to failure. For the overwhelming majority, reading assessment that requires any purportedly distinct levels of thinking is still rooted in an act that begins with the extraction and construction of meaning in response to text. Any differences evidenced among a relatively small number of children are sure to be washed out by the vast majority of children for whom thinking about what they read is as natural as thinking about their life experiences. Thus it may not be possible for mathematical analyses to establish once and for all the existence of different types of thinking in response to text. It may well be that the items themselves are highly interrelated; they simply elicit different responses from different groups of readers.

However, teachers in real-world classrooms must deal with real-world issues. Suffice it to say that it matters little to Jimmy and Sharon in my third-grade class that their inability to evidence any thinking about what they have read has not been empirically validated by mathematical analysis. They simply do not realize that the very type of thinking that they use in their daily interactions with others is that type of thinking called for in the reading that they do in school and home. They struggle with any circumstances that require more than a cursory reaction to text. Their response journals include nothing more than summaries of text, in contrast to the thoughtful responses of their classmates, and they often lapse into silence while other students are discussing their reactions to the ideas presented by the authors of the texts they have read.

The truth is that we have in our instructional repertoires techniques and activities that can help Jimmy and Sharon realize that they can and must apply their thinking skills to the reading that they do. One of the most short-sighted things that we can do as reading professionals is to demand of research and mathematical analysis answers that they simply are ill-equipped to supply. If we refuse to acknowledge the existence of different levels of thinking in reading, we will likely not require of our students anything more than a mastery of factual information. The fact remains that a huge proportion of comprehension items that children encounter in accountability assessments require higher level thinking. If Allington (2001) is correct, the overwhelming majority of questions that teachers ask about what children have read require only memory for details. If that trend continues, we will never discover the needs of children like Jimmy and Sharon and we will never be able to help them grow in their ability to react and respond to text.

Scoring of Retellings

Reliability

Graduate students were instructed to audiotape all retellings and transcribe them verbatim to their examiner's materials. They were then instructed to use the Retelling Rubric that accompanies each passage in the CRI and to determine the extent to which passage elements in the rubric were present in the retelling. Each graduate student was given a copy of the Scoring Guides for Retellings found in the Test Materials section of the CRI Manual. Many students used the automated retelling help feature of the ASII to calculate retelling scores; others used the Scoring Guides.

Retelling Rubrics

Reliability

The retelling rubrics in the CRI 2 were developed to follow the structure of a common story grammar in the case of narrative text and a structure of main ideas (Macro-concepts) and supporting detail (Micro-concepts) in the case of informational text. Our study of authentic student retellings led us to make several modifications and culminated in the development of detailed and mathematically complex Guides for Scoring Retellings. We set out to validate the use of our numerical retelling scores by comparing them to the total percentages correct in the comprehension items that accompany each passage. Our reasoning was that if the retelling scores were unrelated to the reader's comprehension, they would be of little value as a diagnostic tool.

We began our investigation with the notion that a retelling cannot and should not be used as the sole source of comprehension assessment for any student for several reasons. First and foremost among these is the fact that students experience widely varying levels of exposure to story structure specifically and to text structure as a whole. Many children, for example, are taught the elements of a story grammar and exposed to a full range of reading and writing activities in which they are expected to apply it. Other children will have virtually no idea of its existence. Needless to say, the narrative retellings of these two groups will vary widely in terms of overall quality and effectiveness. Still other groups of readers have learned to rely on the structure provided by a set of comprehension questions and have little or no idea of how to structure their own unaided recall of text. For these reasons we hypothesized that the correlation between the retelling scores calculated using the

CRI 2's scoring rubric and the comprehension item percentage scores would be statistically significant and moderate in size.

Our sample of 215 students read 1,255 passages and examiners recorded a retelling for each passage. The retelling scores assigned by the examiners were cross-checked by an expert scorer, using the automatic retelling scoring device included as part of the Automated Scoring and Interpretation Interview (ASII) to ensure consistency of scoring. In 92.5% of the passages, the test administrator and the expert agreed on the scoring of the retelling, establishing the CRI Retelling Rubric as an instrument that can be used reliably by professionals with a reasonable level of preparation in the use of the instrument.

Validity

To establish the validity of the Retelling Rubrics and Scoring Guides of the CRI, we correlated the retelling score with the total comprehension item percentage for each passage. In cases where disagreement existed between the graduate student and the expert scorer, the expert's score was used. An analysis of 905 narrative passages revealed a correlation coefficient of .51 ($p < .001$) between the retelling score and the total comprehension item score. An analysis of 352 informational passages revealed a correlation of .43 ($p < .001$).

These results were certainly in line with our expectations. There is clearly a logical relationship between a reader's unaided recall and ability to respond to comprehension questions. It is very unusual to see a reader fail miserably in responding to comprehension questions after she has delivered a competent and thorough retelling. And there certainly appears to be some measurable common variance that exists between retellings and performance on comprehension questions. However, variations among readers in their experience with retellings and in the type of retelling instruction they may have received makes the use of retellings suspect when they are used as the sole measure of a reader's comprehension. Nevertheless, the common variance of unaided and aided recall lends value to the numerical expression of the quality of retelling assessed by the CRI.

The difference that exists in the correlations between retellings and comprehension items for narrative and informational text is sizeable enough to suggest some variance that is not accounted for by the sheer similarity of the tasks. Informational texts can be organized in several different ways (e.g., cause-effect, examples, comparison, contrast, etc.) and even in combinations of structures. Stories, on the other hand, are characterized by a fairly universal structure often referred to as a story grammar. Some experts have suggested that the ability to comprehend the story structure is common even among young children. It stands to reason that children would be more aware of and comfortable with the narrative as opposed to the informational structure.

This study did not include enough cases to warrant the examination of the relationship between retellings and comprehension scores at various grade levels. Some researchers have reported a shift in the correlation from lower values in the lower grades to higher values in the upper grades (Leslie & Caldwell, 2006).

Fluency Rubric

Reliability

The Fluency Rubric included in the CRI 2 was developed as a consequence of extended analysis of the oral reading of students representing a wide cross-section of grades and ability levels. We set out to develop an instrument that could help teachers distinguish clearly among several different proficiency levels in reading fluency. To be a useful tool, a fluency rubric must enable users to assign a value to a child's oral reading with consistency and clarity. The descriptions included in the rubric must be sufficiently clear to allow users to identify characteristics of a child's oral reading and match them accurately with the weighted descriptions. To test the reliability of the CRI rubric, we randomly selected 30 audiotaped oral readings from among the subjects in the standardization study and compared scores assigned by graduate students to those calculated by expert scorers.

The graduate students who participated in the standardization study were instructed to record the oral reading, retellings, and responses to comprehension questions of the students that they tested. After they had analyzed and scored the results of the CRI, they estimated reading levels, using the criteria described in the CRI Manual. They were then instructed to identify the reader's highest instructional grade level, retrieve the tape of the child's oral reading at that grade level, and match the rubric descriptions to the characteristics of the child's oral reading. They then totaled the point values associated with the descriptions to arrive at a final fluency score.

The 30 audiotaped readings selected for this study were distributed to three experienced and expert CRI users. Each was provided with a printed copy of the targeted text and a copy of the CRI Fluency Rubric. The experts were asked to assess the oral reading and assign appropriate numerical values to the retelling without knowledge of the score originally assigned by the graduate student. We believed that a high level of agreement would demonstrate the usefulness of the rubric descriptions in discriminating among levels of performance in the four categories of reading behavior included in the rubric.

The results of the comparison of scores suggest a high rate of agreement between expert and novice scorers. In 16 of 30 cases, the experts arrived at scores identical to those of the novices; in 12 additional cases, the expert score differed by only a single point. In the remaining 2 cases, the expert's score differed from the novice's score by two points. Thus it seems that the descriptions of differing point values associated with the four dimensions of fluency assessed on the rubric are very clear and enable users to discriminate among distinct levels of fluency. We concluded that the CRI Fluency Rubric can be used with confidence and consistency even by less experienced users.

Validity

Our objective in creating a fluency rubric was to arrive at a numerical expression that could provide CRI users with an immediate and accurate appraisal of a reader's fluency. Validation of the Fluency Rubric was complicated, however, by our insistence that fluency be assessed only at the reader's Instructional Level. We believe that we can obtain only distorted notions of a reader's fluency if we base our assessment on materials that the reader finds too easy to read or too difficult. As a consequence, we were unable to simply correlate the fluency score with the reader's comprehension at that same grade level. The fact that the instructional level represents by definition a constricted range of comprehension scores would skew any attempt to calculate a correlation coefficient.

Instead, we reasoned that because fluency has been shown to be a fairly consistent correlate of reading achievement (Fuchs, Fuchs & Maxwell, 1988; Pinnell et al., 1995), a valid fluency score should be related to grade-level achievement in reading. Consequently, we compared the highest Instructional Level identified by the CRI with each reader's grade level. Our assumption was that, if the rubric is working as it should, readers with a higher fluency score on materials that present some challenges should be achieving at a higher level in reading than dysfluent readers. A child who was instructional at fourth grade but who was attending second grade would receive a score of +2; a child whose Instruction Level was third grade but who was attending fifth grade would receive a score of −2. We then correlated the level of fluency based on the CRI Fluency Rubric to the deviations of grade level and Instructional Level.

Instructional Levels could be calculated for 208 cases and the overall bivariate correlation between CRI fluency scores and grade-level achievement in reading was .67 ($p < .0001$). This correlation was high enough to demonstrate that fluency scores are a valuable dimension of reading assessment and that they are clearly related to reading achievement. At the same time, the correlation is low enough to demonstrate that fluency cannot serve in isolation from other factors as a sufficient measure of reading proficiency.

References

Adams, M. J. (1990). *Beginning to read: Thinking and learning about print.* Cambridge, MA: MIT Press.

Allen, D. D., & Swearingen, R. A. (1991). *Informal reading inventories: What are they really asking?* Paper presented at the 36th annual meeting of the International Reading Association, (Las Vegas, NV, May 6–10). (ERIC Document Reproduction Service No. ED341953)

Allington, R. L. (1983). Fluency: The neglected goal of the reading program. *The Reading Teacher, 36,* 556–561.

Allington, R. L. (2001). *What really matters for struggling readers.* New York: Addison-Wesley.

Allington, R. L., & Johnston, P. (2000, April). *Exemplary fourth grade reading instruction.* Paper presented at the American Educational Research Association, New Orleans.

Alpert, J. (1974). Teacher behavior across ability groups: A consideration of the mediation of Pygmalion effects. *Journal of Educational Psychology, 66,* 348–353.

Alvermann, D. (1988). Effects of spontaneous and induced lookbacks on self-perceived high- and low-ability comprehenders. *Journal of Educational Research, 81*(6).

Alvermann, D. E., & Guthrie, J. T. (1993). The national reading research center. In A. P. Sweet & J. I. Anderson (Eds.), *Reading research into the year 2000* (pp. 129–150). Hillsdale, NJ: Erlbaum.

American Educational Research Association. (2000). *AERA position statement concerning high-stakes testing in preK–12 education.* Retrieved from http://www.aera.net/about/policy/stakes.htm

Anastasi, A., & Urbina, S. (1997). *Psychological testing* (7th ed.). Upper Saddle River, NJ: Prentice Hall.

Anderson, R. C. (1984). Role of the reader's schema in comprehension, learning and memory. In R. C. Anderson, J. Osborn, & R. J. Tierney (Eds.), *Learning to read in American schools: Basal readers and content texts.* Hillsdale, NJ: Erlbaum.

Anderson, R. C., & Freebody, P. (1981). Vocabulary knowledge. In J. T. Guthrie (Ed.), *Comprehension and teaching: Research perspectives.* Newark, DE: International Reading Association.

Anderson, R. C., Osborn, J., & Tierney, R. J. (1984). *Learning to read in American schools: Basal readers and content texts.* Hillsdale, NJ: Erlbaum.

Anderson, R. C., Wilkinson, I. A. G., & Mason, J. M. (1991). A microanalysis of small group, guided reading lesson: Effects of an emphasis on global story meaning. *Reading Research Quarterly, 26*(4), 417–441.

Applegate, A. J. & Applegate, M. D. (2004). The Peter Effect: Reading habits and attitudes of preservice teachers. *The Reading Teacher, 57,* 554–563.

Anderson, R. C., Wilson, P., & Fielding, L. (1988). Growth in reading and how children spend their time outside of school. *Reading Research Quarterly, 23*(3), 285–303.

Applegate, M. D., Quinn, K. B., & Applegate, A. J. (2002). Levels of thinking required by comprehension questions in informal reading inventories. *The Reading Teacher, 56*(2), 174–180.

Applegate, M. D., Quinn, K. B. & Applegate, A. J. (2006). Profiles in Comprehension. *The Reading Teacher, 60,* 48–56.

Armbruster, B. B., & Wilkinson, I. A. (1991). Silent reading, oral reading, and learning from text. *The Reading Teacher, 45,* 154–155.

Athey, I. (1976). Reading research in the affective domain. In H. Singer & R. Ruddell (Eds.), *Theoretical models and processes of reading* (2nd ed.). Newark, DE: International Reading Association.

Ausubel, D. P. (1968). *Educational psychology: A cognitive view.* New York: Holt, Rinehart & Winston.

Bader, L. A. (1998). *Reading and language inventory* (3rd ed.). Upper Saddle River, NJ: Prentice Hall.

Bader, L. A., & Wiesendanger, K. D. (1989). Realizing the potential of Informal Reading Inventories. *Journal of Reading, 32,* 404–408.

Baker, L., & Wigfield, A. (1999). Dimensions of children's motivation for reading and their relationship to reading activity and reading achievement. *Reading Research Quarterly, 34*(4), 452–477.

Baumann, N. (1995). Reading millionaires—it works! *The Reading Teacher, 48,* 730.

Bean R. M., Cassidy, J., Grumet, J. E., Shelton, D. S., Wallis, S., & Rose, R. (2002). What do reading specialists do? Results from a national survey. *The Reading Teacher, 55,* 736–745.

Bean, R. M., Swan, L., & Knaub, R. (2003). Reading specialists in schools with exemplary reading programs: Functional, versatile, and prepared. *The Reading Teacher, 56,* 446–456.

Beck, I. L., & McKeown, M. G. (1991). Reasons social studies texts are hard to understand: Mediating some of the difficulties. *Language Arts, 68*(6), 482–490.

Betts, E. (1954). *Foundations of reading instruction.* New York: American Book Co.

Biemiller, A. (1994). Some observations on beginning reading instruction. *Educational Psychologist, 29*(4), 203–209.

Black, P. (2000). Research and the development of educational assessment. *Oxford Review of Education, 26*(3/4), 407–419.

Black, P., & Wiliam, D. (1998). Assessment and classroom learning. *Assessment in Education, 5*(1), 7–71.

Boodt, G. M. (1984). Critical listeners become critical readers in remedial reading class. *The Reading Teacher, 37,* 390–394.

Bossert, T. S., & Schwantes, F. M. (1995–1996). Children's comprehension monitoring: Training children to use rereading to aid comprehension. *Reading Research and Instruction, 35,* 109–121.

Bransford, J. D. (1984). Schema activation and schema acquisition: Comments on Richard C. Anderson's remarks. In R. C. Anderson, J. Osborn, & R. J. Tierney (Eds.), *Learning to read in American schools: Basal readers and content texts.* Hillsdale, NJ: Erlbaum.

Brophy, J. (1985). Teacher–student interaction. In J. B. Dusek (Ed.), *Teacher expectancies* (pp. 303–328). Hillsdale, NJ: Erlbaum.

Brown, R. G. (1991). *Schools of thought: How the politics of literacy shape thinking in the classroom.* San Francisco: Jossey-Bass.

Burns, P. C., & Roe, B. (1993). *Informal reading inventory.* Boston: Houghton Mifflin.

Carnine, D., & Kindler, B. D. (1985). Teaching low performing students to apply gerfnative and schema strategies to narrative and expository material. *Remedial and Special Education, 6*(1), 20–30.

Cazden, C. (1988). *Classroom discourse: The language of teaching and learning.* Portsmouth, NH: Heinemann.

Cipielewski, J., & Stanovich, K. E. (1992). Predicting growth in reading ability from children's exposure to print. *Journal of Experimental Child Psychology, 54,* 74–89.

Clay, M. (1979). *Reading: The patterning of complex behavior* (2nd ed.). Portsmouth, NH: Heinemann.

Cross, D. R., & Paris, S. G. (1988). Developmental and instructional analysis of children's metacognition and reading comprehension. *Journal of Education Psychology, 80,* 131–140.

CTB McGraw-Hill. (2002). *TerraNova performance assessments: Product detail.* Retrieved from http://www.ctb.com/products_detail.jsp?

Cunningham, A. E., & Stanovich, K. E. (1997). Early reading acquisition and its relation to reading experience and ability 10 years later. *Developmental Psychology, 33,* 934–945.

Davis, F. B. (1968). Research on comprehension in reading. *Reading Research Quarterly, 3,* 449–545.

Davis, Z. T. (1994). Effects of pre-reading story mapping on elementary readers' comprehension. *Journal of Educational Research, 87*(6), 353–360.

Dolch, E. W. (1948). *Problems in reading.* Champaign, IL: Garrard Books.

Donahue, P. L., Voelkl, K. E., Campbell, J. R., & Mazzeo, J. (1999). *NAEP 1998 reading report card for the nation and the states.* (NCES 1999-500) National Center for Educational Statistics, Office of Educational Research and Improvement, U.S. Department of Education.

Driscoll, M. (1994). *Psychology of learning for instruction.* Boston: Allyn & Bacon.

Duffelmeyer, F. A., Robinson, S. S., & Squier, S. E. (1989). Vocabulary questions on informal reading inventories. *The Reading Teacher, 43,* 142–148.

Durkin, D. (1978–1979). What classroom observations reveal about reading comprehension instruction. *Reading Research Quarterly, 14,* 481–538.

Eldredge, J. L., Quinn, B., & Butterfield, D. D. (1990). Causal relationships between phonics, reading comprehension, and vocabulary achievement in the second grade. *Journal of Educational Research, 83*(4), 201–214.

Elmorc, R. S., Peterson, P. L., & McCarthey, S. J. (1996). *Restructuring in the classroom: Teaching, learning and school organization.* San Francisco: Jossey-Bass.

Flippo, R. E. (2001). *Reading researchers in search of common ground.* Newark, DE: International Reading Association.

Flynt, E. S., & Cooter, R. B. (2001). *Reading inventory for the classroom* (4th ed.). Upper Saddle River, NJ: Prentice Hall.

Foorman, B. R., Novy, D., Francis, D., & Lieberman, D. (1991). How letter-sound instruction mediates progress in first grade reading and spelling. *Journal of Educational Psychology, 83,* 456–469.

Fountas, I. C., & Pinnell, G. S. (1996). *Guided reading.* Portsmouth, NH: Heinemann.

Frances, W. N., & Kucera, H. (1982). *Frequency analysis of English usage.* Boston: Houghton Mifflin.

Freppon, P. (1991). Children's concepts of the nature and purpose of reading in different instructional settings. *Journal of Reading Behavior, 23*(2), 139–163.

Fuchs, L. S., Fuchs, D., & Deno, S. L. (1982). Reliability and validity of curriculum-based Informal Reading Inventories. *Reading Research Quarterly, 18,* 6–26.

Fuchs, L. S., Fuchs, D. & Maxwell, L. (1988). The validity of informal measures of reading comprehension. *Remedial and Special Education, 9,* 20–28.

Gagne, E. D. (1985). *The cognitive psychology of school learning.* Boston: Little, Brown.

Gambrell, L. B. (1996). Creating classroom cultures that foster reading motivation. *The Reading Teacher, 50,* 14–25.

Gambrell, L. B., Palmer, B. M., Codling, R. M., & Mazzoni, S. A. (1996). Assessing motivation to read. *The Reading Teacher, 49*(7), 518–533.

Gambrell, L. B., Wilson, R. M., & Gantt, W. N. (1981, July/August). Classroom observations of task-attending behaviors of good and poor readers. *Journal of Educational Research, 74,* 400–404.

Gerke, R. (1980). Critique of informal reading inventories: Can a valid instructional level be obtained? *Journal of Reading Behavior, 12,* 155–157.

Gillis, M. K., & Olson, M. W. (1986). *Informal reading inventories & test type/structure.* Paper presented at the 14th annual meeting of the Southwest Regional Conference of the International Reading Association, San Antonio, TX, January 30–February 1. (ERIC Document Reproduction Service No. ED276971)

Goodman, K. S. (1970). Reading: A psycholinguistic guessing game. In H. Singer & R. B. Ruddell (Eds.), *Theoretical models and processes of reading* (pp. 259–271). Newark, DE: International Reading Association.

Goodman, Y. (1997). Reading diagnosis—qualitative or quantitative. *Reading Teacher, 50*(7), 534–540.

Goodman, Y. M., & Burke, C. (1972). *The reading miscue inventory.* Portsmouth, NH: Heinemann.

Goodman, Y. M., & Goodman, K. S. (1994). To err is human: Learning about language processes by analyzing miscues. In R. B. Ruddell, M. R. Ruddell, & H. Singer (Eds.), *Theoretical models and processes of reading*

(4th ed., pp. 104–123). Newark, DE: International Reading Association.

Gottfried, A. E. (1990). Academic intrinsic motivation in young elementary school children. *Journal of Educational Psychology, 82,* 525–538.

Gray, J. A., & Moody, D. B. (2000). Effects of reading excellence model on children's reading. *Commerce Business Daily Issue.*

Guthrie, J. T. (2001). Benefits of opportunity to read and balanced instruction on the NAEP. *Journal of Educational Research, 94,* 145–163.

Guthrie, J. T., Wigfield, A., Metsala, J. L., & Cox, K. E. (1999). Motivational and cognitive predictors of text comprehension and reading amount. *Scientific Studies of Reading, 3*(3), 231–257.

Hansen, J. (1981). The effects of inference training and practice on young children's reading comprehension. *Reading Research Quarterly, 16,* 391–417.

Harcourt. (2002). *Stanford 9 open-ended reading.* Retrieved from http://www.hbem.com/trophy/schvtest/o-eread.htm

Harris, A. J., & Sipay, E. (1990). *How to increase reading ability* (10th ed.). White Plains, NY: Longman.

Harris, L. A., & Lalik, R. M. (1987). Teachers' use of informal reading inventories: An example of school constraints. *The Reading Teacher, 40,* 624–630.

Helgren-Lempesis, V. A., & Mangrum, C. T. II. (1986). An analysis of alternate-form reliability of three commercially-prepared informal reading inventories. *Reading Research Quarterly, 21,* 209–215.

Hunt, L. C. Jr. (1970). The effect of self-selection, interest, and motivation upon independent, instructional, and frustrational levels. *The Reading Teacher, 24,* 146–151.

Idol, L., & Croll, V. (1987). Story map training as a means of improving reading comprehension. *Learning Disabilities Quarterly, 10,* 214–230.

International Reading Association. (1999). *High stakes assessment in reading: A position statement.* Newark, DE: International Reading Association.

International Reading Association Disabled Reader Subcommittee. (1991). *A nationwide U.S. survey of classroom teachers' and remedial reading teachers' perceptions and knowledge about assessment of disabled readers: A quantitative analysis.* Newark, DE: International Reading Association. (ERIC Document Reproduction Service No. ED337764)

Jitendra, A. K., Nolet, V., Xin, Y. P., Gomez, O., Renouf, K., Iskold, L., et al. (2001). An analysis of middle school geography textbooks: Implications for students with learning disabilities. *Reading & Writing Quarterly, 17,* 151–173.

Johns, J. (1994). *Basic reading inventory.* Dubuque, IA: Kendall-Hunt.

Johns, J. L. (1991). Emmett A. Betts on informal reading inventories. *Journal of Reading, 34,* 492–493.

Johns, J. L., & Magliari, A. M. (1989). Informal reading inventories: Are the Betts criteria the best criteria? *Reading Improvement, 26,* 124–132.

Johnson, M. S., Kress, R. A., & Pikulski, J. J. (1987). *Informal reading inventories* (2nd ed.). Newark, DE: International Reading Association.

Johnson, S. (1982). Listening and reading: The recall of 7- to 9-year-olds. *British Journal of Educational Psychology, 52,* 24–32.

Johnston, P. (1997). *Knowing literacy.* Portland, ME: Stenhouse.

Jongsma, K. S., & Jongsma, E. A. (1981). Test review: Commercial informal reading inventories. *The Reading Teacher, 34,* 697–705.

Juel, C. (1988). Learning to read and write: A longitudinal study of 54 children from 1st to 4th grades. *Journal of Educational Psychology, 80,* 437–447.

Kame'enui, E. J., Carnine, D. W., & Freschi, R. (1982). Effects of text construction and instructional procedures for teaching word meanings on comprehension and recall. *Reading and Research Quarterly, 17,* 367–388.

Kim, Y. H., & Goetz, E. T. (1994). Context effects on word recognition and reading comprehension of good and poor readers: A test of the interactive-compensatory hypothesis. *Reading Research Quarterly, 29,* 179–188.

Kinder, D., Bursuck, B., & Epstein, M. (1992). An evaluation of history textbooks. *Journal of Special Education, 25,* 472–492.

Klesius, J. P., & Homan, S. P. (1985). A validity and reliability update on the informal reading inventory with suggestions for improvement. *Journal of Learning Disabilities, 18,* 71–76.

Knapp, M. S. (1995). *Teaching for meaning in high-poverty classrooms.* New York: Teachers College Press.

Langer, J. A. (1995). *Envisioning literature: Literary understanding and literature instruction.* New York: International Association and Teachers College Press.

Leslie, L., & Caldwell, J. (2001). *Qualitative reading inventory* (3rd ed.). New York: Longman.

Leslie, L. & Caldwell, J. (2006). *Qualitative reading inventory* (4th ed.). New York: Longman.

Lewis, C. S. (1961). *An experiment in criticism.* Cambridge: Cambridge University Press.

Lowell, R. E. (1969). *Problems in identifying reading levels with informal reading inventories.* Paper presented at the International Reading Association conference, Kansas City, MO, April 30–May 3. (ERIC Document Reproduction Service No. ED032199)

Lynch, D. J. (1988). Reading comprehension under listening, silent, and round robin reading conditions as a function of text difficulty. *Reading Improvement, 25,* 98–104.

Manning, M., & Manning G. 81 (1994). Reading: word or meaning centered? *Teaching PreK–8, 25*(2), 98–100.

Manzo, A. V., Manzo, U. C., & McKenna, M. C. (1995). *Informal reading-thinking inventory.* Fort Worth, TX: Harcourt Brace College Publishing.

McKenna, M. C. (1983). Informal reading inventories: A review of the issues. *The Reading Teacher,* (36) 670–679.

Meece, J. L., Blumenfeld, P. C., & Hoyle, R. H. (1988). Students' goal orientation and cognitive engagement in classroom activities. *Journal of Educational Psychology, 85,* 582–590.

Miller, S. D., & Smith, D. E. (1990). Relations among oral reading, silent reading, and listening comprehension of students at differing competency levels. *Reading Research & Instruction, 29,* 73–84.

Morrow, L. M., Tracey, D. H., Woo, D. G., & Pressley, M. (1999). Characteristics of exemplary first-grade literacy instruction. *The Reading Teacher, 52,* 462–476.

National Center for Education Statistics. (2002). *Distribution of questions by reading stance, 2000 NAEP, Grade 4.*

Retrieved from http://nces.ed.gov/nationsreportcard/ reading/distributequest.asp

Nessel, D. (1987). Reading comprehension: Asking the right questions. *Phi Delta Kappan, 68,* 442–445.

Ogbu, J. (1992). Adaptation to minority status and impact on school success. *Theory into Practice, 31,* 287–295.

Oliver, J. E., & Arnold, R. (1978). Comparing a standardized test, an informal inventory and teacher judgment on third grade reading. *Reading Improvement, 15,* 56–59.

Olson, M. W., & Gillis, M. K. (1987). Text type and text structure: An analysis of three secondary informal reading inventories. *Reading Horizons, 28,* 70–80.

Parker, R., & Hasbrouck, J. E. (1992). Greater validity for oral reading fluency: can miscues help? *Journal of Special Education, 25*(4), 492–503.

Pearson, P. D. (1992). Reading. In *The encyclopedia of educational research* (pp. 1075–1085).

Pearson, P. D., & Camperell, K. (1994). Comprehension of text structures. In R. R. Ruddell, M. R. Ruddell, & H. Singer (Eds.), *Theoretical models and processes of reading* (4th ed.). Newark, DE: International Reading Association.

Pearson, P. D., Hansen, J., & Gordon, C. (1979). The effective background knowledge on young children's comprehension of explicit and implicit information. *Journal of Reading Behavior, 11,* 201–209.

Piaget, J. (1973). *The language and thought of the child.* New York: World Books.

Pikulski, J. J. (1990). Informal reading inventories. *The Reading Teacher, 43,* 514–516.

Pinnell, G. S., Pikulski, J. J., Wixson, K. K., Campbell, J. R., Gough, P. B. & Beatty, A. S. (1995). *Listening to children read aloud.* Washington, DC: Office of Educational Research and Improvement, U. S. Department of Education.

Pressley, M., Wharton-McDonald, R., Allington, R. L., Block, C. C., Morrow, L., Tracey, D., et al. (2001). Strategy instruction for elementary students searching informational text. *Scientific Studies of Reading, 5*(1), 35–58.

Quinn, K. B., Slowik, C. C., & Hartman, G. (2000). The relationship between motivation to read and reading achievement. *The Pennsylvania Psychologist, 60,* 23–25.

Rasinski, T. (1989). Fluency for everyone: Incorporating fluency instruction in the classroom. *The Reading Teacher, 42*(9), 690–693.

Report of the National Reading Panel. (2000). *Teaching children to read.* Retrieved from http://www.nichd.nih. gov/publications/nrp/members/htm

Rosenblatt, L. M. (1978). *The reader, the text, the poem: The transactional theory of literary work.* Carbondale: Southern Illinois University Press.

Rosenblatt, L. M. (1983). *Literature as exploration* (4th ed.). New York: Modern Language Association. (Original work published 1938)

Rosenthal, R. (1985). From unconscious experimenter bias to teacher expectancy effects. In J. B. Dusek (Ed.), *Teacher expectancies* (pp. 37–65). Hillsdale, NJ: Erlbaum.

Rosenthal, R., & Jacobson, L. (1968). *Pygmalion in the classroom: Teacher expectations and pupils' intellectual development.* New York: Holt, Rinehart & Winston.

Ruddell, R. B., Draheim, M. E., & Barnes, J. (1990). A comparative study of the teaching effectiveness of influential and noninfluential teachers and reading comprehension development. In J. Zutell & S. McCormick (Eds.), *Literacy theory and research: Analyses from multiple paradigms* (pp. 153–162). Chicago: National Reading Conference.

Rumelhart, D. E. (198). Toward an interactive model of reading. In H. Singer & R. R. Ruddell (Eds.), *Theoretical models and processes of reading* (3rd ed.). Newark, DE: International Reading Association.

Samuels, S. J. (1988). Decoding and Automaticity. *The Reading Teacher, 41,* 756–760.

Schiefele, U. (1991). Interest, learning and motivation. *Educational Psychologist, 26,* 299–324.

Schraw, G., & Bruning, R. (1999). How implicit models of reading affect motivation to read and reading engagement. *Scientific Studies of Reading, 3*(3), 281–302.

Shanker, J. L., & Ekwall, E. E. (1999). *Ekwall-Shanker reading inventory* (4th ed.). Boston: Allyn & Bacon.

Shanker, J. L., & Ekwall, E. E. (2000). *Ekwall-Shanker reading inventory* (4th ed.). Boston: Allyn & Bacon.

Silvaroli, N. J., & Wheelock, W. H. (2001). *Classroom reading inventory* (9th ed.). New York: McGraw-Hill.

Singer, H., & Donlan, W. (1982). Active comprehension: Problem solving with question generation for comprehension of complex short stories. *Reading Research Quarterly, 17,* 166–586.

Stahl, S. A., Duffy-Hester, A. M., & Stahl, K. A. (1998). Theory and research into practice: Everything you wanted to know about phonics (but were afraid to ask). *Reading Research Quarterly, 33,* 338–355.

Stanovich, K. (1986). Matthew effects in reading. *Reading Research Quarterly, 21,* 360–406.

Stanovich, K. E. (1980). Toward an interactive compensatory model of individual differences in the development of reading fluency. *Reading Research Quarterly, 16,* 32–71.

Stauffer, R. G. (1969). *Directing reading maturity as a cognitive process.* New York: Harper & Row.

Swanson, P. N., & De La Paz, S. (1998). Teaching effective comprehension strategies to students with learning and reading disabilities. *Intervention in School and Clinic, 33*(4), 209–218.

Taylor, B., Pearson, D., Clark, K., & Walpole, S. (2000). *Beating the odds in teaching all children to read* (Report #2-006). East Lansing, MI: Center for Improving Early Reading Achievement.

Taylor, S. E., Frackenpohl, H., White, C. E., Nieroroda, B. W., Browning, C. L., & Birsner, E. P. (1989). *EDL Core vocabularies in Reading, Mathematics, Science, and Social Studies.* Orlando, FL: Steck-Vaughn Co.

Tharp, R. G., & Gallimore, R. (1989). Rousing schools to life. *American Educator, 13*(2), 20–25, 46–52.

Thorndike, E. L. (1917). Reading as reasoning: A study of mistakes in paragraph reading. *Journal of Educational Psychology, 8,* 323–332.

Vygotsky, L. (1978). *Mind in society.* Cambridge, MA: Harvard University Press.

Weaver, C., & Smith, L. (1979). A psycholinguistic look at the informal reading inventory part II: Inappropriate inferences from an informal reading inventory. *Reading Horizons, 19,* 103–111.

Wigfield, A., & Guthrie, J. T. (1997). Relations of children's motivation for reading to the amount and breadth of their reading. *Journal of Educational Psychology, 89,* 420–432.

Woods, M. L., & Moe, A. J. (1999). *Analytical reading inventory* (6th ed.). Upper Saddle River, NJ: Prentice Hall.

Test Materials

- Summary of Administration Procedures for The Critical Reading Inventory
- Student Interviews
- Parent/Guardian Interview
- Teacher Interview
- Oral Reading Fluency Rubric
- Critical Reading Inventory Recapitulation Records
- Narrative Retelling Scoring Guide
- Informational Retelling Scoring Guide
- Word Lists

Summary of Administration Procedures for The Critical Reading Inventory

Rapport

- Establish rapport with the child; use the appropriate student interview form to assist in this activity.
- Explain the purpose and process of the assessment, answer any questions, and address any concerns.

Word Lists

- Start at least two levels below the child's current grade level.
- Flash = 1-second exposure using two index cards; record child's exact (phonetic) response in case of a miscue; use "+" to indicate a correct response.
- Untimed = 10- to 15-second exposure to allow the child to "decode" or correct miscues from the flash portion.
- Discontinue once the child has scored 70% or less on the Flash portion.

Passages

- Start with oral reading at the highest level at which the child attained 100% on the Flash portion of the word lists.
- Introduce the process for the passages by reading the introductory statement on the Examiner's Copy of the CRI.
- Record the child's oral reading miscues on the Examiner's Copy, using the notation guidelines in the Oral Reading Miscue Recording chart on the following page; later you will calculate the RAI and MMI for each oral reading passage that the child has completed.
- Remove the story from the child and ask the child to retell the story to you; record his or her retelling verbatim for scoring later. If the child does not do so in the course of the retelling, remind the child, "Tell me what you thought about the passage."
- Ask the comprehension questions and record the child's exact responses. Score as you go if you are an experienced user. Otherwise, estimate the level of the child's performance so that you do not exceed the child's Frustration Level.
- Follow the same procedures for the silent passage at each level (except, of course, for recording the oral reading performance).
- Estimate the average for the oral and the silent comprehension performance after each level is administered.
- Stop when either the oral reading performance RAI score is 90% or less *or* when the average comprehension (oral + silent reading comprehension /2) is 50% or less.
- Proceed to listening comprehension assessment if the child's Instructional Level is below the child's grade level or if you note that word recognition problems are seriously affecting comprehension.
- If you start with a level where the child does not obtain an "independent" score on oral reading performance and/or comprehension average, then go down a level until an independent level is established.

Use the DVD that accompanies this text for guidance on how to use *The Critical Reading Inventory*.

Estimating Reading Levels

	Oral Reading Performance	Comprehension Average
Independent	98–100%	90%
Instructional	93–97%	70–85%
Frustration	92% or below	50% or less

Oral Reading Miscue Recording Procedures for the Critical Reading Inventory

Scoreable Miscues	Coding System for Miscues
• Substitutions/Reversals	Draw a line through word and write phonetic spelling over word
• Omissions	Put an *x* through omitted word
• Insertions	Write inserted word in text using carat
• Teacher-provided	Circle word and note with *TP*

Scoreable Miscues—Special Cases

• Same error repeated more than once, counts only as one miscue
  For example, says *robe* for *rode* three times in the story = 1 miscue
• Skips a whole line of print or several words in a line = 1 miscue
• Reversals = 1 miscue

Nonscoreable but Recorded Oral Reading Behaviors

• Self-corrections	Use check mark or "SC"
• Dialect mispronunciations/omissions	
For example, the child leaves off word endings in both	
speech and oral reading	Note phonetic spelling with "D"
• Proper name mispronunciation	Note phonetic spelling
• Inappropriate pauses or hesitations	Note with slash (/)
• Repetitions	Underline the text
• Finger-pointing	FP
• Head movement	HM
• Subvocalization during silent reading	SV
• Skipped punctuation	Circle punctuation mark
• Word-by-word reading	W×W
• Inappropriate pacing	Slow/Fast

Student Interview, Grades K–4

Name: _____ Grade: ____ Date: _____ Examiner: _____

1. Do you have any brothers or sisters? Any best friends? What about pets?

2. What are some things that you like to do at home?

3. What makes these things fun?

4. Does anyone ever read to you at home? Who? When? What?

5. Do you like to read?

6. Do you have any favorite books or authors? What are they? Why do you like them?

7. Are you a good reader? Why or why not?

8. What do you think is the hardest part about reading?

9. What do you do when you come to a word that you don't know?

10. Where do you get the books you read at home? (Probe further if necessary: library, stores, gifts, etc.)

11. What do you like most about school?

12. What kinds of things do you do when you have reading at school?

13. What would you like to do when you are older?

14. Do you think reading will be important to you?

Student Interview, Grades 5–12

Name:_____ Grade: ____ Date: _____ Examiner: _____

1. What kinds of things do you like to do when you're not in school?

2. How about reading? (If reader does not volunteer the information, probe for how often, what kinds of materials, topics of interest, where materials are obtained, etc.)

3. How do you think you do with reading in school? What about writing?

4. What have you read recently for enjoyment? For school? Did you find them enjoyable? Were they easy for you to understand?

5. What is the hardest part about reading?

6. What are the best and worst things about school?

7. Is writing hard or easy for you? What do you think makes it that way?

8. Are you on any clubs or teams at school? Do you have any hobbies? Do you have a job?

9. How are your grades in school? Do you have any concerns with any subjects?

10. Have you ever thought about what kind of job you'd like to have when you're older?

11. Is there anything else that you'd like to share about yourself?

Parent/Guardian Interview

Name:_____ Grade: ____ Date: _____ Examiner: _____

1. What made you think that it would be a good idea for _____ (student's name) to be tested at this time?

2. How is _____ doing in school, particularly in reading?

3. What kind of reading does _____ do at home?

4. How would you characterize _____'s:

   a Ability

   b. Attitude

   c. Interests

   d. Needs

   e. Behavior

5. What would you say is the major reason for _____'s school performance?

6. How long has he/she had this difficulty?

7. What kinds of help has he/she gotten so far?

8. What are you currently doing at home to help _____ ?

9. Is there anything else you think might be helpful for you to do?

10. What is the school or the teacher doing this year to help _____ ?

11. What else do you think would be helpful for the school or teacher to do?

Teacher Interview

Name:_____ Grade: ____ Date: _____ Examiner: _____

1. What would you say are the greatest needs in reading of the class you have this year?

2. Could you describe for me a typical reading/language arts period in your classroom (this should include time spent, materials used, methods, grouping techniques).

3. How does _____ (student's name) generally react to your instruction?

4. What would you say is the greatest emphasis in your comprehension instruction and assessment? *If response is unclear, you may follow up with:* Do you tend to emphasize recall of information, student response to the text, or both equally?

5. How would you characterize _____'s:

   a. Ability

   b. Attitude

   c. Interests

   d. Needs

   e. Behavior

6. What kinds of activities or strategies have you tried specifically with _____? What seems to work best? What doesn't seem to be working?

7. What do you know about the type of support _____ gets at home?

8. If there were one thing that you could recommend that you think would help _____, what would it be?

Oral Reading Fluency Rubric

Rate the reader's fluency in each of the four categories below. Check only one box in each category.

Oral Reading

_____ (5 pts.) Reading is fluent, confident, and accurate.

_____ (4 pts.) Reading is fluent and accurate for the most part, but reader occasionally falters or hesitates.

_____ (3 pts.) Reader lacks confidence at times and reading is characterized by frequent pauses, miscues, and hesitations.

_____ (2 pts.) Reader consistently lacks confidence and occasionally lapses into word-by-word reading with frequent meaning-violating miscues.

_____ (1 pt.) Largely word-by-word reading with little or no inflection, and numerous meaning-violating miscues, some of which may be nonwords.

Intonation

_____ (5 pts.) Intonations consistently support meaning of the text.

_____ (4 pts.) Intonations are largely meaningful but may include exaggerations or inflections inappropriate for the text.

_____ (3 pts.) Intonation is characterized by some joining of words into meaningful phrases but this element often breaks down when the reader encounters difficulty.

_____ (2 pts.) Intonation is largely flat with lack of enthusiasm.

_____ (1 pt.) Intonation is almost completely absent.

Punctuation

_____ (5 pts.) Natural use of and appreciation for punctuation.

_____ (4 pts.) Solid use of punctuation as an aid to intonation.

_____ (3 pts.) Reaction to punctuation marks results in pauses that are inappropriately long or short.

_____ (2 pts.) Punctuation is occasionally ignored and meaning may be distorted.

_____ (1 pt.) Frequent ignoring of punctuation.

Pacing

_____ (5 pts.) Pacing is rapid but smooth and unexaggerated.

_____ (4 pts.) Reading is well paced with only occasional weakness in response to difficulties with the text.

_____ (3 pts.) Pacing is relatively slow and markedly slower (or markedly faster) when reader encounters difficult text.

_____ (2 pts.) Pacing is either very slow or inappropriately fast.

_____ (1 pt.) Pacing is painfully slow and halting.

_____ **Total Score**

Score Conversion Chart

19–20 pts. = Excellent	13–14 pts. = Fair	7–8 pts. = Weak
17–18 pts. = Very Good	11–12 pts. = Inconsistent	5–6 pts. = Very Weak
15–16 pts. = Good	9–10 pts. = Inadequate	4 pts. or less = Poor

Critical Reading Inventory—Recapitulation Record—Narrative Passages

Name _____ Grade _____ C.A. _____ Date of Testing _____ Examiner _____

Word Lists / *Comprehending and Responding to Text*

Level	Flash	Untimed	Context RAI	Context MMI	Oral Comp. %	Retelling Score	Oral Text-Based	Oral Inference	Oral Critical	Silent Comp. %	Retelling Score	Silent Text-Based	Silent Inference	Silent Critical	Average Oral + Silent	Listening Comp. %
Pre-Primer							/3	/3	/2			/3	/3	/2		
Primer							/3	/3	/2			/3	/3	/2		
1st							/3	/3	/2			/3	/3	/2		
2nd							/4	/3	/3			/4	/3	/3		
3rd							/4	/3	/3			/4	/3	/3		
4th							/4	/3	/3			/4	/3	/3		
5th							/4	/3	/3			/4	/3	/3		
6th							/4	/3	/3			/4	/3	/3		
7th							/4	/3	/3			/4	/3	/3		
8th							/4	/3	/3			/4	/3	/3		
9th							/4	/3	/3			/4	/3	/3		
10th							/4	/3	/3			/4	/3	/3		
11th							/4	/3	/3			/4	/3	/3		
12th							/4	/3	/3			/4	/3	/3		

Level One Numerical Interpretation

Level	Highest Independent Level _____	Highest Instructional Level _____	Frustration Level _____
Word List and Miscue Analysis	Flash ___ MMI ___ · Untimed ___ SC · RAI ___ Nonwords	Flash ___ MMI ___ · Untimed ___ SC · RAI ___ Nonwords	Flash ___ MMI ___ · Untimed ___ SC · RAI ___ Nonwords
Comprehension and Retelling Scores	Comp. % ___ · Retelling ___ · Oral: ___ · Silent: ___ · Average: ___	Comp. % ___ · Retelling ___ · Oral: ___ · Silent: ___ · Average: ___	Comp. % ___ · Retelling ___ · Oral: ___ · Silent: ___ · Average: ___
Oral Comprehension, Fluency, and MMI	Oral comp. % ___ · Fluency · MMI ___ · Silent ___	Oral comp. % ___ · MMI ___ · Silent ___	Oral comp. % ___ · MMI ___ · Silent ___
Question Type	Oral / Silent · Text-Based: ___ · Inference: ___ · Critical: ___	Oral / Silent · Text-Based: ___ · Inference: ___ · Critical: ___	Oral / Silent · Text-Based: ___ · Inference: ___ · Critical: ___

This form is an example of a Narrative Passages Recapitulation Record available electronically for Windows users at *www.prenhall.com/readinginventory/scoringassistant.*

Critical Reading Inventory—Recapitulation Record—Informational Passages

Name _____ Grade _____ C.A. _____ Date of Testing _____ Examiner _____

Word Lists

			Context						Comprehending and Responding to Text							
Level	Flash	Untimed	RAI	MMI	Oral Comp. %	Retelling Score	Oral–Text-Based	Oral–Inference	Oral–Critical	Silent Comp. %	Retelling Score	Silent–Text-Based	Silent–Inference	Silent–Critical	Average Oral + Silent	Listening Comp. %
Pre-Primer							/3	/3	/2			/3	/3	/2		
Primer							/3	/3	/2			/3	/3	/2		
1st							/3	/3	/2			/3	/3	/2		
2nd							/4	/4	/2			/4	/4	/2		
3rd							/4	/4	/2			/4	/4	/2		
4th							/4	/4	/2			/4	/4	/2		
5th							/4	/4	/2			/4	/4	/2		
6th							/4	/4	/2			/4	/4	/2		
7th							/4	/4	/2			/4	/4	/2		
8th							/4	/4	/2			/4	/4	/2		
9th							/4	/4	/2			/4	/4	/2		
10th							/4	/4	/2			/4	/4	/2		
11th							/4	/4	/2			/4	/4	/2		
12th							/4	/4	/2			/4	/4	/2		

Level One Numerical Interpretation

Level	Highest Independent Level	Highest Instructional Level	Frustration Level
Word List and Miscue Analysis	Flash ___ MMI ___ Untimed SC ___ RAI Nonwords ___	Flash ___ MMI ___ Untimed SC ___ RAI Nonwords ___	Flash ___ MMI ___ Untimed SC ___ RAI Nonwords ___
Comprehension and Retelling Scores	Comp. % ___ Retelling ___ Oral: ___ Silent: ___ Average: ___	Comp. % ___ Retelling ___ Oral: ___ Silent: ___ Average: ___	Comp. % ___ Retelling ___ Oral: ___ Silent: ___ Average: ___
Oral Comprehension, Fluency, and MMI	Oral comp. % ___ MMI ___	Oral comp. % ___ Fluency ___ MMI ___	Oral comp. % ___ MMI ___
Question Type	Oral ___ Silent ___ Text-Based: ___ Inference: ___ Critical: ___	Oral ___ Silent ___ Text-Based: ___ Inference: ___ Critical: ___	Oral ___ Silent ___ Text-Based: ___ Inference: ___ Critical: ___

This form is an example of an Informational Passages Recapitulation Record available electronically for Windows users at *www.prenhall.com/readinginventory/scoringassistant.*

Critical Reading Inventory—Completed Sample Recapitulation Record—Narrative Passages

Name __John (Case Study)__ Grade __5__ C.A. __10.8__ Date of Testing __11/15__ Examiner __Examiner__

Word Lists / Comprehending and Responding to Text

Level	Flash	Context Untimed	Context RAI	Context MMI	Oral Comp. %	Retelling Score	Oral-Text-Based	Oral-Inference	Oral-Critical	Silent Comp. %	Retelling Score	Silent-Text-Based	Silent-Inference	Silent-Critical	Average Oral + Silent	Listening Comp. %
Pre-Primer																
Primer							/3	/3	/2			/3	/3	/2		
1st							/3	/3	/2			/3	/3	/2		
2nd	100	100	97	100	100	3.5	4/4	3/3	3/3	100	3.5	4/4	3/3	3/3	100	
3rd	85	95	95	98	50	1.0	2/4	0/3	3/3	40	1.0	2/4	0/3	2/3	45	
4th	55	75					/4	/3	/3			/4	/3	/3		
5th							/4	/3	/3		4.0	/4	/3	/3		100
6th							/4	/3	/3			/4	/3	/3		
7th							/4	/3	/3			/4	/3	/3		
8th							/4	/3	/3			/4	/3	/3		
9th							/4	/3	/3			/4	/3	/3		
10th							/4	/3	/3			/4	/3	/3		
11th							/4	/3	/3			/4	/3	/3		
12th							/4	/3	/3			/4	/3	/3		

Level One Numerical Interpretation

Level	Highest Independent Level __2nd__	Highest Instructional Level __Not established__	Frustration Level __3rd__
Word List and Miscue Analysis	Flash 100 Untimed 100 RAI 97 MMI 100 SC 2 Nonwords 1	Flash — Untimed — RAI — MMI — SC — Nonwords —	Flash 85 Untimed 95 RAI 95 MMI 98 SC 2 Nonwords 7
Comprehension and Retelling Scores	Comp. % Oral 100 / Silent 100 / Average 100 Retelling 3.5 / 3.5 / 3.5	Comp. % Oral — / Silent — / Average — Retelling — / — / —	Comp. % Oral 50 / Silent 40 / Average 45 Retelling 1.0 / 1.0 / 1.0
Oral Comprehension, Fluency, and MMI	Oral comp. % 100 MMI 100	Oral comp. % — Fluency — MMI —	Oral comp. % 50 MMI 98
Question Type	Oral: Text-Based 4/4, Inference 3/3, Critical 3/3 Silent: 4/4, 3/3, 3/3	Oral: Text-Based —, Inference —, Critical — Silent: —, —, —	Oral: Text-Based 2/4, Inference 0/3, Critical 3/3 Silent: 2/4, 0/3, 2/3

This form is an example (John's case study as described on the accompanying DVD) of a completed recapitulation record as scored on the ASII, the Automated Scoring and Interpretation Interview, located at *www.prenhall.com/readinginventory/scoringassistant*.

Narrative Retelling Scoring Guide

Step 1: Record the child's retelling in the space provided on your Examiner's Copy. The retelling should be recorded verbatim and in its entirety. Then determine whether each of the eight elements in the rubric is present and deserves Full Credit, partially present and deserves Half Credit, or absent and deserves No Credit.

Step 2: Total the score for the first two items in the retelling (Key Characters and Character's Problem/Goal). Give one point for each element marked for Full Credit and ½ point for each item marked with ½ Credit. This will be the Starting Score (SS) and it can range from .00 to 2.00. We will then modify that SS based upon the number of steps recalled in the retelling of the Problem-Solving Process.

Step 3: Total the number of steps the reader has identified in the Problem-Solving Process in the same way as in Step Two. We will name this total (PS) and it can range from .0 to 5.0 in half-point increments.

If SS equals 2.0 and PS equals 5.0, then add 1.0 to the SS to make it 3.0 and go to Step 4
If SS equals 2.0 and PS equals 4.5, then add .5 to SS to make it 2.5 and go to Step 4
If SS equals 2.0 and PS is greater than 2.5 and less than 4.5, then keep SS as 2.0 and go to Step 4
If SS equals 2.0 and PS is less than 3.0, then subtract .5 from the SS to make it 1.5 and go to Step 4

If SS equals 1.5 and PS is greater than 4.0, then add .5 to SS to make it 2.0 and go to Step 4
If SS equals 1.5 and PS is greater than 2.5 and less than 4.5, then keep the SS as 1.5 and go to Step 4
If SS equals 1.5 and PS is less than 3.0, then subtract .5 from the SS to make it 1.0 and go to Step 4

If SS equals 1.0 and PS is greater than 3.0, then add .5 to SS to make it 1.5 and go to Step 4
If SS equals 1.0 and PS is greater than .5 and less than 3.5 then keep the SS as 1.0 and go to Step 4
If SS equals 1.0 and PS is less than 1.0, then subtract .5 from the SS to make it .5 and go to Step 4

If SS equals .5 and PS is greater than 2.0, then add .5 to SS to make it 1.0 and go to Step 4
If SS equals .5 and PS is greater than .5 and less than 2.5, then keep the SS as .5 and go to Step 4
If SS equals .5 and PS is less than 1.0, then subtract .5 from the SS to make it .0 and go to Step 4

If SS equals .0 and PS is greater than 2.0, then add .5 to SS to make it .5 and go to Step 4
If SS equals .0 and PS is less than 2.5, then keep the SS as .0 and go to Step 4

Step 4: Is there a well-supported personal response in the retelling?

If yes, and if SS is greater than 2.0, then add 1.0 to SS and this will be the Final Score (FS)
If yes, and if SS is less than 2.5 and PS greater than 1.5, then add .5 to SS and this will be the FS
If no, do not change the SS; simply report it as the Final Score in the appropriate box

Descriptions of Narrative Retelling Scores

Score	Description
4.0	A virtually perfect retelling that includes all story elements and a well-supported Personal Response.
3.5	An exceptionally strong retelling that omits a small but significant part of the Problem Solving Process, but which still includes a well-supported Personal Response.
3.0	A very strong retelling that includes all story elements, including all five steps in the Problem-Solving Process, but which does not include a Personal Response.
2.5	A strong retelling that includes many story elements in a variety of combinations and may include a Personal Response. A reader who achieves this score has clearly comprehended the primary gist of the story.
2.0	A solid retelling which includes most key story elements but which is also characterized by some key omissions.
1.5	A fairly weak retelling which includes some story elements but also omits a good deal of key information and may contain some factual distortions.
1.0	A weak retelling that includes a few story elements but is also characterized by some glaring omissions and factual distortions.
.5	A very weak retelling that includes little more than a few disjointed story elements and factual distortions.
.0	A retelling that may include nothing more than a vague idea of the topic of the story or a character in the story.

Informational Retelling Scoring Guide

Step 1: Record the child's retelling in the space provided on your Examiner's Copy. The retelling should be recorded verbatim and in its entirety. Then determine whether each of the nine elements in the rubric is present and deserves Full Credit, partially present and deserves $\frac{1}{2}$ Credit, or absent and deserves No Credit.

Step 2: Total the score for the three Macro-concepts (the numbered ideas from the passage) and use the table below to calculate the Starting Score (SS) for the retelling. Give one point for each element marked for Full Credit and one half point for each marked with $\frac{1}{2}$ Credit.

If the retelling includes all 3 Macro-concepts, the SS will be 2.0
If the retelling includes two or 2.5 Macro-concepts, the SS will be 1.5
If the retelling includes one or 1.5 Macro-concepts, the SS will be 1.0
If the retelling includes one-half Macro-concept, the SS will be .5
If the retelling includes no Macro-concepts, the SS will be 0.0

Thus the Starting Score can range from .00 to 2.00. We will then modify that SS based upon the number of Micro-concepts (the bulleted concepts from the passage) included in the retelling.

Step 3: Total the number of Micro-concepts included in the retelling. We will name this total (MIC) and it can range from .0 to 5.0 in half-point increments.

If SS equals 2.0 and MIC equals 5.0, then add 1.0 to the SS to make it 3.0 and go to Step 4
If SS equals 2.0 and MIC equals 4.5, then add .5 to SS to make it 2.5 and go to Step 4
If SS equals 2.0 and MIC greater than 2.5 and less than 4.5, then keep SS as 2.0 and go to Step 4
If SS equals 2.0 and MIC less than 3.0, then subtract .5 from the SS to make it 1.5 and go to Step 4

If SS equals 1.5 and MIC greater than 4.0, then add .5 to SS to make it 2.0 and go to Step 4
If SS equals 1.5 and MIC greater than 2.5 and less than 4.5, then keep SS as 1.5 and go to Step 4
If SS equals 1.5 and MIC less than 3.0, then subtract .5 from the SS to make it 1.0 and go to Step 4

If SS equals 1.0 and MIC greater than 3.0, then add .5 to SS to make it 1.5 and go to Step 4
If SS equals 1.0 and MIC greater than .5 and less than 3.5, then keep SS as 1.0 and go to Step 4
If SS equals 1.0 and MIC is less than 1.0, then subtract .5 from the SS to make it .5 and go to Step 4

If SS equals .5 and MIC greater than 2.0, then add .5 to SS to make it 1.0 and go to Step 4
If SS equals .5 and MIC greater than .5 and less than 2.5, then keep SS as .5 and go to Step 4
If SS equals .5 and MIC less than 1.0, then subtract .5 from the SS to make it .0 and go to Step 4

If SS equals .0 and MIC greater than 2.0, then add .5 to SS and go to Step 4
If SS equals .0 and MIC less than 2.5, then go to Step 4

Step 4: Is there a well-supported Personal Response in the retelling?

If yes, and if SS **is greater than** 2.0, add 1.0 to SS and this will be the Final Score (FS)
If yes, and if SS **is less than** 2.5 and MIC greater than 1.5, then add .5 to SS and this will be the FS
If no, do not change the SS; simply report it as the Final Score in the appropriate box

Descriptions of Informational Retelling Scores

Score	Description
4.0	A virtually perfect retelling that includes all Macro- and Micro-concepts and a well-supported Personal Response.
3.5	An exceptionally strong retelling that omits a small but significant part of a Micro-concept, but which still includes a well-supported Personal Response.
3.0	A very strong retelling that includes all Macro- and Micro-concepts, but which does not include a Personal Response.
2.5	A strong retelling that includes many Macro- and Micro-concepts in a variety of combinations and may include a Personal Response. A reader who achieves this score has clearly comprehended the primary gist of the passage.
2.0	A solid retelling which includes most key Macro- and Micro-concepts but which is also characterized by some key omissions.
1.5	A fairly weak retelling which includes some Macro- and Micro-concepts but also omits a good deal of key information and may contain some factual distortions.
1.0	A weak retelling that includes a few Macro- and Micro-concepts but is also characterized by some glaring omissions and factual distortions.
.5	A very weak retelling that includes little more than a few disjointed Macro- and Micro-concepts and factual distortions.
.0	A retelling that may include nothing more than a vague idea of the topic of the passage or a stray Macro- or Micro-concept.

Word Lists Set A

Pre-Primer   **Primer**

	Flash	Untimed		Flash	Untimed
1. the	_____	_____	1. of	_____	_____
2. a	_____	_____	2. have	_____	_____
3. was	_____	_____	3. fig	_____	_____
4. he	_____	_____	4. day	_____	_____
5. go	_____	_____	5. came	_____	_____
6. boy	_____	_____	6. house	_____	_____
7. stop	_____	_____	7. play	_____	_____
8. come	_____	_____	8. little	_____	_____
9. and	_____	_____	9. saw	_____	_____
10. her	_____	_____	10. thing	_____	_____
11. dog*	_____	_____	11. eat*	_____	_____
12. book*	_____	_____	12. wood*	_____	_____
13. big*	_____	_____	13. work*	_____	_____
14. I*	_____	_____	14. move*	_____	_____
15. pet*	_____	_____	15. just*	_____	_____
16. cat*	_____	_____	16. great*	_____	_____
17. for*	_____	_____	17. looked*	_____	_____
18. sad*	_____	_____	18. deep*	_____	_____
19. do*	_____	_____	19. happy*	_____	_____
20. too*	_____	_____	20. who*	_____	_____

Score   __/20   __/20   **Score**   __/20   __/20

              __%   __%   __%   __%

Note: The words marked with asterisks appear in the narrative texts at each grade level.

Word Lists Set A

First Grade	Flash	Untimed	Second Grade	Flash	Untimed
1. family			1. teacher		
2. hear			2. clean		
3. school			3. remember		
4. hard			4. horse		
5. feet			5. anyone		
6. taken			6. birthday		
7. fishing			7. garden		
8. blue			8. street		
9. before			9. guess		
10. children			10. pretty		
11. waited*			11. fastest*		
12. puppy*			12. against*		
13. every*			13. animal*		
14. someone*			14. excited*		
15. goods*			15. laughing*		
16. found*			16. together*		
17. cheese*			17. camp*		
18. would*			18. still*		
19. silly*			19. finish*		
20. sorry*			20. word*		

Score	/20	/20	Score	/20	/20
	%	%		%	%

Note: The words marked with asterisks appear in the narrative texts at each grade level.

Word Lists Set A

Third Grade

	Flash	Untimed
1. enter	_____	_____
2. change	_____	_____
3. lesson	_____	_____
4. think	_____	_____
5. music	_____	_____
6. trust	_____	_____
7. human	_____	_____
8. pencil	_____	_____
9. mail	_____	_____
10. phone	_____	_____
11. kitchen*	_____	_____
12. interested*	_____	_____
13. wildly*	_____	_____
14. breakfast*	_____	_____
15. fence*	_____	_____
16. toward*	_____	_____
17. season*	_____	_____
18. nervous*	_____	_____
19. caught*	_____	_____
20. wrong*	_____	_____

Score   /20   /20
       %   %

Fourth Grade

	Flash	Untimed
1. doesn't	_____	_____
2. concern	_____	_____
3. sample	_____	_____
4. official	_____	_____
5. given	_____	_____
6. present	_____	_____
7. decorate	_____	_____
8. windshield	_____	_____
9. exercise	_____	_____
10. finish	_____	_____
11. science*	_____	_____
12. nothing*	_____	_____
13. eager*	_____	_____
14. irritated*	_____	_____
15. clutter*	_____	_____
16. disappoint*	_____	
17. range*	_____	_____
18. dashed*	_____	_____
19. flown*	_____	_____
20. chores*	_____	_____

Score   /20   /20
       %   %

Note: The words marked with asterisks appear in the narrative texts at each grade level.

Word Lists Set A

Fifth Grade			**Sixth Grade**		
	Flash	Untimed		Flash	Untimed
1. bravely	_____	_____	1. athletic	_____	_____
2. embarrass	_____	_____	2. psychology	_____	_____
3. importance	_____	_____	3. realize	_____	_____
4. guarantee	_____	_____	4. ridiculous	_____	_____
5. magical	_____	_____	5. successful	_____	_____
6. prevent	_____	_____	6. reluctant	_____	_____
7. typical	_____	_____	7. consideration	_____	_____
8. vision	_____	_____	8. mountainous	_____	_____
9. handle	_____	_____	9. partial	_____	_____
10. ledge	_____	_____	10. graceful	_____	_____
11. perhaps*	_____	_____	11. several*	_____	_____
12. province*	_____	_____	12. incredible*	_____	_____
13. decision*	_____	_____	13. tutoring*	_____	_____
14. breathing*	_____	_____	14. fortunately*	_____	_____
15. valuable*	_____	_____	15. authors*	_____	_____
16. disguise*	_____	_____	16. conversations*	_____	_____
17. muttered*	_____	_____	17. self-pity*	_____	_____
18. bounds*	_____	_____	18. pronounce*	_____	_____
19. toughest*	_____	_____	19. calm*	_____	_____
20. sprawled*	_____	_____	20. mockingly*	_____	_____
Score	__/20__	__/20__	**Score**	__/20__	__/20__
	__%__	__%__		__%__	__%__

Note: The words marked with asterisks appear in the narrative texts at each grade level.

Word Lists Set A

Seventh Grade

		Flash	Untimed
1.	fundamental	_____	_____
2.	humane	_____	_____
3.	siege	_____	_____
4.	knuckle	_____	_____
5.	assortment	_____	_____
6.	exposure	_____	_____
7.	vital	_____	_____
8.	waiver	_____	_____
9.	preference	_____	_____
10.	biography	_____	_____
11.	newfound*	_____	_____
12.	intentions*	_____	_____
13.	admiration*	_____	_____
14.	nuisance*	_____	_____
15.	resolution*	_____	_____
16.	seasickness*	_____	_____
17.	uncoordinated*	_____	_____
18.	distract*	_____	_____
19.	mesmerized*	_____	_____
20.	endeavor*	_____	_____

Score   /20   /20

     %   %

Eighth Grade

		Flash	Untimed
1.	jargon	_____	_____
2.	anticipate	_____	_____
3.	jeopardize	_____	_____
4.	calorie	_____	_____
5.	diploma	_____	_____
6.	financial	_____	_____
7.	heredity	_____	_____
8.	logic	_____	_____
9.	plumage	_____	_____
10.	specific	_____	_____
11.	sophisticated*	_____	_____
12.	utter*	_____	_____
13.	demolish*	_____	_____
14.	pharmacies*	_____	_____
15.	chided*	_____	_____
16.	savored*	_____	_____
17.	competition*	_____	_____
18.	interminable*	_____	_____
19.	edible*	_____	_____
20.	cumbersome*	_____	_____

Score   /20   /20

     %   %

Note: The words marked with asterisks appear in the narrative texts at each grade level.

WORD LISTS SET A

Word Lists Set A

Ninth Grade

	Flash	Untimed
1. administer		
2. nautical		
3. squeamish		
4. vestibule		
5. bestow		
6. expenditure		
7. guidance		
8. arbitrary		
9. pennant		
10. comparable		
11. illustrious*		
12. confident*		
13. intrigue*		
14. anticipated*		
15. troublesome*		
16. pretext*		
17. assurance*		
18. vividly*		
19. curvature*		
20. podium*		

Score   __/20__   __/20__
         __%__   __%__

Tenth Grade

	Flash	Untimed
1. chagrin		
2. granulate		
3. pinnacle		
4. mystical		
5. demure		
6. stalwart		
7. thermal		
8. rhapsody		
9. ethical		
10. vitality		
11. startled*		
12. grudgingly*		
13. literally*		
14. scrimped*		
15. resplendent*		
16. unsavory*		
17. saliently*		
18. pathologist*		
19. waif*		
20. hapless*		

Score   __/20__   __/20__
         __%__   __%__

WORD LISTS SET A

Note: The words marked with asterisks appear in the narrative texts at each grade level.

Word Lists Set A

Eleventh Grade

	Flash	Untimed
1. amplitude	_____	_____
2. luxuriant	_____	_____
3. fissure	_____	_____
4. retina	_____	_____
5. guise	_____	_____
6. brevity	_____	_____
7. populace	_____	_____
8. irrepressible	_____	_____
9. versatile	_____	_____
10. dispersion	_____	_____
11. recruiters*	_____	_____
12. regrettable*	_____	_____
13. consequential*	_____	_____
14. frantically*	_____	_____
15. momentous*	_____	_____
16. captivated*	_____	_____
17. hysterically*	_____	_____
18. nonchalantly*	_____	_____
19. provocation*	_____	_____
20. in absentia*	_____	_____

Score	_____ /20	_____ /20
	_____ %	_____ %

Twelfth Grade

	Flash	Untimed
1. diminutive	_____	_____
2. impetuosity	_____	_____
3. candor	_____	_____
4. recluse	_____	_____
5. subterfuge	_____	_____
6. apparition	_____	_____
7. parody	_____	_____
8. vulnerable	_____	_____
9. mediation	_____	_____
10. fiscal	_____	_____
11. sauntered*	_____	_____
12. acknowledged*	_____	_____
13. cajoled*	_____	_____
14. episodes*	_____	_____
15. wheedled*	_____	_____
16. benevolent*	_____	_____
17. regimen*	_____	_____
18. protégés*	_____	_____
19. serenity*	_____	_____
20. propriety*	_____	_____

Score	_____ /20	_____ /20
	_____ %	_____ %

Note: The words marked with asterisks appear in the narrative texts at each grade level.

Word Lists Set B

Pre-Primer			**Primer**		
	Flash	Untimed		Flash	Untimed
1. to	_____	_____	1. fly	_____	_____
2. like	_____	_____	2. jump	_____	_____
3. am	_____	_____	3. went	_____	_____
4. get	_____	_____	4. skate	_____	_____
5. not	_____	_____	5. give	_____	_____
6. can	_____	_____	6. off	_____	_____
7. see	_____	_____	7. could	_____	_____
8. will	_____	_____	8. many	_____	_____
9. me	_____	_____	9. saw	_____	_____
10. you	_____	_____	10. out	_____	_____
11. pet*	_____	_____	11. home*	_____	_____
12. book*	_____	_____	12. food*	_____	_____
13. old*	_____	_____	13. said*	_____	_____
14. bake*	_____	_____	14. some*	_____	_____
15. at*	_____	_____	15. away*	_____	_____
16. be*	_____	_____	16. rod*	_____	_____
17. four*	_____	_____	17. fast*	_____	_____
18. my*	_____	_____	18. took*	_____	_____
19. bus*	_____	_____	19. need*	_____	_____
20. car*	_____	_____	20. read*	_____	_____
Score	/20	/20	**Score**	/20	/20
	%	%		%	%

Note: The words marked with asterisks appear in the narrative texts at each grade level.

Word Lists Set B

	First Grade			**Second Grade**		
		Flash	Untimed		Flash	Untimed
1.	where	_____	_____	1. always	_____	_____
2.	farm	_____	_____	2. walking	_____	_____
3.	surprise	_____	_____	3. pull	_____	_____
4.	friend	_____	_____	4. faster	_____	_____
5.	drop	_____	_____	5. spring	_____	_____
6.	won't	_____	_____	6. when	_____	_____
7.	petting	_____	_____	7. help	_____	_____
8.	made	_____	_____	8. know	_____	_____
9.	bike	_____	_____	9. have	_____	_____
10.	games	_____	_____	10. brother	_____	_____
11.	bringing*	_____	_____	11. daughter*	_____	_____
12.	asked*	_____	_____	12. chance*	_____	_____
13.	ready*	_____	_____	13. aunt*	_____	_____
14.	money*	_____	_____	14. climbed*	_____	_____
15.	sleep*	_____	_____	15. people*	_____	_____
16.	almost*	_____	_____	16. their*	_____	_____
17.	picked*	_____	_____	17. march*	_____	_____
18.	should*	_____	_____	18. large*	_____	_____
19.	many*	_____	_____	19. coach*	_____	_____
20.	heard*	_____	_____	20. weekend*	_____	_____

Score   /20   /20   **Score**   /20   /20

____%   ____%   ____%   ____%

Note: The words marked with asterisks appear in the narrative texts at each grade level.

Word Lists Set B

Third Grade

	Flash	Untimed
1. fright	_____	_____
2. unusual	_____	_____
3. they'll	_____	_____
4. bread	_____	_____
5. forest	_____	_____
6. early	_____	_____
7. hurt	_____	_____
8. water	_____	_____
9. because	_____	_____
10. hour	_____	_____
11. shouldn't*	_____	_____
12. barking*	_____	_____
13. faithful*	_____	_____
14. vacation*	_____	_____
15. roadside*	_____	_____
16. championship*	_____	_____
17. pitcher*	_____	_____
18. trail*	_____	_____
19. hitting*	_____	_____
20. certain*	_____	_____

Score	__/20	__/20
	__%	__%

Fourth Grade

	Flash	Untimed
1. enjoyable	_____	_____
2. wrong	_____	_____
3. quiet	_____	_____
4. morning	_____	_____
5. grandmother	_____	_____
6. huge	_____	_____
7. covered	_____	_____
8. thought	_____	_____
9. creature	_____	_____
10. trouble	_____	_____
11. originality*	_____	_____
12. advice*	_____	_____
13. sobbed*	_____	_____
14. disgusted*	_____	_____
15. rainspouts*	_____	_____
16. wondered*	_____	_____
17. length*	_____	_____
18. startled*	_____	_____
19. afterwards*	_____	_____
20. grown-ups*	_____	_____

Score	__/20	__/20
	__%	__%

Note: The words marked with asterisks appear in the narrative texts at each grade level.

Word Lists Set B

Fifth Grade

	Flash	Untimed
1. wounded	_____	_____
2. defend	_____	_____
3. jungle	_____	_____
4. seasonal	_____	_____
5. differently	_____	_____
6. through	_____	_____
7. projection	_____	_____
8. necessary	_____	_____
9. medicine	_____	_____
10. mysterious	_____	_____
11. marketplace*	_____	_____
12. participate*	_____	_____
13. quitting*	_____	_____
14. calculate*	_____	_____
15. estimated*	_____	_____
16. pressured*	_____	_____
17. teammates*	_____	_____
18. mocking*	_____	_____
19. shoulder*	_____	_____
20. disappointed*	_____	_____

Score	_/20_	_/20_
	_____ %	_____ %

Sixth Grade

	Flash	Untimed
1. applause	_____	_____
2. survival	_____	_____
3. materials	_____	_____
4. perplex	_____	_____
5. license	_____	_____
6. vehicle	_____	_____
7. definite	_____	_____
8. experience	_____	_____
9. predictable	_____	_____
10. conform	_____	_____
11. improve*	_____	_____
12. contribution*	_____	_____
13. probably*	_____	_____
14. difficulties*	_____	_____
15. realized*	_____	_____
16. occasion*	_____	_____
17. mull*	_____	_____
18. emerges*	_____	_____
19. impressed*	_____	_____
20. flinched*	_____	_____

Score	_/20_	_/20_
	_____ %	_____ %

Note: The words marked with asterisks appear in the narrative texts at each grade level.

Word Lists Set B

Seventh Grade

	Flash	Untimed
1. veneer	_____	_____
2. cavity	_____	_____
3. famine	_____	_____
4. incredible	_____	_____
5. guardian	_____	_____
6. relent	_____	_____
7. version	_____	_____
8. dialogue	_____	_____
9. longitude	_____	_____
10. testimony	_____	_____
11. treasure*	_____	_____
12. prospect*	_____	_____
13. defiance*	_____	_____
14. excursion*	_____	_____
15. relieved*	_____	_____
16. moaning*	_____	_____
17. prowess*	_____	_____
18. affection*	_____	_____
19. blurted*	_____	_____
20. unbelievably*	_____	_____

Score   /20   /20
   %   %

Eighth Grade

	Flash	Untimed
1. journalist	_____	_____
2. adequate	_____	_____
3. browse	_____	_____
4. consistent	_____	_____
5. additional	_____	_____
6. gill	_____	_____
7. investment	_____	_____
8. masterpiece	_____	_____
9. resourceful	_____	_____
10. vouch	_____	_____
11. salon*	_____	_____
12. murky*	_____	_____
13. despised*	_____	_____
14. emphatically*	_____	_____
15. seethed*	_____	_____
16. technique*	_____	_____
17. combination*	_____	_____
18. jealousy*	_____	_____
19. competition*	_____	_____
20. binoculars*	_____	_____

Score   /20   /20
   %   %

Note: The words marked with asterisks appear in the narrative texts at each grade level.

Word Lists Set B

Ninth Grade

	Flash	Untimed
1. formidable		
2. refinery		
3. audition		
4. sham		
5. twinge		
6. anecdote		
7. destitute		
8. luminous		
9. inertia		
10. buffer		
11. trivial*		
12. incredulous*		
13. contracted*		
14. luxury*		
15. apprehensive*		
16. muster*		
17. insistent*		
18. surmised*		
19. approximate*		
20. stunned*		

Score   __/20   __/20

     __%   __%

Tenth Grade

	Flash	Untimed
1. fraught		
2. somber		
3. appropriation		
4. opaque		
5. unerring		
6. plausible		
7. bland		
8. tolerable		
9. wan		
10. dynamic		
11. ramshackle*		
12. precinct*		
13. annoyance*		
14. inseparable*		
15. suppressed*		
16. piqued*		
17. therapist*		
18. spontaneous*		
19. urchin*		
20. serene*		

Score   __/20   __/20

     __%   __%

Note: The words marked with asterisks appear in the narrative texts at each grade level.

Word Lists Set B

Eleventh Grade	Flash	Untimed
1. complacent	_____	_____
2. populace	_____	_____
3. inherent	_____	_____
4. myriad	_____	_____
5. ruse	_____	_____
6. askew	_____	_____
7. socialist	_____	_____
8. procure	_____	_____
9. oscillate	_____	_____
10. exhilarated	_____	_____
11. engraved*	_____	_____
12. wistfully*	_____	_____
13. rehabilitation*	_____	_____
14. reminisced*	_____	_____
15. exasperation*	_____	_____
16. confidantes*	_____	_____
17. envisioned*	_____	_____
18. vehemence*	_____	_____
19. fatalistic*	_____	_____
20. ophthalmologist*	_____	_____
Score	___/20	___/20
	___%	___%

Twelfth Grade	Flash	Untimed
1. austerity	_____	_____
2. hieroglyphics	_____	_____
3. mundane	_____	_____
4. rhetoric	_____	_____
5. effervescence	_____	_____
6. predecessor	_____	_____
7. ostracize	_____	_____
8. corollary	_____	_____
9. subsidiary	_____	_____
10. guile	_____	_____
11. manipulative*	_____	_____
12. exploits*	_____	_____
13. whimpered*	_____	_____
14. monumentally*	_____	_____
15. indoctrination*	_____	_____
16. tranquility*	_____	_____
17. pessimism*	_____	_____
18. idyllic*	_____	_____
19. unalterably*	_____	_____
20. diversity*	_____	_____
Score	___/20	___/20
	___%	___%

Note: The words marked with asterisks appear in the narrative texts at each grade level.

Narrative Passages Examiner's Copy

Level	Title	Word Count	Readability
Pre-Primer I	At the Library, p. 98	107	0.0
Pre-Primer II	The Baker, p. 101	120	0.0
Pre-Primer III	No, No, Sue, p. 104	130	0.0
Primer I	The Little Fish, p. 107	175	0.5
Primer II	Learning to Fish, p. 110	157	0.5
Primer III	The Beaver Who Could Read, p. 113	182	0.4
First I	Where Is the Dog?, p. 116	216	1.5
First II	The Pigs Get a Job, p. 119	196	1.5
First III	The Cheese Factory, p. 122	223	1.4
Second I	The Race, p. 125	256	2.4
Second II	The Roller Coaster Ride, p. 128	244	2.3
Second III	Keeping Your Word, p. 131	275	2.2
Third I	The Farm Vacation, p. 134	417	3.5
Third II	The Championship Game, p. 137	418	3.7
Third III	Boy's Best Friend, p. 140	435	3.4
Fourth I	The Vacation, p. 143	412	4.4
Fourth II	Autumn Leaves, p. 146	448	4.3
Fourth III	The Science Fair, p. 149	422	4.4
Fifth I	Getting What You Want, p. 152	479	5.6
Fifth II	The Player, p. 155	473	5.4
Fifth III	The Bully, p. 159	488	5.6
Sixth I	The Motor Bike, p. 162	498	6.6
Sixth II	The Tutor, p. 166	498	6.6
Sixth III	The Dentist, p. 170	477	6.5
Seventh I	The Pet, p. 174	519	7.3
Seventh II	The Fishing Trip, p. 178	513	7.4
Seventh III	Brother's Letter, p. 182	559	7.4
Eighth I	The Friend, p. 186	554	8.6
Eighth II	Exaggeration, p. 190	569	8.3
Eighth III	The Rodeo, p. 194	585	8.4
Ninth I	The Magician, p. 198	667	9.4
Ninth II	Mom's Lesson, p. 202	685	9.3
Ninth III	The Award Ceremony, p. 206	666	9.3
Tenth I	Tutor of the Year, p. 210	673	10.3
Tenth II	The Hero, p. 214	685	10.3
Tenth III	The Duck Hunter, p. 218	716	10.3
Eleventh I	The Injury, p. 222	844	11.3
Eleventh II	The Babysitter, p. 226	757	11.3
Eleventh III	Dreams and Visions, p. 230	722	11.3
Twelfth I	Differences, p. 234	773	12.0
Twelfth II	The Psychology Class, p. 238	802	12.0
Twelfth III	The Retirement Community, p. 242	769	12.0

PRE-PRIMER I: AT THE LIBRARY

Reader's copy on p. 19 of the Reader's Passages

Introductory Statement: "Would you read this passage about a trip to the library (to yourself/out loud). When you are finished, I'll take away the passage. Then I'll ask you to tell me about what you read and what you think of it. After that, I'll ask you some questions about the passage."

Story

"I want a book.

I want a good book.

Please find a pet book for me," said the girl.

"Here is a cat book. I can read you this cat book,"

said Mom.

"No, I do not like that book," said the girl.

"Here is a dog book. I can read you this dog book,"

said Mom.

"No, I do not like that book," said the girl.

"What pet would you like to have?" asked Mom.

"I would like to have a bird," said the girl.

"That's a good pet," said Mom.

"Here is a bird book."

"Oh, I like that book.

Please read me that book!" (107 words)

Scoring Miscues for Oral Reading Option
Mark all scoreable miscues by placing either a plus (for those that maintain meaning) or a zero (for those that violate meaning) in the text margin.

Reading Accuracy Index: _____%
*Total all miscues marked with pluses **and** zeros and enter the corresponding percentage from the Miscue Chart.*

Meaning Maintenance Index: _____%
*Total **only** miscues marked with zeros and enter the corresponding percentage from the Miscue Chart.*

Miscue Chart (if used for oral reading)

Miscues	%	Miscues	%	Miscues	%
1	99	7	93	13	88
2	98	8	93	14	87
3	97	9	92	15	86
4	96	10	91	16	85
5	95	11	90	17	84
6	94	12	89	18	83

Student Retelling

Examiner: "Tell me about what you just read and what you thought about it."

If there is no spontaneous response, repeat the request, "Tell me what you thought about the passage."

Note: Use the Retelling Rubric on p. 99 to assess the child's retelling performance. If you need additional space for retelling responses, use a separate sheet of paper.

RETELLING RUBRIC: NARRATIVE

Place a 0, 1/2, or + to score student responses. See page 80 for information on what these assessment measures mean.

Story Structure:

___ 1. **Key Characters and Setting:** Child and mother in library.

___ 2. **Character's Problem or Goal:** Finding the right book.

3. **Problem-Solving or Goal-Meeting Process:**

___ • Child asks the mother to find a good book.

___ • Mother's suggestions are rejected.

___ • Mother asks child what kind of pet she wants.

___ • Mother finds a book on birds.

___ • The child likes the book.

___ 4. **Personal Response:** Any well-supported positive or negative response to the characters or events in the story, or to the story as a whole.

Retelling Score: _____

Comprehension Questions

_____ 1. **What was the first book about that Mom showed her child?**

Text-Based: A cat book.

_____ 2. **What did the child tell her mother about the cat book?**

Text-Based: He or she didn't like it.

_____ 3. **Do you think the child has a pet at home? Why or why not?**

Inference: Probably not; Mom asked what kind of pet the child would like.

_____ 4. **Do you think Mom and her child started talking about pets *before* they went to the library? Why or why not?**

Critical Response: No—child had no idea what pet she would like to have. Yes—they must have if they are trying to find books about pets.

_____ 5. **Why do you think Mom asked what pet the child would like to have?**

Inference: So the child could find out what book she might like to read.

_____ 6. **What kind of pet did the child say she wanted?**

Text-Based: A bird.

_____ 7. **Why did Mom have to tell her child what the book was about?**

Inference: Child could not read; child was too young.

_____ 8. What could Mom have done *before* they went to the library to help her child get a book?

Critical Response: Talk about the kind of book the child wanted; talk about having a pet to see what the child might want to read about.

Comprehension Analysis:

Text-Based: __/3__
Inference: __/3__
Critical Response: __/2__

Total Comprehension %: _____

PRE-PRIMER II: THE BAKER

Reader's copy on p. 21 of the Reader's Passages

Introductory Statement: "Would you read this passage about a bakery (to yourself/out loud). When you are finished, I'll take away the passage. Then I'll ask you to tell me about what you read and what you think of it. After that, I'll ask you some questions about the passage."

Story

"Come in!" said the baker.

"I like to bake!

Look at the big cakes!

Look at the little cakes!"

"I want a big cake," said Jane.

"The cake is for my birthday party.

Four girls will come.

I will be four years old."

"I want a big cake," said Bill.

"The cake is for my birthday party.

Seven boys will come.

I will be seven years old."

"I want a big cake," said Mom.

"The cake is for my little girl.

She will be two years old.

We will have a party."

"I want the cake now," cried the little girl.

"I don't want a party."

"Look," said the baker.

"Here is a cupcake for you."

"Thank you!" said Mom. (120 words)

Scoring Miscues for Oral Reading Option

Mark all scoreable miscues by placing either a plus (for those that maintain meaning) or a zero (for those that violate meaning) in the text margin.

Reading Accuracy Index: _____%
*Total all miscues marked with pluses **and** zeros and enter the corresponding percentage from the Miscue Chart.*

Meaning Maintenance Index: _____%
*Total **only** miscues marked with zeros and enter the corresponding percentage from the Miscue Chart.*

Miscue Chart (if used for oral reading)

Miscues	%	Miscues	%	Miscues	%
1	99	7	94	13	89
2	98	8	93	14	88
3	98	9	93	15	88
4	97	10	92	16	87
5	96	11	91	17	86
6	95	12	90	18	85

Student Retelling

Examiner: "Tell me about what you just read and what you thought about it."

If there is no spontaneous response, repeat the request, "Tell me what you thought about the passage."

Note: Use the Retelling Rubric on p. 102 to assess the child's retelling performance. If you need additional space for retelling responses, use a separate sheet of paper.

RETELLING RUBRIC: NARRATIVE

Place a 0, 1/2, or + to score student responses. See page 80 for information on what these assessment measures mean.

Story Structure:

___ 1. **Key Characters and Setting:** Baker, children, and mothers in the bakery.

___ 2. **Character's Problem or Goal:** Buying cakes for birthday parties.

3. **Problem-Solving or Goal-Meeting Process:**

___ • A girl wants a big cake for her party.

___ • A boy wants a big cake for his party.

___ • Little girl doesn't want party; she wants cake.

___ • Little girl cries.

___ • The baker gives the little girl a cupcake.

___ 4. **Personal Response:** Any well-supported positive or negative response to the characters or events in the story, or to the story as a whole.

Retelling Score: _____

Comprehension Questions

_____ 1. Where does the story take place?

Text-Based: At a bakery.

_____ 2. Does the baker like his job? Explain.

Text-Based: Yes—he said that he likes to bake cakes.

_____ 3. Why did the baker in this story make big cakes and little cakes?

Inference: If there are more people, you need a bigger cake at the party.

_____ 4. Do you think it was right for the baker to give the little girl a cupcake? Why or why not?

Critical Response: Yes—he was being nice to her; wanted to cheer her up. No—because she cried; she was not polite.

_____ 5. Who would need a bigger cake, Jane or Bill? Why?

Inference: Bill because he has 7 guests at the party; Jane has only 4 guests.

_____ 6. Why does Mom need to buy a cake?

Text-Based: She wants to have a party for the little girl.

_____ 7. Why won't the little girl have as much fun at her party as the older boy and girl will?

Inference: She doesn't want to have a party; she is spoiled; she acts selfish; she is not polite to others.

_____ 8. Who do you think should have thanked the baker for the cupcake, Mom or the little girl? Explain.

Critical Response: Mom—it is the polite thing to do; he gave her daughter a gift. Girl—she got the gift and should have thanked him; encourage the girl to learn manners.

Comprehension Analysis:

Text-Based: __/3__
Inference: __/3__
Critical Response: __/2__

Total Comprehension %: ____

PRE-PRIMER III: NO, NO, SUE

Reader's copy on p. 24 of the Reader's Passages

Introductory Statement: "Would you read this passage about a little girl (to yourself/out loud). When you are finished, I'll take away the passage. Then I'll ask you to tell me about what you read and what you think of it. After that, I'll ask you some questions about the passage."

Story

"Here comes the bus.

Get on the bus, Jane," said Mom.

"You have to go to school and read books."

"I want to go, too," said Sue.

"No, Sue. We have to go home," said Mom.

Sue was sad.

"Here comes your friend, Jane," said Mom.

"You can get in the car, Jane.

You worked hard at school.

You can go to the party."

"I want to go, too," said Sue.

"No, Sue. We have to stay home," said Mom.

Sue was very sad.

Mom was sad, too.

"We can go to the park now," said Mom.

"I have no more work to do."

"Good," said Sue.

Sue was happy.

"Here is the ride you like, Sue," said Mom.

"Get on the ride."

"Good," said Sue.

Sue was very happy. (130 words)

Scoring Miscues for Oral Reading Option

Mark all scoreable miscues by placing either a plus (for those that maintain meaning) or a zero (for those that violate meaning) in the text margin.

Reading Accuracy Index: _____%
*Total all miscues marked with pluses **and** zeros and enter the corresponding percentage from the Miscue Chart.*

Meaning Maintenance Index: _____%
*Total **only** miscues marked with zeros and enter the corresponding percentage from the Miscue Chart.*

Miscue Chart (if used for oral reading)

Miscues	%	Miscues	%	Miscues	%
1	99	7	95	13	90
2	98	8	94	14	89
3	98	9	93	15	88
4	97	10	92	16	88
5	96	11	92	17	87
6	95	12	91	18	86

Student Retelling

Examiner: "Tell me about what you just read and what you thought about it."

If there is no spontaneous response, repeat the request, "Tell me what you thought about the passage."

Note: Use the Retelling Rubric on p. 105 to assess the child's retelling performance. If you need additional space for retelling responses, use a separate sheet of paper.

RETELLING RUBRIC: NARRATIVE

Place a 0, 1/2, or + to score student responses. See page 80 for information on what these assessment measures mean.

Story Structure:

___ 1. **Key Characters and Setting:** Child, sister, and mother near bus and at park.

___ 2. **Character's Problem or Goal:** Child is unable to do what older sister does.

3. **Problem-Solving or Goal-Meeting Process:**

___ • Child is not allowed to get on school bus.

___ • Child is not allowed to go with her sister to a party.

___ • Child is sad and Mother has work to do.

___ • Mother finishes her work and takes child to park.

___ • Child rides and is happy.

___ 4. **Personal Response:** Any well-supported positive or negative response to the characters or events in the story, or to the story as a whole.

Retelling Score: _____

Comprehension Questions

_____ 1. **Why did Jane get on the bus?**

Text-Based: To go to school.

_____ 2. **What will Jane do at school?**

Text-Based: Read books.

_____ 3. **Why did Sue want to go with her sister?**

Inference: She thought there would be fun at the party; she thought she would like to learn to read at school; she wanted to be grown-up like her sister.

_____ 4. **Was Mom being fair to Sue? Explain.**

Critical Response: Yes—she planned to take her to the park. No—she should have had something special for Sue to do when Jane was at school and at the party.

_____ 5. **Why didn't Mom let Sue go to the party with Jane?**

Inference: The party was probably for bigger girls like Jane; Sue was too little to go.

_____ 6. **What made Sue happy? (Must identify one.)**

Text-Based: Going to the park; getting on the ride at the park.

_____ 7. **Had Sue been at the park before? Explain.**

Inference: Yes—Mother said that this was the ride she liked so she must have been on it before.

_____ 8. Did Sue learn anything in this story? Explain.

Critical Response: No—she wasn't allowed to do anything new. Yes—she learned that you have to work before you can play; she can't do everything that older children can do.

Comprehension Analysis:

Text-Based: __/3__
Inference: __/3__
Critical Response: __/2__

Total Comprehension %: _____

Reader's copy on p. 27 of the Reader's Passages

Introductory Statement: "Would you read this passage about a family of fish (to yourself/out loud). When you are finished, I'll take away the passage. Then I'll ask you to tell me about what you and what you think of it. After that, I'll ask you some questions about the passage."

Story

"Come Blue! Come Red!" said Mother Fish.

"Come, let's eat dinner."

Blue went to eat dinner.

Red saw a big fish come by and she chased the big

fish away.

"Go away! This is our home!" said Red.

"What great food!" said Blue.

"Yes, this is good food," said Mother Fish. "Come

and eat, Red."

But Red would not eat because she did not want to

let the big fish come close.

"Come Blue! Come Red!" said Mother Fish.

"Come, let's look at our pretty world."

Blue looked and looked.

Red saw a little fish come by and she chased the little

fish away.

"Go away! This is our home!" said Red.

"Come and look, Red," said Mother.

But Red would not look because she did not want to

let the little fish come close.

"Come Blue! Come Red!" said Mother Fish.

"We will have work to do tomorrow and we need to

sleep."

Mother Fish fell asleep right away.

Blue fell asleep right away.

But Red could not sleep because she was still angry.

(175 words)

Scoring Miscues for Oral Reading Option
Mark all scoreable miscues by placing either a plus (for those that maintain meaning) or a zero (for those that violate meaning) in the text margin.

Reading Accuracy Index: _____%
*Total all miscues marked with pluses **and** zeros and enter the corresponding percentage from the Miscue Chart.*

Meaning Maintenance Index: _____%
*Total **only** miscues marked with zeros and enter the corresponding percentage from the Miscue Chart.*

Miscue Chart (if used for oral reading)

Miscues	%	Miscues	%	Miscues	%
1	99	11	94	21	88
2	99	12	93	22	87
3	98	13	93	23	87
4	98	14	92	24	86
5	97	15	91	25	86
6	97	16	91	26	85
7	96	17	90	27	85
8	95	18	90	28	84
9	95	19	89	29	83
10	94	20	89	30	83

Student Retelling

Examiner: "Tell me about what you just read and what you thought about it."

   If there is no spontaneous response, repeat the request, "Tell me what you thought about the passage."

Note: Use the Retelling Rubric on p. 108 to assess the child's retelling performance. If you need additional space for retelling responses, use a separate sheet of paper.

RETELLING RUBRIC: NARRATIVE

Place a 0, 1/2, or + to score student responses. See page 80 for information on what these assessment measures mean.

Story Structure:

___ 1. **Key Characters and Setting:** Mother Fish, Blue, and Red in the ocean.

___ 2. **Character's Problem or Goal:** Red's anger keeps her from being part of the family activities.

3. **Problem-Solving or Goal-Meeting Process:**

___ • Mother calls Blue and Red to dinner.

___ • Blue comes but Red is chasing a fish away from their home.

___ • Mother calls Blue and Red to explore their world.

___ • Blue comes but Red is chasing another fish away from their home.

___ • When it is time for bed, Red can't sleep because she is still angry.

___ 4. **Personal Response:** Any well-supported positive or negative response to the characters or events in the story or to the story as a whole.

Retelling Score: _____

Comprehension Questions

_____ 1. **Why didn't Red want to eat when Mother called her?**

Text-Based: She was too busy chasing fish away; she was too angry; she didn't want other fish coming by.

_____ 2. **Why was Red so angry with the other fish?**

Text-Based: They were swimming too close by; she was afraid the fish would come into their home.

_____ 3. **Why weren't Mother and Blue angry when other fish swam near their home?**

Inference: They did not think there was any danger; they were used to other fish swimming nearby; they were busy eating and looking at their world.

_____ 4. **Do you think it is a good idea for Red to chase other fish away from their home? Why or why not?**

Critical Response: No—they are doing no real harm; no one else seems worried. Yes—they could be dangerous; may want to take their home.

_____ 5. **Why did Mother Fish and Blue fall asleep right away?**

Inference: Had a busy day; enjoyed what they were doing; were not angry or upset.

_____ 6. **Why couldn't Red fall asleep?**

Text-Based: She was too angry.

_____ 7. Who do you think will get more work done tomorrow, Red or Blue? Why?

Inference: Blue—better rested; not as concerned with other things as Red is.

Comprehension Analysis:

Text-Based: __/3__
Inference: __/3__
Critical Response: __/2__

Total Comprehension %: ____

_____ 8. Do you think Red is brave or just a bully? Why?

Critical Response: Brave—swims at fish that are bigger than she is; defends her mother and sister. A bully—chases other fish for no reason; behaves very rudely.

PRIMER II: LEARNING TO FISH

Reader's copy on p. 30 of the Reader's Passages

Introductory Statement: "Would you read this passage about a fishing trip (to yourself/out loud). When you are finished, I'll take away the passage. Then I'll ask you to tell me about what you read and what you think of it. After that, I'll ask you some questions about the passage."

Story

Pat said, "This is not fun!"

He was learning how to fish with his sister.

But the fish would not bite.

Pat jumped up. He shook the fishing rod.

He tried to get his bait closer to the fish.

"Don't move the rod or you will scare the fish away,"

said Dad.

Pat looked at his sister.

She had caught three fish already.

Then Pat threw some stones into the water.

"You will scare the fish away," said Dad.

Pat was angry. He moved his rod and tried to make a

fish take his bait.

This time Dad just watched.

Pat dropped his rod on the dock and walked away angry.

He sat on the shore and would not talk to his father

or sister.

Just then a big fish took his bait.

Dad called, "Come quick! You've caught a fish!"

But Pat was not fast enough.

The fish pulled the whole rod into the deep water.

(157 words)

Scoring Miscues for Oral Reading Option

Mark all scoreable miscues by placing either a plus (for those that maintain meaning) or a zero (for those that violate meaning) in the text margin.

Reading Accuracy Index: _____%

*Total all miscues marked with pluses **and** zeros and enter the corresponding percentage from the Miscue Chart.*

Meaning Maintenance Index: _____%

*Total **only** miscues marked with zeros and enter the corresponding percentage from the Miscue Chart.*

Miscue Chart (if used for oral reading)

Miscues	%	Miscues	%	Miscues	%
1	99	11	93	21	87
2	99	12	92	22	86
3	98	13	92	23	85
4	97	14	91	24	85
5	97	15	90	25	84
6	96	16	90	26	83
7	96	17	89	27	83
8	95	18	89	28	82
9	94	19	88	29	82
10	94	20	87	30	81

Student Retelling

Examiner: "Tell me about what you just read and what you thought about it."

If there is no spontaneous response, repeat the request, "Tell me what you thought about the passage."

Note: Use the Retelling Rubric on p. 111 to assess the child's retelling performance. If you need additional space for retelling responses, use a separate sheet of paper.

RETELLING RUBRIC: NARRATIVE

Place a 0, 1/2, or + to score student responses. See page 80 for information on what these assessment measures mean.

Story Structure:

___ 1. **Key Characters and Setting:** Pat, his father, and sister fishing.

___ 2. **Character's Problem or Goal:** Pat has a difficult time listening to instructions.

___ 3. **Problem-Solving or Goal-Meeting Process:**

___ • Pat is fishing in the wrong way.

___ • Pat fails but his sister succeeds.

___ • Father gives Pat advice.

___ • Pat won't listen and gets angry at his own failure.

___ • Pat misses his chance to catch a fish.

___ 4. **Personal Response:** Any well-supported positive or negative response to the characters or events in the story or to the story as a whole.

Retelling Score: _____

Comprehension Questions

_____ 1. Why didn't Pat have fun fishing?

Text-Based: Couldn't catch any fish.

_____ 2. What was one thing that Pat did to keep the fish from biting?

Text-Based: Shook the rod; scared fish away; threw stones into the water.

_____ 3. Why would Pat's sister be better at fishing than Pat?

Inference: She had learned how to fish correctly.

_____ 4. How well do you think Dad taught the children to fish? Explain.

Critical Response: Good job—Pat's sister learned well; Pat's problems were his own fault. Poor job—let the kid make mistakes; Dad didn't follow through.

_____ 5. Why would Pat be angry with his sister?

Inference: She was successful and he was not; Pat was jealous of her.

_____ 6. Why did Dad want Pat to stop throwing stones?

Text-Based: Didn't want him to scare the fish.

_____ 7. Why did the fish take the bait when Pat was on the shore but not when he was on the dock?

Inference: No one was moving the rod; no one was scaring the fish; no one was throwing stones into the water.

_____ 8. Do you think Dad will take Pat fishing again? Why or why not?

Critical Response: Yes—he can teach him better when he's older; he has learned his lesson now. No—he missed his chance; ruined the trip for everyone; the others will catch more if he isn't there.

Comprehension Analysis:

Text-Based: ___/3___
Inference: ___/3___
Critical Response: ___/2___

Total Comprehension %: _____

PRIMER III: THE BEAVER WHO COULD READ

Reader's copy on p. 31 of the Reader's Passages

Introductory Statement: "Would you read this passage about a little beaver (to yourself/out loud). When you are finished, I'll take away the passage. Then I'll ask you to tell me about what you read and what you think of it. After that, I'll ask you some questions about the passage."

Story

Chuck the beaver had a friend who was a squirrel.

The squirrel had books in his house.

He showed Chuck how to read.

Chuck learned quickly and he loved to read.

Chuck's father was not happy.

"Get to work, Chuck," said Dad.

"Beavers don't read. Beavers work.

We need a new house."

Chuck was sad because he wanted to read.

But Chuck went to work and he worked hard all day.

Then he saw a sign on a tree near the new house and

he read the words.

Chuck quickly ran home to Father.

"Father, we cannot build here.

I read the sign near our house.

People will come with big trucks and take all the

trees away."

"I know the woods," said Father.

"I will say where our house will be."

But soon the trucks came and Father saw that they

could not build there.

"I was wrong, Son," said Father.

"You saved us by reading.

I am proud of you."

Chuck smiled a huge smile.

"Son, do you think you can teach me, too?"

Chuck smiled an even bigger smile. (182 words)

Scoring Miscues for Oral Reading Option
Mark all scoreable miscues by placing either a plus (for those that maintain meaning) or a zero (for those that violate meaning) in the text margin.

Reading Accuracy Index: _____%
*Total all miscues marked with pluses **and** zeros and enter the corresponding percentage from the Miscue Chart.*

Meaning Maintenance Index: _____%
*Total **only** miscues marked with zeros and enter the corresponding percentage from the Miscue Chart.*

Miscue Chart (if used for oral reading)

Miscues	%	Miscues	%	Miscues	%
1	99	11	94	21	88
2	99	12	93	22	88
3	98	13	93	23	87
4	98	14	92	24	87
5	97	15	92	25	86
6	97	16	91	26	86
7	96	17	91	27	85
8	96	18	90	28	85
9	95	19	90	29	84
10	95	20	89	30	84

Student Retelling

Examiner: "Tell me about what you just read and what you thought about it."

If there is no spontaneous response, repeat the request, "Tell me what you thought about the passage."

Note: Use the Retelling Rubric on p. 114 to assess the child's retelling performance. If you need additional space for retelling responses, use a separate sheet of paper.

RETELLING RUBRIC: NARRATIVE

Place a 0, 1/2, or + to score student responses. See page 80 for information on what these assessment measures mean.

Story Structure:

___ 1. **Key Characters and Setting:** Chuck the Beaver, his friend the squirrel, and Chuck's father in the woods.

___ 2. **Character's Problem or Goal:** Chuck learns to read and that makes his father unhappy.

3. **Problem-Solving or Goal-Meeting Process:**

___ • Chuck's friend teaches Chuck to read.

___ • Chuck's father thinks he should work, not read.

___ • Chuck goes to work and reads a sign.

___ • Chuck tells Father that trucks will come and take away the trees but his father won't listen.

___ • Father realizes that he was wrong and he asks Chuck to teach him to read.

___ 4. **Personal Response:** Any well-supported positive or negative response to the characters or events in the story or to the story as a whole.

Retelling Score: _____

Comprehension Questions

_____ 1. **What did the squirrel do for Chuck?**

Text-Based: The squirrel taught Chuck to read.

_____ 2. **Was Chuck's father always happy that Chuck could read? Explain.**

Text-Based: No, because Chuck's father said that beavers were supposed to work; Chuck's father wanted Chuck to stop reading and help make the new house.

_____ 3. **Was the sign made to help the beavers or people?**

Inference: The sign was made to tell people to stay away because people think beavers cannot read.

_____ 4. **Was it a good thing that Father made Chuck go to work? Explain.**

Critical Response: Yes—he was working near the sign and that was how he got to read it. No—he was making him work and he should have let him read.

_____ 5. **Did Father show that he could learn? Explain.**

Inference: Yes—at first Chuck's father didn't want Chuck to read but then when Chuck's father found out that reading saved them, he learned from his mistakes; Chuck's father wanted to learn to read.

_____ 6. **What did Chuck learn was going to happen in the woods?**

Text-Based: The trucks would come to take away all the trees.

_____ 7. Why didn't Father listen to Chuck when he told him about the sign?

Inference: Father said he knew the woods; he said he knew where they should bulid the house; Father thought he know better than Chuck.

_____ 8. Why would Father want to learn to read now? Explain.

Critical Response: Chuck's father saw the good that came from Chuck's reading; Chuck's father will be able to make better decisions in the future; Father will be smarter and read signs by himself.

FIRST GRADE I: WHERE IS THE DOG?

Reader's copy on p. 34 of the Reader's Passages

Introductory Statement: "Would you read this passage about a girl and her dog (to yourself/out loud). When you are finished, I'll take away the passage. Then I'll ask you to tell me about what you read and what you think of it. After that, I'll ask you some questions about the passage."

Story

Jan waited at the door. She was waiting for the car to

come. Aunt Sara was coming for a visit and she was

bringing Sally. Jan loved to play with Sally and she

loved Aunt Sara, too.

"Here they are!" Jan called to Mother. Jan ran

    outside to meet Sally and Aunt Sara.

"Look what I have," said Sally. Sally showed

Jan her little white puppy.

"Can I hold the puppy?" asked Jan.

"Oh, yes," said Sally.

Sally took the puppy into the house.

Jan and Sally played with the puppy. Then they read

    books and played games. They had fun.

Then Sally went to help her mother. Jan played

    with the puppy. After lunch, Sally looked for her

    puppy. She looked and looked but she could not

    find her.

Aunt Sara and Mother helped her look. They asked

    Jan to help find the puppy.

"She is outside," said Jan.

"How did she get out?" asked Mother.

"She wanted to go out," said Jan.

"So I let her go."

Aunt Sara and Mother ran outside. Everyone looked

    and looked for the puppy. Jan was afraid.

Then Sally saw the puppy sitting under a car.

    Everyone was happy!

"You can not let the dog go out," said Aunt Sara.

"She is too young. She will get lost." (216 words)

Scoring Miscues for Oral Reading Option

Mark all scoreable miscues by placing either a plus (for those that maintain meaning) or a zero (for those that violate meaning) in the text margin.

Reading Accuracy Index: _____%

*Total all miscues marked with pluses **and** zeros and enter the corresponding percentage from the Miscue Chart.*

Meaning Maintenance Index: _____%

*Total **only** miscues marked with zeros and enter the corresponding percentage from the Miscue Chart.*

Miscue Chart (if used for oral reading)

Miscues	%	Miscues	%	Miscues	%	Miscues	%
1	100	9	96	17	92	25	88
2	99	10	95	18	92	26	88
3	99	11	95	19	91	27	88
4	98	12	94	20	91	28	87
5	98	13	94	21	90	29	87
6	97	14	94	22	90	30	86
7	97	15	93	23	89	31	86
8	96	16	93	24	89	32	85

Student Retelling

Examiner: "Tell me about what you just read and what you thought about it."

    If there is no spontaneous response, repeat the request, "Tell me what you thought about the passage."

Note: Use the Retelling Rubric on p. 117 to assess the child's retelling performance. If you need additional space for retelling responses, use a separate sheet of paper.

RETELLING RUBRIC: NARRATIVE

Place a 0, 1/2, or + to score student responses. See page 80 for information on what these assessment measures mean.

Story Structure:

___ 1. **Key Characters and Setting:** Jan and Mother waiting for Sally and Aunt Sara to visit their home.

___ 2. **Character's Problem or Goal:** Jan nearly loses a puppy.

3. **Problem-Solving or Goal-Meeting Process:**

___ • Sally and Aunt Sara bring a new puppy for a visit.

___ • Sally leaves the puppy with Jan.

___ • Jan lets the puppy go outside.

___ • The search for the puppy is successful.

___ • Jan learns that the puppy is too young to go outside alone.

___ 4. **Personal Response:** Any well-supported positive or negative response to the characters or events in the story or to the story as a whole.

Retelling Score: _____

Comprehension Questions

_____ 1. **How do you know that Jan was glad that her aunt and cousin were coming to visit her?**

Text-Based: She was waiting at the door; she said that she loved her aunt; she loved to play with Sally.

_____ 2. **Why didn't Sally know that Jan let the puppy go outside?**

Text-Based: Sally went to help her mother; Sally wasn't with Jan when it happened.

_____ 3. **How did Aunt Sara and Mother feel when they heard that the puppy was outside?**

Inference: Worried because they ran outside and looked for the puppy; unhappy at Jan for letting the puppy out; afraid the puppy was lost.

_____ 4. **Do you think that Jan *should* have been punished for letting the dog go outside? Why or why not?**

Critical Response: Yes—the dog could have been hurt; she should have asked someone; she was very careless. No—she did not really want to hurt the dog; she did not know that she was wrong.

_____ 5. **Why was Jan afraid when she saw everyone looking for the puppy?**

Inference: Afraid she might get into trouble or punished; afraid that the dog may be lost or injured.

_____ 6. **Where did they find the puppy?**

Text-Based: Under the car outside.

7. Why did Mother and Aunt Sara *run* outside to look for the puppy?

    Inference: They were afraid the puppy was gone; they knew the puppy could be hurt.

Comprehension Analysis:

Text-Based: __/3__
Inference: __/3__
Critical Response: __/2__

Total Comprehension %: ____

8. Do you think that it would be good for Jan to have her own pet? Why or why not?

    Critical Response: Yes—she loves animals and would probably care for one if she knew what they needed. No—she was very foolish to do something without knowing how harmful it could be.

FIRST GRADE II: THE PIGS GET A JOB

Reader's copy on p. 35 of the Reader's Passages

Introductory Statement: "Would you read this passage about two pigs who start a business (to yourself/out loud). When you are finished, I'll take away the passage. Then I'll ask you to tell me about what you read and what you think of it. After that, I'll ask you some questions about the passage."

Story

Father Pig had a big apple farm.

He had two sons.

Their names were Pete and Jake.

They worked every day with Father.

Soon Pete and Jake got older.

They were ready to leave home.

Pete bought an apple farm.

Pete said, "I worked for Father every day.

We worked so hard.

I will find a little dog to work for me.

He will work hard."

Pete found a little dog to work for him.

The little dog worked hard.

But Pete wanted more apples.

He told the little dog to work harder.

The little dog came to work early.

The dog picked more apples but he was

   always tired.

The dog did not like his job.

Jake bought an apple farm.

Jake said, "I worked with Father every day.

We had lots of fun working together.

I will find a little cat to work with me."

So Jake asked a little cat to work with him.

Jake and the cat worked together every day.

Jake said, "You can keep the extra apples we pick."

The little cat came to work early.

She took apples home for her mother.

She worked hard but she was happy. (196 words)

Scoring Miscues for Oral Reading Option
Mark all scoreable miscues by placing either a plus (for those that maintain meaning) or a zero (for those that violate meaning) in the text margin.

Reading Accuracy Index: _____%
*Total all miscues marked with pluses **and** zeros and enter the corresponding percentage from the Miscue Chart.*

Meaning Maintenance Index: _____%
*Total **only** miscues marked with zeros and enter the corresponding percentage from the Miscue Chart.*

Miscue Chart (if used for oral reading)

Miscues	%	Miscues	%	Miscues	%	Miscues	%
1	99	9	95	17	91	25	87
2	99	10	95	18	91	26	87
3	98	11	94	19	90	27	86
4	98	12	94	20	90	28	86
5	97	13	93	21	89	29	85
6	97	14	93	22	89	30	85
7	96	15	92	23	88	31	84
8	96	16	92	24	88	32	84

Student Retelling

Examiner: "Tell me about what you just read and what you thought about it."

If there is no spontaneous response, repeat the request, "Tell me what you thought about the passage."

Note: Use the Retelling Rubric on p. 120 to assess the child's retelling performance. If you need additional space for retelling responses, use a separate sheet of paper.

RETELLING RUBRIC: NARRATIVE

Place a 0, 1/2, or + to score student responses. See page 80 for information on what these assessment measures mean.

Story Structure:

___ 1. **Key Characters and Setting:** Pete and Jake, their father and their workers, a cat and dog, on apple farms.

___ 2. **Character's Problem or Goal:** Pete and Jake start apple farms to make a living for themselves.

3. **Problem-Solving or Goal-Meeting Process:**

___ • Pete remembers working hard with Father and Jake remembers the fun of working with Father.

___ • Pete hires a dog and expects him to work hard.

___ • Jake hires a cat and works together with her.

___ • The dog who works for Pete works hard but does not like his job.

___ • The cat who works for Jake works hard and likes her job.

___ 4. **Personal Response:** Any well-supported positive or negative response to the characters or events in the story or to the story as a whole.

Retelling Score: _____

Comprehension Questions

_____ 1. **What did Father Pig do for a living?**

Text-Based: Owned an apple farm.

_____ 2. **Did Pete and Jake remember the same things about working with their father after they left home? How do you know?**

Text-Based: No—Pete remembered working hard but Jake remembered having fun.

_____ 3. **Why didn't the dog who worked for Pete like his job? (If reader responds that the dog worked hard, ask if there is another reason.)**

Inference: Pete was selfish; Pete did not share anything with the little dog; Pete did not work with the dog.

_____ 4. **Who do you think will have a better apple farm, Pete or Jake? Why?**

Critical Response: Jake—treats the cat well, shares with her. Pete—keeps all of the apples; makes the dog work hard.

_____ 5. **Why do you think that Father would be more proud of Jake?**

Inference: Because he treated his worker well; he remembered being happy working with his father; he shared with his worker.

_____ 6. **What did Pete do to get more apples?**

Text-Based: Told the little dog to work harder.

_____ 7. Why didn't the cat who worked for Jake feel as tired as the dog who worked for Pete?

Inference: She was treated better; took extra apples home; decided herself to come to work early.

_____ 8. If you had people working for you, what could you learn from this story?

Critical Response: Don't be too greedy; treat your workers well; people work better when they are happy.

FIRST GRADE III: THE CHEESE FACTORY

Reader's copy on p. 38 of the Reader's Passages

Introductory Statement: "Would you read this passage about two mice (to yourself/out loud). When you are finished, I'll take away the passage. Then I'll ask you to tell me about what you read and what you think of it. After that, I'll ask you some questions about the passage."

Story

Flip and Buzz lived in Mouse Land and worked at the Cheese Factory.

One day they went to work but there was no cheese in the factory.

"Where is all the cheese?" they asked.

They went to see Wise Old Mouse.

He said, "Go see the dogs and they will help you find the cheese."

Flip was very angry. "The dogs were our friends," she said. "Why would they take our cheese?"

"Wise Old Mouse did not say that the dogs took our cheese," said Buzz.

Flip and Buzz went to see the dogs and they asked the first dog that they saw, "Do you know where our cheese is?"

"Go to your factory," said the dog.

"This is silly," said Flip. "We just came from the factory."

"I know," said Buzz. "But the dog sounded as if he knows something."

On the way to the factory, they saw many dogs carrying cheese.

"What are you doing with our cheese?" asked Buzz.

"We heard the rats saying that they were going to steal your cheese. We did not have time to tell you so we hid all the cheese before they got there. Then we

waited for the rats. We told them no one works here anymore and they went away."

"I'm very sorry," said Flip. "You really are our friends after all." (223 words)

Scoring Miscues for Oral Reading Option
Mark all scoreable miscues by placing either a plus (for those that maintain meaning) or a zero (for those that violate meaning) in the text margin.

Reading Accuracy Index: _____%
*Total all miscues marked with pluses **and** zeros and enter the corresponding percentage from the Miscue Chart.*

Meaning Maintenance Index: _____%
*Total **only** miscues marked with zeros and enter the corresponding percentage from the Miscue Chart.*

Miscue Chart (if used for oral reading)

Miscues	%	Miscues	%	Miscues	%	Miscues	%
1	100	9	96	17	92	25	89
2	99	10	96	18	92	26	88
3	99	11	95	19	91	27	88
4	98	12	95	20	91	28	87
5	98	13	94	21	91	29	87
6	97	14	94	22	90	30	87
7	97	15	93	23	90	31	86
8	96	16	93	24	89	32	86

Student Retelling

Examiner: "Tell me about what you just read and what you thought about it."

If there is no spontaneous response, repeat the request, "Tell me what you thought about the passage."

Note: Use the Retelling Rubric on p. 123 to assess the child's retelling performance. If you need additional space for retelling responses, use a separate sheet of paper.

Inference: Trust your friends; don't jump to conclusions; don't be so quick to judge people.

RETELLING RUBRIC: NARRATIVE

Place a 0, 1/2, or + to score student responses. See page 80 for information on what these assessment measures mean.

Story Structure:

___ 1. **Key Characters and Setting:** Flip and Buzz, Wise Old Mouse, dogs and rats in Mouse Land.

___ 2. **Character's Problem or Goal:** Flip and Buzz cannot find the cheese from their factory.

3. **Problem-Solving or Goal-Meeting Process:**

___ • Flip and Buzz discover that cheese from the factory is gone.

___ • Wise Old Mouse tells them to go and see the dogs.

___ • Flip thinks that the dogs have taken the cheese.

___ • The dogs tell about ruining the rats' plan and saving the cheese by hiding it.

___ • Flip admits that she was wrong about the dogs.

___ 4. **Personal Response:** Any well-supported positive or negative response to the characters or events in the story or to the story as a whole.

Retelling Score: _____

---

4. Did Flip show that she was a smart mouse? Explain.

Critical Response: No—she didn't listen carefully and thought that the dogs took their cheese. Yes—she showed that she could learn from her mistakes when she said that she was sorry.

5. Why would the rats believe that no one worked at the cheese factory?

Inference: No one was there and there was no cheese.

Comprehension Questions

1. Why did Flip and Buzz go to visit Wise Old Mouse?

Text-Based: They saw that all the cheese was taken out of the Cheese Factory.

2. What did Wise Old Mouse tell Flip and Buzz to do?

Text-Based: To go to the dogs for help.

6. Why didn't the dogs let the mice know about the rats' plan?

Text-Based: They did not have enough time; they had to hide all the cheese.

_____ 7. Did the rats know that the dogs heard them making plans? Explain.

Inference: No—they would not have believed them when they said that no one worked in the Cheese Factory.

Comprehension Analysis:

Text-Based: __/3__
Inference: __/3__
Critical Response: __/2__

Total Comprehension %: _____

_____ 8. Was the Wise Old Mouse really wise? Explain.

Critical Response: Yes—he made Flip and Buzz solve their own problem but he gave them clues to be sure that they found out. No—or else he would have told them right away what happened to the cheese.

SECOND GRADE I: THE RACE

Reader's copy on p. 40 of the Reader's Passages

Introductory Statement: "Would you read this passage about two cats who race each other (to yourself/out loud). When you are finished, I'll take away the passage. Then I'll ask you to tell me about what you read and what you think of it. After that, I'll ask you some questions about the passage."

Story

Spencer was the fastest animal in the jungle. All of the other animals knew it. Spencer made sure of that. He would say, "No one can beat me! You are all too afraid to race!" It was true. No one wanted to race against Spencer. He always won. Then he would brag even more.

One day another family of cats moved in. Spencer ran up to the new family. He said, "I'm the fastest animal in the jungle. Do you want to race?" The father said, "No, thank you. But maybe our daughter Annie will race with you." Annie smiled and said, "Yes. I'd love to race." Soon the two cats were running for the finish line. Spencer was winning as always. But Annie was very fast. She raced past him and crossed the finish line first.

The other animals cheered in surprise. But Spencer cried, "I want another chance!" They raced again and again. But the result was still the same. There was a new champion in the jungle and her name was Annie.

All the animals came over to talk to Annie. But Spencer went away angry. Annie was a little sad. She hoped that Spencer would be her friend. "Well, at least we won't have to listen to him brag again," said the fox. The next day Spencer was back. The first thing he said was, "I can jump higher than anybody in the jungle! No one can beat me!" The other animals groaned and rolled their eyes. Nothing had changed after all. (256 words)

Scoring Miscues for Oral Reading Option
Mark all scoreable miscues by placing either a plus (for those that maintain meaning) or a zero (for those that violate meaning) in the text margin.

Reading Accuracy Index: _____%
*Total all miscues marked with pluses **and** zeros and enter the corresponding percentage from the Miscue Chart.*

Meaning Maintenance Index: _____%
*Total **only** miscues marked with zeros and enter the corresponding percentage from the Miscue Chart.*

Miscue Chart (if used for oral reading)

Miscues	%	Miscues	%	Miscues	%
1	100	13	95	25	90
2	99	14	95	26	90
3	99	15	94	27	89
4	98	16	94	28	89
5	98	17	93	29	89
6	98	18	93	30	88
7	97	19	93	31	88
8	97	20	92	32	88
9	96	21	92	33	87
10	96	22	91	34	87
11	96	23	91	35	86
12	95	24	91	36	86

Student Retelling

Examiner: "Tell me about what you just read and what you thought about it."

If there is no spontaneous response, repeat the request, "Tell me what you thought about the passage."

Note: Use the Retelling Rubric on p. 126 to assess the child's retelling performance. If you need additional space for retelling responses, use a separate sheet of paper.

RETELLING RUBRIC: NARRATIVE

Place a 0, 1/2, or + to score student responses. See page 80 for information on what these assessment measures mean.

Story Structure:

___ 1. **Key Characters and Setting:** Spencer, other animals, and Annie who moved into jungle.

___ 2. **Character's Problem or Goal:** Spencer wants to be able to brag about his abilities.

3. **Problem-Solving or Goal-Meeting Process:**

___ • Spencer brags and gets others to race with him so that he can brag more.

___ • Annie moves in and Spencer races with her.

___ • Spencer loses the race.

___ • Spencer walks away angrily and Annie is sad because she had wanted a friend.

___ • Spencer returns the next day and brags about jumping.

___ 4. **Personal Response:** Any well-supported positive or negative response to the characters or events in the story or to the story as a whole.

Retelling Score: _____

Comprehension Questions

___ 1. Why didn't any of the animals want to race against Spencer? (Must include both.)

   Text-Based: He always won; he bragged after he won.

___ 2. What did the animals do when Annie won the race? (Must identify one.)

   Text-Based: Cheered; talked with her.

___ 3. Why would Spencer want to race against Annie again?

   Inference: He couldn't accept the fact that someone was faster; thought he could win.

___ 4. Why did Annie agree to race against Spencer when no one else would?

   Inference: She knew she was very fast; she probably knew she could beat him; she wanted to find a friend.

___ 5. If Spencer went to a school for cats, what kind of student do you think he would be? Why?

   Critical Response: Good—because he wants to be the best at everything; he would be willing to try again and again. Bad— because he can't stand it when someone else is better; he walks away when things get tough.

___ 6. What did Spencer do when he came back the next day?

   Text-Based: Started bragging about something else; bragged that he could jump higher than anyone else.

___ 7. Do you think that this was the first time Annie had ever raced against anyone? Why or why not?

   Inference: No—she smiled when Spencer challenged her; she probably knew she could beat him; her father knew that she was fast.

_____ 8. What did the other animals hope would happen after Spencer lost the race?

Text-Based: That Spencer would stop bragging.

_____ 9. Do you think it's a good idea for Annie to want Spencer to be her friend? Explain. (If the reader says that Spencer brags too much, ask, "How would that explain why Annie should not want him as a friend?")

Critical Response: Yes—they both like to run and they are both cats; she is new in the jungle and needs friends. No—he annoys everyone with his bragging; he is a sore loser; he does not care about other people's feelings.

_____ 10. If another new family moved into the jungle, do you think Spencer would ask them to race or not? Explain.

Critical Response: Yes—he did not seem to have learned anything; still bragged even after he lost. No—he has lost once; he may still brag but he didn't like to lose and he may not be as confident as he was once.

Comprehension Analysis:	
Text-Based:	/4
Inference:	/3
Critical Response:	/3

Total Comprehension %: ____

SECOND GRADE II: THE ROLLER COASTER RIDE

Reader's copy on p. 41 of the Reader's Passages

Introductory Statement: "Would you read this passage about a ride on the roller coaster (to yourself/out loud). When you are finished, I'll take away the passage. Then I'll ask you to tell me about what you read and what you think of it. After that, I'll ask you some questions about the passage."

Story

Today it was finally Jessie's birthday. She jumped out of bed and called to her mom. "Mom, can you come here and see how tall I am?" She ran to the wall and waited. Mother marked the spot where Jessie had grown since her last birthday. "I made it!" shouted Jessie. "I'm tall enough to ride the roller coaster now!" On Saturday, Jessie, her mom, and Aunt Jane would go to the park. Then she could take her first ride!

Mom was too afraid to ride so Aunt Jane took Jessie to the line to wait their turn. Jessie and Aunt Jane jumped into a car and pulled the bar over their heads. Then they waited for the ride to start. "Let's get going," thought Jessie. Soon the ride started and Jessie was really excited. She felt very grown up. Then the car climbed higher and higher. It came down and went faster and faster. Jessie was so afraid that she thought she was going to die.

Jessie held Aunt Jane's arm. She covered her face and screamed. Jessie prayed that the ride would end. "Don't let me die," she prayed, "and I'll never ride a roller coaster again." Aunt Jane hugged Jessie. Jessie opened her eyes and she saw people laughing and screaming. Aunt Jane was laughing, too. They were all having fun.

The car slowed and then stopped. The ride was finally over. "Aunt Jane," said Jessie, "can we do it again?" (244 words)

Scoring Miscues for Oral Reading Option
Mark all scoreable miscues by placing either a plus (for those that maintain meaning) or a zero (for those that violate meaning) in the text margin.

Reading Accuracy Index: _____%
*Total all miscues marked with pluses **and** zeros and enter the corresponding percentage from the Miscue Chart.*

Meaning Maintenance Index: _____%
*Total **only** miscues marked with zeros and enter the corresponding percentage from the Miscue Chart.*

Miscue Chart (if used for oral reading)

Miscues	%	Miscues	%	Miscues	%
1	100	13	95	25	90
2	99	14	94	26	89
3	99	15	94	27	89
4	98	16	93	28	89
5	98	17	93	29	88
6	98	18	93	30	88
7	97	19	92	31	87
8	97	20	92	32	87
9	96	21	91	33	86
10	96	22	91	34	86
11	95	23	91	35	86
12	95	24	90	36	85

Student Retelling

Examiner: "Tell me about what you just read and what you thought about it."

If there is no spontaneous response, repeat the request, "Tell me what you thought about the passage."

Note: Use the Retelling Rubric on p. 129 to assess the child's retelling performance. If you need additional space for retelling responses, use a separate sheet of paper.

RETELLING RUBRIC: NARRATIVE

Place a 0, 1/2, or + to score student responses. See page 80 for information on what these assessment measures mean.

Story Structure:

___ 1. **Key Characters and Setting:** Jessie, Aunt Jane, and Mom at amusement park.

___ 2. **Character's Problem or Goal:** Jessie wants to be grown-up enough to ride the roller coaster.

3. **Problem-Solving or Goal-Meeting Process:**

___ • Mother measures Jessie and finds she is tall enough to ride the roller coaster.

___ • Aunt Jane goes with her on the ride.

___ • Jessie becomes frightened and she promises she will never ride again.

___ • She realizes that the ride is safe and fun.

___ • She decides to go on the ride again.

___ 4. **Personal Response:** Any well-supported positive or negative response to the characters or events in the story or to the story as a whole.

Retelling Score: _____

Comprehension Questions

_____ 1. **Why did Jessie want her mother to see how tall she was?**

Text-Based: Wanted to see if she was tall enough to ride the roller coaster.

_____ 2. **Why didn't Mom want to ride on the roller coaster with Jessie?**

Text-Based: She was afraid of roller coasters.

_____ 3. **Do you think that Jessie had ever been to an amusement park before? Why?**

Inference: Yes—she knew that she had to be a certain height to go on certain rides; must have seen a roller coaster at an amusement park before.

_____ 4. **Why would Jessie want so much to ride the roller coaster?**

Inference: Sign that she was growing up; was something she wasn't allowed to do before; she thought it would be fun; she did not know it would be scary.

_____ 5. **As Mom watched Jessie take her first roller coaster ride, do you think she felt more pride or more fear? Why?**

Critical Response: Pride—Jessie was growing up; Jessie was not afraid to try something new. Fear—she was afraid that Jessie would be hurt or become frightened; she was thinking about her own fear of the roller coaster.

_____ 6. **How did Aunt Jane help Jessie during the ride?**

Text-Based: Hugged her; held her close.

_____ 7. **Why did Jessie decide to ride the roller coaster again?**

Inference: She wanted to have more fun; may have wanted to prove to herself that she wasn't afraid; made her feel grown-up; she ended up liking it.

8. What did Jessie do during the ride to help herself stop being afraid? (Must identify one.)

   Text-Based: Hugged Aunt Jane; saw others having fun; prayed; screamed out loud; closed her eyes; covered her face.

9. Do you think Jessie is a girl who thinks about what she's going to do or one who just rushes in without much thought? Explain.

   Critical Response: Thinks—she planned for at least a year; she has been thinking about the roller coaster for a long time. Rushes—she didn't see that the ride was scary; she couldn't wait for the ride to start.

10. Do you think the story would end the same way if Jessie took the ride with her mother instead of Aunt Jane? Explain.

    Critical Response: No—her mother might have been afraid too and neither one would ever ride again. Yes—her mother probably would hide her fear for Jessie's sake.

SECOND GRADE III: KEEPING YOUR WORD

Reader's copy on p. 42 of the Reader's Passages

Introductory Statement: "Would you read this passage about a boy and his dad (to yourself/out loud). When you are finished, I'll take away the passage. Then I'll ask you to tell me about what you read and what you think of it. After that, I'll ask you some questions about the passage."

Story

"You made me sell candy bars all day Saturday," cried Steve to Dad.

"I didn't make you do it," said Dad. "The coach said your team could win a weekend at camp. You gave your word when you said that you would sell candy."

"But Rod didn't sell candy. His father took him swimming all day," said Steve.

"I know," said Dad. "But you kept your word and that's what counts."

The next Saturday Dad took Steve to the food market. Steve worked for four hours and he sold lots of candy bars but he still had many more left to sell. He was very angry when he came home on Monday. "Rod's father took him swimming again!" he said.

This time his father said, "What counts is what you do! I am very proud that you decided to keep your word and it is important that you are proud, too."

In the next two weeks Steve sold all of his candy bars and then the coach called the team together. "I have good news," he said. "We made enough money so that everyone on the team can go to camp."

Steve went to the weekend camp with his team and watched as Rod fished and played ping-pong. Steve did the same things, but he did not have fun.

When Steve came home, he asked his father, "Why did they let Rod go to camp?" Dad said, "I don't think that was right but I didn't make the rules. I hope that you did not let your anger keep *you* from having a great time." Steve thought about what his father said and did not answer. (275 words)

Scoring Miscues for Oral Reading Option
Mark all scoreable miscues by placing either a plus (for those that maintain meaning) or a zero (for those that violate meaning) in the text margin.

Reading Accuracy Index: _____%
*Total all miscues marked with pluses **and** zeros and enter the corresponding percentage from the Miscue Chart.*

Meaning Maintenance Index: _____%
*Total **only** miscues marked with zeros and enter the corresponding percentage from the Miscue Chart.*

Miscue Chart (if used for oral reading)

Miscues	%	Miscues	%	Miscues	%
1	100	13	95	25	91
2	99	14	95	26	91
3	99	15	95	27	90
4	99	16	94	28	90
5	98	17	94	29	90
6	98	18	94	30	89
7	97	19	93	31	89
8	97	20	93	32	88
9	97	21	92	33	88
10	96	22	92	34	88
11	96	23	92	35	87
12	96	24	91	36	87

Student Retelling

Examiner: "Tell me about what you just read and what you thought about it."

If there is no spontaneous response, repeat the request, "Tell me what you thought about the passage."

Note: Use the Retelling Rubric on p. 132 to assess the child's retelling performance. If you need additional space for retelling responses, use a separate sheet of paper.

RETELLING RUBRIC: NARRATIVE

Place a 0, 1/2, or + to score student responses. See page 80 for information on what these assessment measures mean.

Story Structure:

___ 1. **Key Characters and Setting:** Steve, his father, and Rod; at the store selling candy and at camp.

___ 2. **Character's Problem or Goal:** Steve has to deal with his anger about unfairness.

3. **Problem-Solving or Goal-Meeting Process:**

___ • Steve has to sell candy so his team can go to camp.

___ • Steve is angry when he sees that his teammate Rod is not selling candy.

___ • Steve's father tells him that keeping his word is what counts.

___ • The coach tells the children that everyone on the team can go to camp.

___ • Steve watches Rod angrily the whole time at camp and does not have fun.

___ 4. **Personal Response:** Any well-supported positive or negative response to the characters or events in the story or to the story as a whole.

Retelling Score: _____

Comprehension Questions

_____ 1. Why was Steve selling candy bars?

Text-Based: To earn a weekend at a camp.

_____ 2. Why was Steve so angry?

Text-Based: He was selling candy bars and his teammate Rod wasn't.

_____ 3. What was different about Rod's father and Steve's father?

Inference: Rod's father didn't make sure that he sold the candy bars but Steve's father did; Steve's father was teaching him to keep his word.

_____ 4. What lessons did Steve's father want Steve to learn?

Inference: He was trying to teach him how important it is to keep your word; he was trying to teach him not to worry about what other people do; to be sure that he does what is right; he tried to help him learn to be proud of himself.

_____ 5. Was the reward for the weekend camp a fair one? Explain.

Critical Response: Yes—a team could earn a weekend at camp if they sold enough candy bars. No—the reward should have been for only those players who kept their word by selling candy bars.

_____ 6. Why did the coach call the team together?

Text-Based: He told them that they had earned enough money to go to camp.

_____ 7. Why didn't Steve answer when his father asked if he had a good time?

Inference: He knew that he had let his anger about Rod keep him from having a good time at camp.

_____ 8. What did Steve's father say when he heard that Rod went to camp?

Text-Based: He said that he didn't think it was right, but he did not make the rules.

_____ 9. Had Rod done anything wrong? Explain.

Critical Response: No—he probably never promised to sell the candy bars and nobody made him sell them. Yes—he knew that the weekend camp was a reward for selling candy bars and since he wanted the reward, he should have sold the candy bars.

_____10. Do you think that Father should have talked to Steve about being angry *before* Steve went to camp? Explain.

Critical Response: No—he should let Steve learn on his own. Yes—he had already seen Steve get angry when Rod didn't do his work so he should have expected him to do it again; he could have helped Steve learn to ignore Rod and have a good time at camp.

Comprehension Analysis:

Text-Based: __/4__
Inference: __/3__
Critical Response: __/3__

Total Comprehension %: ____

THIRD GRADE I: THE FARM VACATION

Reader's copy on p. 43 of the Reader's Passages

Introductory Statement: "Would you read this passage about a boy's visit to a farm (to yourself/out loud). When you are finished, I'll take away the passage. Then I'll ask you to tell me about what you read and what you think of it. After that, I'll ask you some questions about the passage."

Story

It was five o'clock in the morning when David heard his grandfather call. David never got up this early before but he didn't mind at all! He was visiting his grandfather's farm for the first time and he was excited. He had always wanted to be a farmer and now he would have his chance. Besides, Grandpa had horses too and David looked forward to learning how to ride.

When David ran into the kitchen, Grandfather said, "Eat a good breakfast, Dave. We've got a lot to do this morning. We'll start with the hay."

"Don't rush him!" said Grandma. "Are you sure you want to work with Grandpa all day?" she asked David.

"Sure am!" said David. He gulped down his breakfast and dashed out to help load the hay wagon. He never knew hay was so heavy.

"You finish up here while I get the tractor. We've got some work to do in the garden," said Grandpa.

David walked over to the garden and climbed on to the tractor. Up and down they drove, row after row, turning up the soil as they went. "Lunch time," said Grandpa when the sun was overhead.

"When do the horses get fed?" David asked Grandma as he walked into the kitchen.

"Do you want to do that after lunch? You've worked so much already," said Grandma.

"Don't forget, honey," said Grandpa, "we've got lots to do. That's how life is on the farm."

"That's OK," said David. "Maybe I better stay and help Grandpa."

After lunch, David worked under the hot sun, helping Grandpa dig postholes for a new fence. Then David and Grandpa picked corn and brought it to their roadside stand. David was trudging slowly back toward the house when Grandma called, "Do you want to feed the horses?"

David ran to the barn and helped to feed the horses. "I wish I could ride you," he said to each one as he rubbed its nose. "Maybe Grandpa will teach me!"

David fell asleep immediately that night but when the sun rose the next morning, he was not so eager to get up. He had the feeling that today would be another day just like yesterday. As it turned out, he was right.

"Do you still want to be a farmer?" asked Grandfather at the end of the week. "I'm not so sure," David replied. "If the sun rose at ten o'clock and there wasn't so much hard work, then maybe farming would be more fun." (417 words)

Scoring Miscues for Oral Reading Option
Mark all scoreable miscues by placing either a plus (for those that maintain meaning) or a zero (for those that violate meaning) in the text margin.

Reading Accuracy Index: _____%
*Total all miscues marked with pluses **and** zeros and enter the corresponding percentage from the Miscue Chart.*

Meaning Maintenance Index: _____%
*Total **only** miscues marked with zeros and enter the corresponding percentage from the Miscue Chart.*

Miscue Chart (if used for oral reading)

Miscues	%	Miscues	%	Miscues	%	Miscues	%
1	100	13	97	25	94	37	91
2	100	14	97	26	94	38	91
3	99	15	96	27	94	39	91
4	99	16	96	28	93	40	90
5	99	17	96	29	93	41	90
6	99	18	96	30	93	42	90
7	98	19	95	31	93	43	90
8	98	20	95	32	92	44	89
9	98	21	95	33	92	45	89
10	98	22	95	34	92	46	89
11	97	23	94	35	92	47	89
12	97	24	94	36	91	48	88

Student Retelling

Examiner: "Tell me about what you just read and what you thought about it."

If there is no spontaneous response, repeat the request, "Tell me what you thought about the passage."

Note: Use the Retelling Rubric on p. 135 to assess the child's retelling performance. If you need additional space for retelling responses, use a separate sheet of paper.

RETELLING RUBRIC: NARRATIVE

Place a 0, 1/2, or + to score student responses. See page 80 for information on what these assessment measures mean.

Story Structure:

___ 1. **Key Characters and Setting:** David and his grandparents on the farm.

___ 2. **Character's Problem or Goal:** David gets a chance to find out what it is like to be a farmer.

3. **Problem-Solving or Goal-Meeting Process:**

___ • David wants to learn about farming and to ride horses.

___ • Grandpa has him working hard but Grandma wants him to enjoy himself.

___ • David decides to keep working with Grandpa.

___ • David works hard all week.

___ • David reconsiders his choice.

___ 4. **Personal Response:** Any well-supported positive or negative response to the characters or events in the story or to the story as a whole.

Retelling Score: _____

Comprehension Questions

_____ 1. **Why was David excited about visiting the farm?**

Text-Based: He always wanted to be a farmer; wanted to ride the horses; it was his first time at the farm.

_____ 2. **How did David feel about farming *at the end* of the week?**

Text-Based: He wasn't sure about it; he had changed his mind.

_____ 3. **Do you think that David lived near his grandfather? Explain.**

Inference: Probably not—he was visiting the farm for the first time.

____ 4. Do you think that Grandma was happy about how David's first week at the farm was going? Explain.

Inference: Probably not—he was working very hard and having no fun; he should have been riding the horses.

____ 5. Do you think that Grandpa really wanted David to become a farmer? Why or why not?

Critical Response: Probably not—made him work very hard, possibly because he wanted David to understand how difficult farming was. Probably so—wanted him to understand everything about farming, including the hard work.

____ 6. What did David want most from Grandpa?

Text-Based: To learn how to ride the horses; to learn about farming.

____ 7. Do you think that David ever got to ride the horses that week? Why?

Inference: Probably not; seemed that there was little time for play and Grandpa didn't appear too interested in seeing David ride the horses; other days were just like the first day.

____ 8. Why did David change his mind at the end of the week? (Must identify one.)

Text-Based: Had to get up too early; there was too much hard work.

____ 9. Do you think David and his grandfather had a close relationship? Why or why not?

Critical Response: Yes—David cared for the grandfather; always helped him work even when he would rather ride the horses. No—seemed that they did not talk very much; Grandfather was unaware that David wanted to ride the horses; didn't talk very much about farming.

____ 10. Was Grandpa fair to expect David to do so much work that first week? Why?

Critical Response: No—he seemed to have one task right after another with no rest; it was his first time working on a farm. Yes—David wanted to learn about the farming life; it would be dishonest to present it in any other way.

Comprehension Analysis:

Text-Based: ___/4___
Inference: ___/3___
Critical Response: ___/3___

Total Comprehension %: _____

THIRD GRADE II: THE CHAMPIONSHIP GAME

Reader's copy on p. 45 of the Reader's Passages

Introductory Statement: "Would you read this passage about an important baseball game (to yourself/out loud). When you are finished, I'll take away the passage. Then I'll ask you to tell me about what you read and what you think of it. After that, I'll ask you some questions about the passage."

Story

At the end of a long softball season, Jill's team made it to the championship game. They would play against the top team in the league, the Ramblers. Before the game, the teams practiced throwing and catching the ball. As Jill watched her teammates, she knew that they would have a hard time winning. Three of the girls kept dropping the ball during practice and the team's best pitcher was as awful as Jill had ever seen her. Jill thought that if her team was going to win, she would have to be the one to get the job done. Soon the coach called the players in to sing the national anthem. Jill thought to herself, "This is just like it will be when I get to the pros." She knew the other players were nervous, but not her! She couldn't wait to start the game.

Early in the game, Jill's team took a 1–0 lead. Jill came up to bat with a runner on second base, but when she didn't swing at the ball, the umpire called "Strike three!" She couldn't believe that he would call such a terrible pitch a strike. She really wanted to say to him, "You just called strike three on Jill, the best player on the team." By the third inning, Jill's team was ahead 3–0 and the team was looking good. But Jill still didn't have a hit. Her next time up, she hit the ball a long way and when the ball was caught, she blamed a gust of wind for taking away her home run.

Then the Ramblers scored four runs and took the lead. Soon Jill had her chance to be the star. Her team had two players on base but Jill had two strikes on her. Then she got the pitch she was looking for and she swung with all her might. She couldn't believe that she missed it. Jill sat down, angry that the sun had gotten in her eyes at the wrong time. She just couldn't see the ball. The next player up hit the ball to left field and scored the two runs that the team needed. When the game ended, Jill's team had won 5–4. The team went wild, but Jill didn't feel like celebrating. Even after the team picture, Jill felt terrible. It was her worst game all season and it was the biggest game of the season, too. She wished that she had done better in front of all those people. (418 words)

Scoring Miscues for Oral Reading Option
Mark all scoreable miscues by placing either a plus (for those that maintain meaning) or a zero (for those that violate meaning) in the text margin.

Reading Accuracy Index: _____%
*Total all miscues marked with pluses **and** zeros and enter the corresponding percentage from the Miscue Chart.*

Meaning Maintenance Index: _____%
*Total **only** miscues marked with zeros and enter the corresponding percentage from the Miscue Chart.*

Miscue Chart (if used for oral reading)

Miscues	%	Miscues	%	Miscues	%	Miscues	%
1	100	13	97	25	94	37	91
2	100	14	97	26	94	38	91
3	99	15	96	27	94	39	91
4	99	16	96	28	93	40	90
5	99	17	96	29	93	41	90
6	99	18	96	30	93	42	90
7	98	19	95	31	93	43	90
8	98	20	95	32	92	44	89
9	98	21	95	33	92	45	89
10	98	22	95	34	92	46	89
11	97	23	94	35	92	47	89
12	97	24	94	36	91	48	89

Student Retelling

Examiner: "Tell me about what you just read and what you thought about it."

If there is no spontaneous response, repeat the request, "Tell me what you thought about the passage."

Note: Use the Retelling Rubric on p. 138 to assess the child's retelling performance. If you need additional space for retelling responses, use a separate sheet of paper.

RETELLING RUBRIC: NARRATIVE

Place a 0, 1/2, or + to score student responses. See page 80 for information on what these assessment measures mean.

Story Structure:

___ 1. **Key Characters and Setting:** Jill and her team playing in the championship game.

___ 2. **Character's Problem or Goal:** Jill wants to be the star of the game.

3. **Problem-Solving or Goal-Meeting Process:**

___ • Jill has no confidence that her team can win the game.

___ • Jill thinks she is better than the other players.

___ • She plays badly but makes excuses for it.

___ • Jill's team wins the championship.

___ • Even though her team wins, Jill is unhappy about her play.

___ 4. **Personal Response:** Any well-supported positive or negative response to the characters or events in the story or to the story as a whole.

Retelling Score: _____

Comprehension Questions

_____ 1. Why didn't Jill think that her team was going to win the game? (Must identify one.)

Text-Based: Practice was going badly; three girls were dropping the ball often; pitcher was awful.

_____ 2. Did the other players on the team feel the same way that Jill did about winning the championship? How do you know?

Text-Based: No—They were happy to win while Jill was disappointed in herself.

_____ 3. Do you think that Jill and her teammates were good friends or not? Why?

Inference: Probably not—she didn't seem to know their names; she didn't care too much about the team; she thought that they wouldn't play well.

_____ 4. How important to Jill was winning the championship game? What made you think that?

Inference: Not very important. She was more concerned that she didn't have a hit. When her team was losing she thought about herself, not winning the game.

5. Do you think that Jill has a chance of becoming a professional player? Why or why not?

   Critical Response: No—won't work hard if she thinks everyone else is responsible when she doesn't play well; not a team player. Yes—she is the best player on the team; everyone can have a bad game; she has the confidence she needs.

6. What reasons did Jill give for playing poorly in the game? (Must include two.)

   Text-Based: She made excuses; blamed others or other things for her failures; blamed the umpire; blamed the wind; blamed the sun.

7. Was Jill good at predicting how well her teammates would play? Explain.

   Inference: Not very good; players that she thought would do poorly played well; the team won the game.

8. Why was Jill upset at the end of the game?

   Text-Based: She played badly; she was embarrassed in front of the people; she wished she had played better.

9. Do you think that Jill needs help from her coach? Why or why not?

   Critical Response: Yes—she may not be as good as she thinks she is; she needs to stop making excuses and practice more; she needs to be more of a team player. No—she is already the best player on the team.

10. Why do you think that Jill didn't play as well as she thought she would in the big game?

    Critical Response: May have been overconfident; big crowd may have bothered her; may have tried too hard to be the star; made excuses instead of trying harder.

Comprehension Analysis:

Text-Based: __/4__
Inference: __/3__
Critical Response: __/3__

Total Comprehension %: ____

Reader's copy on p. 46 of the Reader's Passages

Introductory Statement: "Would you read this passage about a boy and his dog (to yourself/out loud). When you are finished, I'll take away the passage. Then I'll ask you to tell me about what you read and what you think of it. After that, I'll ask you some questions about the passage."

Story

Todd ran down to the kitchen and shouted, "Check out this team jacket!" As soon as he heard Todd, Dusty came running and jumped up, trying to lick Todd's face. "Get down right now!" cried Todd. "You'll mess up my new jacket!"

"He's so happy to see you," said Mom. "You shouldn't yell at him. Don't forget, a dog is man's best friend."

But Todd wasn't very interested in Dusty because he was thinking about the mountain bike race next week. This was a special race for third graders and his team really wanted to win. He would be the first rider on his team and he knew he would have to give his team a big lead.

"I have to go and practice. I need to be the fastest rider." Dusty couldn't wait either and he dashed out the door to follow Todd up to the hill. "Keep Dusty at home," Todd called to his mother, but Mother was so interested in making sure that Todd wore his helmet that she forgot to call Dusty.

Todd rode faster and faster as he rode down the bike trail. He knew the course like the back of his hand but knowing the course so well was not enough. Todd went too fast and never saw the rock that he hit with his front wheel. The last thing he remembered was hitting the ground hard.

When Dusty caught up with Todd, he started barking. He wanted Todd to get up and walk but when Todd did not move, Dusty turned suddenly and ran back home.

Mom had a feeling that something was wrong when she heard Dusty barking so wildly. When she ran out of the house and saw Dusty without Todd, she was certain that something was wrong. She quickly called the firehouse for help.

Dusty faced the hill, barking until help came. He ran off before Mom had the chance to say "Find Todd." Mom and the firemen followed Dusty to Todd and then took him to the hospital. Dusty waited in the truck with Todd's broken helmet.

Todd soon woke up and started to talk. The doctor told Todd's mother and father that Todd would be fine. "The helmet took most of the force of his fall," said the doctor. "He was very fortunate that he was wearing it." Todd would only need to rest, but he would not be able to ride for at least a month. Todd was in bed that night when Dusty came into his room. Todd hugged his faithful dog. "Mom is right," said Todd. "A dog is a boy's best friend!" (435 words)

Scoring Miscues for Oral Reading Option
Mark all scoreable miscues by placing either a plus (for those that maintain meaning) or a zero (for those that violate meaning) in the text margin.

Reading Accuracy Index: _____%
*Total all miscues marked with pluses **and** zeros and enter the corresponding percentage from the Miscue Chart.*

Meaning Maintenance Index: _____%
*Total **only** miscues marked with zeros and enter the corresponding percentage from the Miscue Chart.*

Miscue Chart (if used for oral reading)

Miscues	%	Miscues	%	Miscues	%	Miscues	%
1	100	13	97	25	94	37	92
2	100	14	97	26	94	38	91
3	99	15	97	27	94	39	91
4	99	16	96	28	94	40	91
5	99	17	96	29	93	41	91
6	99	18	96	30	93	42	90
7	98	19	96	31	93	43	90
8	98	20	95	32	93	44	90
9	98	21	95	33	92	45	90
10	98	22	95	34	92	46	89
11	97	23	95	35	92	47	89
12	97	24	95	36	92	48	89

Student Retelling

Examiner: "Tell me about what you just read and what you thought about it."

If there is no spontaneous response, repeat the request, "Tell me what you thought about the passage."

Note: Use the Retelling Rubric on p. 141 to assess the child's retelling performance. If you need additional space for retelling responses, use a separate sheet of paper.

RETELLING RUBRIC: NARRATIVE

Place a 0, 1/2, or + to score student responses. See page 80 for information on what these assessment measures mean.

Story Structure:

___ 1. **Key Characters and Setting:** Todd, his mother, Todd's dog Dusty at home and on the bike trail.

___ 2. **Character's Problem or Goal:** Todd must learn what a good friend his dog is.

3. **Problem-Solving or Goal-Meeting Process:**

___ • Todd doesn't want his dog to come when he practices riding his bike for the race.

___ • Mom forgets to keep Dusty at home.

___ • Todd's bike hits a rock and Todd is thrown to the ground.

___ • Dusty finds Todd and runs home for help.

___ • Todd is all right but realizes that his dog is a valuable friend.

___ 4. **Personal Response:** Any well-supported positive or negative response to the characters or events in the story or to the story as a whole.

Retelling Score: _____

Comprehension Questions

_____ 1. **What was Todd showing to his mother in the kitchen?**

Text-Based: His new team jacket.

_____ 2. **What was Todd so excited about?**

Text-Based: Being in the mountain bike race.

_____ 3. **How do you know that Todd took the mountain bike race seriously?**

Inference: He was someone who was willing to practice a lot because he wanted to win.

_____ 4. **Why would Todd think it was OK to practice without wearing his helmet?**

Inference: He had ridden on the course many times before; he was thinking more of speed than of safety.

_____ 5. **Was it wise for Todd to ask Mom to keep Dusty at home?**

Critical Response: Yes—Todd knew that he would be trying to go faster than he had gone before and if Dusty got in the way, he could get hurt. No—if it hadn't been for Dusty, Mom wouldn't have known to get help.

_____ 6. **What made Dusty run back home?**

Text-Based: Todd didn't talk to him as he barked; Todd did not move.

_____ 7. **Why did Todd think that he had to give his team a big lead?**

Inference: He thought that some of the riders on his team were slower than some on the other team.

_____ 8. **How did Mom realize that she needed help?**

Text-Based: She had never heard Dusty barking in that way and then she saw that Todd wasn't with Dusty.

_____ 9. **Which was more helpful to Todd, the helmet or Dusty? Explain.**

Critical Response: The helmet because it kept him from having a serious head injury. Dusty because if he had not come, Todd would not have gotten help so quickly.

_____10. **Besides "always wear your helmet," what do you think was the most important lesson that Todd learned?**

Critical Response: Being careless can take away the chance to meet your goals; a dog is still a friend even if he annoys you sometimes; we don't always appreciate the friends we have.

Comprehension Analysis:

Text-Based: __/4__
Inference: __/3__
Critical Response: __/3__

Total Comprehension %: _____

FOURTH GRADE I: THE VACATION

Reader's copy on p. 47 of the Reader's Passages

Introductory Statement: "Would you read this passage about a family vacation (to yourself/out loud) When you are finished, I'll take away the passage. Then I'll ask you to tell me about what you read and what you think of it. After that, I'll ask you some questions about the passage."

Story

Juan burst into his sister's room. "Only eight more days!" he shouted.

"I started packing already!" said Maria. "I can't wait to see what Florida is like."

Juan and Maria had started every day for the last two weeks talking about their Florida vacation. Mom and Dad were just as eager as they were.

But that evening, Father walked into the house, looking like a ghost. "What's wrong?" Mother asked.

"No more overtime for the rest of the year," he stammered. Mother knew that they were going to use the overtime money to pay for the hotel rooms and the plane tickets to Florida. This was their first family vacation!

Mr. Ruiz struggled as he told the children that they would have to cancel their vacation. Juan ran up to his room crying while Maria hugged her father and sobbed.

"Let me see what I can do," said Mrs. Ruiz as she left the room.

She was smiling from ear to ear when she returned. "I just spoke with my brother Sal and he said that we could use his van to drive to Florida and we can stay with his wife's sister!"

Maria was excited with the news but Juan was angry! That wasn't the fun vacation he had been dreaming of for weeks. He had never flown on an airplane and he had never stayed in a hotel.

During the trip, the family stopped to look at different sights along the way. But every time Juan refused to leave the van. He was irritated with their jabbering about what they had seen at each stop.

The following day, Juan again sat in the van while the others went out to see a nearby river. Suddenly, Maria came rushing back to the van. "Juan! Juan!" she called, "Hurry, there's an alligator!" Juan jumped out of the van and dashed the quarter mile to where his parents were standing.

"You missed it," said his father sadly. "It's gone!"

Maria, Mom, and Dad told Juan how they first saw the alligator sunning itself on the bank of the river. Maria had quietly run back to get Juan but a squawking bird startled the alligator and it dashed into the river.

Everyone saw how disgusted Juan was and no one said a word for over twenty minutes.

"You know, Juan . . . began Mother.

"I know, Mom," said Juan. "I've been missing one of the best chances I've ever had! But I won't do it again!" (412 words)

Scoring Miscues for Oral Reading Option
Mark all scoreable miscues by placing either a plus (for those that maintain meaning) or a zero (for those that violate meaning) in the text margin.

Reading Accuracy Index: _____%
*Total all miscues marked with pluses **and** zeros and enter the corresponding percentage from the Miscue Chart.*

Meaning Maintenance Index: _____%
*Total **only** miscues marked with zeros and enter the corresponding percentage from the Miscue Chart.*

Miscue Chart (if used for oral reading)

Miscues	%	Miscues	%	Miscues	%	Miscues	%
1	100	13	97	25	94	37	91
2	100	14	97	26	94	38	91
3	99	15	96	27	93	39	91
4	99	16	96	28	93	40	90
5	99	17	96	29	93	41	90
6	99	18	96	30	93	42	90
7	98	19	95	31	92	43	90
8	98	20	95	32	92	44	89
9	98	21	95	33	92	45	89
10	98	22	95	34	92	46	89
11	97	23	94	35	92	47	89
12	97	24	94	36	91	48	88

Student Retelling

Examiner: "Tell me about what you just read and what you thought about it."

If there is no spontaneous response, repeat the request, "Tell me what you thought about the passage."

Note: Use the Retelling Rubric on p. 144 to assess the child's retelling performance. If you need additional space for retelling responses, use a separate sheet of paper.

RETELLING RUBRIC: NARRATIVE

Place a 0, 1/2, or + to score student responses. See page 80 for information on what these assessment measures mean.

Story Structure:

___ 1. **Key Characters and Setting:** Juan, Maria, his mother, father on family vacation.

___ 2. **Character's Problem or Goal:** Juan is disappointed with a change in travel plans.

3. **Problem-Solving or Goal-Meeting Process:**

___ • Juan's family plans a trip to Florida.

___ • Trip must be canceled because of money problems.

___ • Mother's arrangements make the trip possible.

___ • Juan is disappointed and refuses to join in the family's fun.

___ • Juan misses seeing the alligator and realizes that he has been wrong.

___ 4. **Personal Response:** Any well-supported positive or negative response to the characters or events in the story or to the story as a whole.

Retelling Score: _____

Comprehension Questions

_____ 1. **Why was everyone in the family excited about the vacation in Florida?**

Text-Based: It was their first family vacation; their first trip to Florida.

_____ 2. **Why did it seem that the family would have to cancel their vacation?**

Text-Based: Mr. Ruiz could get no more overtime at work.

_____ 3. **Why didn't Mrs. Ruiz ask her brother earlier if they could borrow his van?**

Inference: The family planned to fly to Florida.

_____ 4. **What reason would Juan have for being upset when his family talked about what they had seen?**

Inference: Jealous of them; didn't want to be reminded of what he had missed; wanted everyone else to suffer along with him.

5. Who do you think was older, Juan or Maria? Why do you think so?

Critical Response: Maria—seemed more concerned with her father's feelings; handled the disappointment better than Juan did; was willing to enjoy the vacation with her family. Juan—Maria ran back to tell Juan when the family saw the alligator; she would have teased him if he were younger; he stayed in the van by himself.

6. Why was Juan disappointed when he heard that the family would drive the van to Florida? (Must identify one.)

Text-Based: He was looking forward to flying and staying in a hotel for the first time.

7. How did the family show that they cared about Juan's feelings after he missed seeing the alligator?

Inference: They didn't force him to go with them; they didn't preach to him; they stayed silent for 20 minutes after he missed seeing the alligator; they gave him some think time.

8. Why was the family still able to go to Florida without the extra overtime money? (Must include both.)

Text-Based: Mrs. Ruiz got help from her brother: 1) he gave her the van to use, and 2) he found a place for them to stay.

9. Do you think Juan's parents were right to let him sulk for so long? Why or why not?

Critical Response: Yes—maybe they were trying to help him learn a lesson; you can't really force someone to have a good time; he learned something from the experience. No—he was trying to put a damper on everyone else's vacation; he had already made up his mind not to have a good time.

10. What lesson do you think Juan could learn from his experience?

Critical Response: Don't sulk because you could miss some very good things; don't think the worst because sometimes things work out for the best; keep your mind on what is important in life.

Comprehension Analysis:

Text-Based: __/4__
Inference: __/3__
Critical Response: __/3__

Total Comprehension %: _____

Reader's copy on p. 49 of the Reader's Passages

Introductory Statement: "Would you read this passage about two sisters who have a job to do (to yourself/out loud). When you are finished, I'll take away the passage. Then I'll ask you to tell me about what you read and what you think of it. After that, I'll ask you some questions about the passage."

Story

"Libby, come here quick," I called. "The leaves are all falling." It is fall and my little sister, Libby, and I will have to rake the leaves together every day. Mom said that Libby is finally old enough to help with the chores and that I have the job of showing her how to clean up the yard. If we don't rake up the leaves, they will clutter up the lawn, the sidewalks, and even the rainspouts. Mom says that falling leaves are messy and dangerous, especially when they are wet.

"Look at all the leaves, Sue!" shouted Libby. "I want to go out and play right now!" I told her that we couldn't play just then. "Mom wants us to rake the leaves up. If it rains, people walking by our house might slip and fall."

"Please, Sue. Let's just jump in them for a little while," she begged. So I told her that if she would help me clean up afterwards, we could pile them up into a big mound and jump in. She was so excited that she promised to help me.

We went out and raked the leaves into a big pile and then we shouted "one, two, three, jump!" And we jumped on the pile of leaves again and again until the leaves were scattered over the entire yard. Then I told Libby that it was time to rake them up, but Libby just wanted to keep playing. While she played, I had to gather the leaves and put them in the trash bags myself. Then I had to drag all of the bags out to the sidewalk

for the trucks to come and pick them up the next morning. I knew that more leaves would fall tomorrow but I wondered if Libby would help me clean them up then.

The next day, I had piano lessons so I didn't get home until late. I was surprised to find that Libby had gone outside and raked the leaves herself. But then she remembered the fun she had the day before and she jumped in them and they flew all over the yard. When I saw the mess I told Libby that she would have to clean up the leaves. I even offered to help her rake them up before Mom came home. But Libby ran away to play with her friend and I was left to do all of the work again. I really wanted to just leave everything there in the yard but I knew that Mom would be disappointed. Falling leaves can be fun for kids, but grown-ups don't see it that way. I think I'm starting to see the reason. (448 words)

Scoring Miscues for Oral Reading Option
Mark all scoreable miscues by placing either a plus (for those that maintain meaning) or a zero (for those that violate meaning) in the text margin.

Reading Accuracy Index: _____%
*Total all miscues marked with pluses **and** zeros and enter the corresponding percentage from the Miscue Chart.*

Meaning Maintenance Index: _____%
*Total **only** miscues marked with zeros and enter the corresponding percentage from the Miscue Chart*

Miscue Chart (if used for oral reading)

Miscues	%	Miscues	%	Miscues	%	Miscues	%
1	100	13	97	25	94	37	92
2	100	14	97	26	94	38	91
3	99	15	97	27	94	39	91
4	99	16	96	28	94	40	91
5	99	17	96	29	94	41	91
6	99	18	96	30	93	42	91
7	98	19	96	31	93	43	90
8	98	20	96	32	93	44	90
9	98	21	95	33	93	45	90
10	98	22	95	34	92	46	90
11	98	23	95	35	92	47	89
12	97	24	95	36	92	48	89

Student Retelling

Examiner: "Tell me about what you just read and what you thought about it."

If there is no spontaneous response, repeat the request, "Tell me what you thought about the passage."

Note: Use the Retelling Rubric on p. 147 to assess the child's retelling performance. If you need additional space for retelling responses, use a separate sheet of paper.

RETELLING RUBRIC: NARRATIVE

Place a 0, 1/2, or + to score student responses. See page 80 for information on what these assessment measures mean.

Story Structure:

___ 1. **Key Characters and Setting:** Sue and younger sister (Libby) at home.

___ 2. **Character's Problem or Goal:** Sue has difficulty getting her little sister to help her clean up the leaves.

3. **Problem-Solving or Goal-Meeting Process:**

___ • Sue tells Libby about their job raking the leaves.

___ • Libby wants to play and promises to help if Sue agrees.

___ • After they play, Libby leaves Sue with the work.

___ • The next day it happens again.

___ • Sue begins to understand why parents look at leaves differently from the way children do.

___ 4. **Personal Response:** Any well-supported positive or negative response to the characters or events in the story or to the story as a whole.

Retelling Score: ____

Comprehension Questions

_____ 1. Why was it important for the girls to rake up the leaves every day?

Text-Based: Leaves clutter up lawn or sidewalks or downspouts; can be dangerous.

_____ 2. Why is Libby helping this year to clean up the leaves?

Text-Based: She is now old enough to help.

_____ 3. How much older do you think Sue is than her sister Libby? Why do you think this?

Inference: Must be several years; older one is responsible for the other; tells her what Mom wants her to do; decides if they can play in the leaves or not.

_____ 4. Do you think Libby might have a good reason for not wanting to work with Sue? Explain.

Inference: Libby might think she is bossy; makes her do things she doesn't want to do; her sister nags her about their jobs.

_____ 5. What do you think that Sue should do the next time Libby promises to help? Why?

Critical Response: Should refuse to do the work until Libby shows she can keep her promises; should talk to Libby about the importance of keeping your word.

_____ 6. Why couldn't the two girls work together on Tuesday?

Text-Based: Sue had piano lessons.

_____ 7. What do you think Sue meant when she said that she's beginning to see why adults don't see falling leaves as fun?

Inference: They are a lot of work and responsibility; lot of work when no one helps.

_____ 8. Why wasn't Sue happy that Libby raked the leaves by herself while Sue was at her piano lesson?

Text-Based: She played in the leaves and scattered them all over the yard.

_____ 9. Do you think that Sue should have done Libby's work for her? Why or why not?

Critical Response: No— she will only do the same thing again if she gets away with it. Yes—because if she didn't do it, someone might be hurt; she is being responsible.

_____ 10. Do you think that Sue should tell Mom that Libby did not help with the work? Why or why not?

Critical Response: Yes – Libby is not being fair or responsible and will not listen to her sister. No – that would be tattling; she should refuse to let her play until she helps.

Comprehension Analysis:

Text-Based: __/4__
Inference: __/3__
Critical Response: __/3__

Total Comprehension %: _____

FOURTH GRADE III: THE SCIENCE FAIR

Reader's copy on p. 50 of the Reader's Passages

Introductory Statement: "Would you read this passage about a boy and his dog (to yourself/out loud). When you are finished, I'll take away the passage. Then I'll ask you to tell me about what you read and what you think of it. After that, I'll ask you some questions about the passage."

Story

"It is time for the Science Fair," said Mr. Jones. "You should pick something you want to learn about and make sure it is important to you." As soon as Mr. Jones talked about the Science Fair, everyone turned to look at Ben. That was no surprise because Ben had won the first prize last year. He had created an original computer game and his friends loved playing it. No other project in the fair was even close to his.

Ben saw everyone looking at him but he knew down deep that he had lots of help last year. In fact, his father did most of the work. Many times there was nothing for Ben to do and so he went and watched TV. "What will I do this year?" thought Ben. He knew that he was in trouble because his dad had a new job. "He will be away for two months and so this time I will have to make something by myself," he thought.

Ben thought about his problem for many days. He had no idea what he could do but then he remembered Mr. Jones's advice. "This time I am going to do something that I really like even if it isn't great," he thought.

Ben thought about what he loved to do most and that was to play golf with his father. But when he played, he could never hit the ball far. Ben decided that he would learn how to make golf balls fly. He went to the library and found three books on golf. He read the books and made a chart to show what he learned.

Ben went to the golf range three times every week, trying hard to follow the advice from the books. He kept his eyes on the ball and tried not to swing too hard. After each try he charted the length of his drives, keeping a graph that showed how he did every day.

Everyone was surprised when Ben came to the fair with nothing but a simple chart and a graph that plotted his progress. Ben was really proud of the growth he had made. He was disappointed when no one said anything about his hard work or his creativity. His father called that weekend and Ben told him that he was not very happy with the low grade he had received on the science project. "But I did just what Mr. Jones said we were to do. I learned about something that was really important to *me*." (422 words)

Scoring Miscues for Oral Reading Option
Mark all scoreable miscues by placing either a plus (for those that maintain meaning) or a zero (for those that violate meaning) in the text margin.

Reading Accuracy Index: _____%
*Total all miscues marked with pluses **and** zeros and enter the corresponding percentage from the Miscue Chart.*

Meaning Maintenance Index: _____%
*Total **only** miscues marked with zeros and enter the corresponding percentage from the Miscue Chart.*

Miscue Chart (if used for oral reading)

Miscues	%	Miscues	%	Miscues	%	Miscues	%
1	100	13	97	25	94	37	91
2	100	14	97	26	94	38	91
3	99	15	96	27	94	39	91
4	99	16	96	28	93	40	91
5	99	17	96	29	93	41	90
6	99	18	96	30	93	42	90
7	98	19	95	31	93	43	90
8	98	20	95	32	92	44	90
9	98	21	95	33	92	45	89
10	98	22	95	34	92	46	89
11	97	23	95	35	92	47	89
12	97	24	94	36	91	48	89

Student Retelling

Examiner: "Tell me about what you just read and what you thought about it."

If there is no spontaneous response, repeat the request, "Tell me what you thought about the passage."

Note: Use the Retelling Rubric on p. 150 to assess the child's retelling performance. If you need additional space for retelling responses, use a separate sheet of paper.

RETELLING RUBRIC: NARRATIVE

Place a 0, 1/2, or + to score student responses. See page 80 for information on what these assessment measures mean.

Story Structure:

____ 1. **Key Characters and Setting:** Ben, his father, his teacher, and his classmates.

____ 2. **Character's Problem or Goal:** Ben is under pressure to match last year's winning science fair project.

3. **Problem-Solving or Goal-Meeting Process:**

____ • Everyone expects Ben to win this year's Science Fair.

____ • Ben realizes that his father won't be in town to do his project this year.

____ • Ben decides to create a golf project for the Science Fair because that is what he really likes.

____ • Ben's classmates are surprised with his project and the judges gave him a low grade.

____ • Ben tells his father that he got a low grade but enjoyed doing the project.

____ 4. **Personal Response:** Any well-supported positive or negative response to the characters or events in the story or to the story as a whole.

Retelling Score: _____

Comprehension Questions

_____ 1. **Why did all the children look at Ben when Mr. Jones made the announcement?**

Text-Based: Ben had won first prize at the Science Fair last year; everyone expected Ben to win the fair again.

_____ 2. **What was Ben's project that won the top prize in the Science Fair?**

Text-Based: A computer game.

_____ 3. **Do you think Ben should have accepted the Science Fair prize last year? Explain.**

Inference: No—he did not do much of the work; his father worked and he often watched TV.

_____ 4. **Why was Mr. Jones's advice so good for Ben? Explain.**

Inference: It helped Ben come up with a good idea; it is important to learn things that are important to you because you want to learn about them; you will be learning about things that you can use in your real life.

_____ 5. Who do you think made the bigger mistake, Ben for accepting a prize he didn't earn or his father for doing the project for Ben?

Critical Response: Ben—because now people expect more from him; he really lied when he entered the fair. Father—because he set his son up to fail; sent him the wrong message about fair competition.

_____ 6. What was it that Ben loved to do?

Text-Based: Play golf with his father.

_____ 7. Did Ben learn anything besides some science by doing this year's project? Explain.

Inference: He learned that the grade doesn't always show how hard someone worked; school work is more enjoyable when you like what you are doing; he learned how to play golf better.

_____ 8. What did Ben do at the golf range? (Must identify two.)

Text-Based: Practiced what was in the book; kept his eyes on the ball; didn't swing hard.

_____ 9. Were the Science Fair judges fair to Ben this year? Explain.

Critical Response: Yes—they probably didn't know that his father had done the project last year so they expected something very special. No—the chart showed that he had worked hard; he had an original project that showed how much he learned.

_____ 10. Who do you think learned more from what happened in this story, Ben or his father? Explain.

Critical Response: Father—because he now knows that Ben should have done something that he would learn about. Ben—because he learned to be more independent; he learned to do things he's interested in.

Comprehension Analysis:

Text-Based: __/4__
Inference: __/3__
Critical Response: __/3__

Total Comprehension %: ____

FIFTH GRADE I: GETTING WHAT YOU WANT

Reader's copy on p. 51 of the Reader's Passages

Introductory Statement: "Would you read this passage about a girl who gets her wish (to yourself/out loud). When you are finished, I'll take away the passage. Then I'll ask you to tell me about what you read and what you think of it. After that, I'll ask you some questions about the passage."

Story

Many years ago a young woman named Winnie Yua lived in a small Chinese village where her family kept a few rice paddies. Winnie's family was very poor. Winnie was the oldest of five girls and she would help her father take the rice to the city and sell it on market days. Her parents had always hoped to have a son who would be able to go to school and perhaps work in the city for better pay. They never had their son, but their daughters were all good and kind and worked hard on the farm with their parents.

One day in the marketplace, Winnie heard news from the province that the emperor had announced a counting contest. This was exciting news because the winner would get a valuable, secret prize. Winnie knew no one who was nearly as good at counting as she was. But when she asked about how to enter the contest, Winnie learned that only boys were permitted to participate.

"Father, I wish I were a boy. I know that I can count very well. It isn't fair that only boys can compete."

"Winnie, you really need to stop wishing you were a boy. Sometimes I think it is our fault that you feel that way. You are a good daughter and a great help to us. I know it isn't fair that the emperor is only allowing boys to participate but that is the way it is. Perhaps one day things will change but you must accept your fate for now."

Winnie honored and respected her father, but she still wanted a chance to win a valuable prize and help her family. Helping at the market had made her an excellent counter. She could calculate bills and change without an abacus. And she never made a mistake. So Winnie vowed to win the prize and immediately set out to make for herself a special suit of boy's clothing. On the day of the competition, Winnie disguised herself as a young man and entered the contest. As the day went on, Winnie became more and more excited. The others were failing, one by one, but Winnie knew her numbers well. At the end of the contest, she was the only one left. She had achieved her goal!

Now the emperor's minister came forward to award the prize. Winnie's heart was pounding. It seemed as if everyone in the entire city was there to hear the announcement. She prayed that no one would recognize her. All she wanted was to take the money, go home to her own village, and surprise her family, especially her father.

Then the crowd hushed at a signal from the town's guard. Then the minister spoke in a loud voice, "The emperor has decreed that the winner of this contest is the man who will marry his only daughter!" (479 words)

Scoring Miscues for Oral Reading Option
Mark all scoreable miscues by placing either a plus (for those that maintain meaning) or a zero (for those that violate meaning) in the text margin.

Reading Accuracy Index: _____%
*Total all miscues marked with pluses **and** zeros and enter the corresponding percentage from the Miscue Chart.*

Meaning Maintenance Index: _____%
*Total **only** miscues marked with zeros and enter the corresponding percentage from the Miscue Chart.*

Miscue Chart (if used for oral reading)

Miscues	%	Miscues	%	Miscues	%	Miscues	%
1	100	19	96	37	92	55	89
2	100	20	96	38	92	56	88
3	99	21	96	39	92	57	88
4	99	22	95	40	92	58	88
5	99	23	95	41	91	59	88
6	99	24	95	42	91	60	87
7	99	25	95	43	91	61	87
8	98	26	95	44	91	62	87
9	98	27	94	45	91	63	87
10	98	28	94	46	90	64	87
11	98	29	94	47	90	65	86
12	97	30	94	48	90	66	86
13	97	31	94	49	90	67	86
14	97	32	93	50	90	68	86
15	97	33	93	51	89	69	86
16	97	34	93	52	89	70	85
17	96	35	93	53	89	71	85
18	96	36	92	54	89	72	85

Student Retelling

Examiner: "Tell me about what you just read and what you thought about it."

If there is no spontaneous response, repeat the request, "Tell me what you thought about the passage."

Note: Use the Retelling Rubric on p. 153 to assess the child's retelling performance. If you need additional space for retelling responses, use a separate sheet of paper.

RETELLING RUBRIC: NARRATIVE

Place a 0, 1/2, or + to score student responses. See page 80 for information on what these assessment measures mean.

Story Structure:

___ 1. **Key Characters and Setting:** Winnie Yua, her family, and the emperor in a small Chinese village.

___ 2. **Character's Problem or Goal:** Winnie wants a chance to win the counting contest to help her family.

3. **Problem Solving or Goal-Meeting Process:**

___ • Winnie hears about a counting contest with a valuable prize.

___ • Winnie wants to enter but only boys are allowed.

___ • Her father tells her to accept her fate as a girl.

___ • Winnie disguises herself and enters anyway.

___ • Winnie wins but finds that the prize is the emperor's daughter in marriage.

___ 4. **Personal Response:** Any well-supported positive or negative response to the characters or events in the story or to the story as a whole.

Retelling Score: _____

Comprehension Questions

_____ 1. What skill did Winnie have that helped her father on market days?

Text-Based: Counting ability.

_____ 2. What did Winnie have to do to get into the counting contest?

Text-Based: Disguise herself as a boy.

_____ 3. Why would Winnie's father think it was his fault that his daughter wished to be a boy?

Inference: He and his wife had hoped for a son; Winnie may have overheard them.

_____ 4. Was the emperor really unfair to allow only boys in *this* counting contest? Explain.

Inference: No, he knew what the prize would be.

_____ 5. Do you think it was right for Winnie's father to wish that he had a son? Explain.

Critical Response: No—he made his daughter feel unwanted or inferior; he did not take his own advice to accept his fate. Yes—boys had opportunities for education; a boy might be able to earn more and help the family more.

_____ 6. What advice did Winnie's father give her when she said that she wished she were a boy?

Text-Based: Told her she should accept her fate and stop wishing she were a boy.

_____ 7. Why would Winnie be especially eager to tell her father that she had won the contest?

Inference: She thought he would be pleased by her achievement; he had told her to forget about the contest; the family was poor and she thought the prize would help them.

_____ 8. Why did Winnie enter the contest?

Text-Based: Thought she could win a valuable prize; wanted to help the family.

_____ 9. Would you describe Winnie more as a creative person or a dishonest person?

Critical Response: Creative—she solved the problem of getting into the contest; she was attempting to change the way society looked at girls. Dishonest—she ignored her father's advice and disobeyed him; she broke the rules of the contest.

_____ 10. What do you think Winnie should do now that she knows what the prize is?

Critical Response: Apologize for disguising herself; go back to her family without claiming the prize and hope that no one recognized her.

Comprehension Analysis:

Text-Based: __/4__
Inference: __/3__
Critical Response: __/3__

Total Comprehension %: _____

FIFTH GRADE II: THE PLAYER

Reader's copy on p. 52 of the Reader's Passages

Introductory Statement: "Would you read this passage about a basketball player (to yourself/out loud). When you are finished, I'll take away the passage. Then I'll ask you to tell me about what you read and what you think of it. After that, I'll ask you some questions about the passage."

Story

Rasheed was excited to be playing on his first basketball team. He hadn't played much basketball but he had always been big and fast and a good athlete. But this time things were different. The first time he had the ball, Rasheed dribbled it off his foot and out of bounds. The next two times, a quicker player stole it away from him. Finally Rasheed had his first chance to shoot the ball but he missed everything, even the backboard. Soon his teammates stopped passing the ball to him, even when he was open under the basket. His team lost the game badly and Rasheed went home angry with his team and angry with basketball.

That night, Rasheed went to his father and told him that he wanted to quit the basketball team. "I'm no good at basketball and the team is no good either," he said.

"Well, if you want to quit, that's your decision," said Mr. Singer. "But I think if you really want to, you can become a whole lot better and so can your team. Maybe you shouldn't just do things that are easy for you." Rasheed had to think this one over. Rasheed knew that whenever his father said "It's your decision, but . . . " he really meant that he'd like Rasheed to think it over very carefully. Down deep, he knew that his father would be disappointed if he never even tried to become a better player.

Rasheed knew that his father wouldn't be much help at teaching him basketball but he had heard stories about their new neighbor, Mr. Armstrong, being named to the all-state team in high school. When Rasheed asked Mr. Armstrong if he could teach him basketball, Mr. Armstrong's eyes lit up. He said, "You stick with me, kid, and you'll be the best basketball player ever!" Rasheed laughed as the two of them took turns shooting baskets in Mr. Armstrong's back yard. But soon Rasheed was sweating and breathing hard as his new teacher put him through one basketball drill after another. Finally, Mr. Armstrong said, "Time to call it a day! But be here same time tomorrow and we'll do it again." Rasheed worked hard and even after just a few days, he could feel himself becoming more confident in his ability. When it was time for the next game, Rasheed scored eight points, grabbed five rebounds, and didn't lose the ball once. His team still lost the game, but his teammates couldn't believe how much better he had become.

After the game, Mr. Singer put his arm around his son and said, "I'm really proud of the decision you made, Rasheed. You worked awfully hard and it really showed."

"Thanks, Dad. Thanks for not letting me quit the team."

"Who told you that you couldn't quit? It wasn't me!"

Rasheed just smiled. (473 words)

Scoring Miscues for Oral Reading Option
Mark all scoreable miscues by placing either a plus (for those that maintain meaning) or a zero (for those that violate meaning) in the text margin.

Reading Accuracy Index: _____%
*Total all miscues marked with pluses **and** zeros and enter the corresponding percentage from the Miscue Chart.*

Meaning Maintenance Index: _____%
*Total **only** miscues marked with zeros and enter the corresponding percentage from the Miscue Chart.*

Miscue Chart (if used for oral reading)

Miscues	%	Miscues	%	Miscues	%	Miscues	%
1	100	19	96	37	92	55	89
2	100	20	96	38	92	56	88
3	99	21	96	39	92	57	88
4	99	22	95	40	92	58	88
5	99	23	95	41	91	59	88
6	99	24	95	42	91	60	87
7	99	25	95	43	91	61	87
8	98	26	95	44	91	62	87
9	98	27	94	45	90	63	87
10	98	28	94	46	90	64	86
11	98	29	94	47	90	65	86
12	97	30	94	48	90	66	86
13	97	31	93	49	90	67	86
14	97	32	93	50	89	68	86
15	97	33	93	51	89	69	85
16	97	34	93	52	89	70	85
17	96	35	93	53	89	71	85
18	96	36	92	54	89	72	85

Student Retelling

Examiner: "Tell me about what you just read and what you thought about it."

If there is no spontaneous response, repeat the request, "Tell me what you thought about the passage."

Note: Use the Retelling Rubric on p. 156 to assess the child's retelling performance. If you need additional space for retelling responses, use a separate sheet of paper.

RETELLING RUBRIC: NARRATIVE

Place a 0, 1/2, or + to score student responses. See page 80 for information on what these assessment measures mean.

Story Structure:

___ 1. **Key Characters and Setting:** Rasheed, his father, Mr. Armstrong, and basketball team.

___ 2. **Character's Problem or Goal:** Rasheed must deal with his failure in basketball.

3. **Problem-Solving or Goal-Meeting Process:**

___ • Rasheed tries to play basketball and fails.

___ • He wants to quit the team but his father wants him to think about it.

___ • Rasheed asks Mr. Armstrong to help him.

___ • Mr. Armstrong and Rasheed work hard and Rasheed improves.

___ • Rasheed's father is proud of him.

___ 4. **Personal Response:** Any well-supported positive or negative response to the characters or events in the story or to the story as a whole.

Retelling Score: _____

Comprehension Questions

_____ 1. **Why was Rasheed angry after his first game with the basketball team? (Must identify one.)**

Text-Based: His teammates wouldn't pass the ball to him; he played badly; he was embarrassed.

_____ 2. **How do you know that Mr. Armstrong really wanted to help Rasheed become a better player? (Must identify one.)**

Text-Based: His eyes lit up when Rasheed asked him; he worked with Rasheed night after night.

3. What kind of player was Rasheed expecting to be when he first started to play basketball? Why?

   Inference: A good player; was always a good athlete and expected basketball to be easy.

4. Why do you think that Mr. Armstrong would spend so much time and energy on a neighbor's son?

   Inference: Liked to share his knowledge of basketball; enjoyed spending time with Rasheed.

5. Why would Rasheed's father think he should stay on the team, even if he wasn't very good?

   Critical Response: His son shouldn't just quit and walk away; knew his son could be better if he tried; wanted him to learn about how to stick with something and learn.

6. Why didn't Rasheed quit when Mr. Armstrong made him work so hard on basketball drills?

   Text-Based: He had fun; they laughed together; he was learning more about basketball.

7. At the end of the story, Rasheed's father insisted that he hadn't told his son that he could not quit the team. Why do you think he did that?

   Inference: Wanted his son to know that he had made his own decision; didn't want to tell his son what to do; wanted to be sure Rasheed knew he was proud of the decision he made.

8. How did Rasheed's teammates react to him after the second game?

   Text-Based: Surprised at his improvement.

9. Who do you think helped Rasheed more, Mr. Armstrong or his father? Explain.

   Critical Response: Mr. Armstrong—gave him confidence; taught him the value of hard work. Father—let his son make his own decision; taught him to think carefully about what he did; gave his son good advice.

_____10. Do you think it would have been wrong if Rasheed had quit the team? Why or why not?

Critical Response: Yes—he really had not tried to improve; he would have disappointed his father. No—he was not getting better; his teammates did not help him; his teammates ignored him and the team played badly anyway.

Comprehension Analysis:

Text-Based: __/4__
Inference: __/3__
Critical Response: __/3__

Total Comprehension %: _____

FIFTH GRADE III: THE BULLY

Reader's copy on p. 54 of the Reader's Passages

Introductory Statement: "Would you read this passage about a boy and a bully (to yourself/out loud). When you are finished, I'll take away the passage. Then I'll ask you to tell me about what you read and what you think of it. After that, I'll ask you some questions about the passage."

Story

Bill overheard his father talking to Chip's dad, "I'm sure you're proud of how Chip hits the ball." Bill knew that his father admired Chip's athletic skills. "That Chip is really a special kid," his father said, and he said it more often than Bill cared to remember.

"How come you don't spend more time with Chip?" his father asked. "I spend a lot of time with him," said Bill, hoping his father didn't hear the discomfort in his voice. He didn't want to admit that he didn't like Chip at all.

Earlier that same afternoon Bill had been walking with his friend Pedro when Chip turned the corner and saw them. He called out, "Hey Pedro, why don't you learn to talk like a *real* American? If you did, you could help your father talk so people can understand him." Chip laughed loudly and walked off still laughing. This kind of insult was nothing new for Chip, but what really annoyed Bill was that Chip never acted this way in front of adults. But when he was alone with classmates, he had a way of finding their weak spots and making fun of them in front of their friends.

Pedro didn't want Bill to know he was hurt, so he muttered something about having work to do and ran off as fast as he could. Bill wanted to tell Chip where to get off but that might just start a fight. And Chip was too big and strong for Bill to take on.

The next day, Bill was on his way to Pedro's house so Pedro could help him with his math homework. As he turned the corner, he saw Chip and another boy pushing Pedro down on the grass and making fun of him. "Dat' eees not white!" they said, mocking the way Pedro talked. "Don't you even know how to say *right* the right way?"

"Let him alone," shouted Bill, so angry that he didn't care that he was standing up to the two toughest kids in the class. Bill marched right up to Chip's face shouting, "You'd better cut it out now!" Before Bill knew what had happened, Chip had knocked him on the ground, right next to Pedro. Bill never expected to see Pedro jump up and run right into Chip, and he never expected to see Chip sprawled out on the ground. Bill leaped up to his feet and stood shoulder to shoulder with Pedro. He was really surprised when Chip and his friend, seeing how angry Pedro and Bill were, decided to back off and walk quickly away.

Bill decided that it was finally time to tell his father about Chip. "I was always afraid to say anything because I knew how much you liked him," Bill said. His father replied, "I'm sorry, Bill. I should have never pressured you to be his friend. The Chip I liked doesn't really exist!" (488 words)

Scoring Miscues for Oral Reading Option
Mark all scoreable miscues by placing either a plus (for those that maintain meaning) or a zero (for those that violate meaning) in the text margin.

Reading Accuracy Index: _____%
*Total all miscues marked with pluses **and** zeros and enter the corresponding percentage from the Miscue Chart.*

Meaning Maintenance Index: _____%
*Total **only** miscues marked with zeros and enter the corresponding percentage from the Miscue Chart.*

Miscue Chart (if used for oral reading)

Miscues	%	Miscues	%	Miscues	%	Miscues	%
1	100	19	96	37	92	55	89
2	100	20	96	38	92	56	89
3	99	21	96	39	92	57	88
4	99	22	95	40	92	58	88
5	99	23	95	41	92	59	88
6	99	24	95	42	91	60	88
7	99	25	95	43	91	61	88
8	98	26	95	44	91	62	87
9	98	27	94	45	91	63	87
10	98	28	94	46	91	64	87
11	98	29	94	47	90	65	87
12	98	30	94	48	90	66	86
13	97	31	94	49	90	67	86
14	97	32	93	50	90	68	86
15	97	33	93	51	90	69	86
16	97	34	93	52	89	70	86
17	97	35	93	53	89	71	85
18	96	36	93	54	89	72	85

Student Retelling

Examiner: "Tell me about what you just read and what you thought about it."

If there is no spontaneous response, repeat the request, "Tell me what you thought about the passage."

Note: Use the Retelling Rubric on p. 160 to assess the child's retelling performance. If you need additional space for retelling responses, use a separate sheet of paper.

RETELLING RUBRIC: NARRATIVE

Place a 0, 1/2, or + to score student responses. See page 80 for information on what these assessment measures mean.

Story Structure:

___ 1. **Key Characters and Setting:** Bill, his dad, his friend Pedro, and Chip.

___ 2. **Character's Problem or Goal:** Bill is reluctant to tell his father the truth about Chip.

3. **Problem-Solving or Goal-Meeting Process:**

___ • Bill's father wants him to play with a boy he dislikes.

___ • Chip makes fun of Bill's friend Pedro when no adults are around.

___ • Bill is afraid to stand up to Chip.

___ • The next day Chip bullies both Pedro and Bill but they stand up to him.

___ • Bill tells his father about Chip and his father acknowledges that he didn't know the real Chip.

___ 4. **Personal Response:** Any well-supported positive or negative response to the characters or events in the story or to the story as a whole.

Retelling Score: _____

Comprehension Questions

_____ 1. **Why did Bill's father admire Chip?**

Text-Based: He was good at sports; his athletic skills.

_____ 2. **What suggestion did Bill's father make to him?**

Text-Based: That he should spend more time with Chip.

_____ 3. **Why was Bill surprised when Pedro knocked Chip down?**

Inference: Chip was bigger and stronger than Pedro; Pedro had walked away from Chip when he made fun of his father.

4. How would you describe Bill's relationship with his father? Explain your answer.

   Inference: Not too close because he was reluctant to tell his father that he didn't like Chip; he didn't turn to his father for help in math.

5. Which was worse, Chip's prejudice or his dishonesty? Explain.

   Critical Response: His prejudice—because he made fun of Pedro's father's speech and clearly never tried to get to know who they were. His dishonesty—because adults never got to know what he was really like so no one could help him change.

6. Why didn't Bill stand up to Chip at first?

   Text-Based: Chip was too big and strong.

7. Why did Bill and Pedro confront Chip and his friend after they had walked away earlier?

   Inference: Each saw his friend being bullied by them.

8. Why did Chip and his friend walk away instead of fighting?

   Text-Based: They saw that Bill and Pedro were so angry; they were afraid they might lose.

9. Did Bill learn more about himself or about his father from this incident? Explain.

   Critical Response: Himself—because he learned that when a friend of his was in trouble, he was not afraid to defend him even against a very strong kid. His father—because his father really had the same feeling as Bill did when he found out what Chip was really like.

10. How does this story explain the saying, "You can't judge a book by its cover?"

    Critical Response: Chip was successful making people think that he was a nice kid but that was all for show; inside he was a mean kid who tried to make other kids feel bad about themselves.

Comprehension Analysis:

Text-Based: ___/4___
Inference: ___/3___
Critical Response: ___/3___

Total Comprehension %: _____

SIXTH GRADE I: THE MOTOR BIKE

Reader's copy on p. 56 of the Reader's Passages

Introductory Statement: "Would you read this passage about two friends and their families (to yourself/out loud). When you are finished, I'll take away the passage. Then I'll ask you to tell me about what you read and what you think of it. After that, I'll ask you some questions about the passage."

Story

Vic sprinted down the street knowing that Jameer would be waiting for him. For the past several months they had been meeting with Mr. Hunter before school started to discuss the books they were reading. On the way, Vic's mind wandered back to his third grade teacher, Ms. Woodson, and how she had changed his way of thinking. She helped him see that reading and learning could help people improve their lives.

"Guess what?" hollered Jameer when Vic was still a distance away. "I'm getting that incredible motor for my bike that I've been telling you about. Everybody in the family gets something special for their sixteenth birthday and this is my special gift!" Vic was happy for his old friend but he couldn't help feeling just a little envious too. He really wished that he had something exceptional to look forward to on his birthday.

Mr. Hunter started class and the book discussion turned toward the influences and contributions of parents to the lives of authors. Vic realized with a growing sense of discomfort that he had absolutely nothing to add to the conversation. How could he tell them that he hardly ever saw his mother, that she had two jobs and that he was the one who had to supervise his brothers and sisters? By the end of the class, his self-pity was overflowing. Mr. Hunter walked out with Vic at the end of class and said, "My wife and I would like you to have dinner with us next Saturday. See if it's OK for you."

Vic spent the following Saturday evening with the Hunter family. After dinner, Mrs. Hunter sat with Vic and showed him photographs from her childhood. In her entire collection, she had only three photographs of her mother but when Mrs. Hunter got to the first one, her face softened. She told Vic how her mother had worked at two jobs from day to night to be sure that her children always had clothes and food. "This picture was taken shortly before she died," she said. "That was the first time I told her that I resented the fact that she had missed practically every important occasion in my life. That's when she showed me her album. She kept photos and clippings from every one of those events that she had missed because she couldn't take time off from her job. Some people can't express their love with words but they certainly can show it. We just have to have enough insight to read it."

Vic had a lot to mull over that weekend and the next day he called Mrs. Hunter and said, "You know, I learned about reading from Ms. Woodson but she never taught me about the different kinds of reading; I guess we have to read things besides books. I think I'm going to try to get better at reading people. Maybe I've been getting special gifts, just like Jameer, but I never even knew it. Thanks." (498 words)

Scoring Miscues for Oral Reading Option
Mark all scoreable miscues by placing either a plus (for those that maintain meaning) or a zero (for those that violate meaning) in the text margin.

Reading Accuracy Index: _____%
*Total all miscues marked with pluses **and** zeros and enter the corresponding percentage from the Miscue Chart.*

Meaning Maintenance Index: _____%
*Total **only** miscues marked with zeros and enter the corresponding percentage from the Miscue Chart.*

Miscue Chart (if used for oral reading)

Miscues	%	Miscues	%	Miscues	%	Miscues	%
1	100	19	96	37	93	55	89
2	100	20	96	38	92	56	89
3	99	21	96	39	92	57	89
4	99	22	96	40	92	58	88
5	99	23	95	41	92	59	88
6	99	24	95	42	92	60	88
7	99	25	95	43	91	61	88
8	98	26	95	44	91	62	88
9	98	27	95	45	91	63	87
10	98	28	94	46	91	64	87
11	98	29	94	47	91	65	87
12	98	30	94	48	90	66	87
13	97	31	94	49	90	67	87
14	97	32	94	50	90	68	86
15	97	33	93	51	90	69	86
16	97	34	93	52	90	70	86
17	97	35	93	53	89	71	86
18	96	36	93	54	89	72	86

Student Retelling

Examiner: "Tell me about what you just read and what you thought about it."

If there is no spontaneous response, repeat the request, "Tell me what you thought about the passage."

Note: Use the Retelling Rubric on p. 163 to assess the child's retelling performance. If you need additional space for retelling responses, use a separate sheet of paper.

RETELLING RUBRIC: NARRATIVE

Place a 0, 1/2, or + to score student responses. See page 80 for information on what these assessment measures mean.

Story Structure:

___ 1. **Key Characters and Setting:** Vic and his friend Jameer, their teacher and his wife, in school and at dinner.

___ 2. **Character's Problem or Goal:** Vic is struggling with his feelings about his mother's absence.

3. **Problem-Solving or Goal-Meeting Process:**

___ • Vic meets his friend Jameer and hears about his special birthday gift.

___ • Vic compares Jameer's family situation to his own.

___ • Mr. Hunter notices Vic's self-pity and invites him to his home for dinner.

___ • Mrs. Hunter shares her family experiences with Vic.

___ • Vic changes his views about his own mother.

___ 4. **Personal Response:** Any well-supported positive or negative response to the characters or events in the story or to the story as a whole.

Retelling Score: _____

Comprehension Questions

_____ 1. **Why did Vic envy Jameer's family?**

Text-Based: They gave the children special birthday gifts.

_____ 2. **What made Vic feel sorry for himself during Mr. Hunter's class?**

Text-Based: Discussion of the role of parents in the lives of writers.

_____ 3. How do you know that Mr. Hunter took his job as a teacher very seriously?

Inference: Went far beyond the responsibilities of his job; met early with students; shared his family with students; invited Vic to dinner.

_____ 4. Why do you think Mr. Hunter wanted Vic to have dinner with his family?

Inference: Probably noticed that Vic was bothered during the discussion in his class.

_____ 5. Who do you think will have the greater impact on Vic's life, Mr. Hunter or Ms. Woodson? Explain.

Critical Response: Mr. H.—shared his family with Vic; helped him to solve his problems; took personal interest in him. Ms. W.—gave him the incentive to learn to read; would not be in Mr. Hunter's early classes if it weren't for her.

_____ 6. What did Mrs. Hunter do to help Vic understand his mother? (Must identify one.)

Text-Based: She showed him photo albums; she told him stories about her mother.

_____ 7. Do you think Vic's feelings about his mother will change as a result of his conversation with Mrs. Hunter? Why or why not?

Inference: Probably so. He may appreciate her hard work and understand the reasons behind it.

_____ 8. Did Vic learn anything new about reading from Mr. and Mrs. Hunter? Explain.

Text-Based: Yes—he learned about reading people, not just books.

_____ 9. Do you think that it was right for Mrs. Hunter's mother to work so hard that she missed important things in her daughter's life? Why or why not?

Critical Response: Yes—she was providing for her family's needs; showed her love in that way. No—she probably should have balanced working and being with the family; more to being a parent than just providing money.

_____10. Whom would you rather have for a friend, Vic or Jameer? Why?

Critical Response: Vic—sensitive to his friend's feelings; good thinker; open to new learning. Jameer—enthusiastic; good student; honest; shares his feelings with friends and teachers.

Comprehension Analysis:

Text-Based: ___/4___
Inference: ___/3___
Critical Response: ___/3___

Total Comprehension %: _____

SIXTH GRADE II: THE TUTOR

Reader's copy on p. 58 of the Reader's Passages

Introductory Statement: "Would you read this passage about a boy who has to help a younger boy with a problem (to yourself/out loud). When you are finished, I'll take away the passage. Then I'll ask you to tell me about what you read and what you think of it. After that, I'll ask you some questions about the passage."

Story

Jack went to his room very troubled; tomorrow he had to begin participating in the school's tutoring program. As he lay in bed, all the embarrassing reading experiences from grade school bombarded his mind. He remembered having to read aloud in front of the class, stumbling over the words he couldn't pronounce. Now he had to spend one period each day in the second grade class, helping a younger student who was having problems reading. "I'll probably end up making him feel worse than I used to feel!" he thought.

"You'll really enjoy it," said Ms. Anderson, his homeroom teacher, trying to calm Jack as he reluctantly left for his tutoring assignment the following day. "All you have to do is let your student select a book, read it to him, and then discuss it with him. Just ask him to look for different ways that the story had something to do with his life."

Jack hoped that Carl, the little boy to whom he was assigned, wouldn't notice how uncomfortable he felt reading with him. Fortunately, Carl selected a story that Jack had no difficulty reading and one that had an interesting twist, too. The story, *An Extraordinary Egg*, was about a frog who discovered a large egg which her sister, with complete confidence, identified as a chicken egg. When the egg hatches and an alligator emerges, the frogs continue to call it a chicken throughout the entire

story. Carl laughed out loud as Jack read the story; in fact, Jack couldn't help laughing with him.

"The one frog was a real know-it-all," said Carl. "My friend Bob is just the same way because he tries to make me feel stupid. Just because he's a good reader doesn't mean that he knows everything! Do you have any know-it-all friends?"

"Quite a few," said Jack. "When they talk, they act conceited. They try to convince other people that they're great." He was impressed with Carl's insight into his friend and how he used Carl's reading difficulties as a justification to put him down.

"That's exactly what the frog in the story did too," said Carl. "She even laughed at the mother alligator for calling the creature an alligator and not a chicken. Really, somebody should have laughed at her!" Jack suddenly remembered the times that certain of his classmates had laughed at him. "Do you think laughing at people is a very good way to get them to change?" "I guess that probably wouldn't work," said Carl.

"I feel sorry for the frog who was always exploring and discovering things, but nobody at home ever got excited with her. My parents always get excited when I do anything. I think that they want me to feel smart even though I'm not a good reader. You probably never had to worry about that when you were in second grade."

"You can never really know for sure about things like that. Maybe we should talk about school experiences next time." (498 words)

Scoring Miscues for Oral Reading Option
Mark all scoreable miscues by placing either a plus (for those that maintain meaning) or a zero (for those that violate meaning) in the text margin.

Reading Accuracy Index: _____%
*Total all miscues marked with pluses **and** zeros and enter the corresponding percentage from the Miscue Chart.*

Meaning Maintenance Index: _____%
*Total **only** miscues marked with zeros and enter the corresponding percentage from the Miscue Chart.*

Miscue Chart (if used for oral reading)

Miscues	%	Miscues	%	Miscues	%	Miscues	%
1	100	19	96	37	93	55	89
2	100	20	96	38	92	56	89
3	99	21	96	39	92	57	89
4	99	22	96	40	92	58	88
5	99	23	95	41	92	59	88
6	99	24	95	42	92	60	88
7	99	25	95	43	91	61	88
8	98	26	95	44	91	62	88
9	98	27	95	45	91	63	87
10	98	28	94	46	91	64	87
11	98	29	94	47	91	65	87
12	98	30	94	48	90	66	87
13	97	31	94	49	90	67	87
14	97	32	94	50	90	68	86
15	97	33	93	51	90	69	86
16	97	34	93	52	90	70	86
17	97	35	93	53	89	71	86
18	96	36	93	54	89	72	86

Student Retelling

Examiner: "Tell me about what you just read and what you thought about it."

If there is no spontaneous response, repeat the request, "Tell me what you thought about the passage."

Note: Use the Retelling Rubric on p. 167 to assess the child's retelling performance. If you need additional space for retelling responses, use a separate sheet of paper.

RETELLING RUBRIC: NARRATIVE

Place a 0, 1/2, or + to score student responses. See page 80 for information on what these assessment measures mean.

Story Structure:

___ 1. **Key Characters and Setting:** Jack, and young Carl whom he tutors at school.

___ 2. **Character's Problem or Goal:** Jack is afraid he will embarrass himself or the boy he will tutor.

3. **Problem-Solving or Goal-Meeting Process:**

___ • Jack is uncomfortable being a tutor.

___ • He remembers his own problems with reading.

___ • Jack and Carl discuss a book and share ideas.

___ • Both Carl and Jack connect the book to their own lives.

___ • Jack looks forward to working with Carl again.

___ 4. **Personal Response:** Any well-supported positive or negative response to the characters or events in the story or to the story as a whole.

Retelling Score: ____

Comprehension Questions

_____ 1. **Why didn't Jack want to be part of the tutoring program at first?**

Text-Based: He was not very good at reading; remembered being embarrassed.

_____ 2. **Was the tutoring as bad as Jack expected it to be? Why or why not?**

Text-Based: No—the story was easy to read; both of them liked the story and talked about it.

_____ 3. How did the story that they read together help Jack and Carl to be more comfortable with each other?

Inference: Enabled them to talk about the story and relate it to their own feelings; reminded them of people that they knew.

_____ 4. If they ever talk about their experiences with school, what could Jack say to help Carl?

Inference: Should share the difficulties he had; show Carl that anyone can overcome problems with the right kind of help; shouldn't let anyone make you feel inferior.

_____ 5. What do you think Jack learned from his tutoring experience?

Critical Response: Things aren't always as bad as you expect them to be; learning about yourself can be valuable; learning can come from very unexpected sources.

_____ 6. Why does Carl think that he's dumb?

Text-Based: Has difficulty reading; friend makes him feel dumb.

_____ 7. Is Carl's reading problem more about saying words or about understanding ideas? Why?

Inference: Pronouncing words—he is very much able to discuss the ideas in the book.

_____ 8. Does Carl think that Jack is the same kind of reader that he is? Why or why not?

Text-Based: No—thinks he has no problems because he is the tutor; Jack read the story with ease when Carl could not.

_____ 9. Aside from their reading problems they share, how could you explain why Jack and Carl got along so well?

Critical Response: Both had a sense of humor related to the story; both were willing to share the connections with themselves and their lives that they saw in the story.

_____10. Who do you think will learn more from the experience in the story, Jack or Carl? Why?

Critical Response: Jack—he might find that his problems aren't as bad as he thinks; might be able to conquer his doubts. Carl—he may become convinced that he isn't dumb.

Comprehension Analysis:

Text-Based: ___/4___
Inference: ___/3___
Critical Response: ___/3___

Total Comprehension %: _____

SIXTH GRADE III: THE DENTIST

Reader's copy on p. 60 of the Reader's Passages

Introductory Statement: "Would you read this passage about a boy with a toothache (to yourself/out loud). When you are finished, I'll take away the passage. Then I'll ask you to tell me about what you read and what you think of it. After that, I'll ask you some questions about the passage."

Story

Bob bit his lip, trying hard to forget his throbbing toothache as he ran to his friend's home. He had finally become the band's official drummer and no toothache was going to stop him from playing. In spite of his pain, Bob never flinched, making sure no one knew as he concentrated on keeping his drum rolls in rhythm. As he made his way home, the pain in his tooth seemed to become more intense with every step.

"Mom, how can you just let me hurt like this?" he cried as he walked in the door, ran into his bedroom, threw himself on the bed, and sobbed. Mother rushed into the room in a panic and asked, "What's wrong?" "I can't take this pain in my tooth!" Bob cried. "I didn't even know!" his mother exclaimed, as she scurried off to phone their dentist.

When she left, Bob's older sister, Stella, stood at the door muttering, "You are such a baby, making a mountain out of a mole hill!" Bob cried back, "Anybody who had a toothache like this would be crying!" Stella snapped back, "Were you crying like that when you were playing in the band this morning?"

Mother returned with the news that their dentist could see Bob the following morning, and just the knowledge that the problem would be solved, coupled with a few aspirin, was enough to relieve Bob and he headed off to watch television. When Bob left, his sister turned to Mother and said haughtily, "He's such a baby and you're not doing anything to stop it. Isn't it really interesting that he only cries around us?" "Are you forgetting that home is our comfort zone?" said Mother.

The next morning as Bob and his mother drove to the dentist, Bob remained silent for most of the ride. As they neared the dentist's office, he blurted, "Mom, when the nurse asks me if I want you to come back with me to the dentist's chair, I'm going to say 'no' but make sure you come back with me anyway!" Mother smiled, thinking to herself what Stella would be saying if she had heard that. Just as directed, Mother went with Bob after he told the nurse that he didn't need her. On the way home, a pain-free Bob chatted about the funny things the dentist had said and then, smiling, he said, "Mom, when we go back tomorrow and I say you don't have to come back, you *really* don't."

At home, Stella asked mockingly, "You mean you're really going to survive?" Mom waited until Bob left and then asked, "Why are you so hard on him? I remember when you were young and you reacted exactly the same way whenever you had an earache. You'll find that it's time that helps us grow up. Bob is well on his way!" (477 words)

Scoring Miscues for Oral Reading Option
Mark all scoreable miscues by placing either a plus (for those that maintain meaning) or a zero (for those that violate meaning) in the text margin.

Reading Accuracy Index: _____%
*Total all miscues marked with pluses **and** zeros and enter the corresponding percentage from the Miscue Chart.*

Meaning Maintenance Index: _____%
*Total **only** miscues marked with zeros and enter the corresponding percentage from the Miscue Chart.*

Miscue Chart (if used for oral reading)

Miscues	%	Miscues	%	Miscues	%	Miscues	%
1	100	17	96	33	93	49	90
2	100	18	96	34	93	50	90
3	99	19	96	35	93	51	89
4	99	20	96	36	92	52	89
5	99	21	96	37	92	53	89
6	99	22	95	38	92	54	89
7	99	23	95	39	92	55	88
8	98	24	95	40	92	56	88
9	98	25	95	41	91	57	88
10	98	26	95	42	91	58	88
11	98	27	94	43	91	59	88
12	97	28	94	44	91	60	87
13	97	29	94	45	91	61	87
14	97	30	94	46	90	62	87
15	97	31	94	47	90	63	87
16	97	32	93	48	90	64	87

Student Retelling

Examiner: "Tell me about what you just read and what you thought about it."

If there is no spontaneous response, repeat the request, "Tell me what you thought about the passage."

Note: Use the Retelling Rubric on p. 171 to assess the child's retelling performance. If you need additional space for retelling responses, use a separate sheet of paper.

RETELLING RUBRIC: NARRATIVE

Place a 0, 1/2, or + to score student responses. See page 80 for information on what these assessment measures mean.

Story Structure:

___ 1. **Key Characters and Setting:** Bob, his sister, and his mother.

___ 2. **Character's Problem or Goal:** Bob hides his toothache from his friends but cries about it in front of his family.

3. **Problem-Solving or Goal-Meeting Process:**

____ • Bob ignores his toothache in front of the band players.

____ • Bob is angry with his mother for not helping him.

____ • Mother makes an appointment with dentist.

____ • Bob's sister, Stella, is angry that Bob acts like a baby at home.

____ • Mother reminds Stella that she did the same things but that it is time that helps us all to grow.

___ 4. **Personal Response:** Any well-supported positive or negative response to the characters or events in the story, or to the story as a whole.

Retelling Score: _____

Comprehension Questions

_____ 1. **Why did Bob go to band practice in spite of his toothache?**

Text-Based: No—he never told her he had become the band's official drummer.

_____ 2. **Why was it unfair for Bob to be upset with his mother for not relieving his pain?**

Text-Based: He never told her that he had a toothache.

_____ 3. Why would Bob's reaction to his toothache be so different when he was with the band from what it was when he was home?

Inference: He must have thought that complaining in front of others would make him look like a baby; he didn't think that they would be concerned.

_____ 4. Why would Stella be angry with Bob?

Inference: Complaining in front of others would make him look like a baby; he didn't think that they would be concerned about his pain.

_____ 5. Do you think Mother was right to let her children be such babies in response to their pain?

Critical Response: No—she let Bob be upset with her when he really had no reason to be; she should have let him know that it was his responsibility to ask for help. Yes—she expected them to grow out of it and that is what Stella did.

_____ 6. How did Bob act when he heard that his mother would be able to take him to the dentist the next day?

Text-Based: He took some aspirin and then went to watch television.

_____ 7. What would Stella have to do to show her mother that she was becoming more mature?

Inference: She would have to remember what she was like when she was younger: she should stop being critical of people who act the way she had acted.

_____ 8. What did Bob tell his mother to do at the dentist's office the first day?

Text-Based: To come with him even after he tells the nurse that he didn't need her to come with him.

_____ 9. What was more important to Bob, getting rid of his pain or maintaining his image?

Critical Response: Getting rid of his pain—because it was interfering with his playing the drums. His image—because he wouldn't cry in front of his friends; he had to act like he didn't need his mother when he was with the dentist.

_____10. Do you agree with Mother that Bob is well on his way to growing up? Explain.

Critical Response: Yes—he overcame his fear of the new dentist; didn't need his mother's help the second day. No—he never apologized to his mother for being upset with her; he still thinks mainly about himself and not others.

Comprehension Analysis:

Text-Based: __/4__
Inference: __/3__
Critical Response: __/3__

Total Comprehension %: _____

SEVENTH GRADE I: THE PET

Reader's copy on p. 61 of the Reader's Passages

Introductory Statement: "Would you read this passage about a girl and her pet (to yourself/out loud). When you are finished, I'll take away the passage. Then I'll ask you to tell me about what you read and what you think of it. After that, I'll ask you some questions about the passage."

Story

Linda was walking through the woods near her home as she so often did during the summer. All of a sudden she spied a beautifully colored garden snake, slithering among the dried blades of grass. "What an awesome pet that would make!" thought Linda as she scrambled to capture the hapless snake. "My friends will just die when I show them this! Not one of them would have the courage to keep a snake as a pet!"

Linda hurried home to display her newfound treasure to her mother. Somehow she wasn't surprised with her mother's less than enthusiastic reaction to a garden snake as a household pet. "You haven't the slightest idea how to feed or to take care of that animal," said Mom. "If you really wanted to do the right thing, you'd take him right back to where you found him and let him go free."

But Linda had no intentions whatsoever of losing her prize or of giving up the prospect of her friends' admiration and awe. It took quite some time, but she finally convinced her mother that she would learn how to feed the snake and take care of its needs. Although Mother knew her daughter very well, she still agreed to allow Linda to keep the snake, on the condition that Linda would do her research and learn what she needed to know. "Well, who knows? Maybe this time things will be different," thought Mother, as she went about her business feeling disappointed with herself.

The rest of the story is very predictable. Linda's pet elicited the responses she had hoped for from her friends: they were both impressed with and jealous of her exotic pet. But when the novelty wore off and the snake no longer excited the curiosity of her peers, Linda was disappointed. "These people are so picky that nothing keeps them interested!" she told herself on the way home. Then on top of it all, she had to listen to her mother's incessant nagging, "You can't just give the snake scraps of table food when you see that he isn't eating them. He's getting weaker every day, so why don't you for once do the right thing and let him go?" said Mother, unable to hide her irritation.

Linda knew full well that the consequences of outright defiance would be severe, so she simply turned a deaf ear on her mother's complaints. The next day she returned to find that the converted birdcage that she kept the snake in was empty. Running to her mother's room, she demanded to know what had happened to her snake. "You didn't take care of him and you wouldn't do the right thing, so I did it for you," said Mother. "I took the snake back to where he belongs." Linda bolted out of the house furious, muttering to herself that one day she would tell her mother exactly what was on her mind. "She never lets me live my own life the way that I want to live it!" Many days would pass before life in Linda's house settled back to normal. (519 words)

Scoring Miscues for Oral Reading Option
Mark all scoreable miscues by placing either a plus (for those that maintain meaning) or a zero (for those that violate meaning) in the text margin.

Reading Accuracy Index: _____ %
*Total all miscues marked with pluses **and** zeros and enter the corresponding percentage from the Miscue Chart.*

Meaning Maintenance Index: _____ %
*Total **only** miscues marked with zeros and enter the corresponding percentage from the Miscue Chart.*

Miscue Chart (if used for oral reading)

Miscues	%	Miscues	%	Miscues	%	Miscues	%
1	100	17	97	33	94	49	91
2	100	18	97	34	93	50	90
3	99	19	96	35	93	51	90
4	99	20	96	36	93	52	90
5	99	21	96	37	93	53	90
6	99	22	96	38	93	54	90
7	99	23	96	39	93	55	89
8	98	24	95	40	92	56	89
9	98	25	95	41	92	57	89
10	98	26	95	42	92	58	89
11	98	27	95	43	92	59	89
12	98	28	95	44	92	60	88
13	98	29	94	45	91	61	88
14	97	30	94	46	91	62	88
15	97	31	94	47	91	63	88
16	97	32	94	48	91	64	88

Student Retelling

Examiner: "Tell me about what you just read and what you thought about it."

If there is no spontaneous response, repeat the request, "Tell me what you thought about the passage."

Note: Use the Retelling Rubric on p. 175 to assess the child's retelling performance. If you need additional space for retelling responses, use a separate sheet of paper.

RETELLING RUBRIC: NARRATIVE

Place a 0, 1/2, or + to score student responses. See page 80 for information on what these assessment measures mean.

Story Structure:

___ 1. **Key Characters and Setting:** Linda, her mother, Linda's friends, and a snake from the woods.

___ 2. **Character's Problem or Goal:** Linda wants to impress her friends by having a pet snake.

___ 3. **Problem-Solving or Goal-Meeting Process:**

___   • Linda finds a snake in the woods and wants to keep it.

___   • Linda's mother makes her promise to learn to take care of the snake.

___   • Linda's friends lose interest in the snake.

___   • Linda neglects the snake and her mother tries to convince her to take it back to the woods.

___   • Linda is angry when she discovers that her mother set the snake free.

___ 4. **Personal Response:** Any well-supported positive or negative response to the characters or events in the story, or to the story as a whole.

Retelling Score: _____

Comprehension Questions

_____ 1. **How did Linda get her pet?**

Text-Based: She found it in the woods near her home.

_____ 2. **Why was Linda excited about finding the snake?**

Text-Based: She expected her friends to be impressed.

_____ 3. Did Linda's mother have reason to be concerned about Linda's newest request?

Inference: Yes—she knew that Linda wasn't thinking about doing the right thing; Linda wasn't surprised with her mother's reaction so it must have happened before.

_____ 4. Did Mother have faith that Linda would keep her word? Explain.

Inference: No—she was upset with herself because she gave in even when she didn't think that Linda would do what she said she would do.

_____ 5. Did Linda's mother do the right thing when she let the snake go free in the woods?

Critical Response: No—she should have taught her daughter to be more responsible; she should have held Linda to her promises. Yes—because Linda refused to do the right thing; Linda broke her promises; Linda no longer cared for the snake.

_____ 6. How did Linda's friends respond at first to her new pet?

Text-Based: They were impressed with it; they were jealous.

_____ 7. What might have happened if Linda's friends had kept up their excitement with the snake?

Inference: Linda probably would have tried to figure out a way to keep it healthy so that her friends could keep admiring it; Linda may not have lost interest.

_____ 8. What did Linda's mother do with the snake?

Text-Based: She returned it to the woods.

_____ 9. Who do you think struggled more in this story, Linda or her mother? Explain.

Critical Response: Linda—because she wanted so much to get the recognition and admiration of her friends. Her mother—because she knew that she should not give in to Linda but kept doing it anyway.

_____10. What would have to happen before these conflicts between Linda and her mother will come to an end?

Critical Response: Linda and her mother will have to talk openly with each other; her mother needs to set some rules and then help Linda realize that doing the right thing will be expected of her; Linda will have to be more open and tell her mother how she feels; Linda will have to become more responsible.

Comprehension Analysis:

Text-Based: ___/4___
Inference: ___/3___
Critical Response: ___/3___

Total Comprehension %: _____

SEVENTH GRADE II: THE FISHING TRIP

Reader's copy on p. 63 of the Reader's Passages

Introductory Statement: "Would you read this passage about two brothers on a fishing trip (to yourself/out loud). When you are finished, I'll take away the passage. Then I'll ask you to tell me about what you read and what you think of it. After that, I'll ask you some questions about the passage."

Story

Rick could hardly wait for the end of August when his favorite uncle had planned to treat him to his first deep-sea fishing excursion. Rick would finally be angling for really big fish and not just casting for trout! The only dark side to the trip was that his older brother would be going too. Kent was three years his senior and could be a serious nuisance with his non-stop teasing, but Rick was resolved not to let an annoying brother wreck his plans for a fantastic fishing trip.

When the grand day finally arrived, Rick and Kent enthusiastically greeted their Uncle John at the dock. Rick was more than a little relieved to see that their cruiser was both spacious and substantial. "Hope you don't get seasick, squirt," laughed Kent, but Rick remembered his resolution and simply ignored his brother. When the boat finally departed the dock and headed out to deeper water, Rick was spellbound for what seemed like an eternity by the sheer power and beauty of the ocean. He was snapped out of his reverie by the sound of his uncle's voice, reminding the boys to get their fishing gear in order. That's when he first noticed Kent, unsteady on his feet and rapidly turning a sickly shade of green.

Fortunately, Uncle John knew all the signs of impending seasickness and quickly scooped Kent up and carried him below to the boat's lower cabin. The cabin was poorly lit, grimy, and smelled of diesel fumes but Uncle John found Kent a place on one of the wooden benches that lined the cabin, wrapped him in a blanket, and told him to rest as best he could. "There isn't much that we can do until we can get Kent back, so you might as well come up and fish, Rick," he said. When he heard his uncle's words, Kent's eyes widened and he stared desperately at his brother. Rick realized that if the shoe were on the other foot he would be terrified to be left in the cabin alone. Still, he couldn't help thinking that his brother would rather die than admit it.

"That's OK, Uncle John. Maybe I should just stay for a while with Kent." Rick sat for what seemed like hours, with his brother alternating between fitful naps and periods of moaning. Rick couldn't help but feel angry with Kent for ruining his trip, but at the same time, he had never seen his brother quite so sick and helpless. All in all, Rick had the feeling that he was doing the right thing.

By the time Kent began to recover enough to sit up, the boat was already powering back toward the dock. "I don't know why you didn't go and fish with Uncle John, you little jerk," said Kent. "I didn't need you to stay with me. I'd have been fine by myself." Rick turned away hastily so that Kent wouldn't see the anger in his face. It wasn't until years later that the brothers would realize what good friends they had always been. (513 words)

Scoring Miscues for Oral Reading Option
Mark all scoreable miscues by placing either a plus (for those that maintain meaning) or a zero (for those that violate meaning) in the text margin.

Reading Accuracy Index: _____%
*Total all miscues marked with pluses **and** zeros and enter the corresponding percentage from the Miscue Chart.*

Meaning Maintenance Index: _____%
*Total **only** miscues marked with zeros and enter the corresponding percentage from the Miscue Chart.*

Miscue Chart (if used for oral reading)

Miscues	%	Miscues	%	Miscues	%	Miscues	%
1	100	17	97	33	94	49	90
2	100	18	96	34	93	50	90
3	99	19	96	35	93	51	90
4	99	20	96	36	93	52	90
5	99	21	96	37	93	53	90
6	99	22	96	38	93	54	89
7	99	23	96	39	92	55	89
8	98	24	95	40	92	56	89
9	98	25	95	41	92	57	89
10	98	26	95	42	92	58	89
11	98	27	95	43	92	59	88
12	98	28	95	44	91	60	88
13	97	29	94	45	91	61	88
14	97	30	94	46	91	62	88
15	97	31	94	47	91	63	88
16	97	32	94	48	91	64	88

Student Retelling

Examiner: "Tell me about what you just read and what you thought about it."

If there is no spontaneous response, repeat the request, "Tell me what you thought about the passage."

Note: Use the Retelling Rubric on p. 179 to assess the child's retelling performance. If you need additional space for retelling responses, use a separate sheet of paper.

RETELLING RUBRIC: NARRATIVE

Place a 0, 1/2, or + to score student responses. See page 80 for information on what these assessment measures mean.

Story Structure:

___ 1. **Key Characters and Setting:** Rick, Kent, and their uncle John on a fishing trip.

___ 2. **Character's Problem or Goal:** Rick has to choose between enjoying a fishing trip or helping his brother.

3. **Problem-Solving or Goal-Meeting Process:**

___ • Rick is excited about his first deep-sea fishing trip.

___ • Rick ignores his brother Kent's teasing.

___ • Kent becomes seasick and Uncle John takes him to the boat's cabin.

___ • Rick recognizes his brother's fear and stays with him.

___ • Rick becomes angry when Kent tells him that he didn't need to stay with him.

___ 4. **Personal Response:** Any well-supported positive or negative response to the characters or events in the story, or to the story as a whole.

Retelling Score: _____

Comprehension Questions

_____ 1. **What made this fishing trip special for Rick? (Must include one.)**

Text-Based: His favorite uncle was taking him on a fishing trip; it was his first deep-sea fishing trip.

_____ 2. **What was the one thing about the fishing trip that disappointed Rick?**

Text-Based: His older brother would be going with them.

3. Did Rick have any justification for wanting a fishing trip without his brother? Explain.

   Inference: Kent constantly teased Rick; Kent could be an annoyance to Rick.

4. What is there in the story to suggest that the two brothers could ever be friends?

   Inference: They both left their differences behind at the start of the trip and were equally excited; Rick showed his concern for his brother when he remained with him in the lower cabin; Kent sent a signal to his brother that he wanted him to stay.

5. Could Uncle John have helped the boys get along better on the fishing trip? Explain.

   Critical Response: No—because Kent already learned to tease Rick and you can't change that in a day; Rick didn't trust his brother and the uncle couldn't change that in one day. Yes—the uncle could have helped Rick see that Kent's teasing was not meant to be unkind; he could have helped Kent try to show Rick how he appreciated his caring for him.

6. Why didn't Uncle John stay with Kent?

   Text-Based: There was nothing that anyone could do to help him.

7. Why did Kent wait until the end of the trip to tell his brother that he didn't have to stay with him?

   Inference: He didn't tell him because he really wanted him to stay.

8. What reasons did Rick have for resenting his brother? (Must identify two.)

   Text-Based: His brother often teased him; he wouldn't acknowledge that Rick had helped him; Kent caused him to miss out on going fishing.

9. Should Kent have admitted that he wanted his brother to stay with him while he was sick?

   Critical Response: Yes—he should have been honest and accepted Rick's help; it is more mature to admit when you need help. No—he had to maintain his image as an older brother; he needed his brother to think he was tough; he didn't want his brother to think that he was weak.

_____10. Why did it take years for Rick and Kent to develop into friends?

Critical Response: Rick comes to realize that Kent's teasing was not meant to be a put-down; Kent might become more open and honest with his brother; he could reflect on what his brother had really done for him on this trip.

Comprehension Analysis:

   Text-Based: ___/4___
   Inference: ___/3___
   Critical Response: ___/3___

Total Comprehension %: _____

SEVENTH GRADE III: BROTHER'S LETTER

Reader's copy on p. 65 of the Reader's Passages

Introductory Statement: "Would you read this passage about two brothers and their grandfather (to yourself/ out loud). When you are finished, I'll take away the passage. Then I'll ask you to tell me about what you read and what you think of it. After that, I'll ask you some questions about the passage."

Story

It was close to midnight and Luke still wanted to talk. Chad waited patiently, knowing how much his little brother would miss him when he departed the next morning for hockey camp. Chad was a star athlete but Luke, in spite of all of his efforts, was an uncoordinated bookworm with no athletic prowess and few friends, and Chad was more than a little worried about him.

Although Gramps had died several years before his brother was born, Luke had always been fascinated by the stories that Chad told him, so Chad thought that perhaps a few tales of Gramps would distract him. "I really wish you had a chance to know Gramps," began Chad. "Gramps used to write stories and read them to me. His favorites were the ones where he would get inside someone's head and try to see things the way that other person would see them. He told me that if I could do that, it would help me in sports and he was right."

"I always wondered why Gramps didn't become a writer," said Luke.

"When he was in high school he liked writing stories but nobody paid much attention. He knew his family didn't have the money to send him to college so he just wrote for himself."

"Do you think you have lots of friends because you're good in sports?" asked Luke, catching Chad off guard. "No," Chad lied, "I have lots of friends because I try to be myself." "That doesn't work for me," replied Luke, as he began to drift off to sleep.

Early the following week, Chad received a letter from his brother and was overjoyed to hear that Luke had found a new friend. "My friend loves handball and I tried to play but I felt like a failure, and then I sort of did what Gramps said and I made up a story. But in the story I was my friend instead of me so I'd like you to read it and tell me what you think." Chad steeled himself for a lengthy bout of boredom, but he found himself pleasantly surprised. Luke was a very accomplished writer for his age, and he seemed to have the knack of being able to walk in the shoes of other people. Chad actually enjoyed the story immensely but even before he could respond, Chad received yet another story in the mail.

This story was about a great athlete who started out playing hockey but who tired of his old sport, started swimming, and ended up in the Olympics. Luke wrote, "I wrote this because I knew that you could do all of this if you wanted to." Chad was alternately mesmerized and horrified as he read. All of the character failings that Chad thought were so well hidden, like his inability to stick to one endeavor for any considerable period of time, came to life in his brother's story. But it was impossible for Chad not to recognize that he had also been painted with deep affection and admiration by a young artist.

Chad could not wait to write a letter; he had to talk to his brother. "Your stories were incredible," Chad blurted, "unbelievably good. I think you have what it takes to become a really great writer. I'm beginning to wonder who the lucky brother really is." (559 words)

Scoring Miscues for Oral Reading Option

Mark all scoreable miscues by placing either a plus (for those that maintain meaning) or a zero (for those that violate meaning) in the text margin.

Reading Accuracy Index: _____%

*Total all miscues marked with pluses **and** zeros and enter the corresponding percentage from the Miscue Chart.*

Meaning Maintenance Index: _____%

*Total **only** miscues marked with zeros and enter the corresponding percentage from the Miscue Chart.*

Miscue Chart (if used for oral reading)

Miscues	%	Miscues	%	Miscues	%	Miscues	%
1	100	17	97	33	94	49	91
2	100	18	97	34	94	50	91
3	99	19	97	35	94	51	91
4	99	20	96	36	94	52	91
5	99	21	96	37	93	53	91
6	99	22	96	38	93	54	90
7	99	23	96	39	93	55	90
8	99	24	96	40	93	56	90
9	98	25	96	41	93	57	90
10	98	26	95	42	92	58	90
11	98	27	95	43	92	59	89
12	98	28	95	44	92	60	89
13	98	29	95	45	92	61	89
14	97	30	95	46	92	62	89
15	97	31	94	47	92	63	89
16	97	32	94	48	91	64	89

Student Retelling

Examiner: "Tell me about what you just read and what you thought about it."

If there is no spontaneous response, repeat the request, "Tell me what you thought about the passage."

Note: Use the Retelling Rubric on p. 183 to assess the child's retelling performance. If you need additional space for retelling responses, use a separate sheet of paper.

RETELLING RUBRIC: NARRATIVE

Place a 0, 1/2, or + to score student responses. See page 80 for information on what these assessment measures mean.

Story Structure:

___ 1. **Key Characters and Setting:** Luke, his brother Chad, and their grandfather.

___ 2. **Character's Problem or Goal:** Chad is worried that Luke has no friends.

3. **Problem-Solving or Goal-Meeting Process:**

___ • Chad knows that Luke will miss him when he leaves the next day.

___ • Chad tells Luke stories of Gramps to distract him from his sadness.

___ • Chad tells how Gramps used to write stories by changing minds with another person.

___ • Luke writes that same kind of story and Chad finds it surprisingly good.

___ • Luke writes a second story about Chad and Chad realizes how much talent Luke has.

___ 4. **Personal Response:** Any well-supported positive or negative response to the characters or events in the story, or to the story as a whole.

Retelling Score: _____

Comprehension Questions

_____ 1. **Why was Luke awake for so long, talking to his brother?**

Text-Based: He knew that Chad would be leaving the next day; he was sad that his brother was leaving; he knew that he would miss his brother.

_____ 2. **Why was Chad worried about his younger brother?**

Text-Based: Luke had very little athletic ability and few friends.

3. **Why would Gramps think that getting inside another person's head could help a person in sports?**

   Inference: If you know what your opponent intends to do you can be ready for it; if you can predict what others will do, you can stay a step ahead.

4. **Why did Chad lie to his brother when Luke asked him if he thought he had friends because he was good in sports?**

   Inference: He knew that it was true but he did not want to discourage his brother; he didn't want his brother to believe that sports was the only way to popularity.

5. **Who benefited more from his knowledge of Gramps' life, Chad or Luke?**

   Critical Response: Chad—because he had learned to see things from another position in sports and had become very special; Chad had learned to love his grandfather's stories. Luke—because he was able to use his grandfather as a model and develop his writing skills.

6. **What was it about his stories that convinced Chad that Luke was a talented writer?**

   Text-Based: He could see character failings; he could write with great love about his characters; he could walk in the shoes of others.

7. **Do you think Chad followed his own advice when he told Luke the best way to make friends is to be yourself?**

   Inference: No because Chad tried to hide his real character from others.

8. **Why was Chad horrified to read his brother's second story?**

   Text-Based: The story included character flaws that Chad thought were not apparent.

9. **Which of the two characters in this story is more likely to become successful, Chad or Luke?**

   Critical Response: Chad—because he has skills that people already recognize; Chad because he has had experience being very successful and success often brings more success. Luke—because it is easier to become a writer than to be an athlete. Luke because he has insights into other people and can write about them; Chad has no perseverance.

_____10. Who do you think is really the luckier of the two brothers, Chad or Luke?

Critical Response: Luke—because he can walk in the shoes of others; Luke because he has more insight into people. Chad—because he is popular and not a nerd like his brother; Chad because he is a sports hero.

Comprehension Analysis:

Text-Based: _**/4**_
Inference: _**/3**_
Critical Response: _**/3**_

Total Comprehension %: _____

EIGHTH GRADE I: THE FRIEND

Reader's copy on p. 67 of the Reader's Passages

Introductory Statement: "Would you read this passage about a girl and her friend (to yourself/out loud). When you are finished, I'll take away the passage. Then I'll ask you to tell me about what you read and what you think of it. After that, I'll ask you some questions about the passage."

Story

Alex came home from the hair salon, put on her best party dress, and inspected her makeup. Tonight she would be dining at the most exclusive and expensive restaurant at the lake resort where her parents rented a cabin. While it was her old friend Victor, who had always had a crush on Alex, who had invited her to the dinner, it was Victor's visiting cousin Carlos that she was really interested in. The three of them had played tennis that afternoon and Alex couldn't wait to see the handsome and sophisticated Carlos again.

Alex had persuaded her father that she could handle the family's small motorboat by herself for the brief trip to the restaurant dock. After all, she drove the boat more than anyone else in the family did! Alex drove very slowly so that her hairdo would still be perfect when she arrived. Soon she pulled up to the dock in her tiny boat amid all of the expensive yachts and powerboats, and she was glad to see that Victor and Carlos were waiting for her. Both young men were dressed in their finest clothes, but Alex had eyes only for Carlos.

Alex turned the motor off and let the boat slowly drift closer to the dock, eager to display her boating skills. But as she stretched out with the rope to tie up the boat, she nearly lost her balance. Fortunately, she was able to grab and hold on to the end of the pier. To her horror, Alex realized that the boat was drifting further away from the dock with her feet clinging desperately to its rail.

Victor immediately jumped down to the lower dock to try to help, but he was too late. With a sickening splash, Alex fell headlong into the murky water next to the dock. Even though Alex was an excellent swimmer and certainly in no danger, swimming was the furthest thing from her mind. She was completely dismayed at the thought of having to face all of the people who had gathered at the dock watching her. They were all very polite and sympathetic; only Carlos could not hide his amusement. Victor tried to coax Alex toward his outstretched hand, but Alex preferred to stay in the water. With her dream evening completely ruined, Alex simply could not bear the thought of facing the rapidly growing crowd of people on the dock.

Suddenly Victor called, "Hold on, Alex! I'm coming to save you!" She watched in utter disbelief as Victor leaped into the water with a tremendous splash and surfaced next to her with a huge grin. Despite her distress, Alex couldn't help but smile and soon the two of them were hugging each other and laughing so hard that they couldn't stop. When Victor helped Alex from the water, somehow she didn't mind the crowd of now-smiling onlookers nearly as much as she thought she would. Victor whispered to her, "Let's go home and change and then we'll go out and get a pizza." During the boat ride back to her house, Alex watched her old friend laugh and shiver and joke about their experience, trying very successfully to cheer her up. Alex had to admit to herself that, despite the embarrassment, she had learned a great deal that night about true friends. (554 words)

Scoring Miscues for Oral Reading Option
Mark all scoreable miscues by placing either a plus (for those that maintain meaning) or a zero (for those that violate meaning) in the text margin.

Reading Accuracy Index: _____%
*Total all miscues marked with pluses **and** zeros and enter the corresponding percentage from the Miscue Chart.*

Meaning Maintenance Index: _____%
*Total **only** miscues marked with zeros and enter the corresponding percentage from the Miscue Chart.*

Miscue Chart (if used for oral reading)

Miscues	%	Miscues	%	Miscues	%	Miscues	%
1	100	17	97	33	94	49	91
2	100	18	97	34	94	50	91
3	99	19	97	35	94	51	91
4	99	20	96	36	94	52	91
5	99	21	96	37	93	53	90
6	99	22	96	38	93	54	90
7	99	23	96	39	93	55	90
8	99	24	96	40	93	56	90
9	98	25	95	41	93	57	90
10	98	26	95	42	92	58	90
11	98	27	95	43	92	59	89
12	98	28	95	44	92	60	89
13	98	29	95	45	92	61	89
14	97	30	95	46	92	62	89
15	97	31	94	47	92	63	89
16	97	32	94	48	91	64	88

Student Retelling

Examiner: "Tell me about what you just read and what you thought about it."

If there is no spontaneous response, repeat the request, "Tell me what you thought about the passage."

Note: Use the Retelling Rubric on p. 187 to assess the child's retelling performance. If you need additional space for retelling responses, use a separate sheet of paper.

RETELLING RUBRIC: NARRATIVE

Place a 0, 1/2, or + to score student responses. See page 80 for information on what these assessment measures mean.

Story Structure:

____ 1. **Key Characters and Setting:** Alex, her friend Victor, and his cousin Carlos at the lake.

____ 2. **Character's Problem or Goal:** Alex tries to impress Victor's cousin and embarrasses herself.

3. **Problem-Solving or Goal-Meeting Process:**

____ • Alex dresses up for dinner to impress Carlos.

____ • Alex takes the boat to the restaurant and falls into the water.

____ • She is embarrassed and does not want to face the crowd.

____ • Victor jumps into the water to ease her embarrassment.

____ • Alex realizes what a good friend she has in Victor.

____ 4. **Personal Response:** Any well-supported positive or negative response to the characters or events in the story, or to the story as a whole.

Retelling Score: _____

Comprehension Questions

_____ 1. Why did Alex want to impress Carlos instead of Victor?

Text-Based: Carlos was handsome and sophisticated.

_____ 2. How did the accident at the dock happen?

Text-Based: Alex lost her balance; she tried to tie up the boat but slipped into the water; she couldn't stay on the boat.

_____ 3. How did Victor demonstrate his friendship for Alex?

Inference: He cheered her up; made her feel less embarrassed; left the restaurant with her and took her home.

_____ 4. Why did Victor jump into the water?

Inference: His friend was embarrassed and he did it to relieve her embarrassment.

_____ 5. Does the saying "Beauty is only skin deep" apply to this story? Explain.

Critical Response: Alex had a good but less attractive friend in Victor; Carlos was attractive but not what she needed; Carlos was not what he seemed to be; good looks don't always mean good friends.

_____ 6. Why wasn't Alex's father afraid to let Alex take the boat alone to the restaurant?

Text-Based: She was experienced; she drove the boat more than anyone in the family did.

_____ 7. Why was Alex so surprised to see Victor jump into the water with her?

Inference: He was dressed in his best clothes; she didn't realize he was such a good friend.

_____ 8. Why was Alex so embarrassed when she fell into the water?

Text-Based: Many people were watching at the dock; Carlos laughed at her; she ruined her hair and clothes.

_____ 9. Do you think Alex will change her thinking about boyfriends as a result of this experience? Explain.

Critical Response: Yes—she will probably value her friendships more; may not choose her friends for superficial reasons in the future. No—friendship has little to do with choosing boyfriends; she thought about looks and sophistication when thinking about a boyfriend.

_____10. What did Alex learn about friendship that night?

Critical Response: It is about putting someone else first; making sacrifices for others; recognizing a friend's needs.

Comprehension Analysis:

Text-Based: __/4__
Inference: __/3__
Critical Response: __/3__

Total Comprehension %: _____

EIGHTH GRADE II: EXAGGERATION

Reader's copy on p. 69 of the Reader's Passages

Introductory Statement: "Would you read this passage about a girl who exaggerates (to yourself/out loud). When you are finished, I'll take away the passage. Then I'll ask you to tell me about what you read and what you think of it. After that, I'll ask you some questions about the passage."

Story

This was Becky's first trip to the principal's office, and the knot in the pit of her stomach was sending notice that perhaps she had gone too far this time. It had all started so innocently, with Becky bragging to Claire about what a remarkable detective she was. She had convinced herself that the mysterious boy who sat alone in the back of their bus was the person who had been breaking into local pharmacies. "After all, he never talks to anyone! And I heard that the thief has a scar in the middle of his forehead. The other day his cap slid up and I swear that right in the middle of his forehead was the scar. I know that's him!" she told Claire emphatically. How could she have known that Claire would regard it as her civic duty to report the matter to her parents, who had promptly notified the police? If only Claire had asked first, Becky could have told her that even the best of detectives is never totally sure.

Now Becky was in serious trouble and it was all because of Claire and her stupid civic duty! How could she have known that Claire's father was related to the police captain? "She has always been one to make much ado about nothing," thought Becky, the knots still twisting in her stomach.

The situation quickly went from bad to worse when Becky spotted the school counselor walking down the hall into the principal's office. Becky was convinced that the counselor despised her and the thought of having her present during the meeting with the principal made her blood run cold. Everyone knew that counselors could positively demolish your chances to get into college. "That's why a counselor shouldn't be taking such innocent conversation so seriously," thought Becky. She remembered their last meeting and the counselor's stern lecture. "Your gossiping nearly ruined the reputation of a very innocent person," the counselor had told Becky. Becky remembered thinking that a counselor, of all people, should know that kids always talk about other kids. "Why single me out?" Becky thought.

Finally Becky was called into the office, and was immediately dismayed to find that the counselor had been placed in charge of the meeting. Once again she chided Becky for carelessly ruining an innocent person's reputation. But the worst part was the seriousness of having the police investigate a student for criminal activity. The principal sat and silently watched Becky and then finally took over the meeting. At first it was the softness in the principal's voice that captured Becky's attention. Then it was the story she told of the young man whom Becky had accused that really hit home. The principal told of his struggles with depression. She spoke of the concern of his parents that because of his embarrassment with the rumors about him, he had become reluctant to even attend school. Becky fought back the tears as she began to realize how much her loose tongue may have hurt another person. And then suddenly it all became clear to her. How could these people expect her to know everything about everyone's life? She knew nothing about the boy she had accused. If she had, that would have been a very different story. Becky knew better than to reveal her anger openly, but she folded her arms and seethed inside at the unfairness of it all. (569 words)

Scoring Miscues for Oral Reading Option

Mark all scoreable miscues by placing either a plus (for those that maintain meaning) or a zero (for those that violate meaning) in the text margin.

Reading Accuracy Index: _____%

*Total all miscues marked with pluses **and** zeros and enter the corresponding percentage from the Miscue Chart.*

Meaning Maintenance Index: _____%

Total only miscues marked with zeros and enter the corresponding percentage from the Miscue Chart.

Miscue Chart (if used for oral reading)

Miscues	%	Miscues	%	Miscues	%	Miscues	%
1	100	17	97	33	94	49	91
2	100	18	97	34	94	50	91
3	99	19	97	35	94	51	91
4	99	20	96	36	94	52	91
5	99	21	96	37	93	53	91
6	99	22	96	38	93	54	91
7	99	23	96	39	93	55	90
8	99	24	96	40	93	56	90
9	98	25	96	41	93	57	90
10	98	26	95	42	93	58	90
11	98	27	95	43	92	59	90
12	98	28	95	44	92	60	89
13	98	29	95	45	92	61	89
14	98	30	95	46	92	62	89
15	97	31	95	47	92	63	89
16	97	32	94	48	92	64	89

Student Retelling

Examiner: "Tell me about what you just read and what you thought about it."

If there is no spontaneous response, repeat the request, "Tell me what you thought about the passage."

Note: Use the Retelling Rubric on p. 191 to assess the child's retelling performance. If you need additional space for retelling responses, use a separate sheet of paper.

RETELLING RUBRIC: NARRATIVE

Place a 0, 1/2, or + to score student responses. See page 80 for information on what these assessment measures mean.

Story Structure:

___ 1. **Key Characters and Setting:** Becky, her friend Claire, the boy, the counselor, and the principal in the principal's office.

___ 2. **Character's Problem or Goal:** Becky cannot admit that her gossiping is a problem.

3. **Problem-Solving or Goal-Meeting Process:**

___ • Becky is in trouble for accusing a boy of stealing.

___ • Becky tells herself that she is innocent and Claire is the real problem.

___ • The counselor comes to the principal's office and speaks sternly to Becky about her gossiping.

___ • The principal tells Becky about the young man's depression and Becky feels guilty.

___ • Becky becomes angry that people would expect her to know all about the lives of the people she may have hurt.

___ 4. **Personal Response:** Any well-supported positive or negative response to the characters or events in the story, or to the story as a whole.

Retelling Score: _____

Comprehension Questions

_____ 1. **Why did Becky accuse the young boy of being a thief?**

Text-Based: She claimed that she saw a scar on his forehead like the thief supposedly had.

_____ 2. **Why did Claire tell her parents about Becky's accusation?**
Text-Based: She thought that it was her civic duty; her father was related to the police captain.

_____ 3. In what way could the counselor have provided more effective help for Becky?

Inference: *The counselor could have been aware that her sternness with Becky was not working; she should have tried more conversation and fewer lectures.*

_____ 4. In what way were Becky and Claire similar?

Inference: *They both talked behind others' backs; both of them seemed rather impulsive.*

_____ 5. Do you think it is possible that Becky can be someone's good friend in the future? Explain.

Critical Response: *Yes—if she can see her role and responsibility, she might see the need to change. No—if she continues to blame others she will never see her need to change; she doesn't seem to have any idea of the needs of others.*

_____ 6. How did the boy that Becky accused respond to the gossip that was spread about him?

Text-Based: *He became more depressed and didn't want to attend school.*

_____ 7. Why did the principal decide to take over the meeting with Becky?

Inference: *She saw that the approach used by the counselor wasn't working; she thought that she might be able to connect with Becky since the counselor wasn't.*

_____ 8. What did the counselor see as Becky's primary flaw?

Text-Based: *She was a gossip who didn't feel sorry about hurting people.*

_____ 9. How does this story show the power of words?

Critical Response: *Words can be as destructive to people as weapons can be; once words are spoken they can't be taken back.*

_____10. Did Becky learn anything from this experience? Explain.

> *Critical Response: Yes—she realized that her gossip could get her into trouble; she learned not to say something to Claire that she didn't want repeated. No—she made excuses for all her behaviors; she tends to blame others for her problems.*

Comprehension Analysis:

Text-Based: _/4_
Inference: _/3_
Critical Response: _/3_

Total Comprehension %: ____

EIGHTH GRADE III: THE RODEO

Reader's copy on p. 71 of the Reader's Passages

Introductory Statement: "Would you read this passage about a girl and a rodeo (to yourself/out loud). When you are finished, I'll take away the passage. Then I'll ask you to tell me about what you read and what you think of it. After that, I'll ask you some questions about the passage."

Story

Rose sat by the window, unafraid despite the fact that she was flying to Montana alone for the first time. She had taken this flight with her family at least five times, but always their family vacation was over in two weeks. This time she would be spending the entire summer at her uncle's ranch and she could hardly contain her excitement. Rose couldn't wait to show the family how much her riding had improved, and in fact, she knew that she was finally good enough to compete in the rodeo held every year in late August.

She knew that her success in the rodeo would depend on the skills that she sharpened and her skills were now considerable. The hours of practice she had put in with handling a rope were bound to pay off. And although she had never practiced actually roping a steer, she was confident that the combination of her skill with a rope and her favorite horse, Streak, would make an unbeatable team. Rose closed her eyes and gleefully imagined her name being called as the top finisher in the calf roping competition. She especially savored the thought of beating her cousin Cindy.

Rose finally arrived at the ranch and when the interminable welcomes were finally over, she wasted no time running to the corral to see Streak. Rose was an expert in saddling and mounting a horse and she was convinced that before very long, she would be an expert in calf roping. But she was not prepared when

Cindy suggested that riding Streak in the calf roping contest might not be a good idea. She offered to let Rose ride her own horse, Lightning. But Rose brushed off the thought, insisting that Streak was the horse she was most familiar with, and Cindy quickly changed the subject.

Rose immediately began to practice roping real calves but she had much more difficulty than she expected. She could throw the rope around a calf's neck but she could not seem to control the calf after that. Still she resisted Cindy's suggestion. She decided not to share her frustration with anyone. After nearly two weeks of nonstop failure, Rose resolved to study very carefully the technique used by Cindy and Lightning. Almost immediately, she realized that as soon as Cindy threw the rope, Lightning stopped and backed up. This backing up was what kept the rope tight. Suddenly the light bulb went off in Rose's mind. Until that very moment she had been convinced that her success depended solely on her own skills, but suddenly she realized that even this sport was a team effort.

With only three weeks until rodeo night, Rose knew that she would not have enough time to learn to ride Lightning. On the day of the rodeo, she watched her cousin Cindy rope a calf in the quickest time and win the trophy for the Girls' Calf Roping Contest. She fought back her feelings of jealousy and consoled herself with the thought that she would be ready next year.

As she flew back home, Rose thought about the chances she had missed this summer with sadness. She forced herself to remember how funny the rodeo clowns had been. Suddenly, she realized that the only time the clowns were used was during the bull riding competition. Any rider who fell would need the clown to attract the attention of the bull and keep him safe from the bull's sharp horns. "There it is again," Rose thought, "teamwork." (585 words)

Scoring Miscues for Oral Reading Option

Mark all scoreable miscues by placing either a plus (for those that maintain meaning) or a zero (for those that violate meaning) in the text margin.

Reading Accuracy Index: _____%

*Total all miscues marked with pluses **and** zeros and enter the corresponding percentage from the Miscue Chart.*

Meaning Maintenance Index: _____%

*Total **only** miscues marked with zeros and enter the corresponding percentage from the Miscue Chart.*

Miscue Chart (if used for oral reading)

Miscues	%	Miscues	%	Miscues	%	Miscues	%
1	100	17	97	33	94	49	92
2	100	18	97	34	94	50	91
3	99	19	97	35	94	51	91
4	99	20	97	36	94	52	91
5	99	21	96	37	94	53	91
6	99	22	96	38	94	54	91
7	99	23	96	39	93	55	91
8	99	24	96	40	93	56	90
9	98	25	96	41	93	57	90
10	98	26	96	42	93	58	90
11	98	27	95	43	93	59	90
12	98	28	95	44	92	60	90
13	98	29	95	45	92	61	90
14	98	30	95	46	92	62	89
15	97	31	95	47	92	63	89
16	97	32	95	48	92	64	89

Student Retelling

Examiner: "Tell me about what you just read and what you thought about it."

If there is no spontaneous response, repeat the request, "Tell me what you thought about the passage."

Note: Use the Retelling Rubric on p. 195 to assess the child's retelling performance. If you need additional space for retelling responses, use a separate sheet of paper.

RETELLING RUBRIC: NARRATIVE

Place a 0, 1/2, or + to score student responses. See page 80 for information on what these assessment measures mean.

Story Structure:

___ 1. **Key Characters and Setting:** Rose and her cousin Cindy at a ranch in Montana.

___ 2. **Character's Problem or Goal:** Rose wants to win the calf roping contest at the rodeo.

    3. **Problem-Solving or Goal-Meeting Process:**

  ___ • Rose flies to the ranch and dreams of winning the calf roping competition.

  ___ • Rose refuses Cindy's offer to use her horse and doesn't listen to Cindy's advice.

  ___ • Rose learns that the horse is as important as the rider in calf roping.

  ___ • Cindy wins the calf roping competition.

  ___ • On her flight home Rose realizes that success comes from teamwork.

___ 4. **Personal Response:** Any well-supported positive or negative response to the characters or events in the story, or to the story as a whole.

Retelling Score: _____

Comprehension Questions

_____ 1. **What was different about this year's trip to Montana?**

Text-Based: Rose was going alone; she would be staying for the whole summer and not just for two weeks.

_____ 2. **Why did Rose expect to do so well in this year's calf roping competition?**

Text-Based: She had practiced roping and she had great skill riding a horse.

_____ 3. Why didn't Rose accept Cindy's advice?

Inference: She didn't realize how important the horse was; she thought that she could win without Cindy's help; she saw Cindy as her competition, not her friend.

_____ 4. How did Rose show that she had the motivation she needed to achieve her goals?

Inference: She practiced riding horses at her own home; she practiced throwing ropes even when she didn't have a calf; she will work all year so that when she comes back she can win the contest.

_____ 5. Use the information in the story to predict who will win the calf roping competition next year, Rose or Cindy.

Critical Response: Rose—because she is competitive; she is willing to work hard; she has learned what it will take to win. Cindy—because she is more knowledgeable; she doesn't put pressure on herself to win.

_____ 6. What difficulty with calf roping did Rose experience that surprised her?

Text-Based: She wasn't successful holding the calf after she had thrown the rope around its neck.

_____ 7. Why was Cindy's offer to let Rose use her horse such a generous offer?

Inference: If Rose had taken her horse, Cindy would not have had one to ride so Cindy would not have been able to be in the contest.

_____ 8. Why was Rose sad at the end of the summer?

Text-Based: She was sad because she had missed the chance to use the right horse and win the competition.

_____ 9. Who provided the more helpful lesson to Rose, Cindy or the clowns? Explain.

Critical Response: Cindy—since she was finally able to help Rose see that Cindy's horse knew how to work with the rider when Streak didn't. The clowns—since they were the ones who gave Rose the powerful lesson about the importance of teamwork.

_____10. What do you think Rose will value more next year, family or competition? Explain.

Critical Response: Family—she has learned that teamwork is important; she knows that her cousin Cindy will gladly help her. Competition—she will focus her attention on winning because she will remember that she failed.

Comprehension Analysis:

Text-Based: ___/4___
Inference: ___/3___
Critical Response: ___/3___

Total Comprehension %: _____

NINTH GRADE I: THE MAGICIAN

Reader's copy on p. 73 of the Reader's Passages

Introductory Statement: "Would you read this passage about a magician (to yourself/out loud). When you are finished, I'll take away the passage. Then I'll ask you to tell me about what you read and what you think of it. After that, I'll ask you some questions about the passage."

Story

Soon after the death of his father, the longstanding court magician to the Austrian king, Petruccio was named by the king to assume the post and to follow in his illustrious father's footsteps. As the magician, Petruccio would be one of the most important and trusted figures in the king's court, since the king would rely on him for advice ranging from the most trivial of decisions to essential matters of state. He would be expected to foretell future events by reading the stars and he was also supposed to ward off evil spirits who might bring harm to the kingdom.

Petruccio's father had loved his son dearly and sent him to the finest university in the world but his study of logic and science at the university left Petruccio ill-equipped to traffic in spirits and "read" the stars. He wanted nothing to do with the magic and superstition associated with the work that his father had done. How could he be expected to function as a court magician when he did not believe in what he was expected to do? Petruccio's worries and beliefs, however, mattered little to the court officials. The king needed a magician and there was no point in arguing with the king.

When he finally assumed the post of magician, Petruccio noticed danger and intrigue all around him. He was surrounded by men and women who were intensely jealous of the influence he had on the king.

They would be watching Petruccio closely to see if there were some way that they could supplant him as the king's advisor and closest confidant. To make matters worse, it was clear that the king expected the right advice from his magician, and Petruccio had no idea how to provide that advice. But the young man was a swift learner and he quickly realized that the best way to survive life in the king's court was to make the fewest predictions possible. He also developed the skill of taking credit for whatever good befell the kingdom. When the king asked him to predict future events, Petruccio would make predictions for which he had the best chance of being correct. Once the king asked Petruccio to predict whether his soon-to-be-born child would be male or female. Petruccio noted that the king already had four sons and only one daughter and so he correctly predicted the birth of a son. But after several years of good fortune, Petruccio's luck ran out. When the king's favorite aunt fell ill with the fever, Petruccio was asked to predict her fate. He observed that more people who had contracted the disease had died than who had survived. Thus he predicted that the aunt would die.

Petruccio was unfortunately correct, but he had not anticipated that the king would blame him for the death of his beloved aunt. Nor would he have any way of knowing that the king had begun to suspect that his "magician" was a fraud. Having resolved to behead his unlucky court magician, the king called Petruccio before him. On his way to the king's chambers, Petruccio noticed an unusually large number of the king's guards in the halls and even spotted the king's executioner outside the door. With an ironic smile, the king asked him to foretell the manner in which he, Petruccio, would die. But the quick-thinking young man sensed the danger and he said to the king, "Your Majesty, I will die exactly four weeks before you." The king was dumbfounded. He had begun to suspect that his young magician was deceiving him, but how could he risk beheading him now? After all, Petruccio had been right in his predictions many times before. So instead of ordering his execution, the king ordered his guard to place Petruccio under special protection. He even commanded that they take care to be sure that all of Petruccio's needs and desires were met. And so Petruccio lived for many years in comfort and luxury under the watchful care of his king. (667 words)

Scoring Miscues for Oral Reading Option
Mark all scoreable miscues by placing either a plus (for those that maintain meaning) or a zero (for those that violate meaning) in the text margin.

Reading Accuracy Index: _____%
*Total all miscues marked with pluses **and** zeros and enter the corresponding percentage from the Miscue Chart.*

Meaning Maintenance Index: _____%
*Total **only** miscues marked with zeros and enter the corresponding percentage from the Miscue Chart.*

Miscue Chart (if used for oral reading)

Miscues	%	Miscues	%	Miscues	%	Miscues	%
1	100	21	97	41	94	61	91
2	100	22	97	42	94	62	91
3	100	23	97	43	94	63	91
4	99	24	96	44	93	64	90
5	99	25	96	45	93	65	90
6	99	26	96	46	93	66	90
7	99	27	96	47	93	67	90
8	99	28	96	48	93	68	90
9	99	29	96	49	93	69	90
10	98	30	95	50	92	70	89
11	98	31	95	51	92	71	89
12	98	32	95	52	92	72	89
13	98	33	95	53	92	73	89
14	98	34	95	54	92	74	89
15	98	35	95	55	92	75	89
16	98	36	95	56	92	76	89
17	97	37	94	57	91	77	88
18	97	38	94	58	91	78	88
19	97	39	94	59	91	79	88
20	97	40	94	60	91	80	88

Student Retelling

Examiner: "Tell me about what you just read and what you thought about it."

If there is no spontaneous response, repeat the request, "Tell me what you thought about the passage."

Note: Use the Retelling Rubric on p. 199 to assess the child's retelling performance. If you need additional space for retelling responses, use a separate sheet of paper.

RETELLING RUBRIC: NARRATIVE

Place a 0, 1/2, or + to score student responses. See page 80 for information on what these assessment measures mean.

Story Structure:

____ 1. **Key Characters and Setting:** Petruccio (the court magician) and the king, in his kingdom.

____ 2. **Character's Problem or Goal:** Petruccio has to be smart enough to save his own life.

3. **Problem-Solving or Goal-Meeting Process:**

____ • Petruccio is named court magician but does not believe in magic.

____ • He learns to survive by outsmarting everyone.

____ • His luck runs out when the king's aunt dies.

____ • Petruccio outsmarts the king by telling him about his death.

____ • The king protects Petruccio for the rest of his life.

____ 4. **Personal Response:** Any well-supported positive or negative response to the characters or events in the story, or to the story as a whole.

Retelling Score: _____

Comprehension Questions

_____ 1. Why wasn't Petruccio well equipped to be a court magician?

Text-Based: He didn't believe in magic; his studies contradicted magic and superstition.

_____ 2. Why did the king plan to kill Petruccio?

Text-Based: He predicted that the king's favorite aunt would die; the king blamed him for his aunt's death.

_____ 3. Why didn't Petruccio just predict that the king's aunt would live?

Inference: If she died, he would risk being found out; the king may be even angrier; the odds were against it; the king may not trust his predictions anymore.

_____ 4. Do you think that the king had studied science and logic? Explain.

Inference: No—he believed in the superstitions.

_____ 5. Do you think that Petruccio survived mainly because of luck or because of his learning? Explain.

Critical Response: Luck—he had to have some luck even when he made solid predictions. His learning—it enabled him to make better decisions and to save his life in the end.

_____ 6. Why did making fewer predictions increase the magician's chances for survival?

Text-Based: If you don't predict, you can't be wrong.

_____ 7. If the king didn't trust Petruccio anymore, why did he believe in Petruccio's prediction about his own death?

Inference: Probably felt he couldn't take the risk that Petruccio was right this time; too much at stake.

_____ 8. What made Petruccio predict that the king would die four weeks after he did?

Text-Based: Sensed danger; noticed that the king was angry.

_____ 9. Who do you think was more powerful in the kingdom, the king or Petruccio? Why?

Critical Response: Petruccio—he was able to control the king by outsmarting him. The king—he really had power over life and death.

_____10. Do you think that Petruccio's father had prepared him well to be successful in life? Explain.

Critical Response: Yes—he gave him the best education available; he knew that the ability to think clearly would work to his advantage. No—he did not prepare him to become the court magician; did not tell his son what might be expected of him; did not tell him what the king was like.

Comprehension Analysis:

Text-Based: ___/4___
Inference: ___/3___
Critical Response: ___/3___

Total Comprehension %: _____

Reader's copy on p. 75 of the Reader's Passages

Introductory Statement: "Would you read this passage about a girl and her mom (to yourself/out loud). When you are finished, I'll take away the passage. Then I'll ask you to tell me about what you read and what you think of it. After that, I'll ask you some questions about the passage."

Story

Jane smiled when she remembered how foolish she had been to feel apprehensive about high school. She loved everything about it, and best of all, she had been singled out by the most popular girls in the school as a potential initiate in their group. One day Jane was walking through the halls with her fashionable friends, flaunting her new-found popularity, almost sensing the envy of the other girls, when she made her initial social blunder. Spotting her older brother Bruce in the hall heading toward the Special Education classroom, she broke into an enormous smile and waved eagerly to him. When Bruce returned her smile and waved back, one of Jane's companions inquired, "Who's the retarded guy?" Jane was baffled with her own response, as she reddened with embarrassment and heard herself respond in barely a whisper, "That's my brother."

Over the next few weeks, Jane had to face the most serious dilemma of her high school career. It was part of the family legend that Jane's parents would never consent, despite his Down syndrome, to an education that included lower expectations. They were convinced that Bruce could learn to read and write and Bruce, with his own internal sense of pride and with his work ethic, had surpassed even their wildest expectations. When he had turned sixteen and obtained a part-time job at a local pharmacy, an outsider might have thought that he had been elected president. But now Jane was having a troublesome time maintaining that sense of family pride.

She even found, to her horror, that she was pretending to be preoccupied when Bruce waved or hurrying off under any pretext when he stopped to talk to her. Jane couldn't even muster the courage to share her problem with her parents.

And then the situation went from bad to worse with Bruce's dinner announcement that he had won a speaking part in the school's play. Jane could visualize the entire scenario, with Bruce, his name on the program, for all of her friends to gawk at. For Jane, high school had become no longer an exciting but a dreadful place, and the worst part of all was her guilt.

Finally Jane could stand it no longer and, gathering her resolve, spilled the details of her situation to her mother. She asked her to think of some reason that Bruce could not appear in the play, positive that she would understand, but disappointed that the only assurance that her mother would furnish was "Let me see what I can do."

The following week, Jane was annoyed at her mother's insistent invitation to have dinner with her old friend from high school. "I invited her just so that you could meet her," she retorted, when Jane protested about the impending evening of boredom. The evening turned out to be anything but boring.

Mother greeted her guest warmly and then sat in silence as her friend launched into a morbid monologue about being fired from several jobs, blaming everyone from her bosses to her fellow workers, when it was clear to Jane that her insensitivity was the primary cause of her own problems. Then she shifted to her string of three failed marriages, claiming that her life was so hectic that she regrettably had little time to spend with her children. The remainder of the evening consisted largely of more of the same.

When the evening was over, her mother confided to Jane, "You have no idea how hard I tried in school to make sure that girl became my friend. Sometimes I even ignored my own family. Trying to impress her, I hurt the people who stood by me throughout my entire life. I wish I knew then what I know now!"

That night it was guilt and remorse that led Jane to her mother. "Mom," said Jane, "you invited her so I could see and I really did. I wish I had never asked you to keep Bruce out of the play." "I've forgotten it already," she said with the biggest of smiles. "Sometimes our best learning comes from our greatest sorrows." (685 words)

Scoring Miscues for Oral Reading Option
Mark all scoreable miscues by placing either a plus (for those that maintain meaning) or a zero (for those that violate meaning) in the text margin.

Reading Accuracy Index: _____%
*Total all miscues marked with pluses **and** zeros and enter the corresponding percentage from the Miscue Chart.*

Meaning Maintenance Index: _____%
*Total **only** miscues marked with zeros and enter the corresponding percentage from the Miscue Chart.*

Miscue Chart (if used for oral reading)

Miscues	%	Miscues	%	Miscues	%	Miscues	%
1	100	21	97	41	94	61	91
2	100	22	97	42	94	62	91
3	100	23	97	43	94	63	91
4	99	24	96	44	94	64	91
5	99	25	96	45	93	65	91
6	99	26	96	46	93	66	90
7	99	27	96	47	93	67	90
8	99	28	96	48	93	68	90
9	99	29	96	49	93	69	90
10	99	30	96	50	93	70	90
11	98	31	95	51	93	71	90
12	98	32	95	52	92	72	89
13	98	33	95	53	92	73	89
14	98	34	95	54	92	74	89
15	98	35	95	55	92	75	89
16	98	36	95	56	92	76	89
17	98	37	95	57	92	77	89
18	97	38	94	58	92	78	89
19	97	39	94	59	91	79	88
20	97	40	94	60	91	80	88

Student Retelling

Examiner: "Tell me about what you just read and what you thought about it."

If there is no spontaneous response, repeat the request, "Tell me what you thought about the passage."

Note: Use the Retelling Rubric on p. 203 to assess the child's retelling performance. If you need additional space for retelling responses, use a separate sheet of paper.

RETELLING RUBRIC: NARRATIVE

Place a 0, 1/2, or + to score student responses. See page 80 for information on what these assessment measures mean.

Story Structure:

___ 1. **Key Characters and Setting:** Jane, her brother Bruce, Jane's friends, and Jane's mother.

___ 2. **Character's Problem or Goal:** Jane becomes embarrassed with her brother when she tries to be part of the popular crowd.

3. **Problem-Solving or Goal-Meeting Process:**

___ • Jane's popularity makes her happy with high school.

___ • Jane is embarrassed with her brother's disability.

___ • Jane learns that Bruce has a part in the school play and she asks her mother to keep him out of the play.

___ • Jane meets her mother's old friend and learns that her mother regrets valuing her friend's approval more than her own family's.

___ • Jane recognizes that she was wrong to be embarrassed with her brother.

___ 4. **Personal Response:** Any well-supported positive or negative response to the characters or events in the story, or to the story as a whole.

Retelling Score: _____

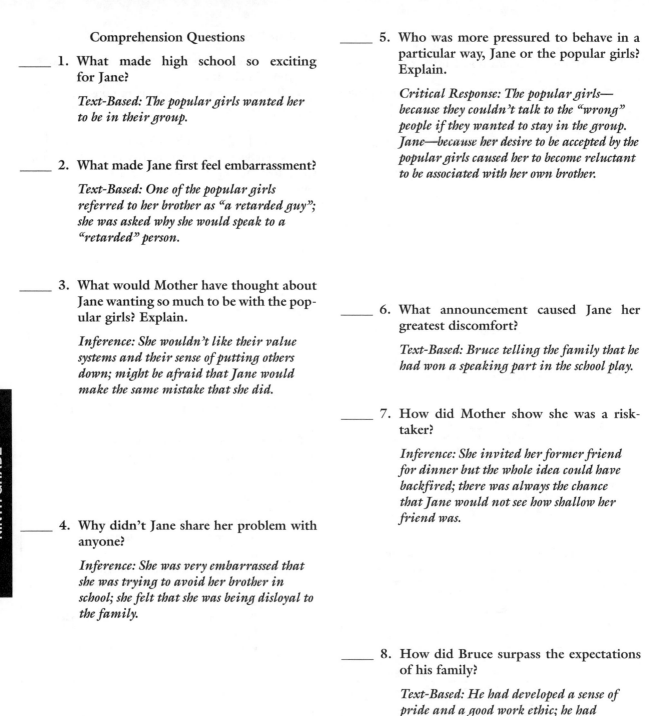

Comprehension Questions

_____ 1. What made high school so exciting for Jane?

Text-Based: The popular girls wanted her to be in their group.

_____ 2. What made Jane first feel embarrassment?

Text-Based: One of the popular girls referred to her brother as "a retarded guy"; she was asked why she would speak to a "retarded" person.

_____ 3. What would Mother have thought about Jane wanting so much to be with the popular girls? Explain.

Inference: She wouldn't like their value systems and their sense of putting others down; might be afraid that Jane would make the same mistake that she did.

_____ 4. Why didn't Jane share her problem with anyone?

Inference: She was very embarrassed that she was trying to avoid her brother in school; she felt that she was being disloyal to the family.

_____ 5. Who was more pressured to behave in a particular way, Jane or the popular girls? Explain.

Critical Response: The popular girls— because they couldn't talk to the "wrong" people if they wanted to stay in the group. Jane—because her desire to be accepted by the popular girls caused her to become reluctant to be associated with her own brother.

_____ 6. What announcement caused Jane her greatest discomfort?

Text-Based: Bruce telling the family that he had won a speaking part in the school play.

_____ 7. How did Mother show she was a risk-taker?

Inference: She invited her former friend for dinner but the whole idea could have backfired; there was always the chance that Jane would not see how shallow her friend was.

_____ 8. How did Bruce surpass the expectations of his family?

Text-Based: He had developed a sense of pride and a good work ethic; he had learned to read.

_____ 9. Are there more similarities or differences between Jane and her mother as a teenager? Explain.

Critical Response: Similarities in that they both wanted to be accepted by others; they both hurt family members. Differences in that Jane had become embarrassed with someone she loved; Jane probably will not do what her mother did in trying to win her friend's approval.

Comprehension Analysis:

Text-Based: __/4__
Inference: __/3__
Critical Response: __/3__

Total Comprehension %: ____

_____10. How does this story explain the saying "Experience is the best teacher"?

Critical Response: Jane's experience with her mother's friend was far more meaningful than stories her mother could have shared.

NINTH GRADE III: THE AWARD CEREMONY

Reader's copy on p. 77 of the Reader's Passages

Introductory Statement: "Would you read this passage about two brothers (to yourself/out loud). When you are finished, I'll take away the passage. Then I'll ask you to tell me about what you read and what you think of it. After that, I'll ask you some questions about the passage."

Story

Fred could never admit to anyone the mixed feelings that he experienced at the approach of the school's Sports Awards Banquet. His younger brother Mike was about to become the school's only freshman ever named as varsity football Player of the Year. Fred vividly remembered the moment when the head football coach shared with him, in confidence, that Mike would receive the award. With his arm around Fred, the coach whispered, "A lot of people will give me credit for bringing a freshman along so quickly, but I know that you've always been his true coach."

As Fred waited for the ceremony to start, he surmised that he would receive the Outstanding Bowler Award. Fred recalled his first encounters with competitive bowling. He was a freshman as well, about to take his own place on the varsity football team when he was diagnosed with scoliosis, a curvature of the spine. Fred's mother had noticed that his clothes were not fitting him properly and she began to worry. Fred brushed off her concerns but the family doctor did not. Then came the round of diagnostic tests and the report that, while he had a mild case, it could worsen if Fred continued playing the sport that he loved. Fred alternated between bouts of self-pity and feelings of resentment that his younger brother could still play. Fred felt guilty that his father wasn't comfortable sharing his enthusiasm about

Mike's success, fearing an affront to Fred, but he still couldn't help himself. Finally, he accepted his father's advice and found a sport that was less risky than football. That was the beginning of his involvement with bowling.

Despite Fred's own disappointment, there was always something about his younger brother's spirit that fueled Fred's desire to mentor him. As he watched Mike play, he could envision himself ready to throw, locating the open receiver, and faking out his opponent. And Mike was the perfect student, always open to any suggestion, soaking up Fred's athletic know-how like a sponge. But it wasn't until Fred had confronted his medical condition and accepted bowling as his sport that he and his brother had become the perfect team. It had all really boiled down to two qualities: Fred's acceptance of his circumstances and his willingness to take a risk. Of course Fred knew that success in bowling would never even approximate the rewards of success in football. But at least now his father could be comfortable enough to openly enjoy his younger son's success.

The football coach was the first to be invited to the microphone and he began by reciting Mike's statistics, pointing out that his success had far surpassed that of any freshman in the history of the school. Then Fred groaned inwardly when Mike was called upon to make an acceptance speech. If they did the same thing for everyone, the banquet would go on all night.

When Mike appeared on stage, he began by saying, "I am really only half-owner of this award," looking directly at Fred as he spoke. "It was my body that was running plays, but it was my brother that my brain was listening to and I never would have had that knowledge without Fred. I asked Coach if his name could be added to this award. I'd like to introduce you to the other Player of the Year, my big brother Fred." As he finished speaking, Mike motioned for Fred to join him at the podium.

Fred was truly dumbfounded by what had just happened but as he stood with his brother's arm around him and looked out at the cheering crowd, he saw something that stunned him even more. He had never once seen his father cry but there he stood, unashamed, with tears streaming down his cheeks. Fred could see his father's pride written all over him and Fred was simply grateful that he had the good fortune or the good sense just for once to put someone else first in his life. (666 words)

Scoring Miscues for Oral Reading Option
Mark all scoreable miscues by placing either a plus (for those that maintain meaning) or a zero (for those that violate meaning) in the text margin.

Reading Accuracy Index: _____ %
*Total all miscues marked with pluses **and** zeros and enter the corresponding percentage from the Miscue Chart.*

Meaning Maintenance Index: _____ %
*Total **only** miscues marked with zeros and enter the corresponding percentage from the Miscue Chart.*

Miscue Chart (if used for oral reading)

Miscues	%	Miscues	%	Miscues	%	Miscues	%
1	100	21	97	41	94	61	91
2	100	22	97	42	94	62	91
3	100	23	97	43	94	63	91
4	99	24	96	44	93	64	90
5	99	25	96	45	93	65	90
6	99	26	96	46	93	66	90
7	99	27	96	47	93	67	90
8	99	28	96	48	93	68	90
9	99	29	96	49	93	69	90
10	98	30	95	50	92	70	89
11	98	31	95	51	92	71	89
12	98	32	95	52	92	72	89
13	98	33	95	53	92	73	89
14	98	34	95	54	92	74	89
15	98	35	95	55	92	75	89
16	98	36	95	56	92	76	89
17	97	37	94	57	91	77	88
18	97	38	94	58	91	78	88
19	97	39	94	59	91	79	88
20	97	40	94	60	91	80	88

Student Retelling

Examiner: "Tell me about what you just read and what you thought about it."

If there is no spontaneous response, repeat the request, "Tell me what you thought about the passage."

Note: Use the Retelling Rubric on p. 207 to assess the child's retelling performance. If you need additional space for retelling responses, use a separate sheet of paper.

RETELLING RUBRIC: NARRATIVE

Place a 0, 1/2, or + to score student responses. See page 80 for information on what these assessment measures mean.

Story Structure:

___ 1. **Key Characters and Setting:** Fred, Mike, their father, and the football coach at the Awards Banquet.

___ 2. **Character's Problem or Goal:** Fred struggles to come to grips with his disappointment.

3. **Problem-Solving or Goal-Meeting Process:**

___ • Fred has mixed feelings about his brother's football success because he can no longer play himself.

___ • Fred accepts his father's advice and takes up competitive bowling.

___ • Fred teaches Mike all that he knows about football.

___ • Mike recognizes his brother's contributions at the Awards Banquet.

___ • Fred sees his father crying and is grateful that he was able to put someone else first in his life.

___ 4. **Personal Response:** Any well-supported positive or negative response to the characters or events in the story, or to the story as a whole.

Retelling Score: _____

Comprehension Questions

_____ 1. How were Fred and Mike similar?

Text-Based: They were both good athletes who made the varsity team in their freshmen year; they both loved football.

_____ 2. Why was scoliosis such a serious illness for Fred?

Text-Based: He had to give up football.

_____ 3. Why couldn't his father share with Fred his enthusiasm about Mike's football success?

Inference: He was afraid of reminding Fred that he couldn't play; didn't want to trigger resentment in Fred for his brother's good fortunes.

_____ 4. Why would it be difficult for Fred to admit that he had mixed feelings about Mike's success?

Inference: He didn't want to be viewed as jealous; Mike was having the chance to do all the things that had been taken away from him; Mike was a member of his family.

_____ 5. Who was the person Fred had put first in his life, Mike or his father? Explain.

Critical Response: Mike—because Fred used all his skills and insights to become Mike's teacher. His father—because Fred allowed him to enjoy Mike's success.

_____ 6. How do you know that Fred was successful at his new sport of bowling?

Text-Based: He expected to win the award for bowling.

_____ 7. What made Fred the perfect coach for Mike?

Inference: He could visualize what he would have done and because he had earned Mike's trust, Mike could trust Fred's judgment.

_____ 8. Why was Fred so surprised to see his father cry at the sports banquet?

Text-Based: He had never seen him cry before.

_____ 9. Which of the brothers do you think will be more successful in life, Mike or Fred? Explain.

Critical Response: Fred—because he has shown that he had adjusted to a very difficult situation. Mike—because he was very open and teachable; he has learned to trust the judgment of others.

_____10. Who had to develop greater inner strength, Fred or his father? Explain.

Critical Response: Fred—because he had to deal with his illness and accept an alternative way. His father—because he had to deal with the heartbreak of seeing his son lose something that he loved; his father had to be firm in giving advice to his son when he was in this difficult situation.

Comprehension Analysis:

Text-Based: ___/4___
Inference: ___/3___
Critical Response: ___/3___

Total Comprehension %: _____

TENTH GRADE I: TUTOR OF THE YEAR

Reader's copy on p. 79 of the Reader's Passages

Introductory Statement: "Would you read this passage about a girl who was a tutor (to yourself/out loud). When you are finished, I'll take away the passage. Then I'll ask you to tell me about what you read and what you think of it. After that, I'll ask you some questions about the passage."

Story

Chet was startled to see Lori biking up his driveway calling, "Get your bike, lazy one, cause you're not the only one who needs exercise." Chet wondered where in the world she had found such a ramshackle second-hand bike. Just a few weeks ago she had given her new bike to a neighborhood family who had come on hard times. Lori was Chet's best friend, and he sometimes recalled with relief the fact that in elementary school he had been confident enough to ignore the teasing of his friends about his supposed "girlfriend." Now his friends agreed, even if sometimes grudgingly, that her wit and contagious laugh simply made her easy to be with.

"I thought that you would be practicing your roller blading today," Chet said as they started down the bike path. "No, I needed a change and besides I thought I'd put my energies into mountain biking," replied Lori. Lori told herself that the fact that Chet could not skate but was an avid biker had nothing to do with the matter, but in reality, she had already decided that biking would be more fun than blading if she could spend that time with Chet.

In fact, when Chet made the varsity basketball team last semester, Lori was left with a great deal of time on her hands. She had always excelled in mathematics and so she volunteered to work with younger students who were having difficulty in geometry and trigonometry. Chet still remembered that excited phone call, with Lori talking nonstop about how much she had helped the student she worked with, the one whom everyone else regarded as a trouble-maker. He couldn't help but remember the day the following year when Lori was honored as the school's Tutor of the Year.

Several days after their afternoon bike ride, Chet appeared in Lori's driveway carrying a pair of second-hand roller blades in an old case. "Turnaround is fair play," he called and then he shouted, "Grab your blades and let's go!" Lori, her mouth wide open, finally blurted out, "You don't even know how to ice skate." "Yes, but don't forget, my friend is the tutor of the year and she'll be able to teach me everything I need to know."

Lori knew that Chet had excelled at any sport he had ever tried, so she was not surprised at his confidence as he strapped on his skates and stood in the deserted parking lot where Lori practiced. But when Chet asked "What do I do now?" Lori looked stunned and replied, "You just kind of move your feet." "Can't you do a little better than that?" he asked, obviously surprised that Lori could not describe the mechanics of skating. An obviously embarrassed Lori quickly scanned the parking lot and finally suggested, "Why don't you just face downhill over there and I'm sure that will get you moving." Lori was right, but she couldn't explain to Chet how to stop either, so Chet spent a good deal of time that afternoon hugging the pavement. Needless to say, he spent even more time teasing Lori about her lack of teaching techniques.

Despite the rocky start, Chet was determined to master roller blading but, as luck would have it, Lori cut her ankle badly on a sharp rock while mountain biking with Chet. She had to avoid the strain of the roller blade boot for three weeks. And while Chet vistited his friend often, he also was determined that he would spend at least an hour each day practicing his roller blading. When Lori's foot had finally healed, Chet coaxed her into an afternoon of roller blading under the pretext that he needed more instruction and practice. He relished the moment as he literally skated circles around his former tutor, having far surpassed her in skill and speed in just three weeks. Lori stood with her jaw wide open, and then grinned at her friend, partly in admiration, partly in envy, and, she had to admit, partly in annoyance as well. (673)

Scoring Miscues for Oral Reading Option
Mark all scoreable miscues by placing either a plus (for those that maintain meaning) or a zero (for those that violate meaning) in the text margin.

Reading Accuracy Index: _____%
*Total all miscues marked with pluses **and** zeros and enter the corresponding percentage from the Miscue Chart.*

Meaning Maintenance Index: _____%
*Total **only** miscues marked with zeros and enter the corresponding percentage from the Miscue Chart.*

Miscue Chart (if used for oral reading)

Miscues	%	Miscues	%	Miscues	%	Miscues	%
1	100	21	97	41	94	61	91
2	100	22	97	42	94	62	91
3	100	23	97	43	94	63	91
4	99	24	96	44	93	64	91
5	99	25	96	45	93	65	90
6	99	26	96	46	93	66	90
7	99	27	96	47	93	67	90
8	99	28	96	48	93	68	90
9	99	29	96	49	93	69	90
10	99	30	96	50	93	70	90
11	98	31	95	51	92	71	89
12	98	32	95	52	92	72	89
13	98	33	95	53	92	73	89
14	98	34	95	54	92	74	89
15	98	35	95	55	92	75	89
16	98	36	95	56	92	76	89
17	97	37	95	57	92	77	89
18	97	38	94	58	92	78	89
19	97	39	94	59	91	79	88
20	97	40	94	60	91	80	88

Student Retelling

Examiner: "Tell me about what you just read and what you thought about it."

If there is no spontaneous response, repeat the request, "Tell me what you thought about the passage."

Note: Use the Retelling Rubric on p. 211 to assess the child's retelling performance. If you need additional space for retelling responses, use a separate sheet of paper.

RETELLING RUBRIC: NARRATIVE

Place a 0, 1/2, or + to score student responses. See page 80 for information on what these assessment measures mean.

Story Structure:

___ 1. **Key Characters and Setting:** Chet and Lori.
___ 2. **Character's Problem or Goal:** Chet wants Lori to teach him to roller blade.
   3. **Problem-Solving or Goal-Meeting Process:**
   ___ • Lori decides to take up bicycling so that she can be with her friend.
   ___ • Chet decides that since Lori is biking with him, he will learn to roller blade with her.
   ___ • Chet is confident that a teacher like Lori can help him learn, but Lori has no idea how to teach someone to roller blade.
   ___ • Lori is hurt and unable to skate.
   ___ • Chet practices his skating and far surpasses his friend in skating ability in a short time.
___ 4. **Personal Response:** Any well-supported positive or negative response to the characters or events in the story, or to the story as a whole.

Retelling Score: _____

Comprehension Questions

_____ 1. Why did Lori decide to take up biking and put aside her roller blading?

Text-Based: She wanted to spend more time with Chet.

_____ 2. Why was Lori riding a secondhand bike when she went to meet Chet?

Text-Based: She had given away her new bike to a family having a hard time.

_____ 3. Why was Chet able to ignore the pressure of his friends and continue his friendship with Lori?

Inference: As an athlete he had developed a lot of confidence; he found that Lori's humor and friendship was too valuable; he didn't pay attention to the teasing.

_____ 4. Why couldn't Lori be more effective in teaching Chet how to roller blade?

Inference: She didn't really have a great deal of skill herself; she didn't really have to think about what she was doing.

_____ 5. Who found greater joy in a challenge, Lori or Chet? Explain.

Critical Response: Lori—because she tutored a young child who was considered to be a trouble maker and had been very successful. Chet—because he was willing to persevere and conquer roller blading after he initially had difficulty.

_____ 6. Why was Chet confident that he would be able to learn roller blading very easily?

Text-Based: He expected that Lori would be able to be a great teacher for him; he had been successful developing athletic skills.

_____ 7. Why would Lori be annoyed that Chet had become so good at roller blading?

Inference: She was clearly better than he was in the beginning but then she saw him outperform her; he didn't have to work as hard as she did to master skating; he was a natural athlete.

_____ 8. Why did Chet really want Lori to go roller blading with him after she recovered?

Text-Based: He wanted to show her that he could now skate better than she could.

_____ 9. Which trait is likely to lead to personal success, Lori's unselfishness or Chet's confidence and athletic skills? Explain.

Critical Response: Lori's unselfishness— because it made her a success at tutoring. Chet's confidence—because his confidence and past success enabled him to have high expectations.

_____10. Who was more disciplined in life, Chet or Lori? Explain.

Critical Response: Lori—she demonstrated the discipline needed for academic success and to learn something that was for her; her discipline enabled her to give up a new bike so that she could live her value system. Chet—because he had maintained a friendship even in the face of peer pressure; he had to use discipline for his athletic success.

Comprehension Analysis:

Text-Based: __/4__
Inference: __/3__
Critical Response: __/3__

Total Comprehension %: ____

NARRATIVE PASSAGES
TENTH GRADE

TENTH GRADE II: THE HERO

Reader's copy on p. 81 of the Reader's Passages

Introductory Statement: "Would you read this passage about a hero (to yourself/out loud). When you are finished, I'll take away the passage. Then I'll ask you to tell me about what you read and what you think of it. After that, I'll ask you some questions about the passage."

Story

Even though nearly three years had passed, Chuck could still feel the pain of his father's disappointment. How could he forget the years that his parents scrimped and worked to send Chuck to the best private school on the island, convinced that a good education would get him into law school in the States? Chuck's father wanted him to become a lawyer, not for the money, but for the chance to return to the island and work to improve the lives of the islanders. When Chuck had dropped out of law school and accepted a position as deputy for freight operations at the island's port facility, his father was devastated and the strain in their relationship had lasted until this very day.

But as painful as these thoughts still were, Chuck almost welcomed them on this day, for they at least took his mind off his most immediate and pressing problem: what to do about Dan. Chuck was the captain of the small but powerful tugboat that guided all military, freight, and vacation cruises into the island. For several weeks he had observed his old school friend, locked in frequent animated conversation at a dockside bar with a particularly unsavory freight hauler, and Chuck couldn't help but become suspicious.

Once his curiosity had been piqued Chuck decided to investigate further, and how he regretted that decision. It was never so much the fact that his investigation brought him into danger for his life, but it was the fact that Dan seemed to be involved up to his ears in a local drug smuggling and distribution ring. Now, as he waited for Ed to arrive at the restaurant for their weekly breakfast, Chuck was both brokenhearted and terribly torn. After all, Chuck couldn't forget that he, Ed, and Dan had been inseparable friends throughout their youth, at least until Chuck had begun to attend his private school.

Finally Ed arrived, resplendent in his dress uniform and armed with his familiar smile. Even though Ed had received the Coast Guard appointment that Chuck had coveted, he could never bring himself to resent his old friend. Ed's smile soon disappeared as Chuck outlined the evidence that he had gathered, and when he had finished, Chuck was deeply surprised that Ed did not hesitate for even an instant. Ed intended to immediately turn in all the evidence to the local authorities. Of course, Chuck knew that the evidence could not be suppressed, and although he was relieved that it would not have to be him that did it, he was also surprised that Ed seemed to have no misgivings about turning in Dan. He had some inkling of the situation when he heard Ed whisper to himself, "Wait till you see what this does for my career!"

In the weeks that followed, Ed became a local hero, his picture plastered all over the island's newspaper. Each time it was Ed who was credited with the removal of millions of dollars of drugs from the local streets of the island. And even though no one seemed to realize that it was Chuck who had unearthed the only significant evidence in the case, Chuck couldn't bring himself to resent that fact. After all, no one could know that he was the one who had turned in an old friend.

The following week, Chuck answered the knock on his apartment door and was stunned to see his father standing in the hall. "If you have the time, I'd like us to have lunch together at our old restaurant," he said. "For you, Dad, I always have the time," Chuck responded with a broad smile. At the restaurant, his father told how he had learned of Chuck's role in breaking up the smuggling ring. "I always wanted you to help the people of this island to have a better life," said Chuck's father, "but I realize that I wanted that to happen on my terms, and not yours. I'm both proud of you and sorry for the way that I've behaved." "Forget it, Dad. It's just great to have you back again." (685 words)

Scoring Miscues for Oral Reading Option
Mark all scoreable miscues by placing either a plus (for those that maintain meaning) or a zero (for those that violate meaning) in the text margin.

Reading Accuracy Index: _____%
*Total all miscues marked with pluses **and** zeros and enter the corresponding percentage from the Miscue Chart.*

Meaning Maintenance Index: _____%
*Total **only** miscues marked with zeros and enter the corresponding percentage from the Miscue Chart.*

Miscue Chart (if used for oral reading)

Miscues	%	Miscues	%	Miscues	%	Miscues	%
1	100	21	97	41	94	61	91
2	100	22	97	42	94	62	91
3	100	23	97	43	94	63	91
4	99	24	96	44	94	64	91
5	99	25	96	45	93	65	91
6	99	26	96	46	93	66	90
7	99	27	96	47	93	67	90
8	99	28	96	48	93	68	90
9	99	29	96	49	93	69	90
10	99	30	96	50	93	70	90
11	98	31	95	51	93	71	90
12	98	32	95	52	92	72	89
13	98	33	95	53	92	73	89
14	98	34	95	54	92	74	89
15	98	35	95	55	92	75	89
16	98	36	95	56	92	76	89
17	98	37	95	57	92	77	89
18	97	38	94	58	92	78	89
19	97	39	94	59	91	79	88
20	97	40	94	60	91	80	88

Student Retelling

Examiner: "Tell me about what you just read and what you thought about it."

If there is no spontaneous response, repeat the request, "Tell me what you thought about the passage."

Note: Use the Retelling Rubric on p. 215 to assess the child's retelling performance. If you need additional space for retelling responses, use a separate sheet of paper.

RETELLING RUBRIC: NARRATIVE

Place a 0, 1/2, or + to score student responses. See page 80 for information on what these assessment measures mean.

Story Structure:

___ 1. **Key Characters and Setting:** Chuck, his father, his friends Ed and Dan.

___ 2. **Character's Problem or Goal:** Chuck agonizes over having to report his former friend.

3. **Problem-Solving or Goal-Meeting Process:**

___ • Chuck knows that he disappointed his father by not becoming a lawyer.

___ • Chuck sees a former friend involved in smuggling drugs.

___ • Chuck contacts their mutual friend Ed who does not hesitate to turn in his old friend to the authorities.

___ • Ed becomes a local hero but Chuck does not resent Ed's publicity.

___ • Chuck's father learns of his role and meets with Chuck to tell him that he is proud of him.

___ 4. **Personal Response:** Any well-supported positive or negative response to the characters or events in the story, or to the story as a whole.

Retelling Score: _____

Comprehension Questions

_____ 1. Why was Chuck's father disappointed in him?

Text-Based: He wanted Chuck to become a lawyer.

_____ 2. What was bothering Chuck even more than his father's disappointment?

Text-Based: He was torn about turning in a former friend.

_____ 3. How would life have been better if Chuck's father had not been so aggressive about directing Chuck's life?

Inference: They wouldn't have lost several years of closeness; the father could have learned about Chuck's desire to serve his community in his own way.

_____ 4. How is Chuck's commitment to friendship demonstrated in this story? (Must identify two.)

Inference: He was reluctant to turn in a former friend; he never had second thoughts about letting his friend Ed enjoy the credit for his work; he did not resent Ed's Coast Guard appointment.

_____ 5. What was Chuck's greatest advantage in life, his education or his value system?

Critical Response: His education because he used it to conduct the investigation; his value system because he didn't let his friendship keep him from doing what was right in protecting innocent people.

_____ 6. Why would Chuck agonize so often doing something that was so obviously right?

Text-Based: He valued friendship; he remembered the friendship he had with his former friend; he dreaded being responsible for turning in a friend.

_____ 7. Why might Chuck be disappointed in Ed?

Inference: He saw the self-centered side of Ed; Ed didn't think twice about his former friendship and thought only of the success that he was about to have; Ed didn't share the credit for the drug-busting operation with Chuck.

_____ 8. How was Chuck right about his career choice as a tugboat operator?

Text-Based: He chose something that he loved doing and he was still able to make a positive contribution to improve the lives of the people on the island.

_____ 9. Are there more similarities or more differences between Chuck and Ed?

Critical Response: Similarities—because they both had careers that helped others. Differences—because Ed wasn't concerned about his past friendship with Dan, but Chuck was.

Comprehension Analysis:

Text-Based: ___/4___
Inference: ___/3___
Critical Response: ___/3___

Total Comprehension %: _____

_____ 10. What trait did Chuck use more effectively, his bravery or his curiosity?

Critical Response: His bravery—since he gained evidence against his former friend in a way that risked his own life; he was brave enough to pursue his own interests even knowing that his father would not approve. His curiosity—because he noticed his former friend talking with the unsavory freight hauler and then he had to find out whether his suspicions were right or wrong.

TENTH GRADE III: THE DUCK HUNTER

Reader's copy on p. 83. of the Reader's Passages

Introductory Statement: "Would you read this passage about a hunter (to yourself/out loud). When you are finished, I'll take away the passage. Then I'll ask you to tell me about what you read and what you think of it. After that, I'll ask you some questions about the passage."

Story

When Grandfather had haltingly confided from his hospital bed that he had been selected by the National Duck Hunting Association for its Lifetime Service Award, Bill had nearly burst with pride, but his enthusiasm quickly waned when Grandfather asked Bill to accept the award in his stead. Bill would have to deliver an acceptance speech! "He knows that my stuttering gets heavy whenever I get nervous, so how could he ask me to make a speech for him?"

"It's such a shame that he had that stroke because getting that award and giving that speech would have been one of the highlights of his life," Bill's mother sighed on their drive home. "If he weren't so self-conscious about how the stroke affected his speech, he could go to the banquet himself." "But where does that leave me?" moaned Bill. "Why don't you talk to Mr. Brock about it?" suggested mother, knowing that Bill admired his former speech therapist and that he always seemed to have good advice for Bill.

Mr. Brock first listened patiently to Bill's worries and self-doubts, and then suggested an intriguing idea. To alleviate his nervousness, Bill could imagine his acceptance speech as a conversation with his grandfather. That way, he could try to block out the audience completely and imagine that he and Grandfather were the only people in the room. Mr. Brock warned Bill that such a technique would take much practice and discipline, but he was confident that Bill could master it.

And so Bill began to prepare for his speech, reflecting on the events in his life with Grandfather that stood out most saliently in his mind. Bill practiced his speech diligently for weeks but when the moment finally arrived, he approached the podium with more dread than confidence. But as Mr. Brock had suggested, Bill firmly focused his attention on a mental picture of his grandfather. He knew that his opening remarks would be the most difficult part of his speech: "My grandfather asked me to accept this award and to take his place at this banquet, but I know that that is impossible. And I know how well you all know him and how much he has loved and contributed to this organization. But what you may not know is what my grandfather has meant in the lives of so many people. So I would like to speak to my grandfather from my heart, just as if he were right here with us."

Bill turned slightly toward the empty chair he had placed near the podium and began to speak. He reminded Grandfather of the time when Bill was six and he had been allowed to watch Grandfather train Molly, his new Labrador retriever. "You told me I had to sit quietly and watch while you threw decoys into the bay and began teaching the proper commands to Molly. And when I couldn't just sit any longer and I called to Molly so that I could hug her, I wasn't really prepared for how stern your lecture was. That was only my first experience with your appreciation for discipline and obedience as the keys to success, but it certainly wasn't my last."

Bill went on to tell his grandfather how grateful he was that he modeled the importance of facing personal challenges, and most of all, for the way in which Grandfather helped Bill face his biggest challenge, stuttering. "It was you who noticed my embarrassment and withdrawal, you who arranged for me to meet with an expert language pathologist, you who helped me understand that stuttering is not an emotional problem. You showed me that there was nothing wrong with me as a person, that it was tension in the speech muscles that caused stuttering, and that hard work and discipline could help me overcome it."

"I always knew you had faith in my ability to face challenges and now I understand why you asked me to be here tonight. I think you knew that this speech would be one of the biggest challenges of my life, but I also know that it was you who gave me the tools I needed to succeed. This audience thanks you for your service to this organization, but I thank you for all that you've meant to my life." (716 words)

Scoring Miscues for Oral Reading Option
Mark all scoreable miscues by placing either a plus (for those that maintain meaning) or a zero (for those that violate meaning) in the text margin.

Reading Accuracy Index: _____%
*Total all miscues marked with pluses **and** zeros and enter the corresponding percentage from the Miscue Chart.*

Meaning Maintenance Index: _____%
*Total **only** miscues marked with zeros and enter the corresponding percentage from the Miscue Chart.*

Miscue Chart (if used for oral reading)

Miscues	%	Miscues	%	Miscues	%	Miscues	%
1	100	21	97	41	94	61	91
2	100	22	97	42	94	62	91
3	100	23	97	43	94	63	91
4	99	24	97	44	94	64	91
5	99	25	97	45	94	65	91
6	99	26	96	46	94	66	91
7	99	27	96	47	93	67	91
8	99	28	96	48	93	68	91
9	99	29	96	49	93	69	90
10	99	30	96	50	93	70	90
11	98	31	96	51	93	71	90
12	98	32	96	52	93	72	90
13	98	33	95	53	93	73	90
14	98	34	95	54	92	74	90
15	98	35	95	55	92	75	90
16	98	36	95	56	92	76	89
17	98	37	95	57	92	77	89
18	97	38	95	58	92	78	89
19	97	39	95	59	92	79	89
20	97	40	94	60	92	80	89

Student Retelling

Examiner: "Tell me about what you just read and what you thought about it."

If there is no spontaneous response, repeat the request, "Tell me what you thought about the passage."

Note: Use the Retelling Rubric on p. 219 to assess the child's retelling performance. If you need additional space for retelling responses, use a separate sheet of paper.

NARRATIVE PASSAGES
TENTH GRADE

RETELLING RUBRIC: NARRATIVE

Place a 0, 1/2, or + to score student responses. See page 80 for information on what these assessment measures mean.

Story Structure:

___ 1. **Key Characters and Setting:** Bill, his mother, his grandfather, and his speech therapist, Mr. Brock.

___ 2. **Character's Problem or Goal:** Bill is asked by his grandfather to deliver a speech.

3. **Problem-Solving or Goal-Meeting Process:**

___ • Bill's grandfather asks him to deliver his acceptance speech.

___ • Bill is worried about his stuttering and his mother suggests he visit his counselor.

___ • Mr. Brock suggests that Bill act as if he is talking to his grandfather during the speech.

___ • Bill gives the speech telling Grandfather how grateful he is for the lessons Grandfather has taught him.

___ • Bill realizes that Grandfather had helped him again by challenging him to overcome his stuttering.

___ 4. **Personal Response:** Any well-supported positive or negative response to the characters or events in the story, or to the story as a whole.

Retelling Score: _____

Comprehension Questions

_____ 1. Why didn't Grandfather deliver his own speech?

Text-Based: He had a stroke.

_____ 2. Why was Bill reluctant to deliver his grandfather's speech?

Text-Based: He stuttered when he became nervous.

_____ 3. In what way was Grandfather more insightful about Bill's life than Bill's mother had been?

Inference: Grandfather was the one who noticed that Bill was becoming self-conscious about his stuttering and he made arrangements for speech therapy.

_____ 4. How had self-discipline paid off in Bill's life?

Inference: It gave him the inner strength to deliver the speech.

_____ 5. Was Mom sympathetic to Bill's reluctance to take his grandfather's role? Explain.

Critical Response: Yes—she made sure that she directed him to his counselor because she knew that the counselor had good advice for Bill. No—she seemed more focused on Grandfather's reluctance to give his own speech than on Bill's reluctance.

_____ 6. What did Mr. Brock, the counselor, do to help Bill deal with his fears?

Text-Based: He told him to imagine that he was talking directly to his grandfather.

_____ 7. Why was the first part of Bill's speech the most difficult for him?

Inference: He had to speak directly to the audience; he wasn't yet speaking as if his grandfather were there.

_____ 8. Why did Bill have an empty chair at the banquet?

Text-Based: The chair was where Grandfather would have sat and it is where Bill could look to act as if he were talking to his grandfather.

_____ 9. Had Grandfather really modeled for Bill the ability to face challenges? Explain.

Critical Response: Yes—he had treated Bill's stuttering as if it were his own problem; he had taken Bill to the best therapist. No—when the real problem of facing his own reluctance to talk surfaced, he passed it on to Bill.

_____10. Which problem caused the greatest challenge, Bill's stuttering or Grandfather's stroke? Explain.

Critical Response: Bill's stuttering—because it kept him from being comfortable with people. Grandfather's stroke—because he was older and had never had a problem.

Comprehension Analysis:

Text-Based: __/4__
Inference: __/3__
Critical Response: __/3__

Total Comprehension %: _____

ELEVENTH GRADE I: THE INJURY

Reader's copy on p. 85 of the Reader's Passages

Introductory Statement: "Would you read this passage about a young man's injury (to yourself/out loud). When you are finished, I'll take away the passage. Then I'll ask you to tell me about what you read and what you think of it. After that, I'll ask you some questions about the passage."

Story

It seemed that the entire town was trying to fit into the Franklin High School football stadium for the final game of the season. But the buzz in the crowd was all about the recruiters from big-name colleges who had come to scout Ron, their local football and baseball hero. It seemed that their small town was finally on the map and it was a fine athlete and a fine young man who had put them there. At the end of the evening few people at the game even remembered the final score. The images that seem engraved on the minds of everyone at the game were the hard tackle, the awkward fall and the stretcher that carried Ron to the ambulance that waited outside the field for just such emergencies. The diagnosis was grim. A torn rotator cuff would need immediate surgical repair and months of rehabilitation and there were no guarantees that Ron would ever regain the athletic skills that had set him apart from every other player in the entire league.

On his way to the hospital, Ron thought about his father who would be anxiously praying and waiting for him there. Ron knew that his father had taken on the extra part time job to earn the money to cover the expenses for Ron's participation in sports. His father had always been proud of his son's athletic success but Ron suspected that he was most grateful for the full scholarship it would bring, a scholarship to a private university that the family could never have afforded.

With that scholarship now in jeopardy, Ron knew that he would have to face some thorny decisions with some far-reaching consequences. But unfortunate decisions and still more regrettable consequences were things that Ron and his father had talked about for as long as Ron could remember. His father had dropped out of football because he hadn't kept up his grades and then he had to watch his best friend, a player whom everyone recognized was not his father's equal, go on to win a football scholarship to a top-grade university and to have a thoroughly successful college career. How many times had he heard his father speculate wistfully on what might have been if he had only stayed with football. After graduation and a tour of duty in Vietnam, his father had returned determined to go on to earn a college degree, but after several months in the local community college, he became jealous of the spending money that his working friends always seemed to have. He dropped out of college and took a full-time job, but he still somehow never seemed to earn enough or succeed enough to match his aspirations. Whenever he could Ron's father would make a point of identifying the consequences he had paid and still continued to pay because of the poor decisions he had made in his youth and Ron knew that his father would be deeply disappointed in him if he made the wrong decision.

After his surgery, Ron's physical therapy was more painful than anything he had ever experienced. He began to wonder whether he really wanted to risk reinjuring the shoulder by trying to rejoin the team, but without football, what could he do to afford college? He had always been an honor roll student, but he knew that he would never qualify for an academic scholarship. Ron began to wonder whether he should drop out of sports altogether. Then he would have more time to devote to his studies. But what about the regrets that were sure to come later? What about the consequences if he made the wrong decision?

His father accompanied Ron, as always, to the doctor's office at the end of Ron's physical therapy program. The doctor told them what Ron had suspected all along: He could return to football but another injury to the shoulder could leave him with permanent damage and pain. Ron and his father drove in silence to the coffee shop where they had spent countless hours over the years discussing life's choices and consequences.

Ron wanted desperately to ask his father what he should do, but he sensed that the time for letting others decide for him had long since passed. Instead, Ron turned to his father and said, "You've never told me which regret was greater, dropping out of football or out of college."

To Ron's surprise, his father replied, "I'm really beginning to wonder if I've wasted too much of my life regretting the things that I've done. If I had stayed in college and in football, I may never have been fortunate enough to meet your mother or to have had a son like you. I may never have been nearly as contented as I've been over the years. I'm beginning to think that maybe it isn't always the choices that you make but what you make of the choices that really matters." Ron nodded; he didn't quite understand yet what his father meant but he had the distinct feeling that he soon would. (844 words)

Scoring Miscues for Oral Reading Option
Mark all scoreable miscues by placing either a plus (for those that maintain meaning) or a zero (for those that violate meaning) in the text margin.

Reading Accuracy Index: _____%
*Total all miscues marked with pluses **and** zeros and enter the corresponding percentage from the Miscue Chart.*

Meaning Maintenance Index: _____%
*Total **only** miscues marked with zeros and enter the corresponding percentage from the Miscue Chart.*

Miscue Chart (if used for oral reading)

Miscues	%	Miscues	%	Miscues	%	Miscues	%
1	100	25	97	49	94	73	91
2	100	26	97	50	94	74	91
3	100	27	97	51	94	75	91
4	100	28	97	52	94	76	91
5	99	29	97	53	94	77	91
6	99	30	96	54	94	78	91
7	99	31	96	55	93	79	91
8	99	32	96	56	93	80	91
9	99	33	96	57	93	81	90
10	99	34	96	58	93	82	90
11	99	35	96	59	93	83	90
12	99	36	96	60	93	84	90
13	98	37	96	61	93	85	90
14	98	38	96	62	93	86	90
15	98	39	95	63	93	87	90
16	98	40	95	64	92	88	90
17	98	41	95	65	92	89	90
18	98	42	95	66	92	90	89
19	98	43	95	67	92	91	89
20	98	44	95	68	92	92	89
21	98	45	95	69	92	93	89
22	97	46	95	70	92	94	89
23	97	47	94	71	92	95	89
24	97	48	94	72	91	96	89

Student Retelling

Examiner: "Tell me about what you just read and what you thought about it."

If there is no spontaneous response, repeat the request, "Tell me what you thought about the passage."

Note: Use the Retelling Rubric on p. 224 to assess the child's retelling performance. If you need additional space for retelling responses, use a separate sheet of paper.

RETELLING RUBRIC: NARRATIVE

Place a 0, 1/2, or + to score student responses. See page 80 for information on what these assessment measures mean.

Story Structure:

____ 1. **Key Characters and Setting:** Ron and his father.

____ 2. **Character's Problem or Goal:** Ron is faced with a difficult decision about his future.

3. **Problem-Solving or Goal-Meeting Process:**

____ • Ron is a star athlete being recruited by college scouts.

____ • An injury jeopardizes his scholarship and future.

____ • Ron is aware of his father's regrets about his own poor decisions and their consequences.

____ • Ron does not want to disappoint his father.

____ • Father tells Ron that he should not have spent so much time on regrets.

____ 4. **Personal Response:** Any well-supported positive or negative response to the characters or events in the story, or to the story as a whole.

Retelling Score: _____

Comprehension Questions

_____ 1. **Why did so many people attend the final football game of the season at Franklin High School?**

Text-Based: Recruiters from colleges had come to see Ron play.

_____ 2. **Why was the torn rotator cuff such a serious injury for Ron?**

Text-Based: He may not recover his athletic skills; he may lose his chance for a scholarship.

_____ 3. **In what ways is Ron's personality like that of his father?**

Inference: Very thoughtful and reflective; afraid of regrets; wants to make the right decision.

_____ 4. **Why would Ron seem to prefer that his father tell him what to do?**

Inference: He trusts his father's judgment; the decisions are serious ones; he won't have to accept the consequences alone that way.

_____ 5. **Do you think his father should have given Ron more specific advice at the end of the story? Explain.**

Critical Response: Yes—he needs the guidance; he is still young to be making that kind of choice; he trusts his father. No—he will have to accept the consequences, not his father; he is old enough to make his own decisions at this point.

_____ 6. **Why didn't Ron's father stay in college when he had the chance?**

Text-Based: He was jealous of his friends who were earning money in their jobs.

7. Do you think as Ron did that his father would have been disappointed in Ron if he made the "wrong decision"? Explain.

Inference: Probably not—too proud of his son; the father had reconsidered his own regrets and decisions.

8. Why was the football scholarship so important to Ron's father?

Text-Based: He could not afford to send his son to a private school.

9. Who do you think learned more from the experience of Ron's injury, Ron or his father? Explain.

Critical Response: Ron—had to grow up fast and make some important decisions; learned about how to reconsider life decisions. His father—had to rethink his life and values; Ron's injury changed him almost completely.

10. Based on what you know about the situation, what do you think would be the best course of action for Ron and why?

Critical Response: Stop sports and concentrate on academics since the injury is so serious; concentrate on baseball which isn't as dangerous a sport; get a loan and attend a state college.

Comprehension Analysis:

Text-Based: __/4__
Inference: __/3__
Critical Response: __/3__

Total Comprehension %: _____

ELEVENTH GRADE II: THE BABYSITTER

Reader's copy on p. 87 of the Reader's Passages

Introductory Statement: "Would you read this passage about a girl who was a babysitter (to yourself/out loud). When you are finished, I'll take away the passage. Then I'll ask you to tell me about what you read and what you think of it. After that, I'll ask you some questions about the passage."

Story

Nancy spent her study hall period frantically working to finish her assignments so that she wouldn't be late for her meeting with her next-door neighbor, Jean. Today was the day that they would be finalizing plans for the birthday party of the great love in Nancy's life, Jean's adorable six year old son, Jeff. And now Nancy sat in Jean's kitchen and assisted Jean in making the arrangements to hire a clown, several ponies, and a tent, since for such a momentous occasion no expense could be spared. As they planned, Nancy and Jean laughed and reminisced about the day nearly six years ago when Nancy, quietly and cautiously standing behind her mother, came to meet their new neighbors with a plate of freshly baked cookies. Nancy was captivated by their tiny child and when Jean asked her if she would like to hold little Jeff, Nancy was thrilled to the soles of her feet. Nancy spent an entire hour cuddling the baby and right then and there a love for the little boy crawled its way into Nancy's heart, a love that was even stronger six years later.

And as an added bonus, Jean had become one of Nancy's closest friends and confidantes. Even when her own beloved mother occasionally lost her patience with Nancy, it seemed that Jean was always there with words of encouragement and advice, and Nancy treasured her friendship, even though Jean

was fifteen years her senior. Nancy's reverie was interrupted by a demanding voice from upstairs: "Hey Nan, I can't get my computer game to work." Nancy promptly stopped filling out invitations and immediately ran upstairs to help Jeff and when she returned, she found Jean shaking her head in mock exasperation. "Did you ever notice that Jeff wouldn't even try to do that to anyone else? Sometimes I feel like scolding him when he takes advantage of you and just assumes you'll drop everything for him." Nancy grinned, confident that both Jean and Jeff loved her and that spoiling Jeff occasionally would do no real harm. But strangely enough, Jean's words made her recall how she had always been puzzled and somewhat resentful that her friends closer to her own age didn't seem to share her affection for Jeff.

The following Saturday, Nancy picked up Jeff at midmorning and Jean reminded him to follow all the rules: "You stay close to Nancy and listen to everything she tells you." Jeff and Nancy smiled patiently at Jean's lecture, both fully aware that between them, there were precious few rules to speak of. Then they departed for the theater for the first part of Jeff's birthday present, a movie that Jeff had been impatient to see. When the feature had concluded and she and Jeff were exiting the theater, Nancy noticed a large travel poster of London, pointed to it and excitedly told Jeff, "That's the place where I'm going this summer!" Nancy spoke breathlessly of her acceptance into a summer program at Oxford and about the kinds of sights she expected to see in London, but when she turned to look at Jeff, he was nowhere to be found.

Nancy's search for her lost charge became more frantic by the moment as she pushed her way past people, calling Jeff's name. With every passing moment she envisioned having to confess to Jean that her son was lost, maybe kidnapped, maybe even worse, and that it was all her fault! Now in tears of panic, Nancy rushed to the theater concession stand and begged hysterically for someone to help her find a missing child. The rush of concerned workers, each of them asking different questions about who the boy was and what he looked like, nearly overwhelmed Nancy.

She was on the verge of completely losing control when she spied Jeff, nonchalantly walking out of the theater's game room. For the first time ever, Nancy scolded Jeff for his lack of consideration, and Jeff responded, "Aw, women make such a big deal out of everything." Behind clenched teeth, Nancy muttered some words of thanks to her would-be helpers, grabbed Jeff's hand, and led him firmly back to the car. "Hey, what about the train ride you promised me?" he cried. "You lost that when you broke the rules!" she retorted. Jeff cried all the way home and there was a time that she would have done anything to dry one of Jeff's tears, but this time Nancy found herself curiously unmoved and she had the distinct feeling that her days of spoiling Jeff were over. (757 words)

Scoring Miscues for Oral Reading Option

Mark all scoreable miscues by placing either a plus (for those that maintain meaning) or a zero (for those that violate meaning) in the text margin.

Reading Accuracy Index: _____%

*Total all miscues marked with pluses **and** zeros and enter the corresponding percentage from the Miscue Chart.*

Meaning Maintenance Index: _____%

*Total **only** miscues marked with zeros and enter the corresponding percentage from the Miscue Chart.*

Miscue Chart (if used for oral reading)

Miscues	%	Miscues	%	Miscues	%	Miscues	%
1	100	25	97	49	94	73	90
2	100	26	97	50	93	74	90
3	100	27	96	51	93	75	90
4	99	28	96	52	93	76	90
5	99	29	96	53	93	77	90
6	99	30	96	54	93	78	90
7	99	31	96	55	93	79	90
8	99	32	96	56	93	80	89
9	99	33	96	57	93	81	89
10	99	34	96	58	92	82	89
11	99	35	95	59	92	83	89
12	98	36	95	60	92	84	89
13	98	37	95	61	92	85	89
14	98	38	95	62	92	86	89
15	98	39	95	63	92	87	88
16	98	40	95	64	92	88	88
17	98	41	95	65	91	89	88
18	98	42	94	66	91	90	88
19	98	43	94	67	91	91	88
20	97	44	94	68	91	92	88
21	97	45	94	69	91	93	88
22	97	46	94	70	91	94	88
23	97	47	94	71	91	95	87
24	97	48	94	72	91	96	87

Student Retelling

Examiner: "Tell me about what you just read and what you thought about it."

If there is no spontaneous response, repeat the request, "Tell me what you thought about the passage."

Note: Use the Retelling Rubric on p. 228 to assess the child's retelling performance. If you need additional space for retelling responses, use a separate sheet of paper.

Place a 0, 1/2, or + to score student responses. See page 80 for information on what these assessment measures mean.

Story Structure:

___ 1. **Key Characters and Setting:** Nancy, her neighbor Jean, and Jeff.

___ 2. **Character's Problem or Goal:** Nancy has to learn that she can't let Jeff do whatever he wants.

___ 3. **Problem-Solving or Goal-Meeting Process:**

___ • Jeff's mother teases Nancy about her spoiling Jeff.

___ • Nancy takes Jeff to the movies and Jeff disappears into the game room.

___ • Nancy panics and asks for help.

___ • When Nancy finds Jeff, his flippant remark angers her.

___ • Nancy takes Jeff home and this time his crying leaves her unmoved.

___ 4. **Personal Response:** Any well-supported positive or negative response to the characters or events in the story, or to the story as a whole.

Retelling Score: _____

Comprehension Questions

_____ 1. **Why was Nancy so eager to finish her homework?**

Text-Based: She wanted to get to her neighbor's house to finalize plans for Jeff's sixth birthday party.

_____ 2. **What arrangements were Nancy and Jeff's mom making?**

Text-Based: They were hiring a clown, several ponies, and a tent.

_____ 3. **Why might Nancy's mother seem to be so different from Jean?**

Inference: Nancy's mother didn't seem to be as patient as Jean; Nancy's mother got upset easily but Jean didn't.

_____ 4. **What advice might Nancy's friends want to give her?**

Inference: Don't let a child of six control her; be more involved socially with friends her own age.

_____ 5. **Was Jeff's mother's approach for dealing with Jeff different from Nancy's approach? Explain.**

Critical Response: Yes—because she would not drop anything she was doing to help him—she would keep doing her own work. No—because she seems to spoil Jeff as much as Nancy does.

_____ 6. **Why was it useless for Jeff's mother to remind Jeff to follow the rules when he was with Nancy?**

Text-Based: There were no rules for him to follow because Nancy let him do whatever he wanted to do.

_____ 7. Why would Jeff be so inconsiderate toward someone who obviously cared for him?

Inference: He had no idea that he was being inconsiderate; no one seemed to give him reason to question his actions.

_____ 8. How did Nancy react to Jeff's disappearance?

Text-Based: She lost her composure, crying hysterically for help; she thought about having to tell his mother that he was kidnapped.

_____ 9. Was it right for Nancy to become so angry at Jeff when he left her in the theater? Explain.

Critical Response: Yes—he had been told to stay close to Nancy and he chose not to do that; he didn't pay any attention to something that was clearly important to her. No—she never gave him any reason to think that he couldn't do whatever he wanted to do; she reacted only to his comment about women.

_____ 10. Did Nancy learn more about herself or about Jeff from this experience?

Critical Response: Herself—because she realized that she had not been in control; realized that she had to behave differently with Jeff. Jeff—because she learned how selfish Jeff could be.

Comprehension Analysis:

Text-Based: ___/4___
Inference: ___/3___
Critical Response: ___/3___

Total Comprehension %: _____

ELEVENTH GRADE III: DREAMS AND VISION

Reader's copy on p. 89 of the Reader's Passages

Introductory Statement: "Would you read this passage about a young man with a dream (to yourself/out loud). When you are finished, I'll take away the passage. Then I'll ask you to tell me about what you read and what you think of it. After that, I'll ask you some questions about the passage."

Story

"Don't touch those slides! I haven't studied them yet!" snapped Len, with enough volume and vehemence to startle his longtime lab partner. When Len realized what he had done and sensed his partner's discomfort, he quickly apologized, muttering something about having a miserable day. Bert knew his old friend well enough to distinguish between a bad day and some deep trouble, but Bert also knew that Len was not about to admit that anything was bothering him. The private boarding school that they both attended on scholarships was a long way from home. But Mr. Lunder, their advanced placement science teacher, had become Len's father in absentia. And though he knew Len would not appreciate the intrusion, Bert made it a point to see if Mr. Lunder had noticed a change in his prize pupil and, if he had, to see if he had discovered its source.

As it seems, Mr. Lunder had indeed noticed a great deal of edginess and anxiety creep into the normally pleasant personality of Len, and he was determined to find out what was wrong. Unfortunately, he also knew that coaxing information out of Len was akin to pulling teeth. With little to lose, Mr. Lunder decided to try the direct approach and ask Len if something was bothering him. He was stunned to listen to Len, without any provocation at all, disclose the fact that his vision had become increasingly blurred over the past several weeks and that Len had become convinced that he was losing his sight altogether.

Later that afternoon, Mr. Lunder left the principal's office with Len in tow, having made all the necessary legal arrangements to take Len to the eye doctor's office. Mr. Lunder tried to distract his melancholy young charge from his gloomy and fatalistic ideas of life and health. He chatted about the advantages Len and his classmates would have as freshmen in college with all of the advanced placement courses they had completed in mathematics and science. Throughout the ride Len nodded dully or responded in monosyllables, his mind millions of miles away in the realm of dejection and despair. Fortunately, it was a completely different Len on the ride home, for the ophthalmologist had diagnosed an eye infection as the cause of the blurred vision, a problem that could be cleared up in less than a week with simple eye drops.

Mr. Lunder fought off the temptation to say "I told you so" to his young charge, and resolved to keep an eye on Len and watch his spirits rise as his vision improved, but unfortunately, the smile did not return. Instead Len appeared at his door two days later and announced that he was dropping out of school and returning home. "It's all over, Mr. Lunder," said Len, fighting back his tears. "My eyes are getting worse and I think I'm in real trouble. All those dreams of going to medical school and getting my mom and sister into a nice neighborhood are all over, and to make matters worse, I'm going to go blind and be a burden on my whole family." This time Mr. Lunder did not bother dissuading Len, but merely obtained authorization to take Len to the famous eye hospital in the city near their school.

Len had a sense of awe just walking into the eye hospital where researchers and physicians conducted the kind of research he had dreamed of doing. He also felt a confidence that he had not felt before, one that was well rewarded. It seems that there had been no eye infection after all, but that the problem lay in the type of contact lens that Len had been wearing for years. His eye had become extremely irritated but would improve rapidly once he began to use the temporary glasses and rid himself of his current supply of contact lenses. "After several months' rest from my contacts, they are going to give me some temporary ones that they will monitor to be sure that I am wearing the right kind," he reported gleefully. Mr. Lunder felt as if a mountain had just rolled off his back as he told Len, "It looks as if your dreams are back on, Len, but one of these days, you and I are going to have to have a long talk." (722 words)

Scoring Miscues for Oral Reading Option
Mark all scoreable miscues by placing either a plus (for those that maintain meaning) or a zero (for those that violate meaning) in the text margin.

Reading Accuracy Index: _____%
*Total all miscues marked with pluses **and** zeros and enter the corresponding percentage from the Miscue Chart.*

Meaning Maintenance Index: _____%
*Total **only** miscues marked with zeros and enter the corresponding percentage from the Miscue Chart.*

Miscue Chart (if used for oral reading)

Miscues	%	Miscues	%	Miscues	%	Miscues	%
1	100	25	97	49	93	73	90
2	100	26	96	50	93	74	90
3	100	27	96	51	93	75	90
4	99	28	96	52	93	76	89
5	99	29	96	53	93	77	89
6	99	30	96	54	93	78	89
7	99	31	96	55	92	79	89
8	99	32	96	56	92	80	89
9	99	33	95	57	92	81	89
10	99	34	95	58	92	82	89
11	98	35	95	59	92	83	89
12	98	36	95	60	92	84	88
13	98	37	95	61	92	85	88
14	98	38	95	62	91	86	88
15	98	39	95	63	91	87	88
16	98	40	94	64	91	88	88
17	98	41	94	65	91	89	88
18	98	42	94	66	91	90	88
19	97	43	94	67	91	91	87
20	97	44	94	68	91	92	87
21	97	45	94	69	90	93	87
22	97	46	94	70	90	94	87
23	97	47	93	71	90	95	87
24	97	48	93	72	90	96	87

Student Retelling

Examiner: "Tell me about what you just read and what you thought about it."

If there is no spontaneous response, repeat the request, "Tell me what you thought about the passage."

Note: Use the Retelling Rubric on p. 232 to assess the child's retelling performance. If you need additional space for retelling responses, use a separate sheet of paper.

RETELLING RUBRIC: NARRATIVE

Place a 0, 1/2, or + to score student responses. See page 80 for information on what these assessment measures mean.

Story Structure:

___ 1. **Key Characters and Setting:** Len, Bert, and Mr. Lunder their science teacher.

___ 2. **Character's Problem or Goal:** Len thinks he is going blind and will never become a doctor.

3. **Problem-Solving or Goal-Meeting Process:**

___ • Len has become very moody.

___ • Mr. Lunder tries to help and the problem is diagnosed.

___ • Len's eye problem returns.

___ • Len is discouraged until an eye specialist finds the real problem.

___ • Mr. Lunder realizes Len needs advice in handling his problems.

___ 4. **Personal Response:** Any well-supported positive or negative response to the characters or events in the story, or to the story as a whole.

Retelling Score: _____

Comprehension Questions

_____ 1. **Why did Bert talk to Mr. Lunder?**

Text-Based: He wanted to see if Mr. Lunder had noticed the change in Len that he had seen.

_____ 2. **How did Len surprise Mr. Lunder?**

Text-Based: Len willingly told him about his blurred vision and his thoughts that he was losing his sight.

_____ 3. **Why had Mr. Lunder made a wise career choice?**

Inference: He was teaching at a boarding school and he was able to take the father role for students like Len.

_____ 4. **How did Len show his willingness to let Mr. Lunder take a father role in his life?**

Inference: He was open in sharing his fears.

_____ 5. **Would it have been a good thing for Mr. Lunder to say "I told you so" after hearing the first doctor's report? Explain.**

Critical Response: Yes—it would have helped Len realize that it is not wise to jump to conclusions. No—it would have put a barrier between him and Len and might have changed the close relationship that Mr. Lunder had developed with Len.

_____ 6. **Why was a college scholarship so important to Len?**

Text-Based: He couldn't afford it and he wanted to be able to help his family move into a good neighborhood.

_____ 7. **Why didn't Mr. Lunder try to convince Len not to drop out of school?**

Inference: He had already realized the need to get Len to the eye hospital.

8. Why did Len have more confidence at the eye hospital than he did when he went to the ophthalmologist?

Text-Based: He was awed by the researchers and physicians who were doing the type of research that he dreamed of doing.

9. Was Bert more open than Len? Explain.

Critical Response: Yes—he approached Mr. Lunder to talk about Len. No—he talked about other people's problems not his own.

10. What do you think Mr. Lunder had in mind when he said that he would have a talk with Len?

Critical Response: He planned to let Len know that he had to be more open in initiating discussions about his fears; not to be so pessimistic.

Comprehension Analysis:

Text-Based: __/4__
Inference: __/3__
Critical Response: __/3__

Total Comprehension %: ____

Reader's copy on p. 91 of the Reader's Passages

Introductory Statement: "Would you read this passage about a young woman (to yourself/out loud). When you are finished, I'll take away the passage. Then I'll ask you to tell me about what you read and what you think of it. After that, I'll ask you some questions about the passage."

Story

Lin sat thinking in silence in the rear seat of the car as her parents drove out of the tree-lined main drive of the idyllic university campus and began the long ride home. But there was no reflection of the campus serenity in Lin's mind that morning. She was trying desperately to control her anger as she relived the events of the past few days, events that dragged her memories back to the days of her youth when she felt so much like an outsider. The cinema in her mind replayed the first time that Lin had met her best friends, Marilyn and Cindy. Lin was seven years old and her family had just moved into their new home when her mother called her to tell her that two girls had knocked at the front door and asked if they could play with Lin.

The three girls sat on the front porch as her new friends bombarded Lin with questions about her life in China. She had all but forgotten the queasy feeling that came over her, like being a strange specimen captured in a bottle to be scrutinized by inquisitive students. "They don't want to be my friends," Lin blurted out to her mother late one afternoon, "they just want to show me how different I am and I don't want to play with them again." But Lin's mother simply said, "Are you talking about how they feel or how you feel?" And so Lin decided not to run away and soon she joined Marilyn and Cindy in their imaginary world in the nearby woods, reading stories of faraway lands. Within months, the girls had become inseparable and they were still the best of friends at the end of their junior year at the university. But it was the memory of being seven years old and feeling so terribly and unalterably different that consumed Lin during the ride home, and not the friendship or the happy ending.

"You're pretty quiet, Lin," Mother said, but Lin was slow to respond, for it had been her mother's idea for Lin to become acquainted with the four Chinese exchange students who began their university studies that semester. At that time Lin thought that serving as their mentor and assisting them in making the transition to American life and customs would be a marvelous way to help the girls, but their initial meeting had not been as fruitful as Lin had hoped it would be. At first, the girls sat in rapt attention and laughed as Lin shared with them stories of how she and her friends had learned to navigate the sometimes rough waters of the often convoluted campus procedures and protocol. But when Lin began to ask about their customs and point out sharp contrasts between Chinese and American ideas of propriety and manners, the girls lapsed into an uncomfortable silence and soon were chattering nervously among themselves about Chinese poets and literature, books that Lin could not even read. The meeting ended awkwardly, with everyone sensing the presence of bruised egos but no one quite sure of their source.

"They seemed to relish making me feel like an outsider and you know, Mother, I can't really comprehend how a working knowledge of Chinese poetry will help them get very far in America."

Her mother replied, "Are you certain that is what they wanted you to feel, Lin? Perhaps it was awkward for them to seem so different from you and all of the other students."

"That's no excuse for being impolite," snapped Lin, "especially when I was going out of my way to try to help them."

Later that week, on the family's long-planned trip to Niagara Falls, Lin stood mesmerized by the swiftness and intensity of the river, all very familiar but yet always somehow new. She felt her mother slip her arm around her and heard her whisper, "The river always knows where it is going, perhaps because it knows where it has been." Lin knew her mother too well to believe that this was mere idle chatter; she had learned long ago that it was worth the effort to think long and hard to uncover the sometimes arcane lesson embedded in her mother's words.

Lin woke the next morning filled with a fresh resolve to help her new friends organize a discussion group to explore Chinese literature and culture, and she knew exactly whom she could invite to participate. The group would dedicate itself to the celebration of diversity, differences, and friendship in the university community, for as her mother knew well, it always helps to know where you've been. (773 words)

Scoring Miscues for Oral Reading Option
Mark all scoreable miscues by placing either a plus (for those that maintain meaning) or a zero (for those that violate meaning) in the text margin.

Reading Accuracy Index: _____%
*Total all miscues marked with pluses **and** zeros and enter the corresponding percentage from the Miscue Chart.*

Meaning Maintenance Index: _____%
*Total **only** miscues marked with zeros and enter the corresponding percentage from the Miscue Chart.*

Miscue Chart (if used for oral reading)

Miscues	%	Miscues	%	Miscues	%	Miscues	%
1	100	25	97	49	94	73	91
2	100	26	97	50	94	74	90
3	100	27	97	51	93	75	90
4	99	28	96	52	93	76	90
5	99	29	96	53	93	77	90
6	99	30	96	54	93	78	90
7	99	31	96	55	93	79	90
8	99	32	96	56	93	80	90
9	99	33	96	57	93	81	90
10	99	34	96	58	92	82	89
11	99	35	95	59	92	83	89
12	98	36	95	60	92	84	89
13	98	37	95	61	92	85	89
14	98	38	95	62	92	86	89
15	98	39	95	63	92	87	89
16	98	40	95	64	92	88	89
17	98	41	95	65	92	89	88
18	98	42	95	66	91	90	88
19	98	43	94	67	91	91	88
20	97	44	94	68	91	92	88
21	97	45	94	69	91	93	88
22	97	46	94	70	91	94	88
23	97	47	94	71	91	95	88
24	97	48	94	72	91	96	88

Student Retelling

Examiner: "Tell me about what you just read and what you thought about it."

If there is no spontaneous response, repeat the request, "Tell me what you thought about the passage."

Note: Use the Retelling Rubric on p. 236 to assess the child's retelling performance. If you need additional space for retelling responses, use a separate sheet of paper.

RETELLING RUBRIC: NARRATIVE

Place a 0, 1/2, or + to score student responses. See page 80 for information on what these assessment measures mean.

Story Structure:

___ 1. **Key Characters and Setting:** Lin, her mother, Cindy and Marilyn, and four Chinese students.

___ 2. **Character's Problem or Goal:** Lin must deal with feelings of not belonging.

3. **Problem-Solving or Goal-Meeting Process:**

___ • Lin is angry at how she is treated by the four Chinese students.

___ • She remembers feeling like an outsider when she first met her best friends.

___ • Lin has a difficult time accepting her mother's suggestion that she might be misreading the Chinese students.

___ • Lin remembers that the students felt uncomfortable when she talked about differences.

___ • Lin's mother's words about the river help her understand that remembering where she has been can help her reconsider her anger.

___ 4. **Personal Response:** Any well-supported positive or negative response to the characters or events in the story, or to the story as a whole.

Retelling Score: _____

Comprehension Questions

_____ 1. **Why did Lin have a difficult time making friends with Marilyn and Cindy?**

Text-Based: She thought they didn't really want to be her friends; she thought they wanted to show how different Lin was.

_____ 2. **What made Lin think that the Chinese students she tried to help were rude?**

Text-Based: They began to talk about Chinese poetry and literature.

_____ 3. **Why *should* Lin have understood how the Chinese students felt?**

Inference: The same thing had happened to her when she was young; emphasis on differences had made her feel uncomfortable; she had become good friends with people she was once suspicious of.

_____ 4. **What do you think was the source of the bruised egos after Lin's first meeting with the Chinese students?**

Inference: Lin thought they were ungrateful and they thought she was insensitive to their feelings.

_____ 5. **Do you think that Lin really learned the lesson her mother intended? Why or why not?**

Critical Response: Yes—she plans to change her approach to the Chinese students; she wants to become friends with them. No—she does not seem to remember her own experiences with friendship.

_____ 6. **What plan did Lin create as a result of her thinking about her mother's words?**

Text-Based: She decided to start a discussion group focusing on Chinese literature and culture.

_____ 7. Why did both Lin and the four Chinese students react so negatively to the "help" they were given?

Inference: Each may have felt that the other was acting superior; each may have felt the other was trying to make them feel bad about their differences.

_____ 8. In what way was Lin's mother influential in helping her resolve problems both early in life and later in life?

Text-Based: She questions Lin's judgment about the motives of others; she makes her rethink the statements she has made.

_____ 9. Was the lesson Lin's mother tried to teach her really difficult to understand? Why or why not?

Critical Response: Yes—she didn't explain what she really meant; lesson was too complicated; Lin hadn't learned the lesson when she was young. No—Lin should know what it's like to be treated as if you were different; Lin was not sensitive enough to learn the lesson; Lin was too self-centered to learn.

_____ 10. Do you think that Lin had forgotten where she had been? Explain.

Critical Response: Yes—she had forgotten her early suspicions about her young friends; she did not learn from her experiences with differences; she did the same thing to the students that she was angry about when she was young. No—she eventually recalled her early experiences; her memories helped her come to grips with her feelings.

Comprehension Analysis:

Text-Based: __/4__
Inference: __/3__
Critical Response: __/3__

Total Comprehension %: _____

TWELFTH GRADE II: THE PSYCHOLOGY CLASS

Reader's copy on p. 93 of the Reader's Passages

Introductory Statement: "Would you read this passage about a young man in a psychology class (to yourself/out loud). When you are finished, I'll take away the passage. Then I'll ask you to tell me about what you read and what you think of it. After that, I'll ask you some questions about the passage."

Story

Marty sauntered into his Child Psychology class and was elated to see the audiovisual equipment already set up and ready to run. Even as a university sophomore, Marty still loved to watch movies during class time. Child Psychology was his favorite class of all, but it always seemed to him that watching a video was much more enjoyable than reading dull books. After a short introduction, the psychology professor began the DVD. The class settled back to observe the exploits of a six year old boy named Mike who was so successful in getting his own way and dominating his parents that he had become the stuff of legends in Child Psychology.

The class watched with increasing amusement as Mike cajoled, whined, whimpered, and cried and essentially did whatever was necessary to impose his will on his parents. His hapless father seemed almost completely overmatched and utterly unable to handle his son. Despite his tough talk to the contrary, he caved in at the slightest hint of Mike's displeasure and gave the boy whatever he desired. The film showed Mike's father undergoing extensive indoctrination in appropriate child rearing practices, even arriving at the point where he could verbalize exactly what he was doing and why it was wrong. The mild amusement of the class gave way to loud bursts of laughter as Mike and his father promptly reverted to their original behavior patterns

the moment the cameras began to roll again. There had been no learning taking place after all.

When the lights came up, the professor acknowledged the appreciative laughter of the class but quickly emphasized that such child rearing practices are no laughing matter for children like Mike. He went on to cite considerable research suggesting that such children often grow up lacking in self-discipline and resolve, with a powerful tendency to attribute their own shortcomings to others. Even worse, many grow into scheming and manipulative adults who use similar though more sophisticated tactics to get their own way in their adult relationships.

When the class had ended, Marty left distraught and ashen because the relationship he had seen depicted on film was so eerily similar to the relationship he had, not only with his father but also with his mother. Marty recalled an endless string of unpleasant episodes he had caused, all for the sake of an ice cream cone or a toy that they were reluctant to immediately procure for him. And he recalled with horror the conversation he had with his father not two days earlier, when he had wheedled some extra spending money by playing on his father's sympathies. Could it be that Marty too was doomed to become a lazy, scheming, manipulative adult whom no one could possibly stomach?

Marty frantically searched his memories of his relationship with his girlfriend, with his old and new classmates, even with his professors. Every instance of concessions that they had made, or arguments that he had won immediately became proof positive in Marty's mind that he was doomed to a life of failure and unhappiness, all because of his own selfishness as a child. When he could stand it no longer, Marty made an appointment to see his psychology professor, convinced that he needed professional help.

The professor listened patiently and quietly as Marty poured out his tale of woe. Then, leaning back in his chair, he said, "First of all, Marty, truly manipulative people have no idea that they are being manipulative. The very fact that you are aware of the possibility is a good sign that you are on the right track. There will always be times when you get your way and the same is true with others, and as long as the score is roughly even, you can be reasonably sure that you are OK. And as far as your parents are concerned, there comes a time in every child's life when he must decide what kind of relationship he will have with his father and mother, no matter what has gone on before. Maybe this is your time."

Marty left the professor's office unburdened by the great weight of guilt that he had piled upon himself, but also filled with a new resolve. Before the end of the day, he had accepted the part-time job that he had flatly refused to consider a few short weeks ago, determined that never again would he solicit his parents for money so that he could evade work. Payday produced a curiously proud moment for Marty when he mailed a generous check to his father, requesting that his parents have dinner at a restaurant together at his expense. "I hope I haven't been too big of a pain in the neck all these years," read the card, "but someday I'm going to make you proud of me." (802 words)

Scoring Miscues for Oral Reading Option
Mark all scoreable miscues by placing either a plus (for those that maintain meaning) or a zero (for those that violate meaning) in the text margin.

Reading Accuracy Index: _____%
*Total all miscues marked with pluses **and** zeros and enter the corresponding percentage from the Miscue Chart.*

Meaning Maintenance Index: _____%
*Total **only** miscues marked with zeros and enter the corresponding percentage from the Miscue Chart.*

Miscue Chart (if used for oral reading)

Miscues	%	Miscues	%	Miscues	%	Miscues	%
1	100	25	97	49	94	73	91
2	100	26	97	50	94	74	91
3	100	27	97	51	94	75	91
4	100	28	97	52	94	76	91
5	99	29	96	53	93	77	90
6	99	30	96	54	93	78	90
7	99	31	96	55	93	79	90
8	99	32	96	56	93	80	90
9	99	33	96	57	93	81	90
10	99	34	96	58	93	82	90
11	99	35	96	59	93	83	90
12	99	36	96	60	93	84	90
13	98	37	95	61	92	85	89
14	98	38	95	62	92	86	89
15	98	39	95	63	92	87	89
16	98	40	95	64	92	88	89
17	98	41	95	65	92	89	89
18	98	42	95	66	92	90	89
19	98	43	95	67	92	91	89
20	98	44	95	68	92	92	89
21	97	45	94	69	91	93	88
22	97	46	94	70	91	94	88
23	97	47	94	71	91	95	88
24	97	48	94	72	91	96	88

Student Retelling

Examiner: "Tell me about what you just read and what you thought about it."

If there is no spontaneous response, repeat the request, "Tell me what you thought about the passage."

Note: Use the Retelling Rubric on p. 240 to assess the child's retelling performance. If you need additional space for retelling responses, use a separate sheet of paper.

Comprehension Questions

_____ 1. Why did the class find the video about Mike so amusing?

Text-Based: It was funny to see a child in charge of the situation; it was obvious to them that Mike was taking advantage of his father.

_____ 2. Why didn't the professor laugh at the video?

Text-Based: He knew the negative consequences of actions such as those demonstrated by Mike.

_____ 3. What would make you believe that Mike's father had not manipulated his parents in the same way that Mike did?

Inference: Research shows that children who act like Mike are the ones that grow up to manipulate, not be manipulated.

_____ 4. What advice would the professor give to Mike to help him avoid becoming manipulative and lazy?

Inference: He has to become self-reflective and think about what he is doing.

_____ 5. Was there any danger that Mike would turn out to be manipulative and lazy? Explain.

Critical Response: Yes—Mike tended to be a bit lazy, preferring to watch videos over reading; he hadn't taken jobs, preferring to tap his parents for money. No—he had used the video to open his eyes to the possibility and once he realized the significance of his actions, he determined to change permanently.

6. Why didn't the professor think that Marty was manipulative in the same way that Marty feared?

Text-Based: The professor knew that truly manipulative people have no idea that they are being manipulative and since Marty was worried about it, that was a good sign that he wasn't manipulative.

7. Why was Marty annoyed with himself when he remembered asking his father for money?

Inference: He saw it as evidence that he was manipulative and lazy.

8. Why was Marty convinced that he needed help from his professor?

Text-Based: He remembered the many times he had manipulated his friends and became fearful that he was doomed for this lifestyle.

9. What would the professor think is more important in the development of personality, the past or the present?

Critical Response: The past—because that's when childhood habits begin that you don't even know that you have. The present— because you have the chance to develop awareness of your behavior and that gives you the opportunity to change it.

10. What kind of friend do you think Marty has been up to this point in his life?

Critical Response: He has been a good friend because he seems to be reflective and think about his actions.
He has been a poor friend because in the past he has been manipulative and self-centered.

Comprehension Analysis:

Text-Based: ___/4___
Inference: ___/3___
Critical Response: ___/3___

Total Comprehension %: ____

TWELFTH GRADE III: THE RETIREMENT COMMUNITY

Reader's copy on p. 95 of the Reader's Passages

Introductory Statement: "Would you read this passage about a couple living in a retirement community (to yourself/out loud). When you are finished, I'll take away the passage. Then I'll ask you to tell me about what you read and what you think of it. After that, I'll ask you some questions about the passage."

Story

Mr. Lancaster strolled the newly paved streets of the Daytona Retirement Community as he had done almost daily for the six months since he and his wife had relocated into their new villa. This was truly Lancaster's fantasy: a new community, a balmy climate (no more Michigan winters for him!), and best of all, no noisy children allowed. Lancaster passed dozens of manicured lawns and professionally landscaped gardens on his regular route through the almost eerie early morning tranquility of the neighborhood. Lancaster was proud that his exercise regimen and limited diet had him in the best physical condition he had seen in decades. And while community maintenance fees were rather steep, he would never have to mow a lawn again or worry if the roof leaked or if the garbage disposal jammed. All it took now was an expeditious phone call and any difficulty with the house or the grounds was immediately resolved.

Even Evelyn seemed to treasure their new life and her new circle of friends, despite her initial stubborn resistance to the move during those difficult days when she begged Lancaster to stay in the old house in Michigan, close to the children and grandchildren. Lancaster chuckled as he thought of his wife's hectic social calendar with the ladies' bridge club, her charity work at the church, her volunteer work at the local elementary school, and the seemingly endless round of planning committee meetings that her benevolent work entailed. True, Lancaster had his beloved golf, but even golfing three or four times a week did not seem to lift Lancaster's game to the level he had anticipated. And although he would never dare admit it to the rest of his regular foursome, he had begun to think that having the leisure to play endless rounds of golf was not all that it was cracked up to be. He had even briefly entertained the idea of seriously pursuing senior tennis, but his old knee injury sounded the alarm and quickly reminded him that he was no longer a spry youngster.

Lancaster stopped himself short; he had caught himself dwelling on the negative instead of the positive yet again. Lancaster had begun to think that his occasional descent into pessimism was something of a character flaw. What more could he possibly desire from his life? His lifestyle was the envy of nearly all of his old friends in Michigan, and Lancaster could not understand why he was beset by those exasperating, gnawing doubts. He knew that Evelyn missed seeing the grandchildren every day, but with phone calls and e-mails and electronically transmitted photographs, they could keep in touch with their children's and their grandchildren's lives almost daily, as Evelyn seldom failed to do. And Lancaster himself could never complain that he was bored, could he? So why did the conviction that he had made a terrible mistake keep cropping up with an increased and disturbing regularity? He had to keep one simple idea very clear in his mind: moving to Florida was not a mistake. He and Evelyn had worked diligently all of their lives to achieve this lifestyle and Lancaster was simply not going to tolerate this weakness. After all, in his professional career, he had drilled into countless protégés the importance of a disciplined mind and now it was time that he started to practice what he had preached.

Lancaster found it monumentally annoying that none of his circle of friends seemed to have any of the kinds of misgivings that haunted him. Only old Wenger would sometimes chide Lancaster with some old nonsense about getting a life and making himself useful, and Wenger would hardly qualify as one of Lancaster's inner circle. Wenger acted as if a forty year career in which Lancaster had risen through the ranks to become chief executive officer of a Fortune 500 company meant nothing! Lancaster knew that he had paid his dues and now it was time to reap the rewards.

Only one element of this entire state of affairs was certain: He could never share with Evelyn the misgivings that had cropped up so often in the past few months. He knew his wife far too well to think that she could easily weather the storm of doubts that would come from second-guessing the decision that had changed their lives so much for the better. One word about his doubts and he would be in for endless soul-searching sessions far into the early hours of morning after morning until they had finally resolved their "problem." No, Lancaster knew that he would have to keep his thoughts to himself. (769 words)

Scoring Miscues for Oral Reading Option

Mark all scoreable miscues by placing either a plus (for those that maintain meaning) or a zero (for those that violate meaning) in the text margin.

Reading Accuracy Index: _____%
*Total all miscues marked with pluses **and** zeros and enter the corresponding percentage from the Miscue Chart.*

Meaning Maintenance Index: _____%
*Total **only** miscues marked with zeros and enter the corresponding percentage from the Miscue Chart.*

Miscue Chart (if used for oral reading)

Miscues	%	Miscues	%	Miscues	%	Miscues	%
1	100	25	97	49	94	73	91
2	100	26	97	50	93	74	90
3	100	27	96	51	93	75	90
4	99	28	96	52	93	76	90
5	99	29	96	53	93	77	90
6	99	30	96	54	93	78	90
7	99	31	96	55	93	79	90
8	99	32	96	56	93	80	90
9	99	33	96	57	93	81	89
10	99	34	96	58	92	82	89
11	99	35	95	59	92	83	89
12	98	36	95	60	92	84	89
13	98	37	95	61	92	85	89
14	98	38	95	62	92	86	89
15	98	39	95	63	92	87	89
16	98	40	95	64	92	88	89
17	98	41	95	65	92	89	88
18	98	42	95	66	91	90	88
19	98	43	94	67	91	91	88
20	97	44	94	68	91	92	88
21	97	45	94	69	91	93	88
22	97	46	94	70	91	94	88
23	97	47	94	71	91	95	88
24	97	48	94	72	91	96	88

Student Retelling

Examiner: "Tell me about what you just read and what you thought about it."

If there is no spontaneous response, repeat the request, "Tell me what you thought about the passage."

Note: Use the Retelling Rubric on p. 244 to assess the child's retelling performance. If you need additional space for retelling responses, use a separate sheet of paper.

Comprehension Questions

_____ 1. Why did Lancaster expect to enjoy his retirement in Florida? (Must include two.)

Text-Based: He had no work; warm weather; no children; new house; free time for golf.

_____ 2. Why had Lancaster's wife argued against the move to Florida?

Text-Based: She didn't want to leave the children and grandchildren.

_____ 3. How was Evelyn's life different from Lancaster's life?

Inference: She accepted change and adjusted to it; she was doing a great deal of worthwhile work.

_____ 4. Why did Lancaster resent Wenger?

Inference: Wenger didn't approve of Lancaster's lifestyle; Wenger felt that Lancaster was doing nothing worthwhile.

_____ 5. Do you think Lancaster used the same approach to problems in his work as a CEO that he does in his personal life? Explain.

Critical Response: Yes—he probably did not make hard decisions and left them to his protégés. No—a successful CEO would have had to face and solve problems; business problems didn't involve the personal feelings that he struggled with.

_____ 6. How did Lancaster and Evelyn keep in touch with their children and grandchildren?

Text-Based: Phone calls, e-mails, and e-photos.

7. What do you think is the basic source of Lancaster's problem?

Inference: He wasn't doing anything worthwhile with his life; he found it difficult to accept the fact that he was not happy.

8. How would you characterize Lancaster's approach to problems in his life?

Text-Based: He avoided problems when he could and refused to accept that his problems existed.

9. Do you think that Lancaster will do anything to increase his happiness in life? Explain.

Critical Response: Yes—he sees the joy that his wife gets from doing worthwhile things and wants to share that with her; he has too many sources of feedback for him to ignore. No—he is not able to be honest with himself and admit that he needs to change.

10. Would you say that Lancaster and his wife have a good marriage? Why or why not?

Critical Response: Yes—they have been together for many years and he seems to have a real concern for her happiness and admires her. No—he has a difficult time communicating with her and avoids sharing his problems with her, and that keeps her at a distance.

Comprehension Analysis:

Text-Based: ___/4
Inference: ___/3
Critical Response: ___/3

Total Comprehension %: ____

Informational Passages Examiner's Copy

Level	Title	Word Count	Readability
Pre-Primer I	All Kinds of Trucks, p. 248	66	0.0
Pre-Primer II	Plants, p. 250	70	0.0
Pre-Primer III	See the Birds, p. 252	73	0.0
Primer I	Turtles, p. 254	110	0.6
Primer II	Planes and Trucks, p. 257	123	0.4
Primer III	Baby Lions, p. 259	110	0.8
First I	Black Bears, p. 262	130	1.6
First II	People in Groups, p. 265	111	1.3
First III	A Bird That Doesn't Fly, p. 268	131	1.6
Second I	Army Ants, p. 271	168	2.4
Second II	The Doctor Fish, p. 274	178	2.6
Second III	A Rose and a Sweet Pea, p. 277	189	2.4
Third I	The Immigrants, p. 280	209	3.8
Third II	Child Slaves, p. 283	206	3.4
Third III	How Banks Work, p. 286	187	3.5
Fourth I	Frida Kahlo, p. 289	220	4.6
Fourth II	Krakatoa, p. 292	215	4.8
Fourth III	Sugar Gliders, p. 295	255	4.6
Fifth I	The Mosquito, p. 298	292	5.4
Fifth II	Oil Spill, p. 301	267	5.7
Fifth III	Bullying, p. 304	299	5.6
Sixth I	A Community of Wolves, p. 307	315	6.4
Sixth II	Are You Afraid of Sharks?, p. 310	353	6.1
Sixth III	Squirrels, p. 313	341	6.3
Seventh I	Mary Jemison, p. 316	367	7.6
Seventh II	Selfish Survival, p. 319	382	7.7
Seventh III	Wayward Whales, p. 322	380	7.5
Eighth I	Dams, p. 325	402	8.4
Eighth II	Jane Addams, p. 328	396	8.5
Eighth III	Possums, p. 331	382	8.5
Ninth I	Insect Camouflage, p. 334	427	9.5
Ninth II	Old Man River, p. 337	428	9.7
Ninth III	The Wise Woman Doctor, p. 340	422	9.7
Tenth I	A Cold Case, p. 344	468	10.4
Tenth II	The Author of Narnia, p. 347	470	10.5
Tenth III	Colored Snow, p. 351	443	10.4
Eleventh I	The Hawaiian Volcano, p. 354	503	11.2
Eleventh II	Politics and Friendship, p. 357	499	11.6
Eleventh III	Context of Philosophies, p. 361	496	11.6
Twelfth I	Quasars, p. 365	516	12.0
Twelfth II	The Search for Pancho Villa, p. 368	528	12.0
Twelfth III	The Continent of Africa, p. 372	554	12.0

PRE-PRIMER I: ALL KINDS OF TRUCKS

Reader's copy on p. 99 of the Reader's Passages

Introductory Statement: "Would you read this passage about trucks (to yourself/out loud). When you are finished, I'll take away the passage. Then I'll ask you to tell me about what you read and what you think of it. After that, I'll ask you some questions about the passage."

Story

A big, red fire truck goes fast.

It helps put out fires.

A small, green truck goes down the street.

It brings boxes to our store.

A tanker truck has a long, long hose.

It brings gas to our gas station.

A large blue truck sprays water.

It cleans our street.

The best truck rings its bell and plays a song.

It brings me a treat. (66 words)

Scoring Miscues for Oral Reading Option
Mark all scoreable miscues by placing either a plus (for those that maintain meaning) or a zero (for those that violate meaning) in the text margin.

Reading Accuracy Index: _____%
*Total all miscues marked with pluses **and** zeros and enter the corresponding percentage from the Miscue Chart.*

Meaning Maintenance Index: _____%
*Total **only** miscues marked with zeros and enter the corresponding percentage from the Miscue Chart.*

Miscue Chart (if used for oral reading)

Miscues	%	Miscues	%	Miscues	%
1	98	7	89	13	80
2	97	8	88	14	79
3	95	9	86	15	77
4	94	10	85	16	76
5	92	11	83	17	74
6	91	12	82	18	73

Student Retelling

Examiner: "Tell me about what you just read and what you thought about it."

If there is no spontaneous response, repeat the request, "Tell me what you thought about the passage."

Note: Use the Retelling Rubric on p. 248 to assess the child's retelling performance. If you need additional space for retelling responses, use a separate sheet of paper.

RETELLING RUBRIC: INFORMATIONAL

Macro-concepts (Numbered and Boldfaced) and Micro-concepts (Bulleted)

Place a 0, 1/2, or + to score student responses. See page 81 for information on what these assessment measures mean.

Story Structure:

____ 1. **There are many kinds of trucks.**
____ 2. **Trucks help people in many ways.**
    ____ • Fire trucks put out fires.
    ____ • Trucks deliver boxes to the stores.
    ____ • Tankers bring gas to the stations.
    ____ • Trucks clean the streets.
____ 3. **Favorite truck is one that brings a treat.**
    ____ • It plays a bell or song.
____ 4. **Personal Response:** Any well-supported positive or negative response to the content or ideas in the text, or to the text as a whole.

Retelling Score: _____

Comprehension Questions

_____ 1. Tell me one way that the passage says how trucks help people.

Text-Based: Put out fires; deliver boxes or gas; clean streets; bring ice cream.

_____ 2. What does the tanker truck use to pump gas?

Text-Based: Long hose.

_____ 3. Why do some trucks in the story need to go faster than others?

Inference: Going to put out fires.

_____ 4. Which truck in the story do you think helps people the most? Why?

Critical Response: Fire truck—saves lives; tanker truck—delivers gas that people need; delivery truck—brings things people need.

_____ 5. Where does the child in the story probably live? Why?

Inference: In or near a city.

_____ 6. Why does the truck in the passage spray water?

Text-Based: It is cleaning the streets.

_____ 7. Why does the child in the story like the last truck best?

Inference: He knows it is the ice cream truck.

_____ 8. The child in the story looks for trucks wherever he goes. Is that a good thing to do? Why?

Critical Response: Yes—he likes trucks; he is interested in trucks. No—he will miss other things that may be better; thinks too much about trucks.

Comprehension Analysis:

Text-Based: __/3__
Inference: __/3__
Critical Response: __/2__

Total Comprehension %: _____

PRE-PRIMER II: PLANTS

Reader's copy on p. 103 of the Reader's Passages

Introductory Statement: "Would you read this passage about plants (to yourself/out loud). When you are finished, I'll take away the passage. Then I'll ask you to tell me about what you read and what you think of it. After that, I'll ask you some questions about the passage."

Story

A man needs food.

He goes to the store.

He buys his food.

A cow needs food.

She walks to the grass.

She eats the grass.

A plant needs food.

It can not move.

It has to make its food.

The roots get the water.

The water moves to the leaf.

The leaf makes food.

The plant eats the food.

People eat the plants.

The plants are good for them. (70 words)

Scoring Miscues for Oral Reading Option
Mark all scoreable miscues by placing either a plus (for those that maintain meaning) or a zero (for those that violate meaning) in the text margin.

Reading Accuracy Index: _____%
Total all miscues marked with pluses and zeros and enter the corresponding percentage from the Miscue Chart.

Meaning Maintenance Index: _____%
Total only miscues marked with zeros and enter the corresponding percentage from the Miscue Chart.

Miscue Chart (if used for oral reading)

Miscues	%	Miscues	%	Miscues	%
1	99	7	90	13	81
2	97	8	89	14	80
3	96	9	87	15	79
4	94	10	86	16	77
5	93	11	84	17	76
6	91	12	83	18	74

Student Retelling

Examiner: "Tell me about what you just read and what you thought about it."

If there is no spontaneous response, repeat the request, "Tell me what you thought about the passage."

Note: Use the Retelling Rubric on p. 250 to assess the child's retelling performance. If you need additional space for retelling responses, use a separate sheet of paper.

RETELLING RUBRIC: INFORMATIONAL

Macro-concepts (Numbered and Boldfaced) and Micro-concepts (Bulleted)

Place a 0, 1/2, or + to score student responses. See page 81 for information on what these assessment measures mean.

Story Structure:

___ 1. **Men and cows need food.**
   ___ • They can move to get their food.
___ 2. **Plants cannot move.**
   ___ • The roots get their water from the soil.
   ___ • The water moves to the leaf.
   ___ • The leaf makes the plant's food.
___ 3. **Plants are good for people.**
   ___ • People use plants for food.
___ 4. **Personal Response:** Any well-supported positive or negative response to the content or ideas in the text, or to the text as a whole.

Retelling Score: _____

Comprehension Questions

_____ 1. Where did the man in the story get food?

Text-Based: From the store.

_____ 2. Where did the cow in the story get food?

Text-Based: It walks to the grass.

_____ 3. How does the story show that walking is important to a cow but not to a plant?

Inference: The cow walks to get food; plant doesn't need to walk to get food.

_____ 4. Use the story to tell who has an easier time getting food, a plant or a cow.

Critical Response: Cow—it can walk to the grass. Plant—it doesn't have to walk; it can make its own food.

_____ 5. Use the story to tell why plants can't get their food like cows do.

Inference: Plants cannot move.

_____ 6. How does the plant get water?

Text-Based: The roots get the water.

_____ 7. Why is the leaf so important to the plant?

Inference: The leaf makes food for the plant; without the leaf the plant cannot get food.

_____ 8. Use the story to tell which is more helpful to plants, the roots or the leaf.

Critical Response: Roots—plant would not be able to make food without roots getting the water. Leaf—it is the place where the food is made.

Comprehension Analysis:

Text-Based: __/3__
Inference: __/3__
Critical Response: __/2__

Total Comprehension %: _____

PRE-PRIMER III: SEE THE BIRDS

Reader's copy on p. 104 of the Reader's Passages

Introductory Statement: "Would you read this passage about birds (to yourself/out loud). When you are finished, I'll take away the passage. Then I'll ask you to tell me about what you read and what you think of it. After that, I'll ask you some questions about the passage."

Story

See the birds.

The birds are in the sky.

The birds fly high.

Some birds are red.

Some birds are yellow.

You can not see the color.

See the birds.

The birds come to eat seeds.

Some birds are red.

Some birds are yellow.

You can see the color.

Do not go by the birds.

The birds will fly.

They may fly into a tree far away.

You will not see the color. (73 words)

Scoring Miscues for Oral Reading Option
Mark all scoreable miscues by placing either a plus (for those that maintain meaning) or a zero (for those that violate meaning) in the text margin.

Reading Accuracy Index: _____ %
*Total all miscues marked with pluses **and** zeros and enter the corresponding percentage from the Miscue Chart.*

Meaning Maintenance Index: _____ %
*Total **only** miscues marked with zeros and enter the corresponding percentage from the Miscue Chart.*

Miscue Chart (if used for oral reading)

Miscues	%	Miscues	%	Miscues	%
1	99	7	90	13	82
2	97	8	89	14	81
3	96	9	88	15	79
4	95	10	86	16	78
5	93	11	85	17	77
6	92	12	84	18	75

Student Retelling

Examiner: "Tell me about what you just read and what you thought about it."

If there is no spontaneous response, repeat the request, "Tell me what you thought about the passage."

Note: Use the Retelling Rubric on p. 252 to assess the child's retelling performance. If you need additional space for retelling responses, use a separate sheet of paper.

RETELLING RUBRIC: INFORMATIONAL

Macro-concepts (Numbered and Boldfaced) and Micro-concepts (Bulleted)

Place a 0, 1/2, or + to score student responses. See page 81 for information on what these assessment measures mean.

Story Structure:

___ 1. **Birds fly in the sky.**
    ___ • Colors are red and yellow.
    ___ • Colors cannot be seen.
___ 2. **Birds come near to eat.**
    ___ • Colors can be seen.
___ 3. **Don't get too close.**
    ___ • Birds will fly away.
    ___ • You can't see their colors.
___ 4. **Personal Response:** Any well-supported positive or negative response to the content or ideas in the text, or to the text as a whole.

Retelling Score: _____

Comprehension Questions

_____ 1. **What colors were the birds in the story? (Must include two.)**

Text-Based: Red and yellow.

_____ 2. **Why did the birds in this story come close by?**

Text-Based: To eat seeds.

_____ 3. **If you like to see the birds, how can you make more of them come close?**

Inference: Put seeds out for them to eat.

_____ 4. **What's more important to the birds in this story, eating or being safe?**

Critical Response: Eating—they come near people so that they can get food. Being safe— they fly away if people come too near.

_____ 5. **Why can't you see the color of the birds in this story when they fly into the trees?**

Inference: They are not near you anymore; they are too far away.

_____ 6. **Why shouldn't you come too close to the birds in this story?**

Text-Based: They will fly away.

_____ 7. **If a bird from this story came near you and you wanted to see its colors, what would be the best thing to do?**

Inference: Don't try to move closer; stay still.

_____ 8. **If you were a farmer, would you be happy to see the birds in this story come to your farm?**

Critical Response: Yes—they are pretty to look at because they have pretty colors. No—they could eat seeds that you have planted.

Comprehension Analysis:

Text-Based: __/3__
Inference: __/3__
Critical Response: __/2__

Total Comprehension %: _____

PRIMER I: TURTLES

Reader's copy on p. 106 of the Reader's Passages

Introductory Statement: "Would you read this passage about turtles (to yourself/out loud). When you are finished, I'll take away the passage. Then I'll ask you to tell me about what you read and what you think of it. After that, I'll ask you some questions about the passage."

Story

Turtles can be big or small.

All turtles can crawl.

Some turtles can swim.

All turtles have shells.

A turtle can hide in its shell and be safe.

Small turtles make good pets.

They can live near a pond or a lake.

They eat worms, bugs, and grass.

Children often catch small turtles and take them home.

They can keep them in a large cage and take care

of them.

They give the turtles water and food.

Large turtles live near the sea.

They catch their food in the sea.

They stay under the water for a long time.

They can swim very fast and can live a long time.

(110 words)

Scoring Miscues for Oral Reading Option
Mark all scoreable miscues by placing either a plus (for those that maintain meaning) or a zero (for those that violate meaning) in the text margin.

Reading Accuracy Index: _____%
*Total all miscues marked with pluses **and** zeros and enter the corresponding percentage from the Miscue Chart.*

Meaning Maintenance Index: _____%
*Total **only** miscues marked with zeros and enter the corresponding percentage from the Miscue Chart.*

Miscue Chart (if used for oral reading)

Miscues	%	Miscues	%	Miscues	%
1	99	9	92	17	85
2	98	10	91	18	84
3	97	11	90	19	83
4	96	12	89	20	82
5	95	13	88	21	81
6	95	14	87	22	80
7	94	15	86	23	79
8	93	16	85	24	78

Student Retelling

Examiner: "Tell me about what you just read and what you thought about it."

If there is no spontaneous response, repeat the request, "Tell me what you thought about the passage."

Note: Use the Retelling Rubric on p. 255 to assess the child's retelling performance. If you need additional space for retelling responses, use a separate sheet of paper.

RETELLING RUBRIC: INFORMATIONAL

Macro-concepts (Numbered and Boldfaced) and Micro-concepts (Bulleted)

Place a 0, 1/2, or + to score student responses. See page 81 for information on what these assessment measures mean.

Story Structure:

___ 1. **Turtles can be big or small.**
___ 2. **Small turtles make good pets.**
  ___ • They are easy to take care of.
  ___ • They are easy to find food for.
___ 3. **Large turtles do not always make good pets.**
  ___ • They live near the sea.
  ___ • They catch their food in the sea.
  ___ • They are hard to take care of.
___ 4. **Personal Response:** Any well-supported positive or negative response to the content or ideas in the text, or to the text as a whole.

Retelling Score: _____

Comprehension Questions

_____ 1. Where could you catch a small turtle?

Text-Based: Near a pond or lake.

_____ 2. Where could you catch a large turtle?

Text-Based: Near the sea.

_____ 3. Would it be easy to find food for a small turtle? Why?

Inference: Yes—bugs, worms, and grass are everywhere.

_____ 4. Which kind of turtle would be better to have for a pet, a small one or a large one? Why?

Critical Response: Small—easy to take care of; could keep him at home. Large—they live a long time; more work but worth it.

_____ 5. Which kind of turtle would be easier to catch, a small one or a large one?

Inference: Small turtle—not as fast; do not live under water; do not swim fast.

_____ 6. Why would it be hard to catch a large turtle?

Text-Based: They swim fast; they live in the sea.

_____ 7. Why don't we see large turtles as often as we see small ones?

Inference: They live near the sea; they stay under water for a long time.

_____ 8. Would it be right to keep a large turtle as a pet?

Critical Response: if you take care of it; if you have enough space. No—it needs too much water; it needs to be free; it needs to swim.

Comprehension Analysis:

Text-Based: _/3_
Inference: _/3_
Critical Response: _/2_

Total Comprehension %: _____

PRIMER II: PLANES AND TRUCKS

Reader's copy on p. 108 of the Reader's Passages

Introductory Statement: "Would you read this passage about planes and trucks (to yourself/out loud). When you are finished, I'll take away the passage. Then I'll ask you to tell me about what you read and what you think of it. After that, I'll ask you some questions about the passage."

Story

A pilot can fly an airplane.

He takes people with him.

He takes goods with him.

He can go a long way but it does not take a long time.

People pay lots of money.

A lady can drive a truck.

She does not take people with her.

She takes goods with her.

She goes a long way too, but it will take a long time.

She carries things people need.

Some people do not like to fly.

They are afraid because the plane flies high and fast.

These people can drive in a car.

They will feel safe.

But they may not be so safe.

There are many cars and trucks on the roads.

There are not many planes in the sky. (123 words)

Scoring Miscues for Oral Reading Option

Mark all scoreable miscues by placing either a plus (for those that maintain meaning) or a zero (for those that violate meaning) in the text margin.

Reading Accuracy Index: _____%
*Total all miscues marked with pluses **and** zeros and enter the corresponding percentage from the Miscue Chart.*

Meaning Maintenance Index: _____%
*Total **only** miscues marked with zeros and enter the corresponding percentage from the Miscue Chart.*

Miscue Chart (if used for oral reading)

Miscues	%	Miscues	%	Miscues	%
1	99	9	93	17	86
2	98	10	92	18	85
3	98	11	91	19	85
4	97	12	90	20	84
5	96	13	89	21	83
6	95	14	89	22	82
7	94	15	88	23	81
8	93	16	87	24	80

Student Retelling

Examiner: "Tell me about what you just read and what you thought about it."

If there is no spontaneous response, repeat the request, "Tell me what you thought about the passage."

Note: Use the Retelling Rubric on p. 257 to assess the child's retelling performance. If you need additional space for retelling responses, use a separate sheet of paper.

RETELLING RUBRIC: INFORMATIONAL

Macro-concepts (Numbered and Boldfaced) and Micro-concepts (Bulleted)

Place a 0, 1/2, or + to score student responses. See page 81 for information on what these assessment measures mean.

Story Structure:

____ 1. **Airplanes are fast.**
    ____ • Airplanes carry people.
    ____ • Airplanes cost lots of money.
____ 2. **Trucks are slower.**
    ____ • Trucks do not cost as much money.
____ 3. **Some people are afraid to fly.**
    ____ • They feel safe in a car.
    ____ • They may not be as safe as they think.
____ 4. **Personal Response:** Any well-supported positive or negative response to the content or ideas in the text, or to the text as a whole.

Retelling Score: _____

Comprehension Questions

_____ 1. What does the pilot take with him that the truck driver does not take?

Text-Based: People.

_____ 2. What docs the truck driver take with her when she drives?

Text-Based: Goods.

_____ 3. Why do people pay more money to use a plane than they do to use a truck?

Inference: Plane is faster; more convenient; people want to go faster.

_____ 4. If someone had to travel to another state, should he or she use a plane or a car? Why?

Critical Response: Plane—it is faster; some people think it is safer. Car—costs less; many people feel safer in a car.

_____ 5. Why would people feel safe in a car but not in an airplane?

Inference: Planes fly fast and high; plane crash is more dangerous; more serious.

_____ 6. If a person has to go a long way, why would he or she want to fly?

Text-Based: To get there faster.

_____ 7. Why would people who drive not be as safe as they think they are?

Inference: There are more cars on the road; there are more accidents.

_____ 8. Who has the more important job, the pilot or the truck driver? Explain.

Critical Response: Pilot—carries more people and truck driver only has herself and her goods. Truck driver—she carries lots of goods that people need.

Comprehension Analysis:

Text-Based: __/3__
Inference: __/3__
Critical Response: __/2__

Total Comprehension %: _____

PRIMER III: BABY LIONS

Reader's copy on p. 109 of the Reader's Passages

Introductory Statement: "Would you read this passage about baby lions (to yourself/out loud). When you are finished, I'll take away the passage. Then I'll ask you to tell me about what you read and what you think of it. After that, I'll ask you some questions about the passage."

Story

Baby lions are called cubs.

Baby lions are furry.

The cubs like to stay with the mother.

Baby lions like to play.

They run.

They jump.

They roll.

Baby lions like to eat.

They eat meat.

They eat grass.

They drink milk.

They drink water.

Baby lions like to sleep.

They sleep in the day.

It is too hot to play.

They like to nap under a tree.

A big lion keeps them safe.

Baby lions like to be clean.

They clean each other.

The mother licks them clean.

Baby lions like to play.

Baby lions like to eat.

Baby lions like to sleep.

Baby lions like to be clean. (110 words)

Scoring Miscues for Oral Reading Option
Mark all scoreable miscues by placing either a plus (for those that maintain meaning) or a zero (for those that violate meaning) in the text margin.

Reading Accuracy Index: _____%
*Total all miscues marked with pluses **and** zeros and enter the corresponding percentage from the Miscue Chart.*

Meaning Maintenance Index: _____%
*Total **only** miscues marked with zeros and enter the corresponding percentage from the Miscue Chart.*

Miscue Chart (if used for oral reading)

Miscues	%	Miscues	%	Miscues	%
1	99	9	92	17	85
2	98	10	91	18	84
3	97	11	90	19	83
4	96	12	89	20	82
5	95	13	88	21	81
6	95	14	87	22	80
7	94	15	86	23	79
8	93	16	85	24	78

Student Retelling

Examiner: "Tell me about what you just read and what you thought about it."

If there is no spontaneous response, repeat the request, "Tell me what you thought about the passage."

Note: Use the Retelling Rubric on p. 260 to assess the child's retelling performance. If you need additional space for retelling responses, use a separate sheet of paper.

RETELLING RUBRIC: INFORMATIONAL

Macro-concepts (Numbered and Boldfaced) and Micro-concepts (Bulleted)

Place a 0, 1/2, or + to score student responses. See page 81 for information on what these assessment measures mean.

Story Structure:

___ 1. **Baby lions like to play and eat.**
  ___ • They run, jump, and roll.
  ___ • They eat meat and grass.
  ___ • They drink milk and water.
___ 2. **Baby lions like to sleep.**
  ___ • They sleep under a tree in the day.
___ 3. **Baby lions like to be clean.**
  ___ • The cubs lick each other and their mother licks them.
___ 4. **Personal Response:** Any well-supported positive or negative response to the content or ideas in the text, or to the text as a whole.

Retelling Score: _____

Comprehension Questions

_____ 1. How do baby lions play? (Must identify two.)

Text-Based: Run; jump; roll.

_____ 2. What do baby lions eat? (Must identify two.)

Text-Based: Meat; grass.

_____ 3. Why doesn't a baby cub take a nap when it is alone?

Inference: Needs a big lion to watch it; needs a big lion to keep it safe.

_____ 4. Who would a baby lion rather be with, another little cub or a big lion?

Critical Response: Another cub—they have fun playing together, they keep each other clean. Big lion—it will protect it; it helps clean it; it gives it food.

_____ 5. How are the baby lions in this story like baby children?

Inference: They take naps; adults keep them safe; adults get them food.

_____ 6. When do baby lions sleep?

Text-Based: In the day.

_____ 7. Why do baby lions like to sleep under a tree?

Inference: It is hot so they go there to be away from the heat; there is shade under the tree.

_____ 8. When might a cub need more help, eating or keeping itself clean? Explain.

Critical Response: Eating—it needs a big lion to get the meat and milk. Keeping itself clean—it needs other cubs or its mother to lick it clean; it can't reach everything with its tongue.

Comprehension Analysis:

Text-Based: __/3__
Inference: __/3__
Critical Response: __/2__

Total Comprehension %: _____

FIRST GRADE I: BLACK BEARS

Reader's copy on p. 111 of the Reader's Passages

Introductory Statement: "Would you read this passage about black bears (to yourself/out loud). When you are finished, I'll take away the passage. Then I'll ask you to tell me about what you read and what you think of it. After that, I'll ask you some questions about the passage."

Story

Black bears live in the U.S.

They live near woods or near mountains.

They live in dens.

The dens can be inside a tree or a cave.

Bears sleep all winter.

In spring, they wake up hungry.

Sometimes they can't find enough food.

They like to eat berries, honey, nuts, and acorns.

But they will eat almost anything.

If they don't find food close to home, they go out

looking.

One bear and her cubs could not find enough to eat.

They came down the mountain.

They broke into someone's house.

This was very dangerous.

They took cookies, dog food, and honey.

The cubs took burgers off the grill.

People found the cubs.

The cubs only weighed 20 pounds.

They should have weighed 50 pounds.

No wonder they were hungry. (130 words)

Scoring Miscues for Oral Reading Option
Mark all scoreable miscues by placing either a plus (for those that maintain meaning) or a zero (for those that violate meaning) in the text margin.

Reading Accuracy Index: _____%
*Total all miscues marked with pluses **and** zeros and enter the corresponding percentage from the Miscue Chart.*

Meaning Maintenance Index: _____%
*Total **only** miscues marked with zeros and enter the corresponding percentage from the Miscue Chart.*

Miscue Chart (if used for oral reading)

Miscues	%	Miscues	%	Miscues	%
1	99	11	92	21	84
2	98	12	91	22	83
3	98	13	90	23	82
4	97	14	89	24	82
5	96	15	88	25	81
6	95	16	88	26	80
7	95	17	87	27	79
8	94	18	86	28	78
9	93	19	85	29	78
10	92	20	85	30	77

Student Retelling

Examiner: "Tell me about what you just read and what you thought about it."

If there is no spontaneous response, repeat the request, "Tell me what you thought about the passage."

Note: Use the Retelling Rubric on p. 263 to assess the child's retelling performance. If you need additional space for retelling responses, use a separate sheet of paper.

RETELLING RUBRIC: INFORMATIONAL

Macro-concepts (Numbered and Boldfaced) and Micro-concepts (Bulleted)

Place a 0, 1/2, or + to score student responses. See page 81 for information on what these assessment measures mean.

Story Structure:

___ 1. **Black bears live in the U.S.**
  ___ • They live in dens.
  ___ • They sleep all winter.
___ 2. **Black bears need to find food.**
  ___ • They wake up hungry.
  ___ • They will eat anything.
___ 3. **Bears will come near people's homes to find food.**
  ___ • This can be very dangerous.
___ 4. **Personal Response:** Any well-supported positive or negative response to the content or ideas in the text, or to the text as a whole.

Retelling Score: _____

Comprehension Questions

_____ 1. Where do black bears in the United States live?

   Text-Based: In woods, near mountains, in dens.

_____ 2. Why did the bears in the story leave their home in the mountain?

   Text-Based: They couldn't find enough to eat.

_____ 3. Use the story to tell why we don't see black bears very often in the city.

   Inference: They live near mountains and woods; don't want their sleep to be disturbed.

_____ 4. Would bears rather eat people's food or food they could find near their homes? Why?

   Critical Response: Food near home—more familiar; less trouble; don't have to travel to eat. People's food—often better than wild food; often easier to find than food in the wild.

_____ 5. Why was it dangerous for the bears in the story to break into homes looking for food?

   Inference: They could be shot and killed; they could damage the homes; they could injure the people living there.

_____ 6. What was wrong with the bear cubs in the story?

   Text-Based: They could not find enough to eat; they were very thin.

_____ 7. How does this story prove that bears eat almost everything?

   Inference: In the story they ate things like cookies, burgers, dog food, and honey; the bears ate people food.

_____ 8. Do you think the bears *should* sleep all winter instead of going out to find food? Explain.

Critical Response: Yes—that is natural for them; they need to sleep in order to survive; there would be little food available in winter anyway. No—if they looked for food all winter they wouldn't be so hungry in the spring.

Comprehension Analysis:

Text-Based: _/3_
Inference: _/3_
Critical Response: _/2_

Total Comprehension %: _____

FIRST GRADE II: PEOPLE IN GROUPS

Reader's copy on p. 113 of the Reader's Passages

Introductory Statement: "Would you read this passage about people living in groups (to yourself/out loud). When you are finished, I'll take away the passage. Then I'll ask you to tell me about what you read and what you think of it. After that, I'll ask you some questions about the passage."

Story

Long ago people lived in groups.

They were called tribes.

They hunted and fished together.

They found plants and berries.

They moved on foot from place to place.

They followed the animals.

They only killed the animals they needed.

They did not grow their own food.

They had to work together to live.

Today people live in groups, too.

They live in cities and towns.

They still like to hunt and fish.

But now they grow their own food on farms.

They also raise their own animals.

But most people buy their food.

They have cars and planes to help them move.

But they still have to work together to live. (111 words)

Scoring Miscues for Oral Reading Option
Mark all scoreable miscues by placing either a plus (for those that maintain meaning) or a zero (for those that violate meaning) in the text margin.

Reading Accuracy Index: _____%
*Total all miscues marked with pluses **and** zeros and enter the corresponding percentage from the Miscue Chart.*

Meaning Maintenance Index: _____%
*Total **only** miscues marked with zeros and enter the corresponding percentage from the Miscue Chart.*

Miscue Chart (if used for oral reading)

Miscues	%	Miscues	%	Miscues	%
1	99	11	90	21	81
2	98	12	89	22	80
3	97	13	88	23	79
4	96	14	87	24	78
5	95	15	86	25	77
6	95	16	86	26	77
7	94	17	85	27	76
8	93	18	84	28	75
9	92	19	83	29	74
10	91	20	82	30	73

Student Retelling

Examiner: "Tell me about what you just read and what you thought about it."

If there is no spontaneous response, repeat the request, "Tell me what you thought about the passage."

Note: Use the Retelling Rubric on p. 266 to assess the child's retelling performance. If you need additional space for retelling responses, use a separate sheet of paper.

RETELLING RUBRIC: INFORMATIONAL

Macro-concepts (Numbered and Boldfaced) and Micro-concepts (Bulleted)

Place a 0, 1/2, or + to score student responses. See page 81 for information on what these assessment measures mean.

Story Structure:

___ 1. **Long ago people lived in tribes.**
  ___ • They moved from place to place.
  ___ • They found food.
  ___ • They hunted animals.
___ 2. **Today people live in cities or towns.**
  ___ • They grow their own food.
  ___ • They buy it in stores.
___ 3. **But people must still work together.**
___ 4. **Personal Response:** Any well-supported positive or negative response to the content or ideas in the text, or to the text as a whole.

Retelling Score: _____

Comprehension Questions

_____ 1. What were people called who lived in groups long ago?

Text-Based: Tribes.

_____ 2. Why did people long ago have to move from place to place?

Text-Based: They needed to find food; they had to follow the animals; they had to catch fish.

_____ 3. Why did people long ago kill only the animals they needed?

Inference: They didn't want to run out of food; they would starve if they killed too many.

_____ 4. Which group of people would need to work together more, people from long ago or people of today?

Critical Response: Long ago—they would need to find hunting places; they would need to find fishing places; they would need to find berries and share their food. Today—people work in the stores to sell; not everybody grows food; we need people to fix the cars and planes; there are more people in cities and towns so they need to work together.

_____ 5. Why didn't people from long ago live in cities and towns?

Inference: They had to keep moving and they would have to leave their homes behind.

_____ 6. How does the story tell us why it is easier to find food today?

Text-Based: People can grow their own food; they can go to the store and buy it; they don't have to go out hunting.

_____ 7. Why didn't the people from long ago grow their own food?

Inference: They had to keep following food supplies; could not wait to harvest the crops.

_____ 8. Use the story to tell whether life would
have been easier today or long ago.

*Critical Response: Long ago—hunting
and fishing would be fun. Today—safer
and easier to get food, shelter.*

Comprehension Analysis:

Text-Based: _/3_
Inference: _/3_
Critical Response: _/2_

Total Comprehension %: _____

INFORMATIONAL PASSAGES
FIRST GRADE

FIRST GRADE III: A BIRD THAT DOESN'T FLY

Reader's copy on p. 114 of the Reader's Passages

Introductory Statement: "Would you read this passage about a bird that doesn't fly (to yourself/out loud). When you are finished, I'll take away the passage. Then I'll ask you to tell me about what you read and what you think of it. After that, I'll ask you some questions about the passage."

Story

There is a bird that doesn't fly.

This bird loves to swim.

This bird lives in the cold.

This bird is a penguin.

Some penguins live at the South Pole.

They like to play and swim.

In the fall, they walk far.

They walk far to lay their egg.

The father penguin keeps the egg safe.

The mother penguin knows the baby will need food.

So, the mother penguin walks far to get food.

When she gets back, the egg is already hatched.

A baby penguin is born.

The father penguin is hungry.

The baby penguin wants food.

Only the mother penguin feeds the baby.

The father penguin has to walk far to get food for
     himself.

The mother and the baby and the father penguin will
     all get to eat. (131 words)

Scoring Miscues for Oral Reading Option

Mark all scoreable miscues by placing either a plus (for those that maintain meaning) or a zero (for those that violate meaning) in the text margin.

Reading Accuracy Index: _____%

*Total all miscues marked with pluses **and** zeros and enter the corresponding percentage from the Miscue Chart.*

Meaning Maintenance Index: _____%

*Total **only** miscues marked with zeros and enter the corresponding percentage from the Miscue Chart.*

Miscue Chart (if used for oral reading)

Miscues	%	Miscues	%	Miscues	%
1	99	11	92	21	84
2	98	12	91	22	83
3	98	13	90	23	82
4	97	14	89	24	82
5	96	15	89	25	81
6	95	16	88	26	80
7	95	17	87	27	79
8	94	18	86	28	79
9	93	19	85	29	78
10	92	20	85	30	77

Student Retelling

Examiner: "Tell me about what you just read and what you thought about it."

If there is no spontaneous response, repeat the request, "Tell me what you thought about the passage."

Note: Use the Retelling Rubric on p. 269 to assess the child's retelling performance. If you need additional space for retelling responses, use a separate sheet of paper.

RETELLING RUBRIC: INFORMATIONAL

Macro-concepts (Numbered and Boldfaced) and Micro-concepts (Bulleted)

Place a 0, 1/2, or + to score student responses. See page 81 for information on what these assessment measures mean.

Story Structure:

___ 1. **Some penguins live at the South Pole.**
___   • They play and swim.
___ 2. **Penguins take care of their babies.**
___   • They walk far to lay eggs.
___   • The mother goes to get food for the baby.
___   • The father keeps the egg safe.
___ 3. **Father needs to eat.**
___   • He walks far to get his food.
___ 4. **Personal Response:** Any well-supported positive or negative response to the content or ideas in the text, or to the text as a whole.

Retelling Score: _____

Comprehension Questions

_____ 1. Where do some penguins live?

Text-Based: At the South Pole.

_____ 2. What do penguins like to do? (Must identify two.)

Text-Based: They play and swim.

_____ 3. Why is walking so important to the mother penguin?

Inference: She has to walk far so that she can lay her eggs; she has to walk far to get food for the babies.

_____ 4. Who has the most important job for the baby penguin, the mother or the father? Explain.

Critical Response: The mother penguin— she is the one who walks far to lay the eggs and then she has to walk far to get food for the babies. The father penguin—he is the one who has to keep the eggs safe and then he has to walk to get food for himself.

_____ 5. Why doesn't the father penguin get food for the baby?

Inference: He must watch the egg; he stays with the egg.

_____ 6. Why is the father penguin hungry when the mother returns?

Text-Based: He could not go and find food because he had to watch the eggs.

_____ 7. How does this story show that the penguin family works well together?

Inference: The mother and father both walk far to lay the egg; they both take care of the baby penguin in different ways.

_____ 8. Whose needs do the penguin parents think are more important, their own needs or the needs of the baby penguin? Explain.

Critical Response: Their needs—because they go get food when they are hungry and they have to walk very far. The baby penguin's needs—because they take care of the baby's needs before they take care of their own.

Comprehension Analysis:

   Text-Based: __/3__
   Inference: __/3__
   Critical Response: __/2__

Total Comprehension %: _____

INFORMATIONAL PASSAGES
FIRST GRADE

SECOND GRADE I: ARMY ANTS

Reader's copy on p. 115 of the Reader's Passages

Introductory Statement: "Would you read this passage about army ants (to yourself/out loud). When you are finished, I'll take away the passage. Then I'll ask you to tell me about what you read and what you think of it. After that, I'll ask you some questions about the passage."

Story

Do you ever run from ants? Some people in South America do. They run from the army ants. The ants are only about the size of your fingernail. But they have large and strong jaws. Army ants march in very large numbers looking for food. They march very slowly in a row four feet wide. But most armies are more than a mile long. All animals must get out of their way. They can bite and kill large animals and they can even kill people.

Army ants are hard to stop. They can climb over walls and trees. Not even water can stop them. They just hold onto each other with their jaws and then roll themselves into a ball. Then they can float across rivers and streams! Sometimes the ants march close to a village. Then the people must all move out. But some of the people are glad to see the ants. The ants clean up the town for them by killing small animals and pests.

(168 words)

Scoring Miscues for Oral Reading Option
Mark all scoreable miscues by placing either a plus (for those that maintain meaning) or a zero (for those that violate meaning) in the text margin.

Reading Accuracy Index: _____%
*Total all miscues marked with pluses **and** zeros and enter the corresponding percentage from the Miscue Chart.*

Meaning Maintenance Index: _____%
*Total **only** miscues marked with zeros and enter the corresponding percentage from the Miscue Chart.*

Miscue Chart (if used for oral reading)

Miscues	%	Miscues	%	Miscues	%
1	99	11	93	21	88
2	99	12	93	22	87
3	98	13	92	23	86
4	98	14	92	24	86
5	97	15	91	25	85
6	96	16	90	26	85
7	96	17	90	27	84
8	95	18	89	28	83
9	95	19	89	29	83
10	94	20	88	30	82

Student Retelling

Examiner: "Tell me about what you just read and what you thought about it."

If there is no spontaneous response, repeat the request, "Tell me what you thought about the passage."

Note: Use the Retelling Rubric on p. 272 to assess the child's retelling performance. If you need additional space for retelling responses, use a separate sheet of paper.

RETELLING RUBRIC: INFORMATIONAL

Macro-concepts (Numbered and Boldfaced) and Micro-concepts (Bulleted)

Place a 0, 1/2, or + to score student responses. See page 81 for information on what these assessment measures mean.

Story Structure:

___ 1. **Army ants in South America can be dangerous.**
___   • The armies have large numbers of ants.
___   • The ants have strong jaws.
___ 2. **People can't avoid them so they must get out of the way.**
___   • The ants can climb over walls.
___   • The ants can float over streams.
___ 3. **Ants can do good as well as harm.**
___   • Ants clean up the town when they pass through.
___ 4. **Personal Response:** Any well-supported positive or negative response to the content or ideas in the text, or to the text as a whole.

Retelling Score: _____

Comprehension Questions

_____ 1. How big is an army ant?

Text-Based: About the size of your fingernail.

_____ 2. How do the ants do something good for the people in the villages?

Text-Based: They clean up the village and remove pests.

_____ 3. Why can't animals just walk around the army of ants to get away from them?

Inference: The row is more than a mile long.

_____ 4. Why don't people in the villages build a wall to protect themselves from the ants?

Inference: The ants would be able to climb over the wall.

_____ 5. If you lived in a village, would you be happy or unhappy to see the ants coming? Explain.

Critical Response: Unhappy—too much danger; very inconvenient to have to move out; where do they stay? Happy—the village and all the houses are free from pests; village is cleaner.

_____ 6. Why do the people in the villages move out when the ants are moving close by?

Text-Based: They would be bitten or killed by the ants.

_____ 7. If the army ants are so small, how would they be able to kill and eat a large animal?

Inference: There are so many of them.

_____ 8. How do army ants cross rivers and streams?

Text-Based: They have to hold on to each other and float; they have to roll each other into a ball.

_____ 9. Why would it be a good idea to jump into a river if the ants were biting you? Why or why not?

Inference: The ants need their jaws to hold onto each other and they wouldn't be able to bite you.

_____ 10. Do you think it would be a good idea for the people in South America to kill all of the army ants?

Critical Response: Yes—then there would be no danger to people and animals. No—the ants kill pests and without them there may be too many pests to control; some animals eat ants.

SECOND GRADE II: THE DOCTOR FISH

Reader's copy on p. 116 of the Reader's Passages

Introductory Statement: "Would you read this passage about a special kind of fish (to yourself/out loud). When you are finished, I'll take away the passage. Then I'll ask you to tell me about what you read and what you think of it. After that, I'll ask you some questions about the passage."

Story

Some animals are a big help to other animals. One animal that helps others is the wrasse. The wrasse is a fish about four inches long. He is very brightly colored. He lives in the South Pacific Ocean. He is like a doctor to other fish.

His office is in the rocks called reefs. Many fish come to the doctor for help. These fish have animals that live on their bodies. They would like to have them taken off. The wrasse eats these tiny animals. He also uses his teeth to clean wounds. He helps the fish to get better.

The doctor can be very busy. Sometimes he works all day. But the doctor gets his pay too! The doctor gets the food he likes from his patients. They also protect the doctor from bigger fish. But the doctor and his patients must be careful. A fish called the blenny looks just like the wrasse. Some fish think they are coming to see the doctor. Then the blenny takes a bite out of them! That makes things worse. (178 words)

Scoring Miscues for Oral Reading Option
Mark all scoreable miscues by placing either a plus (for those that maintain meaning) or a zero (for those that violate meaning) in the text margin.

Reading Accuracy Index: _____%
*Total all miscues marked with pluses **and** zeros and enter the corresponding percentage from the Miscue Chart.*

Meaning Maintenance Index: _____%
*Total **only** miscues marked with zeros and enter the corresponding percentage from the Miscue Chart.*

Miscue Chart (if used for oral reading)

Miscues	%	Miscues	%	Miscues	%
1	99	11	94	21	88
2	99	12	93	22	88
3	98	13	93	23	87
4	98	14	92	24	87
5	97	15	92	25	86
6	97	16	91	26	85
7	96	17	90	27	85
8	96	18	90	28	84
9	95	19	89	29	84
10	94	20	89	30	83

Student Retelling

Examiner: "Tell me about what you just read and what you thought about it."

If there is no spontaneous response, repeat the request, "Tell me what you thought about the passage."

Note: Use the Retelling Rubric on p. 275 to assess the child's retelling performance. If you need additional space for retelling responses, use a separate sheet of paper.

RETELLING RUBRIC: INFORMATIONAL

Macro-concepts (Numbered and Boldfaced) and Micro-concepts (Bulleted)

Place a 0, 1/2, or + to score student responses. See page 81 for information on what these assessment measures mean.

Story Structure:

___ 1. **The wrasse is like a doctor to other fish.**
   ___ • He eats little animals that live on fish.
   ___ • He cleans their wounds.
___ 2. **The doctor fish is paid for his services.**
   ___ • Fish bring him food.
   ___ • They protect the wrasse from harm.
___ 3. **The blenny fools fish into thinking he is a wrasse.**
   ___ • The blenny can be dangerous to fish.
___ 4. **Personal Response:** Any well-supported positive or negative response to the content or ideas in the text, or to the text as a whole.

Retelling Score: _____

Comprehension Questions

_____ 1. **How is the wrasse like a doctor?**

Text-Based: He helps sick fish; he cleans wounds; he has an office; he gets paid.

_____ 2. **How do fish pay the doctor for his help?**

Text-Based: The animals that live on them are food for the wrasse; they will protect the wrasse from other fish.

_____ 3. **How can fish find the wrasse when they need help?**

Inference: They know where the office is located; they can tell by the bright colors of the wrasse.

_____ 4. **What advantages does the blenny have by looking just like the wrasse?**

Inference: Gets food from biting the fish; other fish may even protect him.

_____ 5. **Would a human doctor accept the same kind of pay that the doctor fish does? Explain.**

Critical Response: No—doctors don't need protection from patients. Yes—doctors may accept food or other things in exchange for treatment.

_____ 6. **Where is the doctor fish's office?**

Text-Based: In the rocks; in the reefs.

_____ 7. **Why would other fish protect the wrasse from harm?**

Inference: They may need his help one day.

_____ 8. **Why wouldn't the doctor fish in the story mind that he is very busy some days?**

Text-Based: He gets food from helping the fish; the other fish protect him.

_____ 9. Why wouldn't the wrasse be able to help every *kind* of fish that lives in the ocean?

Inference: He would be too big to help some and too small to help very large fish.

Comprehension Analysis:

   Text-Based: __/4__
   Inference: __/4__
   Critical Response: __/2__

Total Comprehension %: _____

_____ 10. Who do you think gets the better deal, the wrasse or the fish that he helps? Tell why.

Critical Response: The wrasse—food that he likes; he gets protection from bigger fish. Fish—he helps get the animals taken off; they get their wounds cleaned; they get better.

SECOND GRADE III: A ROSE AND A SWEET PEA

Reader's copy on p. 117 of the Reader's Passages

Introductory Statement: "Would you read this passage about two kinds of flowers (to yourself/out loud). When you are finished, I'll take away the passage. Then I'll ask you to tell me about what you read and what you think of it. After that, I'll ask you some questions about the passage."

Story

I have some rose bushes in my yard. They make a border for my flower garden. Their sharp thorns keep animals and pests away. Some of my rose plants are climbers. I put stakes by the plants so they can climb high.

Roses bloom all summer long. Even if I pick some flowers, more will bloom and they will not stop until winter comes. When it gets cold, the cell walls of the rose plant grow thick. This protects them from the cold and they will bloom again the next year.

I have many flowers called "sweet peas" in my garden. They come in many colors, they smell very nice, and they bloom all summer too. Most sweet peas are climbers. Many people love sweet peas and some people call them the "queen of one-year flowers."

In the winter the roots of the sweet pea plants die. If some seeds have fallen, new plants will start to grow in the spring. But not everything about the sweet pea is sweet. If you see a seed, do not eat it. It is full of poison and you may get sick. (189 words)

Scoring Miscues for Oral Reading Option
Mark all scoreable miscues by placing either a plus (for those that maintain meaning) or a zero (for those that violate meaning) in the text margin.

Reading Accuracy Index: _____%
*Total all miscues marked with pluses **and** zeros and enter the corresponding percentage from the Miscue Chart.*

Meaning Maintenance Index: _____%
*Total **only** miscues marked with zeros and enter the corresponding percentage from the Miscue Chart.*

Miscue Chart (if used for oral reading)

Miscues	%	Miscues	%	Miscues	%
1	99	11	94	21	89
2	99	12	94	22	88
3	98	13	93	23	88
4	98	14	93	24	87
5	97	15	92	25	87
6	97	16	92	26	86
7	96	17	91	27	86
8	96	18	90	28	85
9	95	19	90	29	85
10	95	20	89	30	84

Student Retelling

Examiner: "Tell me about what you just read and what you thought about it."

If there is no spontaneous response, repeat the request, "Tell me what you thought about the passage."

Note: Use the Retelling Rubric on p. 278 to assess the child's retelling performance. If you need additional space for retelling responses, use a separate sheet of paper.

RETELLING RUBRIC: INFORMATIONAL

Macro-concepts (Numbered and Boldfaced) and Micro-concepts (Bulleted)

Place a 0, 1/2, or + to score student responses. See page 81 for information on what these assessment measures mean.

Story Structure:

___ 1. **Roses do not die in winter.**
   ___ • Roses can be bushes or climbers.
   ___ • Their thick cell walls protect them from the cold.
___ 2. **Sweet peas die in winter.**
   ___ • Lots of colors make them popular at weddings.
___ 3. **Both flowers have danger.**
   ___ • Roses have thorns.
   ___ • Sweet peas have poisonous seeds.
___ 4. **Personal Response:** Any well-supported positive or negative response to the content or ideas in the text, or to the text as a whole.

Retelling Score: _____

Comprehension Questions

_____ 1. What are the two kinds of rose plants?

Text-Based: Bushes and climbers.

_____ 2. Why would roses be a good border for a flower garden?

Text-Based: Their sharp thorns keep pests away.

_____ 3. What is the most important difference between roses and sweet peas?

Inference: Roses do not die in the winter but sweet pea plants die.

_____ 4. Why would someone plant sweet peas in a garden since they live only one year?

Inference: They make your garden smell nice; they bloom with lots of colors.

_____ 5. If you did not want to work hard in your garden, which flower should you plant, the rose or the sweet pea? Explain.

Critical Response: Rose—don't have to plant it every year. Sweet Pea—if I leave seeds, I won't have to plant them next year.

_____ 6. What name have people given to the sweet pea?

Text-Based: Queen of the one-year flowers.

_____ 7. In what ways are the roses and sweet peas alike?

Inference: They bloom all summer; they are climbers.

_____ 8. Why isn't everything about the sweet peas sweet?

Text-Based: Their seeds have poison that can make you sick.

_____ 9. Why would sweet peas be more popular then roses at weddings?

Inference: Roses have the thorns and could pick people; sweet peas smell nice and have lots of pretty colors.

Comprehension Analysis:

Text-Based: __/4__
Inference: __/4__
Critical Response: __/2__

Total Comprehension %: _____

_____10. Which plant would be more of a problem for your pet, sweet peas or roses? Explain.

Critical Response: Sweet peas because their seeds have poison in them; roses since they have thorns that could hurt animals.

THIRD GRADE I: THE IMMIGRANTS

Reader's copy on p. 118 of the Reader's Passages

Introductory Statement: "Would you read this passage about immigrants (to yourself/out loud). When you are finished, I'll take away the passage. Then I'll ask you to tell me about what you read and what you think of it. After that, I'll ask you some questions about the passage."

Story

Between 1820 and 1920 many people moved to America. Some came to find better jobs. Others came because they were not free in their own lands. Others came because their country's leaders did not like them. Most people just came looking for a better life. They were called immigrants.

Most of these people came to America on sailing ships. Some trips took only a few weeks. Others took months. Some people could afford a cabin for themselves. They were lucky. The rest stayed in large rooms below the deck. The rooms were crowded and often dirty. The food was very poor. The water was sometimes rough. The trip was very dangerous.

The immigrants finally arrived in New York. Then they would wait in line for hours. They had to find out if they were healthy enough to stay. There was a long line for most people. There was a short line for richer people.

Many of these new Americans were not welcome. They could not speak English. They were different and strange. They were willing to work for low wages. But some factory owners would not hire them at all. These owners all seemed to forget one thing. Almost everyone in America had family members who were immigrants themselves. (209 words)

Scoring Miscues for Oral Reading Option

Mark all scoreable miscues by placing either a plus (for those that maintain meaning) or a zero (for those that violate meaning) in the text margin.

Reading Accuracy Index: _____%

*Total all miscues marked with pluses **and** zeros and enter the corresponding percentage from the Miscue Chart.*

Meaning Maintenance Index: _____%

*Total **only** miscues marked with zeros and enter the corresponding percentage from the Miscue Chart.*

Miscue Chart (if used for oral reading)

Miscues	%	Miscues	%	Miscues	%
1	100	12	94	23	89
2	99	13	94	24	89
3	99	14	93	25	88
4	98	15	93	26	88
5	98	16	92	27	87
6	97	17	92	28	87
7	97	18	91	29	86
8	96	19	91	30	86
9	96	20	90	31	85
10	95	21	90	32	85
11	95	22	89	33	84

Student Retelling

Examiner: "Tell me about what you just read and what you thought about it."

If there is no spontaneous response, repeat the request, "Tell me what you thought about the passage."

Note: Use the Retelling Rubric on p. 281 to assess the child's retelling performance. If you need additional space for retelling responses, use a separate sheet of paper.

RETELLING RUBRIC: INFORMATIONAL

Macro-concepts (Numbered and Boldfaced) and Micro-concepts (Bulleted)

Place a 0, 1/2, or + to score student responses. See page 81 for information on what these assessment measures mean.

Story Structure:

___ 1. **People came to America to find a better life.**
  ___ • Some came looking for freedom.
  ___ • Some came looking for jobs.
___ 2. **It was a dangerous journey to America.**
  ___ • Conditions on the ship were poor.
___ 3. **Immigrants had hard life when they arrived.**
  ___ • Many were not welcome.
  ___ • They were mistreated by others.
___ 4. **Personal Response:** Any well-supported positive or negative response to the content or ideas in the text, or to the text as a whole.

Retelling Score: _____

Comprehension Questions

_____ 1. **Why were the rich people in the passage luckier than the poor people?**

Text-Based: Could have their own cabins; did not have to wait in line.

_____ 2. **Why did the immigrants have to wait in line when they got to New York?**

Text-Based: To see if they would be allowed to stay; to see if they were healthy enough to stay.

_____ 3. **Why was the trip to the U.S. more dangerous for the poor?**

Inference: They had dirty place to stay; the food was poor.

_____ 4. **Use the story to tell why people who were already rich would want to come to America.**

Inference: Probably were disliked by leaders or were not free in their countries.

_____ 5. **Based on this passage, do you think life was better for the immigrants in their new country? Why or why not?**

Critical Response: No—some couldn't find jobs; people did not welcome them. Yes—they were free to do what they wanted; no one was oppressing them.

_____ 6. **Why were there two lines in New York?**

Text-Based: One for the rich and one for the poor.

_____ 7. **Why were there shorter lines for the rich people in New York?**

Inference: Had better health after the trip.

_____ 8. **According to the passage, how were many immigrants treated when they got to America?**

Text-Based: They were not welcome; it was hard to find jobs; people thought they were strange.

_____ 9. Why should the United States continue to welcome immigrants?

> *Inference: People still need a better life; most of us have immigrants in our family history; differences among people can be good.*

<table>
<tr><td colspan="2">Comprehension Analysis:</td></tr>
<tr><td>Text-Based:</td><td>/4</td></tr>
<tr><td>Inference:</td><td>/4</td></tr>
<tr><td>Critical Response:</td><td>/2</td></tr>
<tr><td colspan="2">Total Comprehension %: _____</td></tr>
</table>

_____ 10. Would you have hired an immigrant if you were a factory owner? Why or why not?

> *Critical Response: Yes—cheaper labor; give them a chance. No—could not speak English and would not understand instructions.*

THIRD GRADE II: CHILD SLAVES

Reader's copy on p. 119 of the Reader's Passages

Introductory Statement: "Would you read this passage about child slaves (to yourself/out loud). When you are finished, I'll take away the passage. Then I'll ask you to tell me about what you read and what you think of it. After that, I'll ask you some questions about the passage."

Story

Everyone knows that slavery is wrong. But slavery is still very common. And one of its worst forms is child slavery. Poor families are the most likely victims. Farm owners can make families pay for their food and shelter. The family can not earn enough to pay the owners back. So everyone in the family works to try to pay the debt. Most of the time, they will never succeed. But the owners don't care! All those years of cheap work are too valuable.

Often the parents can no longer work. But the children must still work for the owners. The children can not go to school. They can never stop working to pay what they owe. Some owners are at least kind to the children. Then their life is a little better. But other owners are cruel. Children may not get enough food to stay healthy. If the child misses a day of work, the family must pay a fine. Then they will owe even more.

Many countries have laws against children working. But no one in the family knows about the laws. They don't know that their children have rights. And so it is very difficult to stop people from using children as slaves.

(206 words)

Scoring Miscues for Oral Reading Option
Mark all scoreable miscues by placing either a plus (for those that maintain meaning) or a zero (for those that violate meaning) in the text margin.

Reading Accuracy Index: _____%
*Total all miscues marked with pluses **and** zeros and enter the corresponding percentage from the Miscue Chart.*

Meaning Maintenance Index: _____%
*Total **only** miscues marked with zeros and enter the corresponding percentage from the Miscue Chart.*

Miscue Chart (if used for oral reading)

Miscues	%	Miscues	%	Miscues	%
1	100	12	94	23	89
2	99	13	94	24	88
3	99	14	93	25	88
4	98	15	93	26	87
5	98	16	92	27	87
6	97	17	92	28	86
7	97	18	91	29	86
8	96	19	91	30	85
9	96	20	90	31	85
10	95	21	90	32	84
11	95	22	89	33	84

Student Retelling

Examiner: "Tell me about what you just read and what you thought about it."

If there is no spontaneous response, repeat the request, "Tell me what you thought about the passage."

Note: Use the Retelling Rubric on p. 284 to assess the child's retelling performance. If you need additional space for retelling responses, use a separate sheet of paper.

RETELLING RUBRIC: INFORMATIONAL

Macro-concepts (Numbered and Boldfaced) and Micro-concepts (Bulleted)

Place a 0, 1/2, or + to score student responses. See page 81 for information on what these assessment measures mean.

Story Structure:

___ 1. **Child slavery is a terrible thing.**
   ___ • Owners can be cruel to their slaves.
___ 2. **Child slavery usually happens to the poor.**
   ___ • Owners charge families for their food and shelter.
   ___ • Families build up debt.
   ___ • Everyone in family must work to pay off debt.
___ 3. **Child slavery is difficult to stop.**
   ___ • Families often don't know about the laws against it.
___ 4. **Personal Response:** Any well-supported positive or negative response to the content or ideas in the text, or to the text as a whole.

Retelling Score: _____

Comprehension Questions

_____ 1. **Why can't the families pay back what they owe and go work for someone else?**

Text-Based: They don't earn enough money.

_____ 2. **Why don't the owners care that the families cannot pay their debts?**

Text-Based: They make more money from their work.

_____ 3. **Why is it better for the farmers to keep the pay of families very low?**

Inference: So that they can never pay off their debt and they will have to work all of their lives.

_____ 4. **What makes farmers think that they can get away with using children as slaves?**

Inference: Parents don't know about the laws.

_____ 5. **Why would people who read this passage think that slavery of children is worse than any other kind?**

Critical Response: Children are more helpless than adults; have no protection against stronger people; they are being robbed of their futures.

_____ 6. **What happens if a child's parents become too old or sick to work?**

Text-Based: The child must work to pay off their debt.

_____ 7. **Why are poor families the most likely to end up as slaves?**

Inference: They have no power to fight back; do not know about their rights by law; can be easily cheated by owners; have no other source of food or shelter.

_____ 8. **Why are some poor families always in debt?**

Text-Based: They owe the farmer money for their shelter and food; they never earn enough to pay him back.

_____ 9. Why will the child slaves never be able to get better jobs or have a better future?

Inference: Without schooling, they would not be able to do anything else.

Comprehension Analysis:

   Text-Based: __/4__
   Inference: __/4__
   Critical Response: __/2__

Total Comprehension %: _____

_____ 10. What would be the best way of stopping the use of children as slaves?

Critical Response: Making school mandatory; regulating the use of labor by owners; informing the workers of their rights; fining the owners for violations; setting a minimum wage.

Reader's copy on p. 120 of the Reader's Passages

Introductory Statement: "Would you read this passage about how money works (to yourself/out loud). When you are finished, I'll take away the passage. Then I'll ask you to tell me about what you read and what you think of it. After that, I'll ask you some questions about the passage."

Story

Some people save their money by putting it in a bank. The bank pays them for this money. The money that the bank pays is called interest. People can earn about fifteen dollars every year for saving five hundred dollars in the bank. Why would a bank pay people for keeping their money in the bank?

Other people borrow money from the bank. They want to buy things that they need but they do not have the money. They ask the bank to lend them the money. But the money is not free. The people must pay to use it. This means that the people have to pay back all the money that they borrowed. Then they have to pay the bank for letting them use the money. They may have to pay the bank fifty dollars to borrow your five hundred dollars for one year. This is how the bank makes money.

People who save money in a bank earn interest. People who borrow from the bank must pay. Maybe Benjamin Franklin was thinking about that when he said, "A penny saved is a penny earned." (187 words)

Scoring Miscues for Oral Reading Option
Mark all scoreable miscues by placing either a plus (for those that maintain meaning) or a zero (for those that violate meaning) in the text margin.

Reading Accuracy Index: _____%
*Total all miscues marked with pluses **and** zeros and enter the corresponding percentage from the Miscue Chart.*

Meaning Maintenance Index: _____%
*Total **only** miscues marked with zeros and enter the corresponding percentage from the Miscue Chart.*

Miscue Chart (if used for oral reading)

Miscues	%	Miscues	%	Miscues	%
1	99	12	94	23	88
2	99	13	93	24	87
3	99	14	93	25	87
4	98	15	92	26	86
5	98	16	91	27	86
6	97	17	91	28	85
7	97	18	90	29	84
8	96	19	90	30	84
9	96	20	89	31	83
10	95	21	89	32	83
11	94	22	88	33	82

Student Retelling

Examiner: "Tell me about what you just read and what you thought about it."

If there is no spontaneous response, repeat the request, "Tell me what you thought about the passage."

Note: Use the Retelling Rubric on p. 287 to assess the child's retelling performance. If you need additional space for retelling responses, use a separate sheet of paper.

RETELLING RUBRIC: INFORMATIONAL

Macro-concepts (Numbered and Boldfaced) and Micro-concepts (Bulleted)

Place a 0, 1/2, or + to score student responses. See page 81 for information on what these assessment measures mean.

Story Structure:

___ 1. **Some people don't know that money can earn money.**
  ___ • Banks need people to let them use their money.

___ 2. **Banks pay money if you let them use your money.**
  ___ • This money is called interest.
  ___ • People make interest when they put money in the bank.

___ 3. **Banks make people pay interest to use their money.**
  ___ • If people want to buy things, they go to the bank.
  ___ • They must pay interest on the money they use.

___ 4. **Personal Response:** Any well-supported positive or negative response to the content or ideas in the text, or to the text as a whole.

Retelling Score: _____

Comprehension Questions

_____ 1. **Why do people put money in the bank?**

Text-Based: The bank pays them for money.

_____ 2. **How much interest might a person earn for putting five hundred dollars in the bank for a year?**

Text-Based: Fifteen dollars.

_____ 3. **Why would it not be wise to save your money in a piggy bank at home?**

Inference: There is no one to pay interest.

_____ 4. **How can the bank afford to pay you interest for saving your money at their bank?**

Inference: They make money when they lend the money to someone else.

_____ 5. **Who benefits more from a loan, the bank or the person who makes the loan? Explain?**

Critical Response: The person—he can buy things that he didn't have enough money to buy. The bank—it makes lots of money by letting people borrow money.

_____ 6. **How much might a person pay for borrowing five hundred dollars from the bank for one year?**

Text-Based: Fifty dollars.

_____ 7. **Use the story to tell when it would be wise for an adult to borrow money from a bank.**

Inference: They could want something that they did not have enough money to buy.

_____ 8. **Why does the bank give you money for keeping your money in their bank?**

Text-Based: They need to let people use your money; they make more money by lending money to others.

_____ 9. Why wouldn't the bank like it if people did not keep their money in the bank for a long time?

Inference: The bank has to have the money long enough to let people use it and then pay it back.

_____ 10. How does this passage fit Benjamin Franklin's saying, "A penny saved is a penny earned?"

Critical Response: You can earn money by saving your money in a bank; if you do not save enough money, you will have to pay more to get what you want.

FOURTH GRADE I: FRIDA KAHLO

Reader's copy on p. 121 of the Reader's Passages

Introductory Statement: "Would you read this passage about an artist (to yourself/out loud). When you are finished, I'll take away the passage. Then I'll ask you to tell me about what you read and what you think of it. After that, I'll ask you some questions about the passage."

Story

Frida Kahlo was born in Mexico in 1907. She was an intelligent and beautiful young woman. She planned to become a doctor. But when she was 18 years old, she was in a bus accident. The accident broke her back in three places. After a long time in the hospital, she had to stay in bed for months. To pass the time, Frida began to paint. She soon found her talent and her love.

Some of her friends saw that Frida's paintings were very interesting. They helped her to meet Diego Rivera, a famous Mexican painter. Diego helped Frida to develop as a painter. They soon fell in love and married. But their marriage was troubled and painful. Frida soon learned that painting helped her to deal with her feelings. She painted many pictures of herself. She often said that she was the subject she knew best of all.

Frida had many operations on her back. Her great pain and her great strength made their way into her paintings. She had a rare ability to express pain and unhappiness through art. For this reason Frida Kahlo is seen as one of the truly great talents of her time. A museum in Mexico shows only her works. She is one of very few women artists who have ever achieved that honor.

(220 words)

Scoring Miscues for Oral Reading Option
Mark all scoreable miscues by placing either a plus (for those that maintain meaning) or a zero (for those that violate meaning) in the text margin.

Reading Accuracy Index: _____%
*Total all miscues marked with pluses **and** zeros and enter the corresponding percentage from the Miscue Chart.*

Meaning Maintenance Index: _____%
*Total **only** miscues marked with zeros and enter the corresponding percentage from the Miscue Chart.*

Miscue Chart (if used for oral reading)

Miscues	%	Miscues	%	Miscues	%
1	100	13	94	25	89
2	99	14	94	26	88
3	99	15	93	27	88
4	98	16	93	28	87
5	98	17	92	29	87
6	97	18	92	30	86
7	97	19	91	31	86
8	96	20	91	32	85
9	96	21	90	33	85
10	95	22	90	34	85
11	95	23	90	35	84
12	95	24	89	36	84

Student Retelling

Examiner: "Tell me about what you just read and what you thought about it."

If there is no spontaneous response, repeat the request, "Tell me what you thought about the passage."

Note: Use the Retelling Rubric on p. 290 to assess the child's retelling performance. If you need additional space for retelling responses, use a separate sheet of paper.

RETELLING RUBRIC: INFORMATIONAL

Macro-concepts (Numbered and Boldfaced) and Micro-concepts (Bulleted)

Place a 0, 1/2, or + to score student responses. See page 81 for information on what these assessment measures mean.

Story Structure:

___ 1. **Frida Kahlo had a serious accident.**
  ___ • She began painting to pass time in the hospital.
___ 2. **Kahlo met and married a Mexican painter.**
  ___ • He helped her grow as a painter.
  ___ • They were often unhappy together.
  ___ • She used painting to express pain and unhappiness.
___ 3. **She became one of the greatest talents of her time.**
  ___ • She has an entire museum that shows only her works.
___ 4. **Personal Response:** Any well-supported positive or negative response to the content or ideas in the text, or to the text as a whole.

Retelling Score: _____

Comprehension Questions

_____ 1. Why did Frida Kahlo begin to paint?

Text-Based: Pass the time when she was recovering from the accident.

_____ 2. Why did Frida paint many pictures of herself?

Text-Based: She said she was the subject she knew best.

_____ 3. Why could Diego help Frida become a better painter?

Inference: He was already well known and had more experience than she had.

_____ 4. What do you think Frida looked like in her pictures of herself?

Inference: Sad, unhappy, in great pain.

_____ 5. Some people say that without her pain and unhappiness, Frida would never have become a great painter. Do you agree? Why or why not?

Critical Response: Yes—the pain gave her the subject matter; she would not have discovered painting unless she was in the hospital. No—she could have used her talent for different subjects.

_____ 6. Why did her friends introduce her to Diego Rivera?

Text-Based: Saw that her paintings were interesting; recognized her talent.

_____ 7. Why would people say that Frida had a great deal of strength as well as talent?

Inference: She had to endure much pain and painted throughout the years of suffering.

_____ 8. How do we know that Mexico honors Frida Kahlo as a great artist?

Text-Based: There is a museum there that shows only her work.

_____ 9. Why would Mexico honor her by giving Frida her own museum?

Inference: She had exceptional talent; she had rare ability to convey feelings in her art.

_____ 10. How does Frida's life show that the ability to draw and paint does not make anyone a great artist?

Critical Response: Must be able to express emotions like pain and suffering; must enable people to see ideas in the paintings.

FOURTH GRADE II: KRAKATOA
(CRACK-UH-TOE-UH)

Reader's copy on p. 122 of the Reader's Passages

Introductory Statement: "Would you read this passage about a famous volcano (to yourself/out loud). When you are finished, I'll take away the passage. Then I'll ask you to tell me about what you read and what you think of it. After that, I'll ask you some questions about the passage."

Story

Krakatoa was a small island volcano about five miles wide. Over many years it had grown bigger from dozens of small eruptions and lava flows. That was before the morning of August 27, 1883. At the end of that day there was almost no island left. The volcano had exploded. Almost three quarters of the island was gone. Much of it was blown miles into the sky. The dust in the air shaded the sun for months.

It was lucky that no people lived on the island. But there were many islands close by where people did live. The huge waves caused by the blast killed many people. Some waves were as high as twelve-story buildings. They washed whole villages into the sea. Almost 36,000 people died.

The explosion of Krakatoa was heard 2,800 miles away. Windows in homes 100 miles away were broken. Many people think that the explosion was the biggest that ever happened on earth. Over the years a new volcano has risen. It is very close to the old island. Some people believe that it took Krakatoa's place. It has been named "Child of Krakatoa." Many people have read about that first great explosion. Some of them believe that we may not have heard the last of Krakatoa after all.

(215 words)

Scoring Miscues for Oral Reading Option

Mark all scoreable miscues by placing either a plus (for those that maintain meaning) or a zero (for those that violate meaning) in the text margin.

Reading Accuracy Index: _____%
*Total all miscues marked with pluses **and** zeros and enter the corresponding percentage from the Miscue Chart.*

Meaning Maintenance Index: _____%
*Total **only** miscues marked with zeros and enter the corresponding percentage from the Miscue Chart.*

Miscue Chart (if used for oral reading)

Miscues	%	Miscues	%	Miscues	%
1	100	13	94	25	88
2	99	14	93	26	88
3	99	15	93	27	87
4	98	16	93	28	87
5	98	17	92	29	87
6	97	18	92	30	86
7	97	19	91	31	86
8	96	20	91	32	85
9	96	21	90	33	85
10	95	22	90	34	84
11	95	23	89	35	84
12	94	24	89	36	83

Student Retelling

Examiner: "Tell me about what you just read and what you thought about it."

If there is no spontaneous response, repeat the request, "Tell me what you thought about the passage."

Note: Use the Retelling Rubric on p. 293 to assess the child's retelling performance. If you need additional space for retelling responses, use a separate sheet of paper.

Macro-concepts (Numbered and Boldfaced) and Micro-concepts (Bulleted)

Place a 0, 1/2, or + to score student responses. See page 81 for information on what these assessment measures mean.

Story Structure:

___ 1. **The Krakatoa volcano erupted in the 1800s.**
   ___ • Three quarters of the island was blown away.
___ 2. **Krakatoa caused much damage.**
   ___ • Created huge waves.
   ___ • Almost 36,000 people were killed by the flooding from the waves.
   ___ • Some believe it was the biggest explosion ever on earth.
___ 3. **A new volcano has taken Krakatoa's place.**
   ___ • May be another great eruption someday.
___ 4. **Personal Response:** Any well-supported positive or negative response to the content or ideas in the text, or to the text as a whole.

Retelling Score: _____

Comprehension Questions

_____ 1. How much of the island of Krakatoa disappeared in the explosion?

Text-Based: Three quarters.

_____ 2. How many people died in the explosion of Krakatoa?

Text-Based: Almost 36,000.

_____ 3. Why were there no people living on Krakatoa?

Inference: Too many eruptions in the past; island was too small.

_____ 4. Why didn't the people on the other islands get out of the way of the waves?

Inference: Too big or came too quickly; no warning.

_____ 5. Based on this passage, which is more dangerous to people, volcanoes or tidal waves?

Critical Response: Tidal waves—these actually killed the people rather than the volcano. Volcanoes—actually caused the tidal waves.

_____ 6. When did the explosion of Krakatoa take place?

Text-Based: At the end of the 19th century; 1883.

_____ 7. Why would people say that Krakatoa caused the biggest explosion on earth?

Inference: It was heard so far away.

_____ 8. Why was the new volcano named "Child of Krakatoa"?

Text-Based: It grew up very close to the original volcano.

_____ 9. What kind of effect would Krakatoa have had on farmers in the area?

Inference: The shading of the sun would affect crops.

_____ 10. If "Child of Krakatoa" exploded today, would it cause the same damage and death as Krakatoa did? Explain.

Critical Response: No—we have better communication and more warnings; better buildings. Yes—the islands have more people on them now and so more lives could be lost.

FOURTH GRADE III: SUGAR GLIDERS

Reader's copy on p. 123 of the Reader's Passages

Introductory Statement: "Would you read this passage about a special pet (to yourself/out loud). When you are finished, I'll take away the passage. Then I'll ask you to tell me about what you read and what you think of it. After that, I'll ask you some questions about the passage."

Story

Would you want a pet that thinks you are a tree? Then the sugar glider is the pet for you. Sugar gliders are members of the possum family. They are about the size of small flying squirrels and they have arms and legs shaped like bat wings. In the wild they spend their days huddled in their tree nests. They use their wings to glide from branch to branch in their tree without ever touching the ground. In the early evening they look for food and protect their special tree.

They make perfect pets because they enjoy being near their owner's body, sitting on a shoulder or on top of the head or cuddled inside a shirt pocket. To train the baby sugar glider you must wear two T-shirts and put the baby between them. Then you try to forget it is there and go about your regular life. It will explore its new home and the claws on its tiny toes will tickle you. It will take two weeks to train the sugar glider to accept you as its new home. Once that happens, it will always treat you as its own "tree." If you leave your pet in another room, it will glide back to you as soon as it sees you.

Sugar gliders like to eat sweet fruits. But bananas make them sick. Without lots of water, sugar gliders will die, so they must learn to drink from a water bottle. A pet sugar glider can live for 10 to 15 years. (255 words)

Scoring Miscues for Oral Reading Option

Mark all scoreable miscues by placing either a plus (for those that maintain meaning) or a zero (for those that violate meaning) in the text margin.

Reading Accuracy Index: _____%
*Total all miscues marked with pluses **and** zeros and enter the corresponding percentage from the Miscue Chart.*

Meaning Maintenance Index: _____%
*Total **only** miscues marked with zeros and enter the corresponding percentage from the Miscue Chart.*

Miscue Chart (if used for oral reading)

Miscues	%	Miscues	%	Miscues	%
1	100	13	95	25	90
2	99	14	95	26	90
3	99	15	94	27	89
4	98	16	94	28	89
5	98	17	93	29	89
6	98	18	93	30	88
7	97	19	93	31	88
8	97	20	92	32	87
9	96	21	92	33	87
10	96	22	91	34	87
11	96	23	91	35	86
12	95	24	91	36	86

Student Retelling

Examiner: "Tell me about what you just read and what you thought about it."

If there is no spontaneous response, repeat the request, "Tell me what you thought about the passage."

Note: Use the Retelling Rubric on p. 296 to assess the child's retelling performance. If you need additional space for retelling responses, use a separate sheet of paper.

Macro-concepts (Numbered and Boldfaced) and Micro-concepts (Bulleted)

Place a 0, 1/2, or + to score student responses. See page 81 for information on what these assessment measures mean.

Story Structure:

___ 1. **Sugar gliders can fly from tree to tree.**
  ___ • They have wings like bats.
___ 2. **Sugar gliders must be trained to become pets.**
  ___ • Put sugar glider in your shirt.
  ___ • Must wear two shirts to keep from being scratched.
  ___ • In two weeks sugar glider accepts you as home.
___ 3. **Sugar gliders needs right kind of food and drink.**
  ___ • Needs lots of water.
___ 4. **Personal Response:** Any well-supported positive or negative response to the content or ideas in the text, or to the text as a whole.

Retelling Score: _____

Comprehension Questions

_____ 1. How can sugar gliders fly through the air?

Text-Based: Their arms and legs are like bat wings and they use them to glide.

_____ 2. How would you teach the sugar glider to live on you?

Text-Based: Wear two T-shirts and let it live between them.

_____ 3. Why do you have to wear two T-shirts when you are training your sugar glider?

Inference: They have claws and you could be scratched.

_____ 4. Use the story to tell what might happen if a friend put your sugar glider on his shoulder.

Inference: It would glide back to you as soon as it saw you.

_____ 5. What part of training a sugar glider is more important, teaching it to eat or teaching it where to live?

Critical Response: To eat—you must give them particular kinds of fruit and lots of water. Where to live—they must become attached to you in order to live comfortably.

_____ 6. How long does it take to train a sugar glider to get attached to its new home?

Text-Based: Two weeks.

_____ 7. In what ways are tame sugar gliders similar to sugar gliders who live in the wild?

Inference: They use their arms and legs to fly through the air; they like to huddle in their nests; they like to stay in their new "tree" home.

_____ 8. How long could your pet sugar glider live?

Text-Based: About 10 to 15 years.

_____ 9. How does the story show that a sugar glider needs a responsible owner?

Inference: You have to know how to train it to live on you; you have to know what to feed it.

Comprehension Analysis:

Text-Based: __/4__
Inference: __/4__
Critical Response: __/2__

Total Comprehension %: _____

_____ 10. Would be wise to leave your pet sugar glider with your best friend while you go on a vacation? Explain.

Critical Response: Yes—you might have to go places where you couldn't bring it; you might have to leave it in an unfamiliar room alone; you might not be allowed to keep their food and water in the hotel room. No—they are attached to their owner and they can be kept in a pocket where no one can see them; they won't bother you as you go about your vacation fun.

FIFTH GRADE I: THE MOSQUITO

Reader's copy on p. 125 of the Reader's Passages

Introductory Statement: "Would you read this passage about mosquitoes (to yourself/out loud). When you are finished, I'll take away the passage. Then I'll ask you to tell me about what you read and what you think of it. After that, I'll ask you some questions about the passage."

Story

The next time you smack a mosquito on your arm and say to yourself "Got him!" you should think again. Actually, you got *her*! Only the female mosquito does the biting. She is in search of fresh blood to feed the eggs that will soon become more little Draculas. The female mosquito finds her victims by following streams of carbon dioxide. This is the gas that is exhaled by the warm-blooded animals she seeks. The carbon dioxide guides the mosquito to her prey.

Once she has found you, she is hard to stop. Unless you hear the telltale buzzing of her wings, you will probably never know she is there. She lands very lightly on her feet. Once she has landed she inserts her long, needle-like nose into your skin. Her nose is so thin that most people never feel the needle at all. Before she can start sipping your blood, she injects a little saliva to make it thinner. Otherwise it is like trying to drink a thick milk shake through a straw. It is the saliva that the mosquito leaves behind that makes the skin itch and swell.

Some people are lucky enough to feel her and fast enough to smack her. She may leave a smear of blood on their bare arm. But they weren't fast enough. That blood they see is their own! It is no surprise that mosquitoes are not the most popular of insects, unless you happen to be a spider or a bat! In addition to being pests, they also carry and spread diseases like malaria and the West Nile virus. But until we think of a better way to control them, mosquitoes will continue to annoy any animal that has blood and thin skin. (292 words)

Scoring Miscues for Oral Reading Option
Mark all scoreable miscues by placing either a plus (for those that maintain meaning) or a zero (for those that violate meaning) in the text margin.

Reading Accuracy Index: _____%
*Total all miscues marked with pluses **and** zeros and enter the corresponding percentage from the Miscue Chart.*

Meaning Maintenance Index: _____%
*Total **only** miscues marked with zeros and enter the corresponding percentage from the Miscue Chart.*

Miscue Chart (if used for oral reading)

Miscues	%	Miscues	%	Miscues	%
1	100	13	96	25	91
2	99	14	95	26	91
3	99	15	95	27	91
4	99	16	95	28	90
5	98	17	94	29	90
6	98	18	94	30	90
7	98	19	93	31	89
8	97	29	93	32	89
9	97	21	93	33	89
10	97	22	92	34	88
11	96	23	92	35	88
12	96	24	92	36	88

Student Retelling

Examiner: "Tell me about what you just read and what you thought about it."

If there is no spontaneous response, repeat the request, "Tell me what you thought about the passage."

Note: Use the Retelling Rubric on p. 299 to assess the child's retelling performance. If you need additional space for retelling responses, use a separate sheet of paper.

RETELLING RUBRIC: INFORMATIONAL

Macro-concepts (Numbered and Boldfaced) and Micro-concepts (Bulleted)

Place a 0, 1/2, or + to score student responses. See page 81 for information on what these assessment measures mean.

Story Structure:

___ 1. **Only female mosquitoes bite.**
  ___ • They need blood to feed their eggs.
  ___ • They inject saliva to thin the blood.
___ 2. **It is hard to avoid being bitten by mosquitoes.**
  ___ • They land very lightly.
  ___ • They have very thin noses.
___ 3. **Mosquitoes spread diseases.**
  ___ • They spread malaria or West Nile virus.
___ 4. **Personal Response:** Any well-supported positive or negative response to the content or ideas in the text, or to the text as a whole.

Retelling Score: _____

Comprehension Questions

_____ 1. Why does a mosquito's bite itch?

Text-Based: The saliva she leaves behind irritates the skin.

_____ 2. Why does the female mosquito need fresh blood?

Text-Based: She needs the blood to feed her eggs.

_____ 3. When you kill a mosquito, how can you tell if she has bitten you?

Inference: If you see blood, she has probably bitten you.

_____ 4. Why does the mosquito inject saliva before drinking your blood?

Inference: The blood is too thick; her nose is too thin.

_____ 5. Use the story to tell if a mosquito would be more likely to prey on a person or a dog. Why?

Critical Response: Person—skin is easier to get to; dogs have fur to protect them. Dog—it is less likely to feel the mosquito; can't swat them as easily as humans can.

_____ 6. How can you tell if a mosquito is a male or a female?

Text-Based: Only the female bites.

_____ 7. Why can't people avoid being bitten by mosquitoes?

Inference: You can't stop breathing; mosquitoes are everywhere, even indoors; can't feel her when she lands.

_____ 8. What diseases does the mosquito spread? (Must identify one).

Text-Based: Malaria; West Nile virus.

_____ 9. Based on the information in the passage, how does a mosquito possibly spread a disease from one person to another?

Inference: Can spread blood in its saliva from one person to another.

_____ 10. Which is more valuable to the survival of the mosquito, its body structure or its ability to detect carbon dioxide? Explain.

Critical Response: Body structure—light body and thin nose keep it from being detected; has saliva to thin blood. Ability to detect carbon dioxide—enables her to find animals with blood.

FIFTH GRADE II: OIL SPILL

Reader's copy on p. 126 of the Reader's Passages

Introductory Statement: "Would you read this passage about an oil spill (to yourself/out loud). When you are finished, I'll take away the passage. Then I'll ask you to tell me about what you read and what you think of it. After that, I'll ask you some questions about the passage."

Story

On the night of March 24, 1989, a huge oil tanker named the *Exxon Valdez* ran into a reef in Prince William Sound in Alaska. It was carrying oil from the Alaska Pipeline to the mainland U. S. More than 11 million gallons of crude oil spilled from the ship. This was the largest oil spill in U.S. history. The spill was a terrible shock to the residents and Coast Guard that night. They did not know that the spill would soon get much worse.

At first, the Coast Guard tried to burn up the oil. But bad weather made controlled burning difficult. Then cleanup crews tried to scoop the oil from the water. But their equipment quickly became clogged with seaweed and thick oil. To make matters even worse, the spill site could be reached only by boat or helicopter. Crews sent to help clean oil-coated animals were slow to arrive. Then they just could not work fast enough. There were too many birds and animals that needed to be cleaned. The oil spill is estimated to have killed 250,000 sea birds, including 250 bald eagles. Nearly 3,000 sea otters and 22 killer whales were lost in the spill as well.

All in all, 140 miles of coastline were soaked with oil. Nearly 1,500 miles had some oil. Exxon Corporation has spent an estimated 2.5 billion dollars in the clean up of the spill. The fishing industry in Alaska is still not the same. Many fishermen feel that it never will be. Experts predict that the effects of the spill will be felt for decades to come. (267 words)

Scoring Miscues for Oral Reading Option

Mark all scoreable miscues by placing either a plus (for those that maintain meaning) or a zero (for those that violate meaning) in the text margin.

Reading Accuracy Index: _____%
*Total all miscues marked with pluses **and** zeros and enter the corresponding percentage from the Miscue Chart.*

Meaning Maintenance Index: _____%
*Total **only** miscues marked with zeros and enter the corresponding percentage from the Miscue Chart.*

Miscue Chart (if used for oral reading)

Miscues	%	Miscues	%	Miscues	%
1	100	13	95	25	91
2	99	14	95	26	90
3	99	15	94	27	90
4	99	16	94	28	90
5	98	17	94	29	89
6	98	18	93	30	89
7	97	19	93	31	88
8	97	20	93	32	88
9	97	21	92	33	88
10	96	22	92	34	87
11	96	23	91	35	87
12	96	24	91	36	87

Student Retelling

Examiner: "Tell me about what you just read and what you thought about it."

If there is no spontaneous response, repeat the request, "Tell me what you thought about the passage."

Note: Use the Retelling Rubric on p. 302 to assess the child's retelling performance. If you need additional space for retelling responses, use a separate sheet of paper.

Macro-concepts (Numbered and Boldfaced) and Micro-concepts (Bulleted)

Place a 0, 1/2, or + to score student responses. See page 81 for information on what these assessment measures mean.

Story Structure:

___ 1. *Exxon Valdez* spilled a huge amount of oil.
___ • The ship ran into a reef in Alaska.
___ 2. **The oil was very difficult to clean up.**
___ • There were equipment problems.
___ • Bad weather prevented cleanup.
___ 3. **The cost of the spill was huge.**
___ • It cost $2.5 billion.
___ • It caused damage to the area's fishing industry and wildlife.
___ 4. **Personal Response:** Any well-supported positive or negative response to the content or ideas in the text, or to the text as a whole.

Retelling Score: _____

Comprehension Questions

_____ 1. What caused the *Exxon Valdez* to spill its oil?

Text-Based: The ship hit a reef.

_____ 2. Why didn't burning the oil work?

Text-Based: Bad weather made it difficult.

_____ 3. Why did it cost Exxon Corporation so much money to clean up after the spill?

Inference: All the workers and equipment were required to clean hundreds of miles of shoreline.

_____ 4. Why couldn't volunteers who wanted to help clean the animals get to the oil spill very quickly?

Inference: The site could only be reached by boat and helicopter.

_____ 5. Which contributed more to the *Exxon Valdez* disaster, nature or human error? Explain.

Critical Response: Nature—the weather made it difficult to clean up; the reef was part of nature and caused the crash. Human error—captain should have been more careful; should have known reef was there.

_____ 6. Why couldn't the volunteers save more birds than they did?

Text-Based: There were too many birds; they could not work fast enough.

_____ 7. Why wasn't the Coast Guard able to deal with the problem as soon as it happened?

Inference: Spill was too large; it wasn't equipped to deal with it; everything went wrong.

_____ 8. What happened when the Coast Guard tried to scoop the oil from the water?

Text-Based: The equipment became clogged with oil and seaweed.

_____ 9. Why would the fishing industry be affected so many years after the spill?

Inference: So many fish were killed; loss of birds and animals can upset food chain.

_____10. Was it right to make the Exxon Corporation pay for the total cost of oil cleanup? Why or why not?

Critical Response: Yes—it was the company's ship; it had responsibility for any damage that was done. No—it was an accident; it was not anyone's fault.

FIFTH GRADE III: BULLYING

Reader's copy on p. 127 of the Reader's Passages

Introductory Statement: "Would you read this passage about how to deal with a bully (to yourself/out loud). When you are finished, I'll take away the passage. Then I'll ask you to tell me about what you read and what you think of it. After that, I'll ask you some questions about the passage."

Story

Most people experience bullying at some point in their lives. Bullying includes name-calling, making up harmful stories, shoving, or punching. Bullies tease people about how they look, act, or speak. They may even spread rumors and send insults by e-mail.

When you are bullied, you may feel sad and afraid to go to school. Some victims have even turned to violence to get revenge. The murders and suicides at Columbine High School in 1999 are examples.

Sometimes even your friends may not want to help. They are afraid that they will become victims too, but they often feel guilty for not helping.

While it is hard to know what to do, you should tell someone you trust like a parent, coach, or teacher. The important thing is to tell someone who is wise enough to help without making the situation even worse.

At school, try to stay away from the bully. On the bus, change your seat to be near the driver. At lunchtime, look for groups of people you know and try not to sit alone. Whatever you do, always think about your actions. Try to act confident and try not to act upset even though you may feel that way.

It is important to understand that bullies need help, too. They don't often understand the reasons for their actions. Bullies are often in trouble. About 40% of bullies have three or more arrests by age 30. They seldom think about the effects of what they do to others. That is why punishing bullies does not often help. Psychologists have found that bullies have often been victims of abuse during their lives. Bullies must learn that their actions can not be allowed. But remember that in every case of bullying, there are usually two people who need help.

(299 words)

Scoring Miscues for Oral Reading Option
Mark all scoreable miscues by placing either a plus (for those that maintain meaning) or a zero (for those that violate meaning) in the text margin.

Reading Accuracy Index: _____%
*Total all miscues marked with pluses **and** zeros and enter the corresponding percentage from the Miscue Chart.*

Meaning Maintenance Index: _____%
*Total **only** miscues marked with zeros and enter the corresponding percentage from the Miscue Chart.*

Miscue Chart (if used for oral reading)

Miscue	%	Miscue	%	Miscue	%
1	100	13	96	25	92
2	99	14	95	26	91
3	99	15	95	27	91
4	99	16	95	28	91
5	98	17	94	29	90
6	98	18	94	30	90
7	98	19	94	31	90
8	97	20	93	32	89
9	97	21	93	33	89
10	97	22	93	34	89
11	96	23	92	35	88
12	96	24	92	36	88

Student Retelling

Examiner: "Tell me about what you just read and what you thought about it."

If there is no spontaneous response, repeat the request, "Tell me what you thought about the passage."

Note: Use the Retelling Rubric on p. 305 to assess the child's retelling performance. If you need additional space for retelling responses, use a separate sheet of paper.

3. How does the passage show that sometimes we do not think about our fears?

Inference: People who are bullied sometimes are afraid to get help; people who have friends who are bullied are afraid to help because they don't want it to happen to them.

4. How does the passage show the importance of having lots of different types of friends?

Inference: You need to be with people to avoid being bullied; you need friends who can give wise advice.

5. Use the passage to tell which is more important to a victim of a bully, help from others or help from self.

Critical Response: From others—because a counselor or parent could know how to help. There is strength in numbers.
From self—because you have to make wise decisions in acting confident as well as getting help; you need a strategy to help you deal with a bully.

RETELLING RUBRIC: INFORMATIONAL

Macro-concepts (Numbered and Boldfaced) and Micro-concepts (Bulleted)

Place a 0, 1/2, or + to score student responses. See page 81 for information on what these assessment measures mean.

Story Structure:

___ 1. **Most people experience bullying at some time in their lives.**
  ___ • When you are bullied you may feel sad and afraid.
  ___ • Sometimes even your friends are afraid to help.

___ 2. **You should tell someone you trust when you are bullied.**
  ___ • Try to stay with groups of people you know and act confident.

___ 3. **It is important to understand that bullies need help also.**
  ___ • Bullies don't often understand the reason for their actions.
  ___ • Bullies do not often think about the effect their actions have on others.

___ 4. **Personal Response:** Any well-supported positive or negative response to the content or ideas in the text, or to the text as a whole.

Retelling Score: _____

Comprehension Questions

1. Use the passage to tell how victims of bullying often react.

Text-Based: They feel sad; they feel afraid; they may try to get revenge.

2. Why would your friends not want to help if they saw you being bullied?

Text-Based: They may become victims themselves.

6. What advice does the passage give to someone being bullied at school? (Must give two.)

Text-Based: Stay away from the bully; don't sit near the bully; get help from counselor.

_____ 7. Why would we need to understand that bullies need help?

Inference: They often get into trouble; sometimes it is not all their own fault; many have been victims themselves.

_____ 8. Why are bullies so likely to get into trouble with the law?

Text-Based: They don't understand the reasons for their actions; they don't think about how what they do affects others.

_____ 9. What would be a good alternative to punishment for bullies?

Inference: Try to help them to understand their actions; help them realize how others feel when they are bullied; help them try to get to know their victims as people.

_____ 10. Who needs to understand themselves more, a bully or the bully's victim?

Critical Response: A bully—needs to understand how the past is affecting him or her; needs to understand why he or she acts that way. The victim—needs to think about his or her actions; needs to control fears.

Comprehension Analysis:

Text-Based: __/4__
Inference: __/4__
Critical Response: __/2__

Total Comprehension %: _____

SIXTH GRADE I: A COMMUNITY OF WOLVES

Reader's copy on p. 128 of the Reader's Passages

Introductory Statement: "Would you read this passage about wolves (to yourself/out loud). When you are finished, I'll take away the passage. Then I'll ask you to tell me about what you read and what you think of it. After that, I'll ask you some questions about the passage."

Story

Wolves are probably one of the most misunderstood animals on our planet. Many myths and legends depict wolves as tricky, cunning, and dangerous. Who doesn't remember "The Big Bad Wolf" and "Little Red Riding Hood" or the "Werewolf" legend? This image, however, couldn't be further from the truth. Wolves may be dangerous . . . to rabbits, deer, pigs, sheep, and cattle. But you don't have to worry that one will eat you or your granny up!

Actually, wolves are part of a closely knit family that consists of 2 to 10 adults and any young pups. All of the wolves in the pack share responsibility for the young. The wolves travel in packs for the sake of more successful hunting, for mutual protection, and for companionship. Wolves are also territorial. They usually travel within a specific range, sometimes up to 50 square miles.

Many experts believe that it is the wolf's eerie howl that plays on the fears of humans. In fact, their howl is part of a sophisticated communication system within their group. Howling is the wolves' way of "staying in touch" over long distances. If a wolf is separated from her pack, she will begin howling. This is a cry for help as well as a call to reunite. It can, however, be very costly. If a competing pack is within her range, they may seek her out and kill her. Pups are especially vulnerable. They have not yet learned the appropriate times and places for howling.

Other purposes for howling include warning rival packs to keep moving or staking a claim on fresh-killed prey. The so-called *chorus howls* are used to make competing packs think that there are really more wolves in the pack. The next time you hear a wolf howl, you will know it is not a werewolf howling at the moon. Perhaps it is only a lost wolf looking for its pack. (315 words)

Scoring Miscues for Oral Reading Option
Mark all scoreable miscues by placing either a plus (for those that maintain meaning) or a zero (for those that violate meaning) in the text margin.

Reading Accuracy Index: _____%
*Total all miscues marked with pluses **and** zeros and enter the corresponding percentage from the Miscue Chart.*

Meaning Maintenance Index: _____%
*Total **only** miscues marked with zeros and enter the corresponding percentage from the Miscue Chart.*

Miscue Chart (if used for oral reading)

Miscues	%	Miscues	%	Miscues	%	Miscues	%
1	100	12	96	23	93	34	89
2	99	13	96	24	92	35	89
3	99	14	96	25	92	36	89
4	99	15	95	26	92	37	88
5	98	16	95	27	91	38	88
6	98	17	95	28	91	39	88
7	98	18	94	29	91	40	87
8	97	19	94	30	90	41	87
9	97	20	94	31	90	42	87
10	97	21	93	32	90	43	86
11	97	22	93	33	90	44	86

Student Retelling

Examiner: "Tell me about what you just read and what you thought about it."

If there is no spontaneous response, repeat the request, "Tell me what you thought about the passage."

Note: Use the Retelling Rubric on p. 308 to assess the child's retelling performance. If you need additional space for retelling responses, use a separate sheet of paper.

3. According to the passage, how is the wolf pack similar to a human family?

   Inference: Stay together; take care of each other; communicate with each other.

RETELLING RUBRIC: INFORMATIONAL

Macro-concepts (Numbered and Boldfaced) and Micro-concepts (Bulleted)

Place a 0, 1/2, or + to score student responses. See page 81 for information on what these assessment measures mean.

Story Structure:

___ 1. **Wolves are misunderstood and feared by people.**
___   • Wolves live in close-knit families.
___   • Wolves work together and protect each other.
___ 2. **Howling may be part of the reason for fear of wolves.**
___ 3. **Howling is a means of communication among wolves.**
___   • If a wolf is separated from the pack, howling can be a call for help.
___   • Howling can be dangerous to wolves.
___   • Other packs may hear the howl and kill the lone wolf.
___ 4. **Personal Response:** Any well-supported positive or negative response to the content or ideas in the text, or to the text as a whole.

Retelling Score: _____

---

4. Why would chorus howling be a way for wolves to solve their problems with competing packs?

   Inference: Would make a competing pack less likely to attack; makes it seem that they have more wolves.

5. Is the wolf's ability to howl more beneficial or more harmful to the wolf's survival? Explain.

   Critical Response: Beneficial—provides source of communication and safety. Harmful—announces wolf's presence to enemies.

6. What positive purposes does howling serve?

   Text-Based: Communication with the pack; cry for help; attempt to reunite with pack.

Comprehension Questions

1. According to the passage, what advantages are there for wolves traveling in a pack?

   Text-Based: Better hunting, protection, companionship.

2. Why would ranchers or farmers fear and dislike wolves?

   Text-Based: Wolves will kill their livestock for food.

_____ 7. What advantages are there for wolves killing off another pack of wolves?

Inference: Can take over their territory; more food and better hunting.

_____ 8. Why is shooting wolves usually not the solution if a rancher is losing his livestock to wolf attacks?

Text-Based: There are many wolves in the pack; they are territorial and will stay wherever there is food.

_____ 9. According to the passage, do wolves ever provide benefits for farmers and ranchers?

Inference: Yes—they kill rabbits and deer that may eat the farmers' crops.

_____ 10. Do you think that the myths about wolves are fair? Why or why not?

Critical Response: Yes—wolves are clever hunters; they do try to deceive other packs. No—wolves are really families who help and support each other.

Comprehension Analysis:

Text-Based: _/4_
Inference: _/4_
Critical Response: _/2_

Total Comprehension %: _____

GRADE SIX II: ARE YOU AFRAID OF SHARKS?

Reader's copy on p. 129 of the Reader's Passages

Introductory Statement: "Would you read this passage about sharks (to yourself/out loud). When you are finished, I'll take away the passage. Then I'll ask you to tell me about what you read and what you think of it. After that, I'll ask you some questions about the passage."

Story

Every summer in the United States, we hear about shark attacks. On some beaches, it is even common to see sharks swimming offshore. Other beaches will be closed because there are so many sharks swimming near the shore. But how likely is it that if you go for a dip in the ocean you will be attacked by a shark? Not very likely at all!

We are far more likely to be killed by another person than by a shark. Most scientists believe that the few shark attacks that occur are really mistakes. When we tan, the top portion of our foot turns brown while the bottom remains white. This shading is similar to that of many fish. Others think sharks mistake us for sea lions or seals, which are some of their favorite food. When they realize that they have made a mistake, most sharks simply spit out their victims and leave. Just think about it . . . if sharks wanted to have us for dinner on a regular basis, they could just come to any shore in the U.S. and help themselves.

Sharks should probably be more afraid of us than we are of them. The total shark population is in decline as a result of human hunting. For example, in some countries shark fin soup is a delicacy and the fins are very much in demand. The shark fin itself is often used in ceremonial dinners. When local fishermen capture the shark, they will use the entire body, but commercial fishermen have been known to follow the practice of *finning.* They cut off the fins of any sharks caught in their

nets. They then throw the sharks back into the sea, leaving them to bleed to death. And *we're* afraid of *them?*

Since we do not have "shark farms" as we do for catfish or shrimp, constant fishing leads to overkilling of certain kinds of sharks. They simply cannot reproduce quickly enough to keep up with the demand. Although we may fear sharks with good cause, destroying them beyond rescue may be even more harmful to us all in the long run. (353 words)

Scoring Miscues for Oral Reading Option
Mark all scoreable miscues by placing either a plus (for those that maintain meaning) or a zero (for those that violate meaning) in the text margin.

Reading Accuracy Index: _____%
*Total all miscues marked with pluses **and** zeros and enter the corresponding percentage from the Miscue Chart.*

Meaning Maintenance Index: _____%
*Total **only** miscues marked with zeros and enter the corresponding percentage from the Miscue Chart.*

Miscue Chart (if used for oral reading)

Miscues	%	Miscues	%	Miscues	%	Miscues	%
1	100	12	97	23	93	34	90
2	99	13	96	24	93	35	90
3	99	14	96	25	93	36	90
4	99	15	96	26	93	37	90
5	99	16	95	27	92	38	89
6	98	17	95	28	92	39	89
7	98	18	95	29	92	40	89
8	98	19	95	30	92	41	88
9	97	20	94	31	91	42	88
10	97	21	94	32	91	43	88
11	97	22	94	33	91	44	88

Student Retelling

Examiner: "Tell me about what you just read and what you thought about it."

If there is no spontaneous response, repeat the request, "Tell me what you thought about the passage."

Note: Use the Retelling Rubric on p. 311 to assess the child's retelling performance. If you need additional space for retelling responses, use a separate sheet of paper.

3. Why would fishermen bother to cut the fins from sharks that they've caught?

   Inference: They sell them for profit.

4. How would the local fishermen feel about commercial fishermen finning sharks? Why?

   Inference: They would probably disapprove because of the waste of the sharks.

5. Do you think it would be a good idea for people to start shark farms as a solution to the shark-fishing problem? Why or why not?

   Critical Response: Yes—it may reduce some of the fishing of sharks that goes on. No—probably wouldn't work. Takes too long to reproduce sharks.

RETELLING RUBRIC: INFORMATIONAL

Macro-concepts (Numbered and Boldfaced) and Micro-concepts (Bulleted)

Place a 0, 1/2, or + to score student responses. See page 81 for information on what these assessment measures mean.

Story Structure:

___ 1. **We hear about shark attacks every summer.**
   ___ • But attacks are very unlikely.
___ 2. **Scientists believe that most attacks are mistakes.**
   ___ • Sharks mistake us for seals or sea lions.
   ___ • They spit us out when they realize the mistake.
___ 3. **Sharks have more to fear from humans.**
   ___ • Men hunt sharks.
   ___ • Sharks can't reproduce fast enough to keep up with demand.
___ 4. **Personal Response:** Any well-supported positive or negative response to the content or ideas in the text, or to the text as a whole.

Retelling Score: _____

Comprehension Questions

1. According to the passage, why are some beaches in the United States closed every summer?

   Text-Based: Sharks can be seen swimming offshore.

2. According to the passage, why would sharks spit out humans after just one bite?

   Text-Based: They probably do not like the taste; they realize that they have made a mistake.

6. According to the passage, what is the greatest danger to sharks?

   Text-Based: Humans and hunting.

7. Is the author afraid of sharks? Why do you think that?

   Inference: Probably not. He seems to know that there is little danger from sharks.

_____ 8. According to the passage, what is the explanation that most scientists give for shark attacks?

Text-Based: Mistaken identity.

_____ 9. Have scientists discovered why sharks attack humans? Explain.

Inference: No—it is a theory; we cannot be sure.

Comprehension Analysis:

Text-Based: __/4__
Inference: __/4__
Critical Response: __/2__

Total Comprehension %: _____

_____10. Should we make finning of sharks a crime? Why or why not?

Critical Response: No—it's a cultural practice to eat shark fin soup; many sharks are still in the sea. Yes—shark populations are low; sharks are being wasted by careless people.

SIXTH GRADE III: SQUIRRELS

Reader's copy on p. 130 of the Reader's Passages

Introductory Statement: "Would you read this passage about squirrels (to yourself/out loud). When you are finished, I'll take away the passage. Then I'll ask you to tell me about what you read and what you think of it. After that, I'll ask you some questions about the passage."

Story

Watching squirrels can be a very entertaining pastime. To understand squirrels, you must remember that at heart they are concerned with three things: food, shelter, and mating.

Squirrels need one pound of food each week. They manage to balance their eating between immediate and future needs. Food is often in abundance during the late summer and early fall and so squirrels store food for later times when it may be scarce. They are successful at storing food because of their keen memory and good sense of smell. They leave a scent on the food that they bury, using sweat glands located between their foot pads and toes. The scent allows them to quickly locate food that they have hidden.

Squirrels mainly eat nuts, seeds, and fruit. They have sharp front teeth called incisors and powerful jaw muscles. These muscles help them gnaw hard food. Their incisors grow six inches each year. They chew on tree branches to keep their teeth clean, sharp, and short.

Squirrels eat heavily for several hours after sunrise and before sunset. Between feeding times, they usually rest in nests that change with the season. In the winter, large nests are located in a cavity in a tree trunk or on a branch lined with leaves and grasses. In the summer, squirrels stay in smaller ball-shaped nests made of plant materials. The adult squirrel usually lives alone; however, squirrels often share nests during very cold times.

The nest is extremely important to the female since baby squirrels are dependent on her for nearly eight weeks. The nest is located high up in a tree, so life in the crowded space can be very dangerous for baby squirrels.

Parents mate during late winter and babies are born in the spring. The female wants to mate with the older and stronger males so she runs from the young males. Consequently, the squirrels' acrobatic skills are truly spectacular during mating time. They move quickly, jumping from tree to tree without falling. Their tails enable them to balance their bodies in motion.

(341 words)

Scoring Miscues for Oral Reading Option
Mark all scoreable miscues by placing either a plus (for those that maintain meaning) or a zero (for those that violate meaning) in the text margin.

Reading Accuracy Index: _____%
*Total all miscues marked with pluses **and** zeros and enter the corresponding percentage from the Miscue Chart.*

Meaning Maintenance Index: _____%
*Total **only** miscues marked with zeros and enter the corresponding percentage from the Miscue Chart.*

Miscue Chart (if used for oral reading)

Miscues	%	Miscues	%	Miscues	%	Miscues	%
1	100	12	96	23	93	34	90
2	99	13	96	24	93	35	90
3	99	14	96	25	93	36	89
4	99	15	96	26	92	37	89
5	99	16	95	27	92	38	89
6	98	17	95	28	92	39	89
7	98	18	95	29	91	40	88
8	98	19	94	30	91	41	88
9	97	20	94	31	91	42	88
10	97	21	94	32	91	43	87
11	97	22	94	33	90	44	87

Student Retelling

Examiner: "Tell me about what you just read and what you thought about it."

If there is no spontaneous response, repeat the request, "Tell me what you thought about the passage."

Note: Use the Retelling Rubric on p. 314 to assess the child's retelling performance. If you need additional space for retelling responses, use a separate sheet of paper.

_____ 3. **Why are acrobatic skills more important to the female squirrels than to the males?**

Inference: The females are trying to avoid mating with the young males.

_____ 4. **Why are powerful jaw muscles so important to squirrels?**

Inference: They eat hard food; they chew on tree branches.

_____ 5. **What is more important to the squirrels' survival, storing food or choosing a mate?**

Critical Response: Storing food—since food may become scarce. Choosing a strong mate—will ensure stronger children.

_____ 6. **How do squirrels find the food that they have hidden?**

Text-Based: They leave scent on their food that lets them find it later.

_____ 7. **Why would a crowded nest be dangerous to young squirrels?**

Inference: They might fall out of the nest and be killed.

RETELLING RUBRIC: INFORMATIONAL

Macro-concepts (Numbered and Boldfaced) and Micro-concepts (Bulleted)

Place a 0, 1/2, or + to score student responses. See page 81 for information on what these assessment measures mean.

Story Structure:

___ 1. **Squirrels are concerned with food.**
  ___ • Squirrels address present and future needs.
  ___ • They use scent glands to mark and find food they've hidden.
___ 2. **Squirrels are concerned with shelter.**
  ___ • Squirrels have different kinds of nests in different seasons.
___ 3. **Squirrels are concerned with mating.**
  ___ • Females choose stronger mates.
  ___ • They are acrobatic in avoidance of young males.
___ 4. **Personal Response:** Any well-supported positive or negative response to the content or ideas in the text, or to the text as a whole.

Retelling Score: _____

Comprehension Questions

_____ 1. **How do squirrels' habits show they are concerned about the future?**

Text-Based: When food is abundant they hide it for when it is scarce.

_____ 2. **How much do their front teeth grow each year?**

Text-Based: Six inches.

_____ 8. How do the squirrels' nests differ in summer and winter?

Text-Based: In summer they live in a hole in a tree trunk or on a branch lined with leaves. In winter they live in a large ball-shaped nest of leaves and plant materials.

_____ 9. Why would squirrels build larger winter nests and smaller summer nests?

Inference: They often share the winter nest with other squirrels to keep warm.

_____ 10. What do the squirrels seem to rely upon more for healthy living, their bodies or their surroundings?

Critical Response: Their bodies—because they gnaw with teeth, use their memory and sense of smell and their glands. Their surroundings—because their nests come from leaves and trees and they use the branches for gnawing and use trees and plants for food.

Comprehension Analysis:

Text-Based: __/4__
Inference: __/4__
Critical Response: __/2__

Total Comprehension %: _____

SEVENTH GRADE I: MARY JEMISON

Reader's copy on p. 131 of the Reader's Passages

Introductory Statement: "Would you read this passage about an Indian captive (to yourself/out loud). When you are finished, I'll take away the passage. Then I'll ask you to tell me about what you read and what you think of it. After that, I'll ask you some questions about the passage."

Story

Mary Jemison was born in 1743 on board a ship sailing to America. Her family settled in a rural community near what is now Gettysburg, Pennsylvania. Mary's father showed no fear of the reports of Indian raids that he heard from their neighbors. Her mother, however, had always felt differently. On April 5, 1758, her fears came true. A party of French soldiers and Indians raided the Jemison farm. Her terrified mother told Mary to obey her captors, remember her English language, and never forget who she was. Mary was taken away by her captors. Unknown to her, Mary's parents and most of the rest of her family were killed. Mary would have to rely only on her mother's words throughout the long days of captivity.

Mary was given to a pair of Seneca Indian women whose brother had been killed in battle. The women had a simple choice. They could kill Mary in revenge for their lost brother. Or they could adopt her to replace him. They chose to adopt Mary and treated her as their own sister, with a great deal of kindness. Mary missed her parents and family and at first could not be happy. She prayed and practiced her English language every day. But she eventually came to appreciate and respect her two new sisters. At the same time, she began to recognize the qualities that the Indian tribe demonstrated in their daily life. She characterized the Indians as extremely faithful to each other, very honest and honorable in all that they did. Mary married a Seneca warrior in 1765 and had several children of her own.

After the Revolutionary War, Mary was offered her freedom by the tribe. Her son was eager to see his mother go and live with her own people. Mary, however, could not bring herself to leave her son. She also worried about how she and her family would be treated by white people. She was afraid they might view her as a traitor. And so she chose to remain with her Indian family and spend the remainder of her days with them. Mary Jemison died in 1831, having spent more than 70 years as an Indian captive. (367 words)

Scoring Miscues for Oral Reading Option
Mark all scoreable miscues by placing either a plus (for those that maintain meaning) or a zero (for those that violate meaning) in the text margin.

Reading Accuracy Index: _____%
*Total all miscues marked with pluses **and** zeros and enter the corresponding percentage from the Miscue Chart.*

Meaning Maintenance Index: _____%
*Total **only** miscues marked with zeros and enter the corresponding percentage from the Miscue Chart.*

Miscue Chart (if used for oral reading)

Miscues	%	Miscues	%	Miscues	%	Miscues	%
1	100	15	96	29	92	43	88
2	99	16	96	30	92	44	88
3	99	17	95	31	92	45	88
4	99	18	95	32	91	46	87
5	99	19	95	33	91	47	87
6	98	20	95	34	91	48	87
7	98	21	94	35	90	49	87
8	98	22	94	36	90	50	86
9	98	23	94	37	90	51	86
10	97	24	93	38	90	52	86
11	97	25	93	39	89	53	86
12	97	26	93	40	89	54	85
13	96	27	93	41	89	55	85
14	96	28	92	42	89		

Student Retelling

Examiner: "Tell me about what you just read and what you thought about it."

If there is no spontaneous response, repeat the request, "Tell me what you thought about the passage."

Note: Use the Retelling Rubric on p. 317 to assess the child's retelling performance. If you need additional space for retelling responses, use a separate sheet of paper.

Comprehension Questions

_____ 1. **Why was Mary Jemison given to the two Indian women?**

Text-Based: To replace their brother who was killed.

_____ 2. **Why did she choose to stay with the Indians when she was offered her freedom?**

Text-Based: She could not leave her son; she was worried about how people would treat her.

_____ 3. **What would make us think that Mary respected and appreciated her Indian companions?**

Inference: She married one of the Indian warriors.

_____ 4. **Why would her own people treat Mary as if she were a traitor?**

Inference: She joined an Indian tribe and married one of its members; many people saw the Indians as dangerous enemies.

RETELLING RUBRIC: INFORMATIONAL

Macro-concepts (Numbered and Boldfaced) and Micro-concepts (Bulleted)

Place a 0, 1/2, or + to score student responses. See page 81 for information on what these assessment measures mean.

Story Structure:

___ 1. **Mary Jemison was taken from her family by Indians.**
___   • Her family was killed.
___ 2. **Two Indian sisters took Mary into their home.**
___   • They treated her with kindness.
___ 3. **She accepted the Indian way of life.**
___   • She came to appreciate the Indians as honest and faithful.
___   • She married an Indian warrior.
___   • She chose to stay with the Indians and her son when she had the chance to return to her own people.
___ 4. **Personal Response:** Any well-supported positive or negative response to the content or ideas in the text, or to the text as a whole.

Retelling Score: _____

_____ 5. **How might this story have ended differently if Mary knew that her family had been killed?**

Critical Response: She may have resented the Indians; may have tried to escape.

_____ 6. Why was Mary unhappy even though the two women treated her with kindness?

Text-Based: She missed her family and her own home.

_____ 7. Why would Mary's mother tell her to always obey her captors?

Inference: So that she could avoid being mistreated, punished, or killed.

_____ 8. Why could the sisters have chosen to kill Mary instead of adopt her?

Text-Based: To avenge the death of their brother.

_____ 9. Why would Mary's son be eager to see his mother rejoin her own people?

Inference: Thought she would be happy with them; wanted to see her captivity come to an end.

_____ 10. What was more important to Mary's survival, the memory of her mother's advice or the realization that her captors were honorable and honest?

Critical Response: Mother's advice—enabled her to fit in with the Indians. Realization—helped her to accept her new family.

Comprehension Analysis:

Text-Based: __/4__
Inference: __/4__
Critical Response: __/2__

Total Comprehension %: _____

Reader's copy on p. 132 of the Reader's Passages

Introductory Statement: "Would you read this passage about queen bees (to yourself/out loud). When you are finished, I'll take away the passage. Then I'll ask you to tell me about what you read and what you think of it. After that, I'll ask you some questions about the passage."

Story

Throughout a queen bee's relatively short life, she has two essential jobs. The first job is secreting a chemical that spreads among all the worker bees, limiting their interests to nothing but work throughout their lives. The second job is laying eggs, and this task keeps her from having any time to even eat; consequently, she must be fed by a small group of worker bees.

How did this bee become the queen of a hive that contains nearly 20,000 bees? Her ascent to royalty started with a story of death and intrigue. The bee larvae are fed with a creamy white royal jelly that contains high levels of nutrients and acid. The strongest larva is selected as the queen and, once she is hatched, she goes on a murderous rampage, destroying all other potential rivals, hatched or not. To celebrate her victory, the new queen takes what is known as a mating flight. She flies to a large group of drones and while in flight, she mates several times. But in the bee world, the mayhem continues and as each drone mates with the queen, his abdomen is ripped open and he dies. The surviving drones are not welcome in a hive and they cannot feed themselves because their bodies cannot harvest nectar or pollen. They are structured solely for mating and do not even have a stinger. They have outlived their usefulness and die of starvation.

The queen has a pouch that she uses to store the sperm that she has collected and will use throughout her entire life to fertilize her eggs. Her task is made more comfortable by the efforts of dozens of worker bees that keep the hive cool by fanning their wings 11,400 times per minute!

But even the queen is not exempt from the rule of usefulness to the community. If she were to run out of sperm, she would lose her royal status and be replaced at once. One of the newly hatched female bees would be moved by the workers to a special cell. There she would be fed royal jelly while all other larvae are fed a mixture of honey and pollen. Eleven days later, she would hatch, the old queen would be ousted, and the process of survival would carry on. (382 words)

Scoring Miscues for Oral Reading Option
Mark all scoreable miscues by placing either a plus (for those that maintain meaning) or a zero (for those that violate meaning) in the text margin.

Reading Accuracy Index: _____%
*Total all miscues marked with pluses **and** zeros and enter the corresponding percentage from the Miscue Chart.*

Meaning Maintenance Index: _____%
*Total **only** miscues marked with zeros and enter the corresponding percentage from the Miscue Chart.*

Miscue Chart (if used for oral reading)

Miscues	%	Miscues	%	Miscues	%	Miscues	%
1	100	15	96	29	92	43	89
2	99	16	96	30	92	44	88
3	99	17	96	31	92	45	88
4	99	18	95	32	92	46	88
5	99	19	95	33	91	47	88
6	98	20	95	34	91	48	87
7	98	21	95	35	91	49	87
8	98	22	94	36	91	50	87
9	98	23	94	37	90	51	87
10	97	24	94	38	90	52	86
11	97	25	93	39	90	53	86
12	97	26	93	40	90	54	86
13	97	27	93	41	89	55	86
14	96	28	93	42	89		

Student Retelling

Examiner: "Tell me about what you just read and what you thought about it."

    If there is no spontaneous response, repeat the request, "Tell me what you thought about the passage."

Note: Use the Retelling Rubric on p. 320 to assess the child's retelling performance. If you need additional space for retelling responses, use a separate sheet of paper.

RETELLING RUBRIC: INFORMATIONAL

Macro-concepts (Numbered and Boldfaced) and Micro-concepts (Bulleted)

Place a 0, 1/2, or + to score student responses. See page 81 for information on what these assessment measures mean.

Story Structure:

___ 1. **Queen bee has two jobs.**
  ___ • Limiting bee interests and hatching eggs.
___ 2. **Strongest larva becomes queen.**
  ___ • Is fed royal jelly by her subjects.
  ___ • Kills her weaker rivals.
  ___ • Mates with drones who die shortly after.
___ 3. **Queen must remain useful to the hive.**
  ___ • If she stops fertilizing eggs, she will be replaced.
___ 4. **Personal Response:** Any well-supported positive or negative response to the content or ideas in the text, or to the text as a whole.

Retelling Score: _____

Comprehension Questions

_____ 1. **How does the queen bee stay in control of the hive?**

Text-Based: She secretes a chemical that keeps the workers interested only in working.

_____ 2. **Why is the queen bee fed by worker bees?**

Text-Based: She is so busy laying eggs that she has no time to eat.

_____ 3. **How does this passage show that the community is more important to the bees than the individual bee?**

Inference: Each dies when it is no longer useful to the good of the hive.

_____ 4. **Why is it important that the queen be replaced immediately once she can no longer fertilize eggs?**
Inference: The survival of the hive depends on replacing bees; without new bees the hive could not function.

_____ 5. **What is more important to the queen bee's success, her aggressiveness or her ability to fertilize eggs?**

Critical Response: Aggressiveness—she cannot survive unless she eliminates her competitors. Ability to produce eggs—she is ousted as soon as she can no longer fertilize her eggs.

_____ 6. **What happens during the queen's mating flight?**

Text-Based: She leaves the nest and travels to a colony of drones and mates with several who will die.

_____ 7. **If they can't gather their own food, how can the drones survive long enough to mate with the queen?**

Inference: They must rely on others for food; they are fed by the workers until they have outlived their usefulness.

_____ 8. **Why would a new queen have to take over for an existing queen?**

Text-Based: If she were to run out of sperm.

_____ 9. **Why is it that the queen is not really very different from any other bee in the hive?**

Inference: All bees live only to serve the hive or the common good; any larva can become a queen.

_____ 10. **Use the story to tell who provides greater service to the eggs, the queen or the worker bees. Explain.**

Critical Response: The queen has fertilized them. The worker bees keep them cool by fanning their wings.

Comprehension Analysis:

Text-Based: __/4__
Inference: __/4__
Critical Response: __/2__

Total Comprehension %: _____

Reader's copy on p. 133 of the Reader's Passages

Introductory Statement: "Would you read this passage about Beluga (bell-ŏó-gah) whales (to yourself/out loud). When you are finished, I'll take away the passage. Then I'll ask you to tell me about what you read and what you think of it. After that, I'll ask you some questions about the passage."

Story

Whales can be seen in very unexpected places. For example, a large Beluga whale was seen swimming up the Delaware River in Pennsylvania by some fishermen who couldn't believe their eyes. They saw the whale dive into the water, but it didn't reappear for quite some time. This was unusual because Beluga dives usually last only 3 to 5 minutes. Beluga whales, like other marine mammals, have a body structure that is designed for diving. When they dive their heart rate slows down from 100 to about 12 to 20 beats a minute and all of their bodily functions slow down with it.

Reporters from all over came to Pennsylvania to watch the whale. Belugas are easy to observe since they often swim in shallow water where their bodies are barely covered. And they usually swim slowly, about two or three miles per hour. However, if they need to, they can swim at thirteen miles an hour for as long as fifteen minutes.

People began to worry that the whale was lost and would die in the river. Belugas normally live in the Arctic Ocean and the seas that join it. They have a layer of blubber just beneath the skin. This blubber makes up forty percent of the whale's weight and keeps its body from losing heat.

The people in Pennsylvania should not have been that surprised since Belugas often go to rivers to look for food. In fact, Beluga mothers take their young calves to the warmer waters of the Churchill River in Canada. They can be found there from May to August gorging on capland, a small fish that is plentiful there. There are often 50 Belugas in a feeding group that make shallow dives and feast frantically on the capland. Tourists go out in small boats to watch their feeding frenzy. Belugas are also very vocal. They communicate by making high-pitched whistles, squeals, and even bell-like tones. They can find food by making sharp clicking sounds and interpreting the echo they recover. Belugas are often called *sea canaries* because of the chirping sounds they make, but certainly not because of their size!

The whale in the Delaware River finally left. No one, even the scientists, ever really understood why it came there in the first place. (380 words)

Scoring Miscues for Oral Reading Option
Mark all scoreable miscues by placing either a plus (for those that maintain meaning) or a zero (for those that violate meaning) in the text margin.

Reading Accuracy Index: _____%
*Total all miscues marked with pluses **and** zeros and enter the corresponding percentage from the Miscue Chart.*

Meaning Maintenance Index: _____%
*Total **only** miscues marked with zeros and enter the corresponding percentage from the Miscue Chart.*

Miscue Chart (if used for oral reading)

Miscues	%	Miscues	%	Miscues	%	Miscues	%
1	100	16	96	31	92	46	88
2	99	17	96	32	92	47	88
3	99	18	95	33	91	48	87
4	99	19	95	34	91	49	87
5	99	20	95	35	91	50	87
6	98	21	94	36	91	51	87
7	98	22	94	37	90	52	86
8	98	23	94	38	90	53	86
9	98	24	94	39	90	54	86
10	97	25	93	40	89	55	86
11	97	26	93	41	89	56	85
12	97	27	93	42	89	57	85
13	97	28	93	43	89	58	85
14	96	29	92	44	88	59	84
15	96	30	92	45	88	60	84

Student Retelling

Examiner: "Tell me about what you just read and what you thought about it."

If there is no spontaneous response, repeat the request, "Tell me what you thought about the passage."

Note: Use the Retelling Rubric on p. 323 to assess the child's retelling performance. If you need additional space for retelling responses, use a separate sheet of paper.

RETELLING RUBRIC: INFORMATIONAL

Macro-concepts (Numbered and Boldfaced) and Micro-concepts (Bulleted)

Place a 0, 1/2, or + to score student responses. See page 81 for information on what these assessment measures mean.

Story Structure:

___ 1. **People in Pennsylvania came to observe a Beluga swim in the river.**
   ___ • Belugas are easy to observe because they swim slowly in shallow water.
   ___ • Belugas do not dive for a long time.

___ 2. **People worried that the whale was lost.**
   ___ • It was not unusual for whales to enter rivers.

___ 3. **Belugas survive on local fish.**
   ___ • Belugas feed on capland fish.
   ___ • Belugas communicate by making loud chirping sounds.

___ 4. **Personal Response:** Any well-supported positive or negative response to the content or ideas in the text, or to the text as a whole.

Retelling Score: _____

Comprehension Questions

_____ 1. **Why would the fishers be concerned when the Beluga whale did not reappear for quite some time after its dive?**

Text-Based: It was unusual behavior; their dives usually last 3 to 5 minutes.

_____ 2. **Why were so many people concerned about the Beluga whale in Pennsylvania?**

Text-Based: They were afraid that it was lost; afraid it would die.

_____ 3. **What makes Beluga whales such a good subject for scientific study?**

Inference: They are observable because they stay in shallow water; they are slow swimmers.

_____ 4. **Why would a lower heart beat rate help a Beluga whale while it is diving?**

Inference: It uses less oxygen; all of its bodily functions slow down.

_____ 5. **Use the information in the story to decide whether a scientist would rather observe the Beluga in the Delaware River or in the Churchill River.**

Critical Response: The Delaware River— since there was just one whale there; it was very rare in Pennsylvania. The Churchill River—since there are many whales; mothers are also with their young.

_____ 6. Where do Beluga whales mainly live?

Text-Based: *In the Arctic Ocean.*

_____ 7. How can the Belugas' ability to make sounds enhance its chances for survival?

Inference: *It helps them locate food; they can communicate with each other.*

_____ 8. Why would so many Belugas appear at one time in the Churchill River?

Text-Based: *Because of the abundance of food.*

_____ 9. Why would it be problem for a Beluga whale to spend long periods of time in very warm water?

Inference: *Its blubber keeps its body from losing heat and it would overheat.*

_____ 10. Use the information in the passage to decide whether a Beluga is more likely to be a hunter or the hunted. Explain.

Critical Response: *A hunter—because they do eat other fish; they are very aggressive when they eat. The hunted—because they swim slowly and are easily visible.*

Comprehension Analysis:

Text-Based: __/4__
Inference: __/4__
Critical Response: __/2__

Total Comprehension %: _____

EIGHTH GRADE I: DAMS

Reader's copy on p. 134 of the Reader's Passages

Introductory Statement: "Would you read this passage about dams (to yourself/out loud). When you are finished, I'll take away the passage. Then I'll ask you to tell me about what you read and what you think of it. After that, I'll ask you some questions about the passage."

Story

Do you ever smile when you hear people talking about "water shortages"? After all, more than three quarters of the earth's surface is covered with water! The problem, however, is more complex than it seems. Only one fortieth of the world's water is fresh water and less than one third of that exists in fluid form. And as the population grows and cities expand and demand for water increases, people are faced with difficult decisions at every turn.

One solution that has been used throughout the world in rapidly increasing numbers is dams. Dams can convert even modest streams of water into a source of electrical power. They can be used to store water for human consumption or crop irrigation, cooling or transportation. They can even provide recreation on the artificial lakes that are created as a result of dams. Many major cities throughout the world are completely dependent on dams as a source of water. Dams have become an integral part of the successful settlement of the world's population. In fact, they affect, in one way or another, nearly every human being on earth.

But dams are not an unmixed blessing. For nearly every artificial lake we create, there are people and animals that must lose their land and sometimes even their homes. Water stored in artificial reservoirs evaporates more rapidly than water left in its natural state. Many species of fish that migrate to their spawning grounds have suddenly found their way blocked by the creation of dams. And when a dam fails, the loss of life and property can be catastrophic. For all of these reasons and many more, public opposition to the construction of dams can be fierce.

Engineers have developed ingenious ways to overcome some problems, such as building ladders to help migrating fish find their way to the tops of dams. Some problems, of course, can never be overcome. And so the proponents and the opponents of dams fight on. Even the United Nations has tried to ease the tensions between groups. In 2001, it appointed an international commission to share information about the costs and benefits of dams. The commission tries to help countries plan more effectively in the construction of new dams and the removal of unnecessary ones. But with no solution in sight for the world's water demands, the groups must learn to disagree without losing respect for one another's point of view. (402 words)

Scoring Miscues for Oral Reading Option
Mark all scoreable miscues by placing either a plus (for those that maintain meaning) or a zero (for those that violate meaning) in the text margin.

Reading Accuracy Index: _____%
*Total all miscues marked with pluses **and** zeros and enter the corresponding percentage from the Miscue Chart.*

Meaning Maintenance Index: _____%
*Total **only** miscues marked with zeros and enter the corresponding percentage from the Miscue Chart.*

Miscue Chart (if used for oral reading)

Miscues	%	Miscues	%	Miscues	%	Miscues	%
1	100	16	96	31	92	46	88
2	99	17	96	32	92	47	88
3	99	18	95	33	91	48	87
4	99	19	95	34	91	49	87
5	99	20	95	35	91	50	87
6	98	21	94	36	91	51	87
7	98	22	94	37	90	52	86
8	98	23	94	38	90	53	86
9	98	24	94	39	90	54	86
10	97	25	93	40	89	55	86
11	97	26	93	41	89	56	85
12	97	27	93	42	89	57	85
13	97	28	93	43	89	58	85
14	96	29	92	44	88	59	84
15	96	30	92	45	88	60	84

Student Retelling

Examiner: "Tell me about what you just read and what you thought about it."

If there is no spontaneous response, repeat the request, "Tell me what you thought about the passage."

Note: Use the Retelling Rubric on p. 326 to assess the child's retelling performance. If you need additional space for retelling responses, use a separate sheet of paper.

RETELLING RUBRIC: INFORMATIONAL

Macro-concepts (Numbered and Boldfaced) and Micro-concepts (Bulleted)

Place a 0, 1/2, or + to score student responses. See page 81 for information on what these assessment measures mean.

Story Structure:

___ 1. **One common solution to water shortage problems is dams.**
   ___ • Dams can store water and produce electricity.
   ___ • Most major cities are dependent on dams for their water.

___ 2. **Many people are opposed to the building of dams.**
   ___ • Many lose their lands or homes.
   ___ • Wildlife can be endangered by dams

___ 3. **Engineers try to solve problems caused by dams.**
   ___ • The U.N. named a commission to study dams and to share information with the nations of the world.

___ 4. **Personal Response:** Any well-supported positive or negative response to the content or ideas in the text, or to the text as a whole.

Retelling Score: _____

Comprehension Questions

_____ 1. How does population growth make decisions about dams more difficult?

   Text-Based: The demand for water increases.

_____ 2. Why would people build dams even if they have plenty of water from existing sources?

   Text-Based: To generate electrical power; for recreation; to create artificial lakes.

_____ 3. What kinds of problems related to the building of dams cannot be overcome by engineers?

   Inference: Overpopulation; loss of land or homes because of the creation of lakes.

4. Why would fish need ladders because of the presence of dams?

   Inference: They cannot get to the higher water on the other side of the dams without ladders.

5. What is the greatest danger to people when the dam is built, the loss of land or the danger to wildlife?

   Critical Response: Land—people may lose their homes; people are displaced. Wildlife—wildlife cannot be replaced if they become extinct; we don't always know how wildlife will react to loss of their homes.

6. What are some reasons for the public's opposition to the building of dams? (Must identify two.)

   Text-Based: Danger of dam failure; loss of land; loss of homes; danger to wildlife; evaporation problems.

7. Why would the United Nations need to set up a special commission on the building of dams?

   Inference: Opposing groups couldn't get along; the commission could help countries to plan.

8. Why would people see dams as a solution to some of the world's energy problems?

   Text-Based: Dams can be used to generate electricity.

9. Why is it important for the supporters and critics of dams to respect each other's point of view?

   Inference: It is unlikely that either side is completely right; complex problems can't be solved without some cooperation between opposing groups.

10. Who do you think has more powerful support for their position, those opposed to building dams or those in favor of them? Use information from the passage to support your position.

    Critical Response: Opposed—dams are dangerous; dams destroy parts of the environment; dams kill animals and their habitats. In favor—people need water to live; energy is important to people's lives.

Comprehension Analysis:

   Text-Based: __/4__
   Inference: __/4__
   Critical Response: __/2__

Total Comprehension %: _____

EIGHTH GRADE II: JANE ADDAMS

Reader's copy on p. 135 of the Reader's Passages

Introductory Statement: "Would you read this passage about Jane Addams (to yourself/out loud). When you are finished, I'll take away the passage. Then I'll ask you to tell me about what you read and what you think of it. After that, I'll ask you some questions about the passage."

Story

Jane Addams was born in Cedarville, Illinois, in 1860, just before the start of the Civil War. She grew up in a trying time in America, but spent her youth in a tranquil, privileged home. Jane dreamed of going away to a "real" college, like Smith College in Massachusetts, but she never had that opportunity. Instead, she complied with the wishes of her family and attended a local college, Rockford Female Seminary. But Jane's disappointment was short-lived. At Rockford she met a girl who would become her lifelong friend and co-worker, Ellen Starr.

Jane and Ellen shared a deep concern for the problems experienced by immigrants to the United States. Together they founded a social settlement called Hull House, on Chicago's West Side. Hull House served the needs of immigrants from many nations and of many colors. Jane and her co-workers offered child care, clubs, activities, and citizenship classes. They even provided an employment service as well as music and art activities. These were designed to help immigrants value and celebrate their own heritage. Hull House was also a much-needed safe meeting place for the new trade and labor unions. But above all, it was a place where immigrants could find help in learning about American ways.

Jane Addams became one of the most influential American women of her time. Her work extended far beyond Chicago and Hull House. She became part of the national and international reform movement for social justice. Jane helped establish the first juvenile court and helped develop the first legislation to protect women and children from abuse. Jane was also part of the creation of the Federal Children's Bureau in 1912 and the first child labor laws in 1916.

Jane was the first president of the National Conference for Social Work. She was among the founders of the National Association for the Advancement of Colored People in 1909. She played the same role for the American Civil Liberties Union in 1920. Both of these groups are still active today.

Jane Addams was part of an international group of women who opposed World War I and fought for peace and freedom. Jane received worldwide recognition. She was awarded the Nobel Peace Prize in 1931. She was the first American woman to receive it.

She may never have achieved her goal of going away to college. Yet, Jane Addams made the world a better place! (396 words)

Scoring Miscues for Oral Reading Option
Mark all scoreable miscues by placing either a plus (for those that maintain meaning) or a zero (for those that violate meaning) in the text margin.

Reading Accuracy Index: _____%
*Total all miscues marked with pluses **and** zeros and enter the corresponding percentage from the Miscue Chart.*

Meaning Maintenance Index: _____%
*Total **only** miscues marked with zeros and enter the corresponding percentage from the Miscue Chart.*

Miscue Chart (if used for oral reading)

Miscues	%	Miscues	%	Miscues	%	Miscues	%
1	100	16	96	31	92	46	88
2	99	17	96	32	92	47	88
3	99	18	95	33	92	48	88
4	99	19	95	34	91	49	88
5	99	20	95	35	91	50	87
6	98	21	95	36	91	51	87
7	98	22	94	37	91	52	87
8	98	23	94	38	90	53	87
9	98	24	94	39	90	54	86
10	97	25	94	40	90	55	86
11	97	26	93	41	90	56	86
12	97	27	93	42	89	57	86
13	97	28	93	43	89	58	85
14	96	29	93	44	89	59	84
15	96	30	92	45	89	60	85

Student Retelling

Examiner: "Tell me about what you just read and what you thought about it."

If there is no spontaneous response, repeat the request, "Tell me what you thought about the passage."

Note: Use the Retelling Rubric on p. 329 to assess the child's retelling performance. If you need additional space for retelling responses, use a separate sheet of paper.

RETELLING RUBRIC: INFORMATIONAL

Macro-concepts (Numbered and Boldfaced) and Micro-concepts (Bulleted)

Place a 0, 1/2, or + to score student responses. See page 81 for information on what these assessment measures mean.

Story Structure:

____ 1. **Jane Addams was born to a wealthy and privileged family.**
- ____ • She wanted to attend Smith College but her family wanted her to attend a local school for women.
- ____ • She met her lifelong friend and collaborator Ellen Starr at Rockford.

____ 2. **Jane Addams had a deep concern for immigrants and the poor.**
- ____ • She founded Hull House with Ellen to serve the needs of immigrants in Chicago.
- ____ • She fought for social justice for children and minorities.

____ 3. **Jane Addams became one of the most influential people of her time.**
- ____ • Was the first American woman to win the Nobel Peace Prize.

____ 4. **Personal Response:** Any well-supported positive or negative response to the content or ideas in the text, or to the text as a whole.

Retelling Score: _____

Comprehension Questions

_____ 1. **When was Jane Addams born?**

Text-Based: In 1860; just before the start of the Civil War.

_____ 2. **Where did Jane Addams go to college?**

Text-Based: Rockford Female Seminary.

_____ 3. **Why would Addams's family prefer that she attend Rockford Female Seminary?**

Inference: It was closer to home; it was an all women college.

_____ 4. Why is it surprising that she was so concerned about poor immigrants?

Inference: She was from a wealthy privileged family.

_____ 5. Do you think Addams's family was right in not allowing her to attend Smith College?

Critical Response: Yes—if she hadn't gone to Rockford Female Seminary she would never have met Ellen Starr and would probably have never started Hull House; she developed a concern for social justice. No—she should have been allowed to attend the school of her own choice; she could have received a better education there.

_____ 6. Why would children need an advocate like Jane Addams?

Inference: They could become victims of abuse; they were sometimes exploited for their labor.

_____ 7. What did Addams do that indicates she was a forerunner of the civil rights movement?

Text-Based: She was a cofounder of the NAACP; she was a cofounder of the American Civil Liberties Movement.

_____ 8. What kinds of services did Hull House provide for the immigrants in Chicago? (Must include two.)

Text-Based: Helped immigrants learn American ways; offered child care, clubs, activities, and citizenship classes; provided an employment service; provided music and art activities celebrating their own heritage; provided a safe meeting place for the new trade and labor unions.

_____ 9. Aside from her friendship with Ellen Starr, how did Jane Addams's experiences at Rockford Seminary affect her life?

Inference: She developed a sense of social justice; she made the lives of immigrants more meaningful.

_____ 10. Which was a greater accomplishment for Jane, founding Hull House or winning the Nobel Peace Prize? Explain.

Critical Response: Hull House—she helped many more people in much more practical ways; Hull House was her lifelong work. Peace Prize—she was the first American woman to ever receive it and this gained her international recognition.

Comprehension Analysis:

Text-Based: __/4__
Inference: __/4__
Critical Response: __/2__

Total Comprehension %: _____

Reader's copy on p. 136 of the Reader's Passages

Introductory Statement: "Would you read this passage about possums (to yourself/out loud). When you are finished, I'll take away the passage. Then I'll ask you to tell me about what you read and what you think of it. After that, I'll ask you some questions about the passage."

Story

The possum, sometimes called North America's kangaroo, is its only marsupial animal. A female possum gives birth to over 20 babies, each no bigger than a honeybee. Only the first thirteen that crawl their way to the mother's pouch and attach themselves to one of her available nipples will survive. They remain in the pouch for 3 months and then crawl out and cling to the mother's fur. When they become too heavy to hold on, they fall off to the ground. At that time they are fully weaned and can begin their own search for food and shelter.

The study of possum habits shows that they do not need a permanent home. They usually spend only 2 or 3 days in another animal's hideout. Then they leave to find another. Their paws are too soft to dig holes to live in, but they seem to adapt anywhere they find the food, water, and shelter they need. Possums do not hibernate but they find winter very challenging. Their tails are particularly prone to frostbite since they have no fur covering. As a result, they often change their nocturnal habits in winter and eat during the day when it is warmer. The possum is very docile and, in addition to its many natural predators in the wild, humans, cats, and cars take their toll on possums. In fact, most possums never reach adulthood, living only 1 to 2 years.

Trappers who hoped to establish a fur industry brought the possum to New Zealand. At the height of the fur trade, 20 million possums were trapped yearly. However, the possum, with no natural enemies in New Zealand, quickly became a national pest. It loved the juicy new growth on several native trees. And because it returns to the same tree night after night until the leaves are gone, the destruction to vegetation was unbelievable. Seventy million possums nightly destroy 20 tons of growth, or the equivalent of 190 million hamburgers.

In spite of the deep resentment felt for possums in New Zealand, residents in several counties in Florida pay tribute to them. During the Depression, when little food was available, people survived because of the abundance of possum. The residents of Chipley, Florida, show their appreciation through their yearly celebration of the Possum Festival. (382 words)

Scoring Miscues for Oral Reading Option
Mark all scoreable miscues by placing either a plus (for those that maintain meaning) or a zero (for those that violate meaning) in the text margin.

Reading Accuracy Index: _____%
*Total all miscues marked with pluses **and** zeros and enter the corresponding percentage from the Miscue Chart.*

Meaning Maintenance Index: _____%
*Total **only** miscues marked with zeros and enter the corresponding percentage from the Miscue Chart.*

Miscue Chart (if used for oral reading)

Miscues	%	Miscues	%	Miscues	%	Miscues	%
1	100	15	96	29	92	43	89
2	99	16	96	30	92	44	88
3	99	17	96	31	92	45	88
4	99	18	95	32	92	46	88
5	99	19	95	33	91	47	88
6	98	20	95	34	91	48	87
7	98	21	95	35	91	49	87
8	98	22	94	36	91	50	87
9	98	23	94	37	90	51	87
10	97	24	94	38	90	52	86
11	97	25	93	39	90	53	86
12	97	26	93	40	90	54	86
13	97	27	93	41	89	55	86
14	96	28	93	42	89		

Student Retelling

Examiner: "Tell me about what you just read and what you thought about it."

    If there is no spontaneous response, repeat the request, "Tell me what you thought about the passage."

Note: Use the Retelling Rubric on p. 332 to assess the child's retelling performance. If you need additional space for retelling responses, use a separate sheet of paper.

RETELLING RUBRIC: INFORMATIONAL

Macro-concepts (Numbered and Boldfaced) and Micro-concepts (Bulleted)

Place a 0, 1/2, or + to score student responses. See page 81 for information on what these assessment measures mean.

Story Structure:

___ 1. **Female possums give birth to 20 babies.**
   ___ • Only 13 babies will survive.
   ___ • Possums will live in the homes of other animals for 2 or 3 days and then move on.
   ___ • Winter is hard for possums so most live only 1 or 2 years.
___ 2. **Possums became a pest in New Zealand.**
   ___ • Possums were brought in for fur but had no enemies.
   ___ • Possums multiplied and would eat huge quantities of vegetation.
___ 3. **People in Florida fed on possums and now celebrate with a Possum Festival.**
___ 4. **Personal Response:** Any well-supported positive or negative response to the content or ideas in the text, or to the text as a whole.

Retelling Score: _____

Comprehension Questions

_____ 1. Why do only 13 possum babies survive when over 20 are born?

Text-Based: The mother has only 13 nipples.

_____ 2. Why don't possums dig their homes in the ground?

Text-Based: Their paws are too soft.

_____ 3. How does the story show the adaptability of the possum?

Inference: In the winter they eat during the day when it is warmer; they live in the houses of other animals.

_____ 4. If possums seldom survive beyond 1 or 2 years, how can it be that they are so abundant?

Inference: They have a high birthrate; they don't have to build their own homes; they had no natural enemies in New Zealand.

_____ 5. What causes the greater challenge for possums, their physical structure or their social behaviors?

Critical Response: Their physical structures—because many die after birth since there are only 13 nipples; they can't dig holes; they have a hard time in the cold winters. Their social behaviors—because they must live in other animal's homes; they get different homes every few days; they are very docile and not good fighters.

_____ 6. What habit of possums has created a major problem in New Zealand?

Text-Based: Possums were destroying many native trees.

_____ 7. How does the story show that the best-laid plans do not always work?

Inference: The plan to produce a fur business backfired and the possums became a very destructive pest.

_____ 8. Why did the possum population explode in New Zealand?

Text-Based: They had no natural enemies.

_____ 9. Use the story to tell what the authorities in New Zealand might do to help them deal with the possum problem.

Inference: They could import animals that would be natural enemies to the possum.

_____ 10. Who has the right attitude about possums, the people in New Zealand or the people in Florida? Explain.

Critical Response: The people in New Zealand—because the possum destroyed their native trees. The people in Florida—because many people would have starved to death during the Depression if there hadn't been possums available for them to eat.

Comprehension Analysis:

Text-Based: __/4__
Inference: __/4__
Critical Response: __/2__

Total Comprehension %: _____

Reader's copy on p. 137 of the Reader's Passages

Introductory Statement: "Would you read this passage about insects (to yourself/out loud). When you are finished, I'll take away the passage. Then I'll ask you to tell me about what you read and what you think of it. After that, I'll ask you some questions about the passage."

Story

When it comes to adapting to life on earth, there may be no species that does it better than the insect. If you are tempted to think that humans are at the top of the list, it may be time to reconsider. It is estimated that for every person on the face of the earth, there are one million insects and, if taken together, they would outweigh us by about 12 to 1. And their sheer ability to adapt to their surroundings makes them arguably the most successful creatures alive.

Take, for example, insect larvae. Unlike primitive insects whose young resemble the adults into which they will grow, more complex insects go through radically different stages of development. Grubs turn into beetles, maggots develop into flies, and caterpillars morph into butterflies. But the very complexity of their development presents some monumental problems. Unlike the insect that they will soon become, larvae have none of the traditional means of escaping predators; they are not built to move or flee; they are built only to eat and grow. Their lack of mobility is of little consequence to grubs and maggots; they do their eating out of sight of the world. Caterpillars, however, are a different matter since their banquet table is in the woods, in full view of dozens of hungry potential predators. How then can they ever win the perpetual battle to be a diner rather than a dinner?

The answer is quite simple: Caterpillars are among the greatest camouflage artists the world has ever seen. For example, the larvae of geometer moths have taken on the size and shape of tree twigs and are virtually undetectable while feeding on leaves. The Tiger Swallowtail larvae look remarkably like fresh bird droppings on a leaf, effectively discouraging predators from even considering them as food. Some caterpillars have eye-like markings on the side of their head. When disturbed by a hungry bird, they weave from side to side, mimicking a dangerous tree snake.

Other caterpillars use equally ingenious escape mechanisms. When detected, the Looper caterpillar will jump off the branch where it is feeding and its predator will search futilely for it on the ground below. But the Looper is really an accomplished bungee jumper who watches the search below while hanging from the branch by a thread of silk.

We have just scratched the surface of the enormous array of survival techniques used by insects. It may be that when it comes to sheer problem-solving and adaptability, humans, especially soldiers, may have much to learn from the lowly insect. (427 words)

Scoring Miscues for Oral Reading Option
Mark all scoreable miscues by placing either a plus (for those that maintain meaning) or a zero (for those that violate meaning) in the text margin.

Reading Accuracy Index: _____%
*Total all miscues marked with pluses **and** zeros and enter the corresponding percentage from the Miscue Chart.*

Meaning Maintenance Index: _____%
*Total **only** miscues marked with zeros and enter the corresponding percentage from the Miscue Chart.*

Miscue Chart (if used for oral reading)

Miscues	%	Miscues	%	Miscues	%	Miscues	%
1	100	15	96	29	93	43	90
2	100	16	96	30	93	44	90
3	99	17	96	31	93	45	89
4	99	18	96	32	93	46	89
5	99	19	96	33	92	47	89
6	99	20	95	34	92	48	89
7	98	21	95	35	92	49	89
8	98	22	95	36	92	50	88
9	98	23	95	37	91	51	88
10	98	24	94	38	91	52	88
11	97	25	94	39	91	53	88
12	97	26	94	40	91	54	87
13	97	27	94	41	90	55	87
14	97	28	93	42	90		

Student Retelling

Examiner: "Tell me about what you just read and what you thought about it."

If there is no spontaneous response, repeat the request, "Tell me what you thought about the passage."

Note: Use the Retelling Rubric on p. 335 to assess the child's retelling performance. If you need additional space for retelling responses, use a separate sheet of paper.

RETELLING RUBRIC: INFORMATIONAL

Macro-concepts (Numbered and Boldfaced) and Micro-concepts (Bulleted)

Place a 0, 1/2, or + to score student responses. See page 81 for information on what these assessment measures mean.

Story Structure:

___ 1. **Insects may be the most successful creature on earth.**
  ___ • They outnumber humans a million to one.
___ 2. **The complexity of the development of some insects causes problems.**
  ___ • They cannot flee from predators.
  ___ • Problem is greatest for caterpillars who eat in full view of their predators.
___ 3. **Caterpillars have found ways to avoid their predators.**
  ___ • Some do it by imitating things in the environment.
  ___ • Some do it by developing escape techniques.
___ 4. **Personal Response:** Any well-supported positive or negative response to the content or ideas in the text, or to the text as a whole.

Retelling Score: _____

Comprehension Questions

_____ 1. According to the passage, why aren't humans at the top of the adaptability list?

Text-Based: Insects outnumber humans a million to one; insects outweigh humans 12 to 1; insects are better at adapting.

_____ 2. Why is camouflage the only effective way to help caterpillars survive?

Text-Based: They are too slow to escape; they are built only to feed, not to escape predators.

3. What could human soldiers possibly learn from observing insects?

   Inference: Ideas to avoid detection; ideas about blending in with the environment; ideas about avoiding enemies.

4. Why didn't caterpillars simply learn to defend themselves instead of developing so much camouflage?

   Inference: They have no mobility; they have nothing to defend themselves with; their bodies are not built for defending themselves.

5. Which caterpillar is likely to be the most effective defense against predators, the tree snake imitator or the bungee jumper?

   Critical Response: Tree snake—because if the predator looks up, he'll see the bungee jumper. The bungee jumper—if the predator watches the tree snake for a while, he'll realize that it is just a caterpillar.

6. Why is lack of mobility of little consequence to grubs or maggots?

   Text-Based: They are out of sight of predators.

7. What can human beings learn about survival from observing insects?

   Inference: To avoid trouble at all costs; to have a strategy to outsmart an enemy.

8. What is the biggest disadvantage to being a complex insect?

   Text-Based: They have no means of escaping predators; they are helpless at certain stages of their development.

9. Why do predators look on the ground for the Looper caterpillar?

   Inference: They expect that there is nowhere else that an insect who has jumped from a branch could possibly be.

10. If the earth changed in a way that made it inhospitable to life, who would have a better chance of surviving, humans or insects?

    Critical Response: Insects—there are more of them; they adapt to change very quickly. Humans—they are intelligent and can control their world in ways impossible to insects.

Comprehension Analysis:

Text-Based: __/4__
Inference: __/4__
Critical Response: __/2__

Total Comprehension %: _____

Reader's copy on p. 138 of the Reader's Passages

Introductory Statement: "Would you read this passage about the Mississippi River (to yourself/out loud). When you are finished, I'll take away the passage. Then I'll ask you to tell me about what you read and what you think of it. After that, I'll ask you some questions about the passage."

Story

For many midwestern Americans living along the floodplains of the Mississippi River, the Great River was the source of their livelihood. The commercial traffic that flowed daily on the river provided goods and employment for thousands of people. But as William Faulkner wrote, the river was like a mule that would work for you for ten years just for the privilege of kicking you once.

And one of the river's hardest kicks was delivered in 1993 when a huge flood caused widespread destruction, leaving nearly 75,000 people without homes in nine states. The flood caused over 15 billion dollars in damage. To be sure, the Mississippi had flooded before and old-timers in the town could remember many flood years in their lifetimes. But 1993 seemed to almost everyone to be the worst of them all. This flood broke high-water records all across the Midwest. But to the people living along the floodplains, the Great Flood of 1993 was simply another of life's challenges to be met and overcome. They would rebuild their homes with help from the Federal Emergency Management Agency (FEMA). After the inconveniences and obstacles had been overcome, life would go on just as it had so many times in the past.

But no one could foresee that this time things were different. The U.S. Congress was apparently tired of flood emergency claims year after year and so instead, it announced a grand social experiment. It would no longer help the citizens living on floodplains to rebuild their homes in the same place. Congress instructed FEMA to help them rebuild their homes and towns in locations that were not as prone to flooding. In 1993 alone, over 10,000 homes were relocated but hardships, as always, seemed to relocate along with the homes. Many citizens complained that their new homes, built on more expensive land, drove up their mortgage debt. Others felt the loss of friends as towns and communities went their separate ways rather then relocating together.

But, as is so often the case, there were also many success stories. Many towns managed to stay intact and to plan newer and better communities. Many local leaders emerged to help their friends and fellow townspeople ease the stresses of the drastic changes in their lives. It is too early to tell whether the experiment has worked for the greater good of all, but one certainty has emerged from the flood of 1993. The U.S. Congress will probably never again help flood victims stay in the same places just to wait for the next great flood to strike.

(428 words)

Scoring Miscues for Oral Reading Option
Mark all scoreable miscues by placing either a plus (for those that maintain meaning) or a zero (for those that violate meaning) in the text margin.

Reading Accuracy Index: _____%
*Total all miscues marked with pluses **and** zeros and enter the corresponding percentage from the Miscue Chart.*

Meaning Maintenance Index: _____%
*Total **only** miscues marked with zeros and enter the corresponding percentage from the Miscue Chart.*

Miscue Chart (if used for oral reading)

Miscues	%	Miscues	%	Miscues	%	Miscues	%
1	100	15	96	29	93	43	90
2	100	16	96	30	93	44	90
3	99	17	96	31	93	45	89
4	99	18	96	32	93	46	89
5	99	19	96	33	93	47	89
6	99	20	95	34	92	48	89
7	98	21	95	35	92	49	89
8	98	22	95	36	92	50	88
9	98	23	95	37	91	51	88
10	98	24	94	38	91	52	88
11	97	25	94	39	91	53	88
12	97	26	94	40	91	54	87
13	97	27	94	41	90	55	87
14	97	28	93	42	90		

Student Retelling

Examiner: "Tell me about what you just read and what you thought about it."

If there is no spontaneous response, repeat the request, "Tell me what you thought about the passage."

Note: Use the Retelling Rubric on p. 338 to assess the child's retelling performance. If you need additional space for retelling responses, use a separate sheet of paper.

RETELLING RUBRIC: INFORMATIONAL

Macro-concepts (Numbered and Boldfaced) and Micro-concepts (Bulleted)

Place a 0, 1/2, or + to score student responses. See page 81 for information on what these assessment measures mean.

Story Structure

___ 1. **The Mississippi River flooded in the late 1900s.**
  ___ • Worst flood ever.
  ___ • Left thousands homeless.
  ___ • They expected that the government would help them rebuild as always.
___ 2. **Government decided to help people move, not rebuild.**
  ___ • Many were unhappy, but there were many successes too.
___ 3. **It is too early to tell if the experiment was a success.**
  ___ • Government will probably never just re-build homes again.
___ 4. **Personal Response:** Any well-supported positive or negative response to the content or ideas in the text, or to the text as a whole.

Retelling Score: _____

Comprehension Questions

_____ 1. **What was different about the 1993 flood from those that went before?**

  Text-Based: More serious; families did not move back to the same place.

_____ 2. **Why weren't all of the people happy about getting a new home after the flood?**

  Text-Based: Mortgages were higher; land was more expensive.

_____ 3. What made many people think that the relocation experiment would succeed?

Inference: Leaders emerged who helped people and helped keep communities together; people came together to help each other.

_____ 4. What did William Faulkner mean when he said, "The river is like a mule that will work for you for 10 years just for the privilege of kicking you once"?

Inference: River provided many good things, but then became a huge problem when it was least expected.

_____ 5. Do you think that Faulkner was right? (Explain concept if child got previous item incorrect.)

Critical Response: Yes—the problems that occurred with the flood outweighed the good that had been done before it; the flood was worse than the good things. No—the river had provided many years of jobs and good things and one incident couldn't outweigh them all.

_____ 6. What did the people along the river expect FEMA to do after the 1993 floods?

Text-Based: Help them rebuild their homes in the same place.

_____ 7. Why wouldn't the government just help people to rebuild their homes wherever they wanted?

Inference: Cost too much to keep rebuilding after every flood.

_____ 8. What did Congress tell FEMA to do instead?

Text-Based: Help them rebuild in different locations away from the river.

_____ 9. Why would people want to rebuild along the river after so many floods?

Inference: It was their home town; they knew their neighbors and were comfortable where they were.

_____ 10. Do you think that the U.S. Congress was right to experiment with people's lives? Explain.

Critical Response: Yes—if it worked, they would save a great deal of money; the idea was a good one and would make things better for everyone. No—people should be free to live where they want; government should not be playing with people's lives.

Comprehension Analysis:

Text-Based: /4

Inference: /4

Critical Response: /2

Total Comprehension %: _____

NINTH GRADE III: THE WISE WOMAN DOCTOR

Reader's copy on p. 139 of the Reader's Passages

Introductory Statement: "Would you read this passage about a woman physician (to yourself/out loud). When you are finished, I'll take away the passage. Then I'll ask you to tell me about what you read and what you think of it. After that, I'll ask you some questions about the passage."

Story

Many people characterize medieval Europe almost exclusively as the Dark Ages. Historians, on the other hand, know that there were many bright spots. And one of the brightest was the medical center at Salerno in southern Italy. This center had earned a worldwide reputation as the home of the first formal medical school. Contrary to all social customs, women studied and learned here side-by-side with men, using Greek, Arabic and Jewish texts. One of these women was Trotula di Ruggerio, known more affectionately as the "wise woman teacher." Trotula's primary interest was attempting to lessen women's suffering. She did this by listening closely to what her patients had to say about their ailments. She believed that it was the doctor's responsibility to ensure the comfort of patients and to foster healing. Some practices she recommended included warm herbal baths, diets, and massages. She also advocated plenty of rest to foster positive attitudes. Not only were Trotula's practices innovative for her times, but her views challenged some very central social assumptions. For example, she believed that problems with fertility could be caused by the male, not just the female, as was commonly believed.

Trotula is widely credited for having written key textbooks used during her life and for many years after her death. Her most notable work, *The Diseases of Women*, was written for male students, since information about the female body was not widely known. In many ways, Trotula was ahead of her time, especially her use of drugs to lessen the pain of childbirth. This practice illustrates her willingness to challenge the predominant religious views of her time. The Church held that women were destined by God to suffer during childbirth.

She is credited with performing life-saving surgeries for both infants and mothers during childbirth. Her books are recognized as pioneering two fields of study, obstetrics and gynecology.

It would be wonderful to report that the social gains and opportunities for education at Salerno continued for many years to come. Unfortunately, in 1194 King Henry VI destroyed the medical school at Salerno. From that point on, women were not permitted to study medicine. In fact, they were deprived of any type of education. Those women who continued practicing healing skills through the use of herbs and oils were often persecuted as witches. Many of Trotula's books were lost and some of her works were credited to male physicians. But most historians today accept Trotula as the author of these medical books because of the openness and frankness with which she wrote. (422 words)

Scoring Miscues for Oral Reading Option
Mark all scoreable miscues by placing either a plus (for those that maintain meaning) or a zero (for those that violate meaning) in the text margin.

Reading Accuracy Index: _____%
*Total all miscues marked with pluses **and** zeros and enter the corresponding percentage from the Miscue Chart.*

Meaning Maintenance Index: _____%
*Total **only** miscues marked with zeros and enter the corresponding percentage from the Miscue Chart.*

Miscue Chart (if used for oral reading)

Miscues	%	Miscues	%	Miscues	%	Miscues	%
1	100	19	95	37	91	55	87
2	99	20	95	38	91	56	87
3	99	21	95	39	91	57	86
4	99	22	95	40	91	58	86
5	99	23	95	41	90	59	86
6	99	24	94	42	90	60	86
7	98	25	94	43	90	61	86
8	98	26	94	44	90	62	85
9	98	27	94	45	89	63	85
10	98	28	93	46	89	64	85
11	97	29	93	47	89	65	85
12	97	30	93	48	89	66	84
13	97	31	93	49	88	67	84
14	97	32	92	50	88	68	84
15	96	33	92	51	88	69	84
16	96	34	92	52	88	70	83
17	96	35	92	53	87		
18	96	36	91	54	87		

Student Retelling

Examiner: "Tell me about what you just read and what you thought about it."

If there is no spontaneous response, repeat the request, "Tell me what you thought about the passage."

Note: Use the Retelling Rubric on p. 341 to assess the child's retelling performance. If you need additional space for retelling responses, use a separate sheet of paper.

RETELLING RUBRIC: INFORMATIONAL

Macro-concepts (Numbered and Boldfaced) and Micro-concepts (Bulleted)

Place a 0, 1/2, or + to score student responses. See page 81 for information on what these assessment measures mean.

Story Structure:

___ 1. **The medical center at Salerno was the first medical school.**
  ___ • Women and men studied together.
  ___ • Trotula di Ruggerio was one of the women better known as the "wise woman teacher."

___ 2. **Trotula is credited with writing books that attempted to lessen women's suffering.**
  ___ • Her most notable book was *The Diseases of Women*.
  ___ • Her books pioneered the fields of obstetrics and gynecology.

___ 3. **The medical school at Salerno was destroyed.**
  ___ • Women were no longer permitted to study medicine.

___ 4. **Personal Response:** Any well-supported positive or negative response to the content or ideas in the text, or to the text as a whole.

Retelling Score: _____

Comprehension Questions

_____ 1. **What was so unusual about the medical school at Salerno?**

Text-Based: Men and women studied side-by-side.

_____ 2. **What was Trotula's primary approach to the treatment of her patients?**

Text-Based: She listened to her patients; she tried to make them as comfortable as possible.

_____ 3. Why would people be likely to regard "wise woman teacher" as a good name for Trotula?

Inference: She was a competent doctor and shared her knowledge with other people; she earned the respect of the medical field.

_____ 4. Why did it take great courage for Trotula to practice medicine?

Inference: It violated social customs; she spoke up against the church; she challenged medical assumptions about fertility.

_____ 5. Which was more important to her success, her interactions with her patients or her courage in defying social customs?

Critical Response: Interaction with her patients—since she learned about their ailments as she talked to them. Her courage in defying social customs—made it possible for her to become a doctor.

_____ 6. Why did the Church disagree with Trotula's use of drugs to lessen the pain of childbirth?

Text-Based: It believed God ordained woman's suffering during childbirth.

_____ 7. What advantage existed for male medical students to study side-by-side with females?

Inference: They could learn more about women's diseases.

_____ 8. How did Trotula show that she valued what she had learned in the study of medicine?

Text-Based: She wrote books for future medical students.

_____ 9. Why was the persecution of women who practiced healing such a clear example of human foolishness?

Inference: They had evidence that women could be successful doctors; the people were deprived of the learning that a woman doctor had acquired.

_____10. Which challenge was more significant to Trotula's career, Salerno's willingness to challenge social norms, or Trotula's willingness to challenge religious norms?

Critical Response: Salerno's challenge to social norms—since without that Trotula would never have been able to study. Trotula's challenge to religious norms— since women were relieved of a great deal of pain.

Comprehension Analysis:

Text-Based: __/4__
Inference: __/4__
Critical Response: __/2__

Total Comprehension %: _____

Reader's copy on p. 141 of the Reader's Passages

Introductory Statement: "Would you read this passage about criminal investigations (to yourself/out loud). When you are finished, I'll take away the passage. Then I'll ask you to tell me about what you read and what you think of it. After that, I'll ask you some questions about the passage."

Story

On television shows about cold cases, detectives always seem to solve the mystery within the show's one hour time limit, but this is a far cry from reality. Actually, some of history's most infamous cases have never been solved at all. Jack the Ripper was never caught and the Boston Strangler case was never officially closed, even though a man confessed to the crimes.

The real job of cold case crime solving is often tedious, detailed work. It involves careful analysis of physical evidence from the crime scene with thorough investigative interviewing techniques. Technology including the Automated Fingerprint Identification System, along with DNA and chemical analysis, can help. Their results may not tell the police who the criminal was, but they may lead detectives to the elimination of possible suspects and witnesses. After extensive background checks and interviews, suspects and witnesses eventually may implicate the perpetrator.

A prime example of a case that combined all of these techniques is that of Robert Spangler, a convicted serial killer who had evaded justice for years. In 1978, neighbors discovered a 45-year-old woman, her 17-year-old son, and her 15-year-old daughter dead from apparent gunshot wounds. A suicide note was found by the mother's body. Police who interviewed the father, Robert Spangler, found gunshot residue on his hands. Even with two questionable polygraph tests,

this was not enough evidence to charge him with murder since it is imperative that police provide credible evidence for an indictment. But with no statute of limitations on murder, time is on the side of the legal system. Tests that were not available to police at the time of a murder can be used on the physical evidence that still exists.

In 1993, 15 years later, Spangler married for the third time. While on a hiking trip in the Grand Canyon, he reported that his wife was missing. Park rangers later found her body, and classified her death as an accidental fall. Unknown to Spangler, they were very suspicious.

The park rangers requested help from local police and the Federal Bureau of Investigation (FBI). Because there was limited physical evidence, the FBI focused on interviewing techniques and background information analysis. Finally, agents interviewed Spangler and confronted him with their belief that he was a unique murderer. Spangler, suffering from terminal cancer, confessed to killing his first wife, his two children, and his third wife.

For more than 20 years after his first murder, Spangler was a free man. During that time he took at least one more life. Slow but thorough detective work coordinated at the local and federal level eventually led to his arrest and conviction. About 35 to 40% of homicides go cold in any given year. When they are solved, it is often through long, complex investigation and that kind of work is never completed in one hour! (468 words)

Scoring Miscues for Oral Reading Option
Mark all scoreable miscues by placing either a plus (for those that maintain meaning) or a zero (for those that violate meaning) in the text margin.

Reading Accuracy Index: _____%
*Total all miscues marked with pluses **and** zeros and enter the corresponding percentage from the Miscue Chart.*

Meaning Maintenance Index: _____%
*Total **only** miscues marked with zeros and enter the corresponding percentage from the Miscue Chart.*

Miscue Chart (if used for oral reading)

Miscues	%	Miscues	%	Miscues	%	Miscues	%
1	100	19	96	37	92	55	88
2	100	20	96	38	92	56	88
3	99	21	96	39	92	57	88
4	99	22	95	40	92	58	88
5	99	23	95	41	91	59	88
6	99	24	95	42	91	60	87
7	99	25	95	43	91	61	87
8	98	26	95	44	91	62	87
9	98	27	94	45	90	63	87
10	98	28	94	46	90	64	86
11	98	29	94	47	90	65	86
12	97	30	94	48	90	66	86
13	97	31	93	49	90	67	86
14	97	32	93	50	89	68	86
15	97	33	93	51	89	69	85
16	97	34	93	52	89	70	85
17	96	35	93	53	89		
18	96	36	92	54	89		

Student Retelling

Examiner: "Tell me about what you just read and what you thought about it."

If there is no spontaneous response, repeat the request, "Tell me what you thought about the passage."

Note: Use the Retelling Rubric on p. 345 to assess the child's retelling performance. If you need additional space for retelling responses, use a separate sheet of paper.

RETELLING RUBRIC: INFORMATIONAL

Macro-concepts (Numbered and Boldfaced) and Micro-concepts (Bulleted)

Place a 0, 1/2, or + to score student responses. See page 81 for information on what these assessment measures mean.

Story Structure:

___ 1. **Real cold cases are very different from those we see on TV.**
  ___ • Some cold cases are never solved.
  ___ • Real cold case investigations involve analysis of technology and human nature.

___ 2. **A classic cold case was that of Robert Spangler.**
  ___ • Spangler was a serial killer who was free for 20 years.
  ___ • Officers became suspicious when his third wife died "accidentally."
  ___ • FBI obtained a confession from Spangler.

___ 3. **About 35 to 40% of murder cases go cold every year.**

___ 4. **Personal Response:** Any well-supported positive or negative response to the content or ideas in the text, or to the text as a whole.

Retelling Score: _____

Comprehension Questions

_____ 1. What is the difference between TV cold cases and real-life cases?

Text-Based: TV cases are solved in one hour, but are never solved that way in real life.

_____ 2. Even if they do not identify a murderer, how do DNA testing and fingerprint identification technology help police?

Text-Based: They can eliminate suspects and witnesses; they can help save a great deal of time and effort.

3. Why did Robert Spangler confess to the murder of his wives and children?

   Inference: He was surprised by the accusation of the agents; he was dying of cancer and had nothing to lose.

4. Why is it fair to say that an unsolved murder case is never closed?

   Inference: The statute of limitations never runs out on murder cases.

5. What quality do you believe would be more important to a cold case detective, knowledge of technology or knowledge of human nature? Explain.

   Critical Response: Technology—new technologies can help solve crimes; technology can be used to re-examine old cases. Human nature—the ability to interview suspects is essential in murder cases; a knowledge of what motivates people can solve cases.

6. How long did it take law enforcement officers to convict Robert Spangler of murder?

   Text-Based: Twenty years.

7. Why would the police have been suspicious of Spangler when he reported his wife missing at the Grand Canyon?

   Inference: His family already died once under suspicious circumstances.

8. How many homicide cases go cold in any given year?

   Text-Based: About 35 to 40%.

9. Why would the Grand Canyon park rangers ask the FBI and police for help in the investigation of the death of Spangler's third wife?

   Inference: FBI would have more technology and experience; park rangers deal with few murders.

10. Do you believe that the police who first arrested Robert Spangler did a good job? Explain.

    Critical Response: Yes—they found the gunshot residue on his hands; they gave him polygraph tests. No—they let him get away; they should have asked for help; they should have used more up-to-date technology.

Comprehension Analysis:

Text-Based: __/4__
Inference: __/4__
Critical Response: __/2__

Total Comprehension %: _____

TENTH GRADE II: THE AUTHOR OF NARNIA

Reader's copy on p. 143 of the Reader's Passages

Introductory Statement: "Would you read this passage about C. S. Lewis, the author of the Narnia stories (to yourself/out loud). When you are finished, I'll take away the passage. Then I'll ask you to tell me about what you read and what you think of it. After that, I'll ask you some questions about the passage."

Story

Many people are surprised that one of the world's most beloved writers of children's literature was actually very uncomfortable around children. And in reality, the life of C. S. Lewis included many such contradictions. Although Lewis was born in Ireland, he received most of his education in private boarding schools in England. He served England in World War I on the front lines in France, despite the fact that as an Irish national, he could have been exempted from service.

Lewis began his professional career as a tutor at Oxford University, surrounded by world-renowned scholars. He immediately began to fulfill his life's ambitions of becoming an author and scholar. By all accounts he was wildly successful in both areas. He wrote a series of children's stories which he called *The Chronicles of Narnia*. He also wrote science fiction novels for adults, and books about faith and belief. Many of his books became extraordinarily popular all over the world, a sticking point for some of his Oxford colleagues. By 1947, Lewis was famous enough to appear on the cover of *Time* magazine. And in 1956, Lewis published a study of 16th-century literature that to this very day is considered the definitive work on the subject. Yet Lewis never reached another of his major dreams, an appointment as a full professor at Oxford.

A lifelong bachelor, Lewis began correspondence with an American woman named Joy Davidman who often questioned him about ideas in his books. Lewis found that he enjoyed these challenging intellectual matches. Joy later took up residence in England but because of her involvement with the communist movement during her youth, she was threatened with deportation. Lewis went through a legal marriage ceremony to enable Joy to remain in England. Lewis and Joy did not live together but maintained their deep friendship. But when Joy was diagnosed with terminal cancer, Lewis realized something more. He was in love and wanted a real church wedding. They spent more than three delightful years living together after a near-miraculous remission of her cancer. When Joy at last succumbed to the disease, Lewis penned a journal that was later published as *A Grief Observed*. This book is a meditation on the mystery of life and triumph over sorrow that has served as a source of comfort to millions of readers.

Nine years before his death, C. S. Lewis was finally offered the post that had eluded him throughout his professional life, the position of full professor. But it was Oxford's historical rival, the University of Cambridge, that made the offer. Faced with the prospect of losing one of its most distinguished and famous faculty members, Oxford quickly replicated Cambridge's offer. It was too little too late. Lewis happily spent the remainder of his career as a professor of medieval literature at Cambridge University. (470 words)

Scoring Miscues for Oral Reading Option
Mark all scoreable miscues by placing either a plus (for those that maintain meaning) or a zero (for those that violate meaning) in the text margin.

Reading Accuracy Index: _____%
*Total all miscues marked with pluses **and** zeros and enter the corresponding percentage from the Miscue Chart.*

Meaning Maintenance Index: _____%
*Total **only** miscues marked with zeros and enter the corresponding percentage from the Miscue Chart.*

Miscue Chart (if used for oral reading)

Miscues	%	Miscues	%	Miscues	%	Miscues	%
1	100	19	96	37	92	55	88
2	100	20	96	38	92	56	88
3	99	21	96	39	92	57	88
4	99	22	95	40	92	58	88
5	99	23	95	41	91	59	87
6	99	24	95	42	91	60	87
7	99	25	95	43	91	61	87
8	98	26	94	44	91	62	87
9	98	27	94	45	90	63	87
10	98	28	94	46	90	64	86
11	98	29	94	47	90	65	86
12	97	30	94	48	90	66	86
13	97	31	93	49	90	67	86
14	97	32	93	50	89	68	86
15	97	33	93	51	89	69	85
16	97	34	93	52	89	70	85
17	96	35	93	53	89		
18	96	36	92	54	89		

Student Retelling

Examiner: "Tell me about what you just read and what you thought about it."

If there is no spontaneous response, repeat the request, "Tell me what you thought about the passage."

Note: Use the Retelling Rubric on p. 348 to assess the child's retelling performance. If you need additional space for retelling responses, use a separate sheet of paper.

RETELLING RUBRIC: INFORMATIONAL

Macro-concepts (Numbered and Boldfaced) and Micro-concepts (Bulleted)

Place a 0, 1/2, or + to score student responses. See page 81 for information on what these assessment measures mean.

Story Structure:

___ 1. **Lewis became a very successful writer.**
  ___ • Many of his books became extremely popular.
  ___ • Some faculty at Oxford resented his success.
___ 2. **Lewis fell in love and married late in life.**
  ___ • Lewis married Joy to save her from being deported.
  ___ • When she was diagnosed with cancer, Lewis realized that he was in love with her.
___ 3. **Lewis finally became a full professor at Cambridge.**
  ___ • When Oxford heard of Cambridge's offer to Lewis, it tried to keep him but it was too late.
___ 4. **Personal Response:** Any well-supported positive or negative response to the content or ideas in the text, or to the text as a whole.

Retelling Score: _____

Comprehension Questions

_____ 1. **Why is it surprising that Lewis wrote books for children?**

   Text-Based: He was uncomfortable around children.

_____ 2. **How did Lewis meet his future wife, Joy Davidman?**

   Text-Based: She wrote letters questioning him about ideas in his books.

3. What in the passage suggests that Lewis believed in the values that England was fighting for in World War I?

   Inference: He could have been exempt from serving because he was an Irish national.

4. Why would Cambridge offer Lewis the post of full professor when Oxford would not?

   Inference: It respected his gifts; he was a world renowned scholar; his fame could bring recognition to Cambridge.

5. Which had greater contradictions, Lewis's personal life or his professional life? Explain.

   Critical Response: His personal life—since he was a confirmed bachelor but had a civil marriage to keep a friend from being deported. His professional life—he was successful but not recognized at Oxford; he wrote scholarly books as well as novels and children's stories.

6. Why did Lewis agree to a civil marriage to Joy Davidman?

   Text-Based: She was threatened with deportation; they were good friends.

7. Why would his colleagues at Oxford refuse to recommend Lewis for a full professor post?

   Inference: They may have been jealous of his fame; they didn't respect popular books.

8. Which of Lewis's works became a scholarly classic?

   Text-Based: His work on 16th-Century literature.

9. Why wouldn't Lewis realize that he was in love with Joy before she became ill? Explain.

   Inference: He was a confirmed bachelor; he had to face the fact that he might lose her, he took her for granted.

_____10. Which university really deserved to be most strongly linked with Lewis, Oxford or Cambridge?

Critical Response: Oxford—he spent most of his career there; he was there when he became so popular. Cambridge—it recognized his value and offered him the post of full professor that he had wanted and deserved.

INFORMATIONAL PASSAGES
TENTH GRADE

TENTH GRADE III: COLORED SNOW

Reader's copy on p. 145 of the Reader's Passages

Introductory Statement: "Would you read this passage about colored snow (to yourself/out loud). When you are finished, I'll take away the passage. Then I'll ask you to tell me about what you read and what you think of it. After that, I'll ask you some questions about the passage."

Story

If you were hiking on the alpine slopes of the Sierra Nevada Mountains in California, you might come upon patches of pink snow with red streaks. If you walked on these patches of snow, the soles of your shoes would turn bright red and the cuffs of your pants would turn pink. For years this mysterious pink snow was a puzzle to mountain climbers and naturalists alike. In May 1818, Captain John Ross, traveling off the northwestern coast of Greenland, noticed white cliffs that were streaked with what looked like crimson blood. A report of his finding, published in the *London Times,* caused some readers to conclude that the red color was rust from a meteoric iron deposit. It was not until the end of the 19th century that this colored snow was recognized to be "blooms" of microscopic algae, or snow algae.

During the winter months snow algae are dormant. They do not begin germination until spring thawing when the nutrients in the melting snow reach them. This germination results in the releasing of smaller swimming cells that find their way to the surface. Researchers are not certain if the dissolved nutrients from the melting snow cause the cells to move to the surface. Some speculate that it has to do with the length of daylight and light density. The spores of the algae have thick walls and fatty deposits that enable them to withstand both the extreme cold temperature of winter and the high summer temperatures that would kill regular vegetative cells. The cells of some algae secrete mucilage that enables them to stick to one another and prevents them from being washed away.

Since the atmosphere is thinner in the higher altitudes, snow algae are exposed to damaging ultraviolet radiation. How can a plant thrive in such a severely cold environment with such bright light and high ultraviolet radiation? The cells of the snow algae contain carotenoid, a bright red pigment. This carotenoid serves as protection from the intense solar radiation at the surface of the mountain snow. The carotenoid is similar to that found in tomatoes, red peppers, carrots, and avocados. While carotenoids are widely used for food coloring, certain types have been found to possess cancer-fighting properties and some scientists believe that they have the potential to reduce risks of heart disease and eye degeneration.

Scientists have also discovered that a compound in grape skins inhibits clogging of the arteries; some scientists are hoping that the antioxidants produced by snow algae can have the same effect. It is clear that this once-confusing phenomenon has become a source of hope for researchers interested in finding cures for life-threatening diseases. (443 words)

Scoring Miscues for Oral Reading Option
Mark all scoreable miscues by placing either a plus (for those that maintain meaning) or a zero (for those that violate meaning) in the text margin.

Reading Accuracy Index: _____%
*Total all miscues marked with pluses **and** zeros and enter the corresponding percentage from the Miscue Chart.*

Meaning Maintenance Index: _____%
*Total **only** miscues marked with zeros and enter the corresponding percentage from the Miscue Chart.*

Miscue Chart (if used for oral reading)

Miscues	%	Miscues	%	Miscues	%	Miscues	%
1	100	19	96	37	92	55	88
2	100	20	95	38	91	56	87
3	99	21	95	39	91	57	87
4	99	22	95	40	91	58	87
5	99	23	95	41	91	59	87
6	99	24	95	42	91	60	86
7	98	25	94	43	90	61	86
8	98	26	94	44	90	62	86
9	98	27	94	45	90	63	86
10	98	28	94	46	90	64	86
11	98	29	93	47	89	65	85
12	97	30	93	48	89	66	85
13	97	31	93	49	89	67	85
14	97	32	93	50	89	68	85
15	97	33	93	51	88	69	84
16	96	34	92	52	88	70	84
17	96	35	92	53	88		
18	96	36	92	54	88		

Student Retelling

Examiner: "Tell me about what you just read and what you thought about it."

If there is no spontaneous response, repeat the request, "Tell me what you thought about the passage."

Note: Use the Retelling Rubric on p. 352 to assess the child's retelling performance. If you need additional space for retelling responses, use a separate sheet of paper.

RETELLING RUBRIC: INFORMATIONAL

Macro-concepts (Numbered and Boldfaced) and Micro-concepts (Bulleted)

Place a 0, 1/2, or + to score student responses. See page 81 for information on what these assessment measures mean.

Story Structure:

___ 1. **Red snow in the Sierra Mountains was a mystery for many years.**
  ___ • Some thought it was rust from iron in meteors.
___ 2. **Scientists found that the color came from microscopic algae.**
  ___ • Snow algae become active in spring.
___ 3. **Snow algae must withstand extreme weather conditions.**
  ___ • Algae spores have thick walls to protect against cold.
  ___ • Carotenoids protect algae from intense sunlight.
  ___ • Carotenoids may become a medical treatment.
___ 4. **Personal Response:** Any well-supported positive or negative response to the content or ideas in the text, or to the text as a whole.

Retelling Score: _____

Comprehension Questions

_____ 1. **Where in the United States could you see colored snow?**

  Text-Based: Sierra Nevada Mountains in California.

_____ 2. **What did some people believe was the source of red snow?**

  Text-Based: Rust from iron left by a meteor.

_____ 3. **What does the red color do to help snow algae survive?**

  Inference: Reflects the bright sunshine; protects cells from intense light.

_____ 4. Why would scientists think that colored snow might help the treatment of disease?

Inference: It is similar to carotenoids that fight diseases in humans.

_____ 5. Which is more important to the germination of some snow algae, the weather or the cell's structure? Explain.

Critical Response: The weather—without the melting of snow the cells would not swim to the top of the surface. The cell's structure—the cells secrete mucilage that enables them to stick together and not wash away.

_____ 6. What enables the spores of the algae to withstand extreme temperatures?

Text-Based: Their thick walls; deposits of fat.

_____ 7. Use the text to tell why the author connects snow algae to tomatoes?

Inference: They have a similar carotenoid; there is hope that it will have cancer-fighting properties.

_____ 8. Why are snow algae exposed to very damaging ultraviolet radiation?

Text-Based: Atmosphere is thinner in the higher altitudes where the algae live.

_____ 9. Why would it be important that snow algae cells be able to stick together?

Inference: Keeps them from being washed away by melting snow.

_____10. Does the text suggest that researchers have more answers or more questions about snow algae? Explain.

Critical Response: Questions—they aren't sure what causes cells to move to the surface; Answers—they are beginning to conduct research that shows the potential of algae for the cure of diseases, medicinal cures.

Comprehension Analysis:

Text-Based: _/4_
Inference: _/4_
Critical Response: _/2_

Total Comprehension %: _____

ELEVENTH GRADE I: THE HAWAIIAN VOLCANO

Reader's copy on p. 147 of the Reader's Passages

Introductory Statement: "Would you read this passage about volcanoes in Hawaii (to yourself/out loud). When you are finished, I'll take away the passage. Then I'll ask you to tell me about what you read and what you think of it. After that, I'll ask you some questions about the passage."

Story

If you asked a hundred people where to find the most magnificent and tranquil tropical paradise on earth, it is a good bet that many would name the Hawaiian Islands. Few of them, however, would realize the extent to which the islands are a product of the pure, raw violence of nature. Incessant volcanic activity over a period of hundreds of thousands of years actually created the islands where no land had been before. A hot spot of magma (fluid rock material) thrust lava through the ocean floor to create a seamount, an undersea volcano. As the lava was cooled by the ocean water, it formed a massive mountain whose tip finally emerged from the sea. Mauna Loa, the most famous of the four active volcanoes in the Hawaiian chain, is really the world's highest mountain. If measured from the ocean floor to its summit, it towers 56,000 feet, dwarfing its more renowned brother, Mount Everest.

The lava flows from the volcano known as Kilauea began in 1983 and continue to this very day. Eventually, the lava reaches the cliffs and flows into the ocean below, where it hardens and adds yet more land to the Hawaiian Islands. Sometimes the cooled lava forms what is called a bench, an outcropping of hardened lava that is nonetheless very unstable. In fact, about 45 acres of such benches recently collapsed into the Pacific, adding yet more volume to the Big Island's coast. But

before the real estate agents celebrate and the tourists flock to the newly created swimmer's paradise, they may need to remember the ferocity of nature in the islands.

The chemical reaction caused by the heat, chloride, and oxygen produces vast quantities of hydrochloric acid that can irritate the skin, and the superheated water that results from contact with the lava can cause third-degree burns. It will be many years after Kilauea ceases to erupt before anyone will be able to take advantage of the creative generosity of nature in that part of Hawaii.

You can visit both Mauna Loa and Kilauea at Volcanoes National Park and observe firsthand the creative work of Kilauea. There you can even walk on newly hardened lava, but be sure to wear tough shoes with thick soles. Much of the lava is rough and jagged with sharp edges, and there is also shiny, smooth lava that can crumble with the lightest pressure; in other words, don't walk there!

Some intrepid visitors can take a *doors off* helicopter ride for a bird's-eye view of the volcano and its surrounding lava fields. Vents of hot steam, molten lava, laze (lava haze), and vog (volcanic smog) are all part of the ride. Brace yourself to feel the heat and 120 mile per hour winds, and to see a stunning spectacle of lava emptying off the cliffs into the ocean below. You may even find yourself believing in the ancient goddess Pele who is said to live inside Kilauea and carry on her work of reshaping and recreating the Hawaiian Islands. (503 words)

Scoring Miscues for Oral Reading Option
Mark all scoreable miscues by placing either a plus (for those that maintain meaning) or a zero (for those that violate meaning) in the text margin.

Reading Accuracy Index: _____%
*Total all miscues marked with pluses **and** zeros and enter the corresponding percentage from the Miscue Chart.*

Meaning Maintenance Index: _____%
*Total **only** miscues marked with zeros and enter the corresponding percentage from the Miscue Chart.*

Miscue Chart (if used for oral reading)

Miscues	%	Miscues	%	Miscues	%	Miscues	%
1	100	19	96	37	93	55	89
2	100	20	96	38	92	56	89
3	99	21	96	39	92	57	89
4	99	22	96	40	92	58	88
5	99	23	95	41	92	59	88
6	99	24	95	42	92	60	88
7	99	25	95	43	91	61	88
8	98	26	95	44	91	62	88
9	98	27	95	45	91	63	87
10	98	28	94	46	91	64	87
11	98	29	94	47	91	65	87
12	98	30	94	48	90	66	87
13	97	31	94	49	90	67	87
14	97	32	93	50	90	68	86
15	97	33	93	51	90	69	86
16	97	34	93	52	90	70	86
17	97	35	93	53	89		
18	96	36	93	54	89		

Student Retelling

Examiner: "Tell me about what you just read and what you thought about it."

If there is no spontaneous response, repeat the request, "Tell me what you thought about the passage."

Note: Use the Retelling Rubric on p. 355 to assess the child's retelling performance. If you need additional space for retelling responses, use a separate sheet of paper.

RETELLING RUBRIC: INFORMATIONAL

Macro-concepts (Numbered and Boldfaced) and Micro-concepts (Bulleted)

Place a 0, 1/2, or + to score student responses. See page 81 for information on what these assessment measures mean.

Story Structure:

___ 1. **Volcanic activities created the Hawaiian Islands.**
   ___ • Mauna Loa is the world's biggest volcano.
___ 2. **Kilauea has been emitting lava since 1983.**
   ___ • Lava flows add land to the islands.
   ___ • Land they add will be too dangerous to use for many years.
___ 3. **Visitors can see Mauna Loa and Kilauea up close.**
   ___ • You can walk on freshly solidified lava.
   ___ • You can take an adventurous helicopter ride over the volcano.
___ 4. **Personal Response:** Any well-supported positive or negative response to the content or ideas in the text, or to the text as a whole.

Retelling Score: _____

Comprehension Questions

_____ 1. **How long did it take to create the Hawaiian Islands?**

Text-Based: Hundreds of thousands of years.

_____ 2. **What did the passage say that a seamount was?**

Text-Based: An undersea volcano.

_____ 3. **Why isn't a lava bench considered a valuable addition to the land of the Hawaiian Islands?**

Inference: Too unstable, too close to heat and lava.

4. What will have to happen before anyone can settle on the new land created by Kilauea? (If child says, "The volcano must stop erupting," ask, "What will that do?")

    Inference: The lava and the water will have to cool off; the acid will have to wash away.

8. How could volcanoes create a chain of islands in the ocean?

    Text-Based: Lava flow rose higher and higher as it cooled until it rose higher than the ocean.

9. What might happen to people who stepped in shiny new lava?

    Inference: The lava would break and the person could be burned or injured.

5. What is likely to be more dangerous, bathing near freshly hardened lava or a helicopter ride above Kilauea?

    Critical Response: Bathing—the water can burn; the acid can damage your skin and eyes. Ride—if volcano erupts, it can kill you; high winds near the volcano are very dangerous.

10. Is it worth the risk of a helicopter ride to see a volcano up close? Explain.

    Critical Response: Yes—it is a once in a lifetime adventure; if you are curious, it is the best way to see the volcano. No—it is too dangerous to be that close to a volcano; all it would take is one eruption and you could be killed.

6. Why would people say that the Hawaiian Islands are the product of the violence of nature?

    Inference: The islands wouldn't exist without volcanoes erupting; the islands are growing today because of active volcanoes.

Comprehension Analysis:

    Text-Based: ___/4___
    Inference: ___/4___
    Critical Response: ___/2___

Total Comprehension %: _____

7. Why do people think Mount Everest is the highest mountain, and not Mauna Loa?

    Text-Based: Mauna Loa is mostly under water.

Reader's copy on p. 149 of the Reader's Passages

Introductory Statement: "Would you read this passage about James Madison and Alexander Hamilton (to yourself/out loud). When you are finished, I'll take away the passage. Then I'll ask you to tell me about what you read and what you think of it. After that, I'll ask you some questions about the passage."

Story

There is an old saying that conflict can either deepen or destroy a friendship. Anyone tempted to doubt the truth of that maxim need only examine the relationship that existed between James Madison and Alexander Hamilton. Seldom have we encountered a more unlikely pair of friends. Madison was born to a wealthy family in Virginia, and received an education commensurate with his privilege. Hamilton was the child of an unwed mother and a father heavily in debt. But Hamilton possessed astounding skills and when, at the age of 15, he published an article, he stunned his readers with his proficiency in language. A group of wealthy readers decided to bankroll the fledgling writer and sent him to the American colonies for his first taste of formal education.

Madison began his distinguished political career at the age of 25 when he helped draft a new constitution for Virginia. It was then that Madison met Thomas Jefferson and their lifelong friendship began. Three years later, Madison's election to the Continental Congress afforded him the opportunity to promote his dream of a unified country, in contrast to a loosely confederated group of individual states.

In the meantime, Hamilton had embarked on a distinguished military career and when he too began his term of service with Congress, he met James Madison. The two men immediately recognized the congruity of their ideas, particularly the need for a strong federal government to guide the colonies.

Both Madison and Hamilton were named as delegates to the Annapolis Convention in 1786. It was there that the two most formidable intellectuals of their time cemented their relationship. Madison began to realize that Hamilton's passionate political style stood in sharp contrast to his own subtle style. Nonetheless, when Hamilton sought out his assistance in preparing the influential *Federalist Papers*, Madison rushed to his side. The *Papers* were a set of elegantly framed essays that succeeded in convincing New York's political leaders of the need for a strong federal government.

During George Washington's presidency, Hamilton became the country's first secretary of the treasury, charged with creating a plan for the payment of the nation's foreign debt. Hamilton proposed that all the new states pay equal portions of the war debt. The proposal generated much anger, but the strongest opposition to his plan came from none other than James Madison. Madison's home state of Virginia had already paid much of its war debt and he believed that Hamilton's plan would punish those states that had acted responsibly.

Hamilton knew that he would need Virginia's support, but Madison refused to budge. Finally, Hamilton asked Thomas Jefferson, Madison's closest friend, for help. Jefferson promised his support on condition that the nation's capital would be located on the Potomac River, near his native Virginia. Hamilton agreed and his plan passed; however, he had paid a great price, both politically and personally. His longstanding relationship with Madison was now over. Madison went out of his way to avoid Hamilton for the rest of his life. (499 words)

Scoring Miscues for Oral Reading Option

Mark all scoreable miscues by placing either a plus (for those that maintain meaning) or a zero (for those that violate meaning) in the text margin.

Reading Accuracy Index: _____%

*Total all miscues marked with pluses **and** zeros and enter the corresponding percentage from the Miscue Chart.*

Meaning Maintenance Index: _____%

*Total **only** miscues marked with zeros and enter the corresponding percentage from the Miscue Chart.*

Miscue Chart (if used for oral reading)

Miscues	%	Miscues	%	Miscues	%	Miscues	%
1	100	19	96	37	93	55	89
2	100	20	96	38	92	56	89
3	99	21	96	39	92	57	89
4	99	22	96	40	92	58	88
5	99	23	95	41	92	59	88
6	99	24	95	42	92	60	88
7	99	25	95	43	91	61	88
8	98	26	95	44	91	62	88
9	98	27	95	45	91	63	87
10	98	28	94	46	91	64	87
11	98	29	94	47	91	65	87
12	98	30	94	48	90	66	87
13	97	31	94	49	90	67	87
14	97	32	94	50	90	68	86
15	97	33	93	51	90	69	86
16	97	34	93	52	90	70	86
17	97	35	93	53	89		
18	96	36	93	54	89		

Student Retelling

Examiner: "Tell me about what you just read and what you thought about it."

If there is no spontaneous response, repeat the request, "Tell me what you thought about the passage."

Note: Use the Retelling Rubric on p. 358 to assess the child's retelling performance. If you need additional space for retelling responses, use a separate sheet of paper.

RETELLING RUBRIC: INFORMATIONAL

Macro-concepts (Numbered and Boldfaced) and Micro-concepts (Bulleted)

Place a 0, 1/2, or + to score student responses. See page 81 for information on what these assessment measures mean.

Story Structure:

___ 1. **Hamilton and Madison were very unlikely friends.**
   ___ • Madison's family was wealthy; Hamilton's family was very poor.

___ 2. **Hamilton and Madison shared the vision of a unified country.**
   ___ • Hamilton and Madison collaborated on the *Federalist Papers*.

___ 3. **Hamilton and Madison disagreed on how to pay the war debt.**
   ___ • Hamilton wanted the states to share the debt equally and Madison disagreed.
   ___ • Hamilton made a deal with Jefferson to gain his support.
   ___ • Hamilton and Madison ended their relationship because of their disagreement.

___ 4. **Personal Response:** Any well-supported positive or negative response to the content or ideas in the text, or to the text as a whole.

Retelling Score: _____

Comprehension Questions

_____ 1. **What benefit did Madison's wealth provide him?**

Text-based: He received the best possible education.

_____ 2. **How did Hamilton's writing skills benefit him?**

Text-based: He published an article that impressed readers; readers sent him to the colonies and paid for his education.

3. Why might people have been impressed when they read Hamilton's article?

   Inference: He was only 15 years old; he was very young to be so accomplished a writer.

4. How can you explain how such different people could have become such good friends?

   Inference: Both had strong views about how the new country needed to succeed; both believed in a strong central government; both believed Congress needed to raise taxes; both were willing to defend their views.

5. Would you think that the political writing and work of Madison and Hamilton were a success or a failure? Explain.

   Critical Response: Success—because they convinced people of the need for a strong central government. Failure—because they let differences of opinions destroy their friendship.

6. What enabled Madison and Hamilton to cement their friendship?

   Text-Based: Their common interest in a strong central government.

7. Why could the reader conclude that Jefferson did not feel as strongly as Hamilton did about the taxation plan?

   Inference: He voted for it as a favor and not as a matter of a belief; he voted for it in exchange for a favor.

8. What position did Hamilton have in Washington's government?

   Text-Based: Country's first secretary of the treasury.

9. How could Madison be justified in his opposition to Hamilton's plan for dealing with the national debt?

   Inference: He thought that states like Virginia that had paid their debts were being punished.

_____10. Use the information in the passage to decide which man remained truer to his beliefs, Madison or Hamilton? Explain.

Critical Response: Madison—because he opposed a plan even though it was proposed by a friend. Hamilton—because he thought that dealing with the debt was so important that he was willing to negotiate about the location of the capital.

Comprehension Analysis:

Text-Based: __/4__
Inference: __/4__
Critical Response: __/2__

Total Comprehension %: _____

INFORMATIONAL PASSAGES
ELEVENTH GRADE

Reader's copy on p. 151 of the Reader's Passages

Introductory Statement: "Would you read this passage about Gramsci and Tocqueville (to yourself/out loud). When you are finished, I'll take away the passage. Then I'll ask you to tell me about what you read and what you think of it. After that, I'll ask you some questions about the passage."

Story

In what ways do our personal experiences determine our views of the world? Consider the lives of two individuals with some common experiences but very different philosophies.

Antonio Gramsci was born in Italy in 1891. When he was six years old, the arrest of his father thrust the family into poverty. At the age of twenty, Gramsci was fortunate enough to obtain a scholarship to study at the University of Turin. Gramsci gradually became aware of Italy as a backward country controlled by corrupt politicians. He came to accept the socialist theory of Karl Marx. By the age of 24, he had become a forceful social, economic, and political critic. His revolutionary spirit was kindled by the success of the Bolshevik revolution in Russia. In an attempt to gain greater insight into communist theory, Gramsci moved to Moscow in 1921. But he was soon disillusioned by the terror and tyranny that characterized both Lenin and Stalin. When he returned home and found the same tactics used by Mussolini, his outspoken criticism resulted in his arrest. He was sentenced to prison in 1928. He spent the final nine years of his life writing about his socialist vision. He had come to believe that workers and peasants cannot bring about revolutions. He became an advocate of nonviolent socialist revolutions. He believed that these revolutions could be brought about only through an undermining of the values of the controlling majority.

Alexis de Tocqueville, on the other hand, was born in 1805 in Paris to an aristocratic family who had barely escaped the guillotine during the French Revolution of 1780. After a childhood haunted by fears of imprisonment, he was sent to college at the age of sixteen. He soon began to question the wisdom of the French aristocratic structure, even though his father held an influential position as a prefect. During the Revolution of 1830, his father lost that position and Tocqueville completely distanced himself from his aristocratic heritage. He believed that France was traveling a road toward internal revolution and destruction. Under the guise of studying the American penal system, Tocqueville requested permission to travel to the United States. His ultimate goal was to study democracy and his observations led to the publication of two volumes titled *Democracy in America*.

Tocqueville's interest in democracy continued when he returned to France. At the age of 39 he became part owner of a radical newspaper. Nonetheless, he remained opposed to Gramsci's kind of political agitation that could result in revolution. He tried to show his loyalty to France shortly before Napoleon's coup by helping restructure the government. However, Napoleon's distrust resulted in the overnight imprisonment he dreaded as well as a physical breakdown. In 1852, Tocqueville removed himself from political life and spent his final seven years writing. He had observed firsthand the great paradox of democracy. Without majority rule there can be no democracy, and once in power, the majority will always have the potential to tyrannize the minority. (496 words)

Scoring Miscues for Oral Reading Option

Mark all scoreable miscues by placing either a plus (for those that maintain meaning) or a zero (for those that violate meaning) in the text margin.

Reading Accuracy Index: _____%

*Total all miscues marked with pluses **and** zeros and enter the corresponding percentage from the Miscue Chart.*

Meaning Maintenance Index: _____%

*Total **only** miscues marked with zeros and enter the corresponding percentage from the Miscue Chart.*

Miscue Chart (if used for oral reading)

Miscues	%	Miscues	%	Miscues	%	Miscues	%
1	100	19	96	37	93	55	89
2	100	20	96	38	92	56	89
3	99	21	96	39	92	57	89
4	99	22	96	40	92	58	88
5	99	23	95	41	92	59	88
6	99	24	95	42	92	60	88
7	99	25	95	43	91	61	88
8	98	26	95	44	91	62	88
9	98	27	95	45	91	63	87
10	98	28	94	46	91	64	87
11	98	29	94	47	91	65	87
12	98	30	94	48	90	66	87
13	97	31	94	49	90	67	86
14	97	32	94	50	90	68	86
15	97	33	93	51	90	69	86
16	97	34	93	52	90	70	86
17	97	35	93	53	89		
18	96	36	93	54	89		

Student Retelling

Examiner: "Tell me about what you just read and what you thought about it."

If there is no spontaneous response, repeat the request, "Tell me what you thought about the passage."

Note: Use the Retelling Rubric on p. 362 to assess the child's retelling performance. If you need additional space for retelling responses, use a separate sheet of paper.

RETELLING RUBRIC: INFORMATIONAL

Macro-concepts (Numbered and Boldfaced) and Micro-concepts (Bulleted)

Place a 0, 1/2, or + to score student responses. See page 81 for information on what these assessment measures mean.

Story Structure:

___ 1. **Personal experiences affect the way people view the world.**

___ 2. **Gramsci believed in nonviolent social revolution.**

   ___ • Gramsci accepted the political theories of Marx and moved to Russia.

   ___ • Gramsci was imprisoned in Italy when he criticized Mussolini.

___ 3. **Tocqueville accepted the paradox of democracy.**

   ___ • Tocqueville was part of the privileged French aristocracy.

   ___ • Tocqueville left France to study democracy in the United States.

   ___ • Tocqueville was removed from political influence by Napoleon.

___ 4. **Personal Response:** Any well-supported positive or negative response to the content or ideas in the text, or to the text as a whole.

Retelling Score: _____

Comprehension Questions

_____ 1. **What caused Gramsci's poverty?**

Text-Based: His father was arrested.

_____ 2. **What haunted Tocqueville's childhood?**

Text-Based: The fear of being imprisoned.

_____ 3. What enabled Gramsci's studies at the University of Turin to alter his life?

Inference: He studied Marx's socialist theory; he observed the corruption of his country's leaders.

_____ 4. In what way was conflict with the government central to the lives of both Gramsci and Tocqueville?

Inference: Gramsci experienced the tyranny in both Italy and Russia; he spent 5 years in prison. Tocqueville knew the fear of abusive power even though his family was saved from the guillotine; he was arrested briefly.

_____ 5. Who was affected more by firsthand experiences of oppression, Gramsci or Tocqueville?

Critical Response: Gramsci—was imprisoned for nine years; he saw cruelty and oppression in Moscow. Tocqueville—he had to overcome his aristocratic background; was removed from any position of influence by Napoleon himself.

_____ 6. What led to the corruption of Gramsci's homeland of Italy?

Text-Based: It was a poor backward country; corrupt politicians gained power.

_____ 7. How does the passage show that both Gramsci and Tocqueville were aware of the power of the word?

Inference: Both actively used writing to share their ideas with others.

_____ 8. Why was Tocqueville able to travel to the United States?

Text-Based: He said that he was going to study the prison system.

_____ 9. How does the passage show the potential for imprisonment to kindle drive?

Inference: The political stand taken by both Gramsci and Tocqueville contributed to their imprisonment; their views held such importance to them that they wrote about them despite the danger.

_____10. Whose philosophy matches more closely with his life experiences, Gramsci's or Tocqueville's? Explain.

Critical Response: Gramsci's—since he experienced the inability for commoners to cause a revolution. Tocqueville's—since he saw that government without the voice of the common person was not effective.

Comprehension Analysis:

Text-Based: _/4_
Inference: _/4_
Critical Response: _/2_

Total Comprehension %: _____

INFORMATIONAL PASSAGES
ELEVENTH GRADE

TWELFTH GRADE I: QUASARS

Reader's copy on p. 153 of the Reader's Passages

Introductory Statement: "Would you read this passage about quasars (to yourself/out loud). When you are finished, I'll take away the passage. Then I'll ask you to tell me about what you read and what you think of it. After that, I'll ask you some questions about the passage."

Story

Ever since the dawn of humanity, searching the skies with more and more sophisticated instruments has led to a spate of new discoveries almost too breathtaking to keep up with. In the 1940s, for example, radio astronomers found that many celestial objects were emitting radio waves; most of these sources were common stars. But some faint blue-colored objects in the astronomical landscapes were very difficult to explain. They looked like stars but they emitted a huge quantity of very intense radio and ultraviolet waves, much more than could be expected from a typical star.

It was not until 1963 that Dr. Maarten Schmidt explained the phenomenon by examining the strange light spectrum emitted by one of the "stars." Schmidt deduced that the unusual red-shifted spectrum lines (the measure of an object's recession velocity) were part of a simple hydrogen spectrum. However, the only way that the objects could produce this type of spectrum was if they were traveling away from earth at a speed of almost 30,000 miles per second! And if that were correct, the objects would be more than 3 billion light years away, making them the most distant and, arguably, the most fascinating objects ever discovered in our universe. Because they were not true stars, scientists dubbed the strange objects quasars (for quasi-stellar radio sources).

Scientists were at a loss to explain how telescopes on earth could still detect such distant objects. To be detectable from earth, quasars would have to emit light as intense as that produced by 1,000 entire galaxies. In fact, the brightest quasar in the sky emits more than 2 trillion times the light of our sun, yet many quasars take up only about the space of our own solar system. Scientists today believe that the brightness of a quasar can be accounted for by the presence of super-sized black holes in the midst of huge galaxies. Black holes suck in passing stars and clouds of gas and, in doing so, heat huge quantities of matter to such an extent that they emit stupendous amounts of light. One amazing fact is that in order to create the light emitted by the brightest quasars in the sky, the black hole would have to consume as many as 10 stars the size of our sun every year.

Today scientists know of the existence of more than 60,000 quasars, with the most distant an astonishing 13 billion light years removed from earth. Because quasars are so distant, they must have been created in the very early stages of the development of the universe. Indeed, it would be logical to conclude that since it is taking billions of years for the light of some quasars to reach us, those quasars are no longer in existence. Only their light, still traveling over the vast expanses of the universe, is reaching us today. It is certainly true that quasars still raise more questions than scientists have answers for, but quasars are objects that unequivocally challenge the imagination of scientists and laypeople alike as we seek more and more answers to the mysteries of the universe. (516 words)

Scoring Miscues for Oral Reading Option
Mark all scoreable miscues by placing either a plus (for those that maintain meaning) or a zero (for those that violate meaning) in the text margin.

Reading Accuracy Index: _____%
*Total all miscues marked with pluses **and** zeros and enter the corresponding percentage from the Miscue Chart.*

Meaning Maintenance Index: _____%
*Total **only** miscues marked with zeros and enter the corresponding percentage from the Miscue Chart.*

Miscue Chart (if used for oral reading)

Miscues	%	Miscues	%	Miscues	%	Miscues	%
1	100	19	96	37	93	55	89
2	100	20	96	38	93	56	89
3	99	21	96	39	92	57	89
4	99	22	96	40	92	58	89
5	99	23	96	41	92	59	89
6	99	24	95	42	92	60	88
7	99	25	95	43	92	61	88
8	98	26	95	44	91	62	88
9	98	27	95	45	91	63	88
10	98	28	95	46	91	64	88
11	98	29	94	47	91	65	87
12	98	30	94	48	91	66	87
13	97	31	94	49	91	67	87
14	97	32	94	50	90	68	87
15	97	33	94	51	90	69	87
16	97	34	93	52	90	70	86
17	97	35	93	53	90		
18	97	36	93	54	90		

Student Retelling

Examiner: "Tell me about what you just read and what you thought about it."

If there is no spontaneous response, repeat the request, "Tell me what you thought about the passage."

Note: Use the Retelling Rubric on p. 366 to assess the child's retelling performance. If you need additional space for retelling responses, use a separate sheet of paper.

RETELLING RUBRIC: INFORMATIONAL

Macro-concepts (Numbered and Boldfaced) and Micro-concepts (Bulleted)

Place a 0, 1/2, or + to score student responses. See page 81 for information on what these assessment measures mean.

Story Structure:

___ 1. **Scientists discovered objects in the sky emitting large amounts of radio waves.**
  ___ • Concluded that they were 3 billion light years away.
  ___ • They were not true stars so they were called quasars.
___ 2. **Quasars would have to be incredibly bright to be seen from so far away.**
  ___ • Quasars produce the light of 1,000 galaxies.
  ___ • Scientists believe they are black holes heating up matter as they suck it in.
___ 3. **Many quasars are no longer in existence.**
  ___ • Only the light is still traveling toward us for 3 billion years.
___ 4. **Personal Response:** Any well-supported positive or negative response to the content or ideas in the text, or to the text as a whole.

Retelling Score: _____

Comprehension Questions

_____ 1. **What did the passage say was so different about quasars that first made scientists curious about them?**

  Text-Based: They emitted huge amounts of radio waves.

_____ 2. **Why aren't quasars considered true stars?**

  Text-Based: They are the size of the entire solar system.

_____ 3. Why would scientists find it hard to believe that quasars were 3 billion light years from the earth?

Inference: Their light was still visible from earth.

_____ 4. Why would the distance of quasars cause scientists to conclude that they were formed in the early stages of the universe?

Inference: They must have been created early to have traveled such a huge distance; if they were moving at 30,000 miles per second, it would have taken huge amounts of time to travel 3 billion light years.

_____ 5. Based on the information in this passage, how much progress do you think scientists have made in explaining the mysteries of the universe?

Critical Response: Not much—we don't even know what else is out there to be discovered; we can not yet see all of the universe. A great deal—scientists have discovered and explained many new phenomena; our technology has improved tremendously and so has our understanding.

_____ 6. How could we see quasars if most of them are no longer in existence?

Text-Based: Their light is still traveling for billions of years.

_____ 7. If many quasars are not in existence today, how could scientists explain how they died?

Inference: Black holes ran out of materials to suck in.

_____ 8. How does the name fit the nature of quasars?

Text-Based: They are not real stars—they are quasi-stars.

_____ 9. Why didn't astronomers discover the existence of quasars before the 1940s?

Inference: Radio technology had not yet been invented.

_____ 10. Some commentators have observed that it is a good thing that quasars are so far from the earth. Do you agree? Why or why not?

Critical Response: Agree—so much heat and light would be dangerous; don't want to be too close to a black hole; might get sucked in by the black hole. Disagree—they would be easier to study if they were closer; we might uncover more of the mysteries of the universe.

Comprehension Analysis:

Text-Based: _/4_
Inference: _/4_
Critical Response: _/2_

Total Comprehension %: _____

Reader's copy on p. 155 of the Reader's Passages

Introductory Statement: "Would you read this passage about America's search for Pancho Villa (to yourself/ out loud). When you are finished, I'll take away the passage. Then I'll ask you to tell me about what you read and what you think of it. After that, I'll ask you some questions about the passage."

Story

America's hunt for the infamous Mexican revolutionary Pancho Villa in 1916 in reality was the result of a series of botched political, economic, and military decisions. The United States had huge business interests in Mexico, interests that were threatened by the Mexican Revolution of 1910. Anxious to protect these interests, President Woodrow Wilson decided to throw his support behind one of the leaders of the revolution, Venustiano Carranza, the Mexican president. Carranza was the man he believed to be most sympathetic to the American agenda. But Carranza regarded his American allies as something of a mixed blessing. While grateful for any support he could muster, Carranza remained fearful of alienating his own people by showing favor to the hated neighbor to the north. He refused to give in to some of Wilson's demands. In retaliation, Wilson then began to supply another revolutionary, Pancho Villa, with arms and supplies. It was Wilson's hope that Villa might overthrow Carranza and be more favorably inclined to the United States if he came into power.

But Villa's potential as a threat to the Mexican leader failed to materialize quickly enough to satisfy the American president. Wilson decided to make his peace with Carranza and recognize his government. Villa was infuriated at the desertion of Wilson and the loss of the support to which he had become accustomed.

In retaliation, he and his men killed 16 Americans traveling on a train in Mexico. But his boldest attack occurred on American soil in the town of Columbus, New Mexico, and left 19 Americans dead. Villa hoped that by provoking a counterattack by the Americans, he could turn popular opinion against Carranza and expose his ties to the United States. Then Villa would be waiting in the wings to assume the leadership of all of Mexico.

America, in its turn, launched what came to be known as the Punitive Expedition against Villa and his men. Wilson sent General John J. Pershing and 5,000 soldiers, equipped with trucks, armored vehicles, and even airplanes, into Mexico to hunt down and destroy Villa and his army. Suddenly the overwhelming popularity that had never come about during all the years of Wilson's support materialized. Pershing naturally underestimated Villa's enormous support among the Mexican people. They consistently protected their local Robin Hood, giving Villa advance notice of Pershing's movements. They even supplied false information about Villa's whereabouts to Pershing's troops. After nearly two years of trying, Pershing had nothing to show for his efforts. He had not even come close to locating Villa. The Punitive Expedition was finally called off.

Despite the miserable failure of the expedition in achieving its primary end, many historians consider it a resounding success in the larger scheme of things. With the threat of World War I looming, American troops had the chance to familiarize themselves with their new weapons and technology. In particular, their use of reconnaissance aircraft, despite its failure in the short term, led to a great deal of success in the preparation for the war against Germany. John J. Pershing went on to become leader of the American forces in Europe and the most celebrated military leader of the war. (528 words)

Scoring Miscues for Oral Reading Option

Mark all scoreable miscues by placing either a plus (for those that maintain meaning) or a zero (for those that violate meaning) in the text margin.

Reading Accuracy Index: _____ %
*Total all miscues marked with pluses **and** zeros and enter the corresponding percentage from the Miscue Chart.*

Meaning Maintenance Index: _____ %
*Total **only** miscues marked with zeros and enter the corresponding percentage from the Miscue Chart.*

Miscue Chart (if used for oral reading)

Miscues	%	Miscues	%	Miscues	%	Miscues	%
1	100	19	96	37	93	55	90
2	100	20	96	38	93	56	89
3	99	21	96	39	93	57	89
4	99	22	96	40	92	58	89
5	99	23	96	41	92	59	89
6	99	24	95	42	92	60	89
7	99	25	95	43	92	61	88
8	98	26	95	44	92	62	88
9	98	27	95	45	91	63	88
10	98	28	95	46	91	64	88
11	98	29	95	47	91	65	88
12	98	30	94	48	91	66	88
13	98	31	94	49	91	67	87
14	97	32	94	50	91	68	87
15	97	33	94	51	90	69	87
16	97	34	94	52	90	70	87
17	97	35	93	53	90		
18	97	36	93	54	90		

Student Retelling

Examiner: "Tell me about what you just read and what you thought about it."

If there is no spontaneous response, repeat the request, "Tell me what you thought about the passage."

Note: Use the Retelling Rubric on p. 369 to assess the child's retelling performance. If you need additional space for retelling responses, use a separate sheet of paper.

RETELLING RUBRIC: INFORMATIONAL

Macro-concepts (Numbered and Boldfaced) and Micro-concepts (Bulleted)

Place a 0, 1/2, or + to score student responses. See page 81 for information on what these assessment measures mean.

Story Structure:

___ 1. **The U.S. problem with Villa was the result of a series of mistakes.**
  ___ • The U.S. first supported Carranza for Mexican president and then turned to Villa.
  ___ • When Villa did not become strong enough, Wilson returned to Carranza.
___ 2. **Villa retaliated against Wilson's disloyalty.**
  ___ • Attacked Americans on American soil.
___ 3. **The United States sent General Pershing and 5,000 troops to find Villa.**
  ___ • The people protected Villa.
  ___ • Punitive Expedition never found Villa but it did help the United States prepare for World War I.
___ 4. **Personal Response:** Any well-supported positive or negative response to the content or ideas in the text, or to the text as a whole.

Retelling Score: _____

Comprehension Questions

_____ 1. **What would President Carranza gain by refusing to give in to President Wilson's demands?**

Text-Based: Show his people that he was not favoring the United States.

_____ 2. **Why did President Wilson abandon Pancho Villa after first giving him arms and supplies?**

Text-Based: He did not become a threat to the Mexican president; it became clear that Villa would not become Mexico's leader.

3. What did presidents Wilson and Carranza have in common with respect to their political decisions?

   Inference: Both had their own interests in mind at all times; neither one trusted the other.

4. Did Mexico have any reason for hating the United States?

   Inference: Yes. The United States was interfering in their affairs; the U.S. president did not seem to care about who was in charge of Mexico, but only if they were favorable to the United States.

5. Was Pancho Villa successful in his quest for power in Mexico? Explain.

   Critical Response: Yes—he achieved success with the people and through his popularity; he had power because Pershing could not locate him. No—he did not attain his ultimate goal of the presidency; he was on the run constantly from the U.S. troops and could not even show his face without being in danger.

6. How did the United States benefit from the Punitive Expedition?

   Text-Based: It learned to use its new technology and equipment; learned about aerial surveillance techniques; practiced for the First World War.

7. Why would the people of Mexico consider Pancho Villa another Robin Hood?

   Inference: He was hunted down by more powerful enemies; he was much loved by the common people; people saw him as a hero who would protect them.

8. Why did Pancho Villa turn against the United States?

   Text-Based: It recognized the government of Carranza; it stopped providing him with aid.

9. With 20–20 hindsight, how should Pershing have gone about finding and arresting Villa?

   Critical Response: Could have used spies to infiltrate his organization; could pay Mexican people for information on Villa's whereabouts; could have tried to undermine the trust people had in Villa; could have offered bribes for information.

_____10. How does the saying "You reap what you sow" fit both President Wilson and Pancho Villa?

Inference: Wilson strengthened Villa and then had to pay the price; Villa's lack of political skill kept him from becoming a threat to Carranza.

Comprehension Analysis:

Text-Based: __/4__
Inference: __/4__
Critical Response: __/2__

Total Comprehension %: _____

Reader's copy on p. 157 of the Reader's Passages

Introductory Statement: "Would you read this passage about Africa (to yourself/out loud). When you are finished, I'll take away the passage. Then I'll ask you to tell me about what you read and what you think of it. After that, I'll ask you some questions about the passage."

Story

Africa is a large continent made up of 54 countries. Many countries in Africa struggle with poverty, rebellions, famine, and disease while other countries have strong governments and economies with many resources.

Since 2003, the Darfur region of the country of Sudan has had continual strife between the Muslim government and rebel groups such as the Justice and Equality Movement and the Sudan Liberation Movement Army. Many of the tribal, civilian inhabitants of this region of Sudan have been massacred. Others live in encampments without fresh water and food, often separated from their families. A recent peace agreement holds out hope that this civil conflict will soon end; however, the International Committee of the Red Cross reports that the internally displaced people are still struggling to survive.

In the North Central African country of Niger, famine is wreaking havoc. Countless children are dying of malnutrition and disease and their distraught parents are helpless since they, too, are without food.

Robert Mugabe, the first and only president of Zimbabwe since it gained independence from Britain in April 1980, has become a tyrant. Mugabe has been burning makeshift homes and vegetable gardens in areas that did not support him in Zimbabwe's most recent election. Fuel and food shortages are also prevalent.

In one of Zimbabwe's largest cities, Bulawayo, a loaf of bread costs 3,000 Zimbabwe dollars, or U.S. $3. But with most people earning the equivalent of only U.S $18 per month, that is a huge sum of money. More than 70% of Zimbabweans are unemployed and the inflation rate is currently over 600%. Once considered the "breadbasket" of southern Africa, Zimbabwe has suffered tremendously because of the mismanagement of its current dictator.

Throughout the continent of Africa, various contagious diseases are widespread. Out of the 20 countries in the world with the highest HIV/AIDS rates, 19 of them are in Africa, mostly in the sub-Saharan areas. In addition to rampant malaria, common illnesses like polio, measles, cholera, typhoid fever, and diphtheria are still prevalent in Africa's population. The tragedy is that the vast majority of these diseases are preventable through vaccination. But in many African nations, vaccines and medicines that we take for granted are not even widely available.

Many organizations are working to combat the problems of famine, disease, and civil strife. However, as of yet, there is still much to do.

Some African nations are making significant progress toward prosperity and stability. In Botswana, another South African nation, agricultural and mining industries produce income to provide education and health care for their populace. Other countries have developed a strong ecotourism industry. These countries are helping protect natural wildlife and their habitats, while providing opportunities for both research and entertainment.

Many African nations have rich natural resources such as titanium, oil, diamonds, and other gems, along with minerals used in computers, cell phones, and medical equipment. Some countries, such as the Democratic Republic of the Congo, are fighting over them; others, such as Botswana, are utilizing them in responsible and controlled ways that support their economies and protect their supplies.

If it takes a village to raise a child, imagine what it will take to help countries in turmoil to prosper. Perhaps a careful examination of the countries that have succeeded on this vast African continent can help others to achieve the same successes. (554 words)

Scoring Miscues for Oral Reading Option
Mark all scoreable miscues by placing either a plus (for those that maintain meaning) or a zero (for those that violate meaning) in the text margin.

Reading Accuracy Index: _____%
*Total all miscues marked with pluses **and** zeros and enter the corresponding percentage from the Miscue Chart.*

Meaning Maintenance Index: _____%
*Total **only** miscues marked with zeros and enter the corresponding percentage from the Miscue Chart.*

Miscue Chart (if used for oral reading)

Miscues	%	Miscues	%	Miscues	%	Miscues	%
1	100	19	97	37	93	55	90
2	100	20	96	38	93	56	90
3	99	21	96	39	93	57	90
4	99	22	96	40	93	58	90
5	99	23	96	41	93	59	89
6	99	24	96	42	92	60	89
7	99	25	95	43	92	61	89
8	99	26	95	44	92	62	89
9	98	27	95	45	92	63	89
10	98	28	95	46	92	64	88
11	98	29	95	47	92	65	88
12	98	30	95	48	91	66	88
13	98	31	94	49	91	67	88
14	97	32	94	50	91	68	88
15	97	33	94	51	91	69	88
16	97	34	94	52	91	70	87
17	97	35	94	53	90		
18	97	36	94	54	90		

Student Retelling

Examiner: "Tell me about what you just read and what you thought about it."

If there is no spontaneous response, repeat the request, "Tell me what you thought about the passage."

Note: Use the Retelling Rubric on p. 373 to assess the child's retelling performance. If you need additional space for retelling responses, use a separate sheet of paper.

RETELLING RUBRIC: INFORMATIONAL

Macro-concepts (Numbered and Boldfaced) and Micro-concepts (Bulleted)

Place a 0, 1/2, or + to score student responses. See page 81 for information on what these assessment measures mean.

Story Structure:

_____ 1. **Many African countries struggle with problems.**
  _____ • Sudan is engaged in civil war.
_____ 2. **Tyrants like Mugabe in Zimbabwe are another problem.**
  _____ • Mismanagement by the dictator has led to much suffering.
  _____ • A large number of diseases also plague Africans.
_____ 3. **Some African nations are making progress.**
  _____ • Botswana has industries that pay for education and health care.
  _____ • Many nations have rich natural resources.
_____ 4. **Personal Response:** Any well-supported positive or negative response to the content or ideas in the text, or to the text as a whole.

Retelling Score: _____

Comprehension Questions

_____ 1. Who are the most likely victims of war and unrest in Africa?

Text-Based: The people; civilians; the poor; children.

_____ 2. What seems to be the primary objective of the regime of Robert Mugabe of Zimbabwe?

Text-Based: To get revenge on nonsupporters; to exploit his people for his own interests.

_____ 3. What would the people of Sudan have to do in order to make progress in lessening the suffering of its people?

Inference: Establish peace; work together to bring the scattered people home; put aside differences for the common good.

_____ 4. Why couldn't the government of Robert Mugabe exist as a democracy in Africa?

Inference: People would not elect him because of his mismanagement and cruelty; he would lose his power.

_____ 5. What would you characterize as Africa's most serious problem, its lack of effective leadership or its poverty?

Critical Response: Lack of leadership— since the resources seem to be there. Poverty—because the people are not healthy enough to participate in the building of countries.

_____ 6. Why are many African countries so susceptible to so many diseases?

Text-Based: They cannot afford vaccines; vaccines are unavailable; medicine is not available.

_____ 7. Why do organizations that have tried to help the African countries still have so much to do?

Inference: Too many problems in too many places; too many different types of problems; too little in the way of resources.

_____ 8. Why can't a typical citizen of Zimbabwe afford to feed himself and his family?

Text-Based: Food is too expensive and wages are too low.

_____ 9. What do the African countries that have experienced success have in common?

Inference: They use resources wisely; they use what they have; they use resources to help their people.

_____10. What is the most important lesson that struggling African countries can learn from successful ones?

Critical Response: Cooperation among people; concern for human life; responsible use of resources.

Comprehension Analysis:

Text-Based: __/4__
Inference: __/4__
Critical Response: __/2__

Total Comprehension %: _____